Cooking Light
COOKBOOK 1991

Cooking Light

COOKBOOK 1991

Oxmoor House®

Copyright 1990 by Oxmoor House, Inc.
Book Division of Southern Progress Corporation
P.O. Box 2463, Birmingham, Alabama 35201

Library of Congress Catalog Number: 87-61020
ISBN: 0-8487-1029-0
ISSN: 1043-7061

Manufactured in the United States of America
First Printing 1990

Executive Editor: Ann H. Harvey
Director of Manufacturing: Jerry R. Higdon
Associate Production Manager: Rick Litton
Art Director: Bob Nance

Cooking Light® Cookbook 1991

Editor: Cathy A. Wesler, R.D.
Copy Chief: Mary Ann Laurens
Copy Editors: Diane Lewis Swords, Melinda E. West
Editorial Assistants: Sue L. Killingsworth, Kelly E. Hooper, Pam Beasley Bullock
Production Assistant: Theresa L. Beste
Director, Test Kitchens: Vanessa Taylor Johnson
Assistant Director, Test Kitchens: Gayle Hays Sadler
Test Kitchen Home Economists: Caroline Alford, R.D., Angie Neskaug, Christina A. Pieroni,
    Kathleen Royal, Jan A. Smith
Senior Photographer: Jim Bathie. Additional photography by Colleen Duffley: pages 34, 36,
    38, 40, 74
Photo Stylist: Kay E. Clarke. Additional styling by Virginia R. Cravens: pages 2, 33, 34, 36,
    38, 40, 42, 60, 70, 73, 74, 79, 82, 85, 88
Designer: Faith Nance
Recipe and Menu Developers: Phyllis Young Cordell, Marilyn Wyrick Ingram, OTT
    Communications, Inc., Beatrice Ojakangas, Jane Ingrassia Reinsel, Elizabeth J. Taliaferro,
    Lisa Weiss
Exercise Models: Judith A. Mason, Alan T. Rogers

Consultants: Maureen Callahan, M.S., R.D.; University of Alabama School of Medicine at
    Birmingham: Julius Linn, M.D.; Susan Brown, Assistant Editor

Cover: *Ruby Strawberries (page 236)*.
Back cover: *Cheesy Broccoli-Corn Strudel (page 140)*.
Page 2: *Chicken Breasts with Wild Mushrooms (page 88), Saffron Orzo (page 89), and
    Roasted Asparagus with Orange Sauce (page 89)*.

To subscribe to *Cooking Light* magazine, write to *Cooking Light*, P.O. Box C-549,
    Birmingham, Alabama 35283.

Contents

Living Well Is The Best Reward

To say that you are "living well" conveys many meanings. But with *Cooking Light Cookbook 1991*, living well means being healthy and staying healthy.

Research shows that lifestyle—how you live and what you eat—clearly affects your risk for developing disease. To help you avoid those risks, we've included in this all-new volume the latest breakthroughs in nutrition, including highlights on cholesterol, heart disease, and cancer. But healthy eating is only part of the healthy lifestyle equation.

Regular exercise has proven benefits; researchers now know that even moderate to leisurely exercise is beneficial in the prevention of disease. And Americans are paying attention to this research. They are spending more money than ever to get fit—$728 million on exercise machines alone. Exercise walking attracted a reported 7.6 million new participants in 1988, according to the National Sporting Goods Association. Bicycling was next in line, with 6.5 million new participants. There's no doubt that more people than ever are becoming exercise conscious.

Let *Cooking Light* assist you in achieving better health. Along with recipes, menus, and a calorie/nutrient chart, you will find an abundance of information on nutrition and fitness and the role they play in bringing about a healthier lifestyle.

Sit back and relax as you enjoy a colorful, nutritious meal. Lobster Tails Oriental (page 132) and Minted Mandarin Peas (page 214) are accompanied by steamed new potatoes and mineral water.

Update '91

As we approach the 21st century, more Americans are moving away from fat-laden diets and sedentary lifestyles that contribute to clogged arteries and dulled senses. The results are astounding. Since 1968, the number of deaths resulting from diseases of the heart and blood vessels has dropped almost 40 percent, and government experts expect the declines to continue.

These statistics reflect not only better technology and treatments but also major changes in the typical diet, amount of exercise, and smoking habits of Americans. In countries where people have not made these striking lifestyle changes, death rates from heart and vascular diseases continue to soar.

The National Report Card

The recent U.S. Department of Agriculture (USDA) survey shows Americans are eating more fish (a low-fat choice) and eating fewer eggs than 10 years ago. The USDA has also found that consumption of low-fat milk surpassed that of whole milk, and, for the first time, Americans are eating more poultry than beef and more vegetables than they consumed 20 years ago. While Americans are indeed eating less cholesterol-rich food and less fat, studies cite the need to cut fat even more. Only one of every two people surveyed could name foods high in fat; even fewer could name the foods high in saturated or unsaturated fats.

The survey also pointed out that Americans need to look at their overall diet and quit focusing on quick fixes. A Gallup poll taken in 1989 for the American Dietetic Association and the International Food Information Council concurred. Their findings: Americans are eating more oat bran and taking more vitamins because of health concerns, but only 8 percent are consuming more vegetables and only 6 percent more fruits or fruit juices. The USDA says more than half of those polled agreed with the statement that fruits and vegetables are "not at all important" in a balanced diet.

America's Objectives

The Department of Health and Human Services (HHS) unveiled goals for improving America's health by the year 2000. In 1985, only 22 percent of Americans got a half-hour of regular, moderate physical activity each day. By the year 2000, the government hopes to increase that figure by 30 percent. A second goal for the 1990s is to trim the number of obese Americans from the current 26 percent to no more than 20 percent. HHS hopes to see smoking cut from an average 29 percent of the population to 14 percent.

Reversing the trend in cancer deaths also is on the federal agenda—in 1970, 130 people per 100,000 died of cancer; the number rose to 133 per 100,000 in 1987. The goal is to return to the 1970 rate. Officials hope to see heart disease deaths continue their decline. In 1987, 135 people per 100,000 died from this disease, and by the year 2000 HHS wants to see that figure at 100 per 100,000. To achieve these goals, HHS has devised 298 goals, many of which focus on healthy eating and exercise. By making the 1990s a decade of prevention, the goals are attainable.

Controversy Over Cholesterol

Although the death rates from heart and vascular diseases continue to fall, some researchers still question the cholesterol-diet connection. The controversy was fueled by journalist Thomas Moore's book *Heart Failure*, excerpts of which appeared in *Atlantic Monthly* magazine. Moore argued that it's unclear whether diet affects blood cholesterol levels all that much and whether lowering cholesterol really improves life expectancy.

While Moore correctly criticized several studies that were not conclusive, he failed to look at the broad spectrum of studies that, when taken as a whole, make a strong case for the link between diet, cholesterol, and heart disease.

When animal and cross-cultural studies are included, it seems clear that by eating the right foods, most people can lower cholesterol levels and decrease the risk of having heart attacks.

A recent study has shown conclusively that lowering cholesterol extends life. The reason most studies have not reached this conclusion is that they were conducted over too short a period of time, and heart disease is a lifelong process. But once measures are taken earlier to control cholesterol levels, the clearer the diet-longevity link will become.

This was borne out by a 10-year follow-up of one of the studies Moore criticized—the Multiple Risk Factor Intervention Trial (MR FIT). After six years, the data did not show that efforts to reduce cholesterol—losing weight, stopping smoking, and exercising—extended life. But after 10 years, more of those who had changed their habits were alive than were those who had not.

A Life-Long Benefit

One other cholesterol issue was resolved in 1990—whether or not elderly people can benefit from reducing cholesterol. The Honolulu Heart Program involving 1,480 men showed that although the beneficial effects are not as striking in men over 65 as in middle-aged men, older people can still benefit from heart disease prevention tactics.

In recognition of the importance of the cholesterol-heart disease link, the National Cholesterol Education Program now recommends a low-fat, low-cholesterol diet for all Americans over the age of two, not just those with high cholesterol levels. The consensus of the experts is that all Americans need to get their daily fat intake down to 30 percent of total calories. No more than 10 percent of calories should come from saturated fat.

Yet another study has confirmed the benefits of even greater reductions of dietary fat for people who have had heart problems. Scientists at the University of Southern California followed 82 men for two years after coronary artery bypass surgery. The men who lacked new fatty build-up in arteries had reduced their total fat consumption to about 28 percent of total calories. But the total fat consumption of the group that developed new fatty lesions averaged 34 percent.

Heart Disease and Weight

Evidence now clearly links obesity in women to coronary artery disease. Forty percent of the heart-related problems of women participating in an 8-year Harvard study were attributed to excess weight. The evidence suggests that middle-aged women who are 20 pounds heavier than they were in adolescence are twice as likely to have a heart attack as are women of the same height and age who have not gained weight. Even losing just 5 percent of the extra weight helps.

Controlling weight pays off, resulting in a lower blood pressure and cholesterol level, less chance of diabetes, and lower cancer risk, especially for women during the years after menopause. In the multicenter Women's Health Trial, women who reduced fat from 40 percent to just under 20 percent of total calories reduced cancer risk four- to five-fold.

Most people are overweight because they eat too much and exercise too little, but new evidence links a tendency to be overweight to genetics. In a study of more than 600 twins in Sweden, researchers learned that twins had similar weights in adulthood, whether they lived with biological or adopted parents. In another study, sets of twins were fed an extra 1,000 calories a day. Some sets gained up to three times as much weight as other sets on the same diet, but if one brother gained, his twin gained a similar amount.

The inherited trait to gain weight is not absolute—it's not like inheriting blue eyes and blond hair. You only inherit the tendency, which you can overcome with diet and exercise. The study simply reinforces what we've all known: Some people have more trouble losing weight and keeping it off than others.

More About Fiber

Oat bran mania subsided a bit in 1990 after a Harvard study found that eating oat bran failed to lower cholesterol in people whose levels were already in the desirable range. Additional studies have shown, however, that oat bran and other foods high in soluble fiber may lower cholesterol slightly in people with high levels, especially when fiber is substituted for fatty foods.

Substituting fiber for fatty foods also can help in weight-loss efforts, according to University of Minnesota scientists. They found that people who ate a bowl of high-fiber cereal for breakfast ate less at lunch than those who ate low-fiber cereals.

Rice bran cereals, breads, and snacks are pushing oat bran products off the grocery shelves. Animal studies have shown that rice bran lowers total cholesterol and harmful low-density lipoprotein (LDL) cholesterol levels. LDLs carry cholesterol to cells to manufacture cell walls and hormones. LDLs narrow the blood vessels by dumping excess cholesterol into artery walls. Preliminary studies at Louisiana State University showed that rice bran lowered total and LDL cholesterol levels by about the same amount as oat bran.

But it's not the fiber in rice bran that does the trick—it's the oil. Rice oil blocks absorption of some cholesterol from the intestine and interferes with its production in the liver. Nutrition experts caution, however, that neither adding nor leaving off one food will make your diet a healthy one.

On the cancer front, wheat bran cereal reduced the number and size of precancerous growths called polyps in the colons of people with a family tendency toward this problem. People in the study ate 22 grams of wheat fiber a day, which is within the range the National Research Council recommends. Unfortunately, the average American consumes half of that in his diet.

If you're adding fiber-rich foods to your child's diet, consider this: Current National Research Council guidelines for fiber are geared to adults, not children. One reason is that high-fiber foods are usually low in calories. Children have small stomachs, and bulky, high-fiber foods can keep them from getting adequate nutrients for growth. Studies show children can get enough fiber in a balanced diet of four to six servings of fruits and vegetables a day.

Fruits and Vegetables Help

Fruits and vegetables are a good source of soluble fiber, and scientists have discovered that ellagic acid found naturally in strawberries and apples may reduce risks of some types of cancer. This acid reduces the cancer-causing effects of toxic chemicals present in the environment. USDA researchers are scrutinizing the genetics of this acid in hopes of growing more varieties of fruits high in ellagic acid.

Vegetables may provide protection against lung cancer, according to a University of Hawaii investigation. Researchers found that people who ate many different vegetables were less likely to have lung cancer. An especially helpful measure for lungs may be eating dark green, leafy vegetables such as spinach that are rich in folic acid. A University of Alabama at Birmingham study showed that folic acid can slow and perhaps even reverse precancerous changes in the lungs of smokers. But the most important practice people can follow to protect their lungs is to avoid cigarette smoking completely.

FDA Approval Given

The fight to cut fat in foods is moving ahead with the Food and Drug Administration's (FDA) approval of the first fat substitute made from milk and egg protein. A new ice cream made with a fat substitute is on the market, and other frozen desserts are coming. Look for fat substitutes soon in mayonnaise, sour cream, and dips—they won't be in foods that require warming, however, because the substitutes gel when heated.

These products have about half the calories of their fat-containing counterparts. Note, however, that some sherbets, sorbets, and low-fat

or nonfat yogurts contain even fewer calories and less fat. While these fat-substitutes appear safe, no studies have shown that their use leads to weight loss or lower cholesterol levels.

Science Looks at Drinking

Avoiding too much alcohol is a good health habit, especially if you're a woman. A multicenter study found that women have less of a critical stomach enzyme that metabolizes alcohol than do men. Consequently, women absorb more alcohol and thus feel its effects more quickly than men; they also experience more ill effects from the same amount.

One of the USDA Dietary Guidelines says, "If you drink alcohol, do so in moderation." According to the committee that devised the guidelines, moderation means no more than two drinks a day for men and one for women. Pregnant women should avoid alcohol altogether.

The caffeine issue is less clear, but many Americans have switched to decaffeinated coffee because of the possibility that caffeine causes birth defects and raises cholesterol levels. Scientists confirmed last year that the cholesterol-raising effects appear to be related to the way coffee is brewed. A Norwegian study showed that drinking boiled, unfiltered coffee, which is popular in Europe, raised cholesterol levels. Filtering coffee appears to prevent a cholesterol-raising factor from reaching the cup.

Much to decaffeinated coffee drinkers' dismay, a study from the Stanford University Lipid Research Clinic showed that decaffeinated coffee raised LDL cholesterol, the "bad" cholesterol, but other studies are necessary to confirm this finding. For now, drinking no more than two or three cups of regular or decaffeinated coffee a day seems safe for most people.

The Revised RDAs

The revised Recommended Dietary Allowances (RDAs) of vitamins and minerals were released late in 1989 by the National Academy of Sciences. The new recommendations include slightly lower RDAs for vitamins A, B_{12}, C, folic acid, and iron for women. Vitamin K was added to the RDA list, and the calcium requirement was raised for young adults. The 1980 version suggested 1,200 milligrams of calcium a day for people aged 19 to 22; today's version raises that age to 24, the age for peak bone formation.

A Tufts University study indicated that the RDA of vitamin D may be too low to protect older women from losing calcium from bone during late winter. During these gray, cold months there's often not enough sunlight to stimulate the skin to produce the vitamin. The study of 333 women past menopause found that those who consumed at least 10 percent more vitamin D than the RDA didn't have the seasonal dip in calcium that many women experience during late winter. Egg yolks, liver, tuna, and cod liver oil are good dietary sources of vitamin D.

Selenium, a trace mineral thought to be important to metabolism, now has an RDA—70 micrograms for men and 55 for women. You can get this small amount from seafood, whole grain cereals, meat, egg yolks, chicken, and milk.

Today's Exercise Evidence

Research on more than 13,000 men and women at the Institute for Aerobics Research in Dallas proved fitness extends life. Although not the first study to arrive at these conclusions, it is one of the best. It's also one of the first longevity studies to include women and require specific measures of exercise capacity. The study showed that the most fit people lived the longest, while the least fit had the highest death rates. Surprisingly, even in the second-least-fit group, death rates were sharply lower than in the group that exercised almost none at all. Scientists concluded that even moderate exercise greatly lowered the rate of cardiovascular disease and cancer.

Lifelong Exercise

Exercise may keep your mind fit as well as your body. The Boston Longitudinal Study of Aging revealed that healthy older people who exercise at the same level as younger people react as quickly mentally as do their younger counterparts.

Elderly people who exercise also react faster and can break a fall better than those who are sedentary, according to researchers at the Washington University Medical Center in St. Louis. Elderly people who walked regularly were 40 percent more likely to have good reaction time than non-exercisers.

And exercise also may play a role in cancer prevention. A 21-year Japanese study has shown that the risks of developing colon cancer rise sharply as resting heart rates—a measure of fitness—increase. Exercise, in addition to lowering heart rates, speeds waste material through the colon and reduces the time that cancer-causing compounds remain in contact with the colon wall.

Easier Exercising

A more evenhanded approach to exercising has now been accepted. In 1990, the American College of Sports Medicine (ACSM) released an updated version of its position on the quantity and quality of exercise for healthy adults. It added for the

first time a section on the benefits of strength training because of its importance to well-rounded fitness.

To encourage more people to get involved in exercise, ACSM distinguished between levels of fitness necessary for athletic performance and levels needed for improving health. It advises that many people can improve health by exercising longer than 15 or 20 minutes but taking it easier—perhaps a brisk 40-minute walk every day instead of an intense 20-minute run three times a week.

The message for most people is that you don't have to exercise to exhaustion to be healthy. The ACSM committee of experts concluded that low to moderately intense exercise is best for most adults. High-intensity workouts increase your risk of injury.

Similarly, the government continues its push to get more people into the exercise mainstream. The Director of the President's Council on Physical Fitness wants to draw inner-city children and people who haven't gotten the fitness message into the exercise circle. He's also concerned because only one state, Illinois, out of the 50 requires daily physical education for all children, kindergarten through grade 12. Look for his upcoming drive to get parents involved in building family fitness.

Getting the whole family out means people of all ages, which is especially important in light of new evidence that staying physically fit reduces the risk of having a stroke. An 8-year study at the Institute for Aerobics Research in Dallas showed that people with low fitness levels were three times as likely to suffer a stroke as those who were more fit.

Slim, Relaxed, and Laughing

Staying slim is an attractive by-product of exercising regularly, and the importance of keeping

weight down is underscored in the 1989 American Cancer Society's (ACS) Dietary Guidelines for reducing cancer risks.

The first ACS recommendation is to avoid obesity because of its link to many types of cancer. ACS also urges cutting down on total fat intake for the same reasons. Eating more fruits and vegetables as well as other high-fiber foods such as whole grain cereals is the central point of the guidelines.

Because heavy drinkers have unusually high cancer risks, ACS urges limiting alcohol consumption, if you drink at all. Finally, the experts recommend limiting the amount of smoked, salt-cured, and nitrite-cured lunch meats and other foods because of their links to stomach and other cancers.

To round out your eating and exercise program, you'll want to include time for relaxation and laughter every day. This may help you live longer and certainly will help relieve stress. In a study of men with advanced coronary artery disease, those who included stress management and relaxation as part of their dietary and exercise program did better than those who didn't. Dean Ornish, M.D., director of the study, says, "Clearly we know that the mind can create problems for the heart. We are now beginning to see the mind also can heal the heart."

A Stanford researcher points out that laughter not only makes us feel good, but also it is good exercise for the heart. Three minutes of hearty laughter is roughly equivalent to 10 minutes of rowing. The evidence is mounting that relaxation and humor are vital to good health.

Get away from the television and other distractions and give yourself a few minutes of quiet today. There's no doubt that the beacons of current scientific knowledge shine on healthy, light eating; moderate exercising; regular relaxation; and a generous dose of humor.

The Food
& Fitness
Connection

Carrot Bran Muffins (page 106), Crisp Mix (page 199), and fresh fruit are portable take-alongs for an adventurous outing. Packed in waterproof containers, they will remain dry for a healthy afternoon snack.

In 1988, the Surgeon General urged Americans to cut back on fat, particularly saturated fat. Soon afterwards, a similar report came from a group of scientists convened by the National Research Council. Their specific advice: Cut fat intake to no more than 30 percent of total calories. However, about 37 percent of the total calorie intake of most Americans is fat.

Although translating this numerical advice into actual foods isn't always easy, you'll find throughout *Cooking Light* meal-planning specifics that simplify the problem. For a concise review of nutrition fundamentals, take a look at Nutrition Basics on the next page.

Studies continue to show that lifestyle—how you live and what you eat—clearly affects your health. Research also shows that exercise can lower blood pressure, blood cholesterol, and the risk for developing a number of chronic diseases. Therefore, it makes sense to try to establish a commitment to fitness. Turn to page 18 for ideas in putting together a workable fitness plan. Armed with these motivating health facts, it will be easy to keep fitness part of your winning health strategy.

Discover the benefits of cross-training. Learn what the experts say about mixing and matching different activities as a way to help you stick with an exercise program. Finally, check out the latest in exercise information, everything from buying the right shoes to keeping in step with fitness, bench-style.

In the *Cooking Light* Kitchen (pages 26 and 27), you'll find helpful tips on how to make low-fat recipe substitutions. Try using the featured herbs in your recipes, and learn how to keep the recipes light while retaining the flavor. This primer on fresh herbs tells you how to use their unusual flavors to perk up the lean and light cuisine.

Throughout *Cooking Light* you will find nutrition and fitness guidelines that make for a healthy lifestyle. Share these food and fitness facts with your family, and you will encourage even the heartiest eater to become more health conscious. You'll find these facts flagged with the following symbols:

NUTRITION   FITNESS

Nutrition Basics for *Cooking Light*

Making a conscious decision to eat healthier is a step in the right direction when it comes to staying healthy. But if you're like most people, wanting to eat better and actually understanding how to do so are not the same. Although advice about nutrition seems to change daily, don't get tripped up by the barrage of changing health messages.

Health professionals continue to encourage Americans to reduce their fat intake to no more than 30 percent of the total calories consumed per day. In addition, no more than 10 percent of the calories should be from saturated fat. The recommended limit for cholesterol is 300 milligrams per day; for sodium, 3,300 milligrams. Lost in the shuffle is how these specific numbers translate into foods—the practical advice that helps you decide what foods to put into the grocery cart each week. You can relax, though, because finding the best food choices can become second nature. All you need to do is brush up on the basics.

While the recommended amounts may sound confusing, *Cooking Light* can help you understand these basics and show you how to achieve the recommendations of health professionals.

THE FUNDAMENTAL FOUR

Years ago, health professionals created a food classification system—called the Basic Four—to simplify the task of planning a well-balanced diet. Foods with similar nutrient profiles were grouped together under one category. Today, this system is still your best guide for planning a healthy diet. Of course, there have been a few updates to bring the system into the nineties, but first, it's back to the basics.

Leading the list is the breads and cereals group, which includes products such as rolls, muffins, biscuits, and pancakes made from enriched or whole-grain wheat, rice, or corn. Most grain products provide a healthy dose of the B vitamins and are rich in complex carbohydrates. As a bonus, many contain little fat.

The second classification is made up of many vitamin-rich fruits and vegetables. Fruits and vegetables are excellent sources of carbohydrate, fiber, and vitamins A and C.

The third classification, the meat group, contains high-protein foods, including beef, pork, poultry, peanut butter, and dried beans, all equally important. These foods are excellent sources of protein, iron, thiamin, riboflavin, niacin, and vitamin B_{12}, a vitamin found only in animal products.

The final group, the milk group, provides carbohydrate, protein, calcium, riboflavin, and vitamin D. Foods in this group include milk, cheese, cottage cheese, and ice cream.

Under the Basic Four system, the number of servings is specified. Each day, for example, a healthy adult should eat at least four fruit and vegetable servings, four bread and cereal servings, two meat servings, and two milk servings. But the servings-per-group concept does have limitations. The system does not account for the fat or calories of each group, and many foods overlap two or more food groups. To gain a better understanding of a food's nutritional place in the diet, you should consider more than the Basic Four.

CONSIDERING NUTRIENT DENSITY

Part of the secret to healthy eating is to go one step beyond the Basic Four. Select foods from each group that deliver the most nutrients at the lowest calorie cost. Nutritionists refer to this concept as comparing the nutrient density of the food. The idea is similar to comparison shopping. If you're looking for a good source of calcium, several foods may come to mind: whole milk, skim milk, ice cream, and cheese. Skim milk, however, offers the needed calcium at the lowest calorie cost and lowest fat content. The point is not to exclude any food from the diet. Rather, it's to put each food into perspective.

If, for example, you eat a meal high in fat at lunch, you should focus at supper on foods that offer any nutrients you missed at lunch and that have less fat. Indeed, too much fat at meals is what leads most Americans away from the guidelines recommended by nutrition experts.

A CALORIE ISN'T A CALORIE

Heart disease is only one of the problems associated with consuming a lot of fat. The caloric density of fat can also be a problem, especially to those watching their weight. Fat contains 9 calories per gram, twice as much as in carbohydrate and protein. And, to compound the problem, the body is more efficient at processing fat. So, if a person eats 300 extra calories of fat, the body stores 291 of those calories as fat. A mere 9 calories are used during the process. The body is far less efficient in processing carbohydrate calories. In comparison, with 300 extra calories of carbohydrate, 25 percent, a full 75 calories, will be used to help the body convert this nutrient to body fat. This is just one more good reason to choose foods lower in fat and higher in complex carbohydrate.

SEVEN TENETS OF HEALTHFUL EATING

To help Americans eat healthier, the National Academy of Sciences released some concrete guidelines in its recent report, *Diet and Health*.
● Eat your vegetables and fruits. Go beyond the Basic Four guidelines and aim for at least five servings (½ cup) each day. Mix and match selections to get healthy amounts of vitamins A and C.
● Include plenty of whole grain foods at meals. Dish up six or more servings (½ cup) a day, preferably whole grain breads and cereals.
● Enjoy plenty of calcium-rich foods. Besides obvious sources such as low-fat dairy products, calcium is found in leafy green vegetables—broccoli, spinach, and kale—and in salmon and tofu.
● Downplay salt. Maximum salt allowance: 6 grams a day, which equals only 2,400 milligrams sodium. Limit highly salted convenience foods, such as luncheon meats, and pickled or canned items processed with salt. Spice up meals with other seasonings: lemon, garlic, basil, and oregano.
● Keep fat calories to 30 percent or less. For most Americans, this means cutting back by trimming

visible fat from beef, peeling the skin from chicken, and consuming foods lower in fat. Not every food needs to meet this 30 percent recommendation, however. Balance an indulgence such as premium ice cream with a broiled fish dinner.
● If you do drink, limit alcohol to one ounce of pure alcohol per day. That equates to either two cans of beer, two small glasses of wine, or two average cocktails. Caution—pregnant women need to avoid alcohol altogether.
● Work to maintain weight. That involves a commitment to exercise and balanced eating. Both go hand-in-hand when it comes to staying healthy.

WHAT'S MISSING IN YOUR DIET?

Government surveys show that many Americans, both men and women, fall short of meeting the RDA for several key nutrients: folic acid, magnesium, vitamin B_6, and zinc. If you are a woman, add calcium and iron to this growing list. Then make sure to load up the grocery cart with at least a few of the following foods, all good sources of the missing nutrients.
• Folic acid: Legumes, sunflower seeds, wheat germ, asparagus, English peas, dark green leafy vegetables such as spinach.
• Magnesium: Nuts and seeds, peanut butter, legumes, fish, shrimp, oysters, spinach, potatoes, wheat germ, whole grains.
• Vitamin B_6: Fish, red meat, poultry, liver, soybeans, bananas, wheat germ, whole grains.
• Zinc: Oysters, red meat, poultry, clams, yogurt, sesame seeds, pecans, wheat germ.
• Calcium: Milk, yogurt, cheese, canned salmon, some tofu.
• Iron: Liver, red meat, poultry, fish, shellfish, dried beans, enriched breads and enriched cereals.

PUTTING IT ALL TOGETHER

Eating for good health need not be a tedious task based on counting and measuring. Numbers, after all, are simply meant as guidelines. If you choose foods with an eye toward the nutrients they contain and, at the same time, those that downplay fat, you are well on your way toward achieving a nutritional balance.

Computing Nutrition

Your Daily Needs

To estimate your daily calorie requirement, multiply your current weight by 15. Remember that this is only a rough guide because calorie requirements vary according to age, body size, and level of activity. If a change of weight is desired, add or subtract 500 calories per day to allow for weight gain or loss of 1 pound a week. However, a diet of less than 1,200 calories a day is not recommended unless medically supervised. For more information concerning your individual requirements, consult a registered dietitian (R.D.).

Implement the *Cooking Light* 50-20-30 guidelines (page 32) by calculating the amount of carbohydrate, protein, and fat for optimal health. Multiply your calorie requirement by the percentages 50, 20, and 30 to give the calories from each nutrient. Divide the carbohydrate and protein calories by 4 (4 calories per gram) and the fat by 9 (9 calories per gram) to determine how many grams of each nutrient you need.

For example, here's how to calculate the distribution of a 2,000-calorie diet:

50% carbohydrate = 1,000 calories ÷ 4 = 250 grams carbohydrate

20% protein = 400 calories ÷ 4 = 100 grams protein

30% fat = 600 calories ÷ 9 = 67 grams fat

Therefore, for a person eating 2,000 calories a day, 1,000 calories would meet the 50 percent carbohydrate guideline, while no more than 400 calories and 600 calories would be from protein and fat, respectively.

When planning your meals, refer to the daily amounts of nutrients to help you make the most of the nutrient values that follow *Cooking Light* recipes. Although there is no RDA for sodium or cholesterol, suggested intake is listed below along with the RDA for iron and calcium.

Iron	15 mg
Calcium	800 mg
Sodium	3,300 mg or less
Cholesterol	300 mg or less

Every Recipe Analyzed

Calories per serving and a nutrient breakdown accompany every recipe. The nutrients listed include grams of carbohydrate, protein, and fat along with milligrams of cholesterol, calcium, iron, and sodium.

Determining Calorie Percentages

Use *Cooking Light* nutrient breakdowns to calculate the percentage of calories contributed by carbohydrate, protein, and fat. Let's say you are looking at the recipe for Spicy Chili Mac (complete recipe on page 146), and you want to determine the percentage of fat in one serving.

First, find the number of grams of fat per serving. This is calculated in the analysis to be 5.4 grams. To find the percentage of calories from fat, multiply grams of fat by 9 (the number of calories per gram of fat) to get fat calories per serving. Then divide this quantity by the total calories. You'll find that fat contributes 16 percent of the calories in one serving.

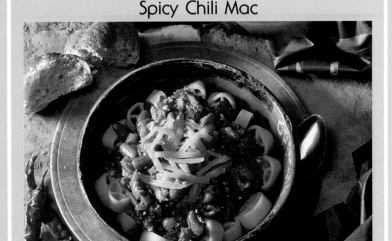

Spicy Chili Mac

PROTEIN 18.1 / FAT 5.4 / CARBOHYDRATE 50.5 / CHOLESTEROL 4 / IRON 7.8 / SODIUM 205 / CALCIUM 196

To calculate the calories contributed by carbohydrate and protein, multiply grams of carbohydrate or protein per serving by 4 (the number of calories per gram of carbohydrate or protein). Divide the quantity by total calories.

Menus and Menu Plans Meet 50-20-30 Guidelines

For a healthy meal, add a dinner roll to a serving of Spicy Chili Mac to meet the recommended percentages: more than 50 percent carbohydrate, 20 percent protein, and no more than 30 percent fat. All recipes will not fall so neatly within the guidelines. The goal is to achieve the recommended balance of nutrients on a daily basis, taking into consideration three meals and a snack. Use "Healthy American Meals" (page 31) and "Light Recipes" (page 91) to create meals that meet the 50-20-30 guidelines.

How the Recipes Are Analyzed

The recipes are developed for people interested in lowering their intake of calories, sodium, fat, and/or cholesterol to maintain healthy eating patterns. If you are following a medically prescribed diet, consult a registered dietitian to see how *Cooking Light* recipes can fit into your specific meal plan.

The calorie and nutrient breakdown of each recipe is derived from computer analysis, based primarily on information from the U.S. Department of Agriculture. The values are as accurate as possible and are based on these assumptions:

• All nutrient breakdowns are listed per serving.
• All meats are trimmed of fat and skin before cooking.
• When a range is given for an ingredient (for example, 3 to 3½ cups flour), the lesser amount is calculated.
• A percentage of alcohol calories evaporate when heated, and this reduction is reflected in the calculations.
• When a marinade is used, only the amount of marinade used (not discarded) is calculated.
• Garnishes and other optional ingredients are not calculated.
• Fruits and vegetables listed in the ingredients are not peeled unless otherwise specified.

Exercise—The Perfect Partner

Whether the goal is to lose weight or just to stay in shape, a well-rounded exercise program is one of the most important factors to being healthy. Healthful eating, after all, is but one part of the healthy lifestyle equation. How active you are, say leading health professionals, is just as important as what you eat.

Strong scientific evidence supports the fact that regular exercise can reduce the risk for a host of serious illnesses, including heart disease, high blood pressure, osteoporosis, and America's number one problem—obesity. Why then do so many Americans find it difficult to commit to some type of regular exercise program?

Experts think the lack of commitment may stem from the approach people take toward exercise. Not everyone can run a 6-minute mile or tackle 50 sit-ups at a fast pace. But that's no reason to give up on fitness. Studies show that something as simple as walking for 10 minutes per day can offer cardiovascular benefits. Clearly, workouts don't need to be long and grueling in order to achieve positive results. That's why the approach to fitness in the 90s places emphasis on moderation and variety.

Create a mixed package of exercise activities—sports or fitness programs tuned to your individual body, fitness level, and personal enjoyment—and chances are you will stick with the schedule. Gardening, golf, and even household chores such as making a bed can each contribute to the net fitness goal. Indeed, there's more than one way to get your motor running.

STARTING OVER, STAYING WITH IT

Studies show that 60 to 70 percent of Americans give up on a new exercise regimen within the first month. Fitness experts have an idea about how to lessen that "drop-out" rate. The key to the success of any exercise program, they say, is to find a number of activities that you enjoy. Never mind what is popular or at what sport your best friend excels. Instead, concentrate on the exercise program that is right for you.

Like enjoying food, enjoying exercise is definitely a matter of taste. Even the time of the exercise session—day, night, or during the lunch hour—is a personal preference. If you are easily distracted from working out, perhaps you might want to try a morning routine. It seems that morning fitness enthusiasts are three times more likely to stay with the programs than those who exercise later in the day. Another tip: Build variety into that morning schedule. Variety keeps boredom at bay, which will help you stick with your exercise program and thus end up being healthier.

ANAEROBIC OR AEROBIC?

Fitness experts point out that aerobic and anaerobic exercises differ in more ways than just oxygen requirements. Anaerobic sports depend on brief bursts of effort. A short run such as a 10-yard dash, the swinging of a golf club or a tennis racquet, the pummeling of a volleyball over a net, or the lifting of weights are all anaerobic activities. As such, they don't depend on cardiovascular fitness. Although the oxygen demands may be high, the period of need is brief, and the oxygen debt can be replenished during a period of rest. What these endeavors do require is strength. And the only way to build up that strength is to practice the anaerobic activity.

Aerobic activity, on the other hand, is built on cardiovascular endurance. Demand for oxygen is constant, which is why the heart must pump harder. Aerobic sports, such as jogging, cycling, swimming, cross-country skiing, or swimming, condition the heart and help it work more efficiently. For this reason, fitness experts place more emphasis on aerobic sports. However, if you want to build strength as well as endurance, be sure to include both types of exercise in your workout schedule because anaerobic exercise builds strength and aerobic builds endurance.

CROSS-TRAINING

In the past, "being fit" involved choosing one sport or activity and sticking with it for the long haul. Today, cross-training is the order of the day. And you don't need to be an athlete to reap the rewards. The approach is straightforward and the premise is simple: Employ a mix and match of different exercises to tone the body from head to toe. Each activity uses different muscles, making it likely that the whole body gets a workout, not just the arms or legs. Cycling, for example, provides an excellent workout for the heart but neglects upper-body muscles, unless a stationary bike with moveable handlebars is utilized. Flexibility, another crucial component of a total body fitness program, is also not increased when cycling.

With cross-training, cycling or any other cardiovascular exercise forms the core of the training program. The other components include exercises that build flexibility and muscle strength. Add calisthenics to build flexibility, and add weight resistance for muscle strength. Some people find weight training to be another valid option. It's an excellent activity for developing muscle strength. Whatever your choice, the point is to build a partnership of activities that satisfy all four components of the cross-training program: cardiovascular strength, flexibility, muscle strength, and endurance. The cross-training chart can help you figure out whether the activities you enjoy fulfill these key components. Keep in mind that working out safely, however, is just as important as finding the right variety.

Cross-training is a personalized approach to achieving fitness. The challenge is putting together a comprehensive exercise program that promotes lifelong fitness and provides optimum conditioning. If you select activities that contribute to the four components and that you enjoy, achieving total body fitness can be a realistic goal.

DEFINING "MUSCLE-BOUND"

Fear of "bulking up" prevents many people from lifting weights and using weight-training techniques to their advantage. What they don't realize is that to make muscles bigger—the size and shape bodybuilders flaunt—requires lifting increasing amounts of weight repeatedly. While bodybuilders place the emphasis on increasing the amount of weight they can lift, strength training approaches the muscle workout differently. The focus is on increasing the number of times a weight is lifted (repetitions) rather than the amount of the weight. The muscle responds quite differently to this approach; instead of bulking up, muscles become sleek, toned, and much more efficient.

Weight training, or strength training as it's also called, is a critical component when trying to get in the best shape possible to play a sport. When the strength of muscles is increased, the speed at which you can move is actually increased, making you faster in general. Improving muscle strength through weight training definitely gives athletes—both amateur and weekend enthusiasts—the competitive edge.

BUILDING A CROSS-TRAINING PROGRAM

The following chart rates sports and activities in the four components of a well-rounded cross-training program. Four bullets indicate an excellent rating; one bullet is considered poor.

SPORT/ACTIVITY	CARDIO-VASCULAR	STRENGTH	MUSCLE ENDURANCE	FLEXIBILITY
Aerobic dance	••••	••	•••	••
Bicycling	••••	••	•••	•
Bowling	•	•	•	•
Calisthenics		••••	••••	••••
Fencing	••	••	•••	••
Golf	••	•	•	••
Hiking	•••	••	••••	••
Horseback riding	•	••	••	••
Judo or karate	•	••	••	••
Racquetball	•••	•	•••	
Rowing, crew	••••	••	••••	
Skating, ice	•••	•	•••	
Skating, roller	••	•	••	
Skiing, cross-country	••••	••	•••	•
Skiing, downhill	•	••	••	•
Softball, slow	•	•	•	•
Swimming	••••	••	•••	••
Tennis	••	•	••	
Walking	•••	•	••	
Weight Training	•	••••	•••	•

From *Fitness For Life*, (2nd Ed.) by Charles B. Corbin and Ruth Lindsey. Copyright © 1983, 1979 by Scott, Foresman and Company. Reprinted by permission.

WARMING UP, WORKING OUT

Adding new sports and activities to your fitness routine is crucial to achieving the overall fitness that cross-trainers experience. But with every new activity comes the risk of injury. Seldom-worked muscles and joints need time to get with the program. You might want to call this the 10-20-10 rule. It takes at least 10 minutes of stretching and warm-up exercises to get muscles ready for action. Without the warm-up, muscles are subject to being torn, pulled, or stretched out of shape. The warm-up phase is not a time to build intensity.

Instead, intensity should be reached during the aerobic portion of your exercise program and should be maintained at peak levels during the 20- to 30-minute aerobic phase for maximum cardiovascular benefits. In fact, to work the heart completely, the heart rate must reach into the 70 to 85 percent target heart rate zone.

Without counting numbers, reaching the target heart rate zone equates to working up a healthy sweat but still being able to breathe normally. An easy test: While exercising—jogging, dancing, or doing bench aerobics—you should be able to talk with a companion or sing along with the music without becoming short of breath. But for a more accurate check on your heart rate, refer to the target heart rate chart.

Finally, once the workout is over, it is important to cool down at a slow pace for 10 minutes. The cool down gradually brings the heart back to normal rhythm and helps relax muscles. This 10-20-10 rule is not carved in stone. It's possible to extend the warm-up portion or to work the heart longer. But for a safe, effective exercise session, it's always necessary to warm up and cool down.

AN ADDED BONUS

Besides strengthening muscles and building endurance, exercise also burns energy. Some exercises, such as cross-country skiing, swimming, and racquetball, actually burn more than 600 calories per hour. Obviously, this makes it possible to "burn off" fat with just exercise alone. Say a person skis, swims, or plays racquetball for a full hour every day. By week's end, it would be possible to lose a full pound of fat since one pound of fat represents 3,500 excess calories. By burning only 400 calories per week with exercise, more than five pounds of stored body fat could be lost in a year. All of these calculations, of course, bar any change in eating habits.

Unfortunately, most time schedules don't allow for this kind of commitment. A more realistic approach to weight loss or weight control is to combine exercise with smart food choices. Toning the body from head to toe, once you add variety to the routine, can easily become a lifetime commitment. Paging through *Cooking Light*, you will find many delicious low-fat, low-calorie menus and recipes. Enjoy the variety, add a healthy dose of activity, brisk walking three times a week, and you will be well on your way to achieving overall body fitness. In no time, you will discover that food, fitness, and fun definitely do go together.

COUNTING THE BEATS

To determine your heart rate, locate your radial artery (on the thumb side of your wrist) and take your pulse during your exercise session. Take the pulse count for 10 seconds and then multiply that number by 6 to get your actual heart rate. If that number is above your target heart rate (THR) zone, slow down. If the number is below the zone, step up the pace.

Age	Predicted Maximum Heart Rate (in minutes)	Number of Heartbeats in 10 Seconds 70% - 85%		Target Heart Rate Zone (in minutes) 70% - 85%	
20	200	23	28	140	170
25	195	23	28	137	166
30	190	22	27	133	162
35	185	22	26	130	157
40	180	21	26	126	153
45	175	20	25	123	149
50	170	20	24	119	145
55	165	19	23	116	140
60	160	19	23	112	136

MATHEMATICAL FORMULA:
Maximum Heart Rate (MHR) = 220 minus age
MHR x 70% and 85% = THR in minutes

Stepping Up With Bench Aerobics

Bench aerobics combines the fun and cardiovascular benefits of aerobic dance with a workout that firms the muscles in the buttocks, thighs, and calves. Combinations of leg and arm movements as you step on and off the bench provide a high intensity, low impact workout. While benching has caught on at health clubs, it also can be done easily at home.

Start by wearing comfortable clothing and aerobic dance or cross-training shoes. Don't wear running shoes because their tread may catch on the bench.

As you step onto the bench, place your heel first and roll onto ball of foot. As you step off the bench, step onto the ball of foot and roll back onto the heel. Be sure to keep your eyes on the bench because it is easy to catch your foot. Watching the bench also will help you keep your feet in the right place.

Take a few minutes to learn each movement and do the moves slowly to keep your balance. Learn the leg movements first, and then add the arm movements. Check your heart rate; if it's too high, come off the bench and continue exercising on the floor.

Your workout session should include warming up, stretching, benching, doing muscle-strengthening exercises, cooling down, and stretching again. For the cool down, repeat the warm-up exercises, decreasing the intensity. But before you start this or any other fitness program, be sure to check with your physician.

Warm up—Start with legs shoulder-width apart, knees slightly flexed, and arms above head. Step to the side, leaning on one leg, and reach up with the opposite hand. Raise the heel of your free foot to protect your back. Alternate sides, reaching up high with your right arm as you lunge to the left. Repeat for 1 to 2 minutes.

Warm up—March briskly, bringing each knee high. Swing arms with each step, keeping elbows at 90-degree angles. Continue for 1 to 2 minutes.

Stretch—Stand with one leg slightly in front with foot flexed upward. Bend both knees slightly and rest arms on thighs for support. Hold for 30 seconds. Repeat with opposite leg.

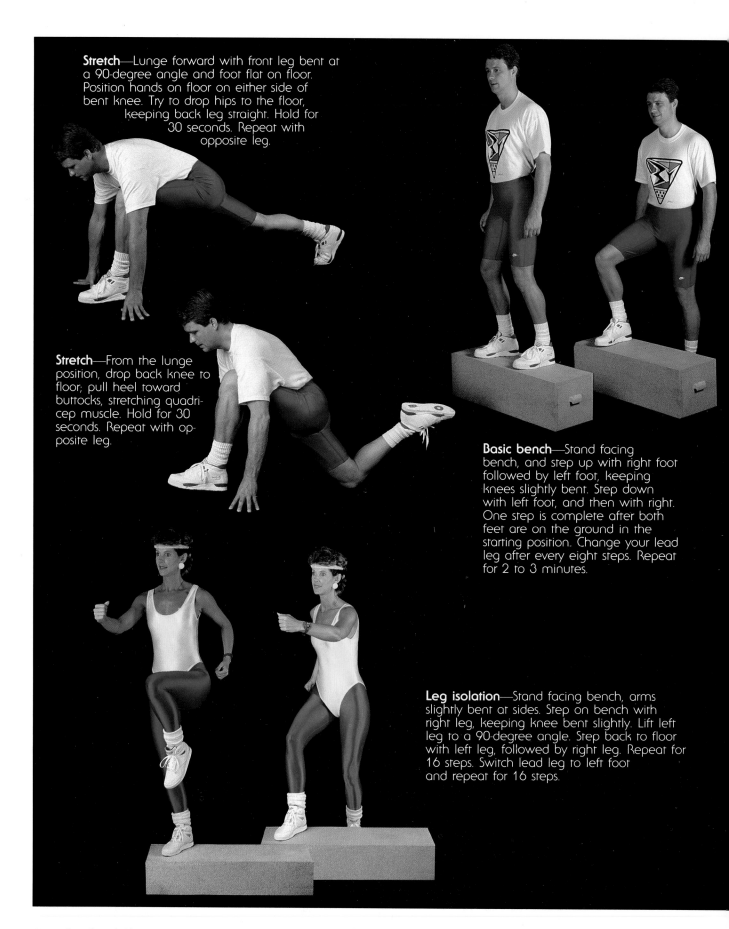

Stretch—Lunge forward with front leg bent at a 90-degree angle and foot flat on floor. Position hands on floor on either side of bent knee. Try to drop hips to the floor, keeping back leg straight. Hold for 30 seconds. Repeat with opposite leg.

Stretch—From the lunge position, drop back knee to floor; pull heel toward buttocks, stretching quadricep muscle. Hold for 30 seconds. Repeat with opposite leg.

Basic bench—Stand facing bench, and step up with right foot followed by left foot, keeping knees slightly bent. Step down with left foot, and then with right. One step is complete after both feet are on the ground in the starting position. Change your lead leg after every eight steps. Repeat for 2 to 3 minutes.

Leg isolation—Stand facing bench, arms slightly bent at sides. Step on bench with right leg, keeping knee bent slightly. Lift left leg to a 90-degree angle. Step back to floor with left leg, followed by right leg. Repeat for 16 steps. Switch lead leg to left foot and repeat for 16 steps.

Travel the bench—Stand on floor at center of bench and turn slightly toward righthand corner of bench with feet together, arms at sides. Step onto the bench, leading with right foot. Place left foot on far lefthand side of bench, shifting weight as you place foot. Step off bench with right foot, and then with left foot, returning to starting position. Repeat for 2 to 3 minutes. When comfortable with steps, add weights and arm movements.

Aside the bench—Stand beside bench, toes parallel to bench. Put arms at sides with elbows bent. Step onto bench with closest leg, followed by other leg, keeping knees slightly bent. As you step up, raise elbows and hands to shoulder height. Step off opposite side of bench, leading with first leg and return arms to starting position. Repeat, starting with opposite leg. Repeat sequence for 2 to 3 minutes.

Muscle strength—Lie with your back pressed down on bench and your feet flat on floor. Hold weights at chest level with arms bent at right angles. Inhale. As you exhale, push up and straighten arms without locking your elbows. Inhale as you return arms to starting position. Repeat 10 to 15 times.

Muscle strength—Lie with your back flat against floor and your feet on bench. Inhale. As you exhale, slowly curl your head, shoulders, and upper back off floor. Inhale as you slowly roll back to the starting position. Repeat 10 to 15 times.

Set Yourself Up for Success

When tension builds up and you feel that you are ready to explode, take a breather. But make it an exercise "breather." Studies show that exercise can reduce blood pressure and cause other healthy physiological changes to occur. In other words, activity can have a calming effect on the heart.

The type of exercise doesn't seem to matter. Something like yoga—a form of meditation that requires deep breathing and mental focusing—has been shown to increase calmness and lower the heart rate and blood pressure. Aerobic dancing, walking, and swimming have the same effect.

Since high blood pressure is one of the major risk factors for heart disease, exercise is paramount to prevention of this illness. Moreover, if high blood pressure is left untreated, it can wreak havoc on the heart, causing a multitude of unhealthy changes in heart tissue. So don't let your blood pressure zoom through the roof. When things take a stressful turn at home or at the office, take an activity break. With a little self-discipline, you can put forth the effort necessary to maintain health and fitness.

DEBUNKING ENERGY MYTHS

No matter how energetic you are, the daily grind can sap your get-up-and-go. Scientists have shown that anxiety, pressures, and the trials and tribulations of normal life can cause problems. But you can short circuit that drain on your energy. Fatigue, in fact, is often the sign of an underexercised body. The simple remedy: activity.

Slouching on the couch or reaching for a candy bar may seem like sure ways to regain lost energy, but they aren't, according to researchers at Stanford University. They offered groups of office workers the choice of a candy bar or a 10-minute walk to revive afternoon energy slumps. Workers who opted for the candy bar noticed an immediate surge of energy. Later, however, they complained that their energy had dropped to even lower levels than at the start. Although the walkers did not experience the energy "high" that the candy bar munchers

described, they felt more energetic overall. What's more, their energy lasted throughout the rest of the afternoon. So while most of us would like to count on candy and other sweets, the real energy booster is free, plain and simple. It's exercise.

SMART PLANNING

Whether you want to start a new food and fitness regimen or fine-tune an existing program, the key to success lies primarily in how you go about it. In today's fast-paced, high-pressure world, smart planning is needed to cope with the pressures, stresses, and unknowns that each day brings. Remember, however, that what works for one person when it comes to exercise or eating style may not work for someone else. Travel, the amount of time available, and daily responsibilities at work and at home all play a role in what a person can handle. But the need for establishing some type of program is obvious.

Luckily, achieving a healthy lifestyle is simpler than you may think. Unfortunately, however, most people lose the fitness battle at the very start. Trying to do too much too fast is a sure way to sabotage even the best of intentions. Scale down your efforts and make changes gradually in your lifestyle. One-at-a-time shifts or changes in the way you eat and live, after all, can add up to big benefits over the long haul. The key to making these changes is moderation.

LITTLE CHANGES ADD UP

The road to good health is paved with hundreds of choices. Picture the road as a chain with many links, connections that can be hooked together in dozens of different ways. Changes that last tend to come about in small increments. Gradually build on these changes in a way that suits your lifestyle, and chances are you'll reach your goals. Just don't set an unrealistic deadline for reaching those goals.

For example, several studies have found that most Americans routinely choose the same 10 to 12 meals over and over again. Perhaps it's fried chicken one night; macaroni and cheese the next. The point is that most of us fall into established patterns when choosing food. By making a few minor adjustments, you can update this eating style and bring it into the more health-conscious 90s. The changes may be as simple as trimming the fat from your current recipe (using a lower-fat cheese and less of it in a macaroni and cheese dish, for example) or trying a new recipe that's lower in fat. You will find throughout the pages of *Cooking Light* a wide variety of pasta recipes that contain cheese as an ingredient but still keep the fat and calories low.

MIND MATTERS

Even under the best of circumstances, sticking with a food and fitness plan is not easy, but the health benefits far outweigh the work you put into a program. Scientific studies prove that physical activity and good nutrition can help stave off chronic illness and even prolong life. What the studies fail to show is the "good feeling" that comes from keeping active and eating right. Experts call this "life quality."

In a recent study, Fortune 500 executives reported feeling much more energetic when they exercised and ate well. Indeed, the new power lunch of the 90s is a salad and fresh fruit. The power exercise to accompany it—walking. You can do it anywhere, almost anytime. No special equipment is required, and the chance for injury is slim.

Whatever activity or eating style you choose, keep in mind the overall effect it will have on your body. Health professionals know that simple day-to-day practices—what you eat, when you eat, and what activities you spread throughout your busy schedule—have a big impact on health. Building good health habits takes commitment. But if you reshape your lifestyle slowly, chances are you won't want to go back to old, less healthy habits. Fitness, when you make it a personal strategy, can turn out to be just as much fun as it is healthful. The overall quality of life improves more than scientific studies can even measure.

ON THE ROAD TO GOOD HEALTH

To get started on the road to good health, read the following tips on how to trim the fat and boost the activity in your daily schedule. Select six changes that will be easy for you to make. Start there and then gradually include the other healthful suggestions in your daily routine.

• Think fresh fruit for dessert. Enjoy strawberries lightly dusted with powdered sugar, for example, rather than higher-fat strawberry shortcake.
• Remember to remove the skin from turkey and chicken. Leaving the skin on poultry doubles the fat content; skin is pure saturated fat.
• Crowd out fatty foods by filling up on complex carbohydrates: pastas, breads, cereals, grains, and vegetables.
• Zero in on hidden sources of fat in your diet—snack crackers, processed luncheon meats, convenience foods, and pastries—and begin to limit or eliminate them one by one.
• Experiment with herbs—tarragon, basil, chives, dillweed, and cilantro—as seasonings instead of using butter and rich sauces.
• Gradually work your way from whole milk to 2% to 1% and skim. Substitute skim milk, low-fat cheese, and nonfat or low-fat yogurt for higher-fat dairy products.
• Switch to low-fat cooking methods: bake, steam, roast, grill, or broil foods rather than fry or cook them with large amounts of fat.
• Save high-fat treats or indulgences for once a month instead of once a week.
• Take a brisk 20-minute walk before work, before dinner, or some time during the day.
• Schedule an exercise "appointment" on your calendar at least three times a week. If you block out time for activity, chances are you will do it.
• Join family or friends in an active pursuit every week. Social get-togethers need not revolve solely around food.
• Park your car away from store entrances when shopping and walk the extra distance. Walk short distances when possible rather than drive.

The *Cooking Light* Kitchen

As you become familiar with techniques and ingredients for lighter cooking, preparing nutritious recipes will become second nature. When you cook, try steaming, sautéing, broiling, boiling, grilling, or stir-frying foods instead of deep-fat or pan-frying. Avoid boiling foods in large amounts of water because this depletes water-soluble nutrients in the foods. Prevent meat from cooking in excess fat when roasting by placing it on a rack in a roasting pan.

Observing these cooking techniques will give you a good start toward preparing foods that are lower in fat and calories. And by steaming or cooking vegetables in just a little water, you'll retain water-soluble vitamins such as vitamin C.

Cooking methods alone, however, will not make a recipe low in fat or cholesterol. By making smart low-fat substitutions in the ingredients, you can make a recipe more nutritious without decreasing the flavor of the food.

Each ingredient must be evaluated to determine its function in the recipe so that the modifications can be made without changing the basic structure of the dish. For example, vegetable cooking spray can be used in place of lard or vegetable shortening to grease a pan or skillet. However, this substitution would not be appropriate when shortening is an ingredient in a baked product. Instead, try substituting vegetable oil, using one-third less than the amount of solid fat.

PUTTING *COOKING LIGHT* INTO ACTION

Each recipe in *Cooking Light* has been developed and tested to meet strict standards for sound nutrition, excellent flavor, and visual appeal. And to add to the visual appeal, garnishing and serving suggestions have been provided to assist you in creating great-looking, great-tasting meals.

As a *Cooking Light* cook, you may want to lighten your own recipes to meet today's nutrition-conscious standards. The following chart provides examples of substitutions for foods high in calories or fat, and shows the fat, calories, and cholesterol you save by making these changes. And to add flavor to your foods, include fresh herbs for a taste that everyone will enjoy.

LIGHTENING THE INGREDIENT LIST

Making a favorite recipe lighter in calories and lower in fat isn't difficult. All it takes is learning how to make low-fat substitutions. The following chart should help get you started; it gives you a play by play on the savings in calories, fat, and cholesterol you net with each substitution.

FOOD ITEM	AMOUNT	CAL.	FAT	CHOL.	SUBSTITUTE	AMOUNT	CAL.	FAT	CHOL.	SAVINGS		
			gm	mg				gm	mg	CAL.	FAT	CHOL.
Whole milk	8 oz.	149	8	34	Skim milk	8 oz.	86	tr	5	63	8	29
Cream cheese	1 oz.	99	10	31	Light cream cheese	1 oz.	62	5	16	37	5	15
Ricotta cheese	½ c.	214	16	63	Ricotta, part-skim	½ c.	170	10	38	44	6	25
Cheddar cheese	1 oz.	114	9	30	40% less-fat Cheddar	1 oz.	71	4	15	43	5	15
Sour cream	½ c.	246	24	51	Nonfat yogurt	½ c.	64	tr	3	182	24	48
Fudge sauce	2 Tbl.	128	5	—	Chocolate syrup	2 Tbl.	98	tr	—	30	5	—
Whole egg	1	75	5	213	Egg whites	2	32	0	0	43	5	213
Baking chocolate	1 oz.	141	15	0	Cocoa powder	¼ c.	96	1	—	45	14	—
Beef, prime rib	3 oz.	293	25	—	Beef, round roast	3 oz.	162	5	71	131	20	—
Bacon strips	3	109	9	16	Canadian bacon	1 oz.	45	2	14	64	7	2
Walnuts	2 oz.	384	37	—	Raisins	2 oz.	170	0	0	214	37	—

tr = Trace amount of nutrient   Dash (—) indicates insufficient data available

KEEP IT LIGHT AND KEEP THE FLAVOR

Basil has broad, shiny leaves and comes in several varieties, each with a clove-like, anise flavor. Basil is a versatile Italian seasoning and is used to flavor egg dishes, meats, pesto, salads, and vegetables, especially eggplant and tomatoes.

Chives have long, slender, hollow blades and a pleasant, delicate, onion-like flavor. Chives are used to flavor poultry, tuna, appetizers, cream soups, potatoes, green salads, vegetables, spreads, sauces, and vinaigrettes.

Dillweed has fine, feathery leaves and a sweet caraway flavor. Dillweed is used to flavor chicken, egg dishes, fish, chowders, salad dressings, mustard sauces, and vegetables, especially carrots, peas, and cucumbers.

Parsley has curly or flat bright green leaves and slender, stringy stalks. Parsley has a delicate, fresh, celery-like flavor that enhances almost any food. It is used to flavor meats, fish, egg dishes, soups, stuffings, salads, and sauces.

Rosemary has hard, spiky leaves that have a strong, piney flavor. Rosemary is used in marinades to flavor grilled meats, chicken, fish, beef stews, soups, long-simmered sauces, and vegetables, especially cabbage and potatoes.

Sage has long, aromatic, velvety leaves that have a strong, warm, musky flavor. Sage is used to flavor meats, poultry, egg dishes, soups, stews, tomato and meat sauces, stuffings, and vegetables, especially eggplant and tomatoes.

Spearmint has large, pointed bright green leaves, a sweet, pungent aroma, and a cool, refreshing, minty flavor. It is used to flavor lamb, stuffings, fruit salads, tabbouleh salad, tea, fruit beverages, and vegetables, especially carrots, peas, and tomatoes.

Tarragon has long, slender, dark greenish-gray leaves and a sweet-spicy, licorice flavor. Tarragon is used to flavor veal, fish, shellfish, poultry, egg salad, chowders, tomato soup, salad dressings, vinegars, marinades, and vegetables, especially asparagus and mushrooms.

Thyme has small, pointed, gray-green leaves, and a sweet, pleasantly pungent flavor. It is used to flavor roasted meat, fish, chicken, egg dishes, soups, stews, stuffings, barbecue and other sauces, salad dressings, marinades, and vegetables, especially tomatoes and zucchini.

What's New in the Marketplace?

Physiologists have recently learned more about how the foot functions during different sporting activities and have concluded that sport shoes need to be individually structured. In other words, the best shoe for jogging may not be the best shoe for tennis or hiking or basketball. It may seem that the shoe industry is getting carried away—there are shoes for water sports, racquet sports, cycling, running, and walking—but fitness experts find clear advantages for each shoe type.

Of course, none of this is to say that you can't use a cross-training shoe if you participate in several different sporting activities. But if you are an avid runner, walker, or racquet sport player, your feet will benefit from the shoe that suits your sport. First, however, there are some guidelines that apply when buying any athletic shoe.

Pay attention to how your foot is structured. For example, people who have either a high or low arch need to look for shoes that compensate for this feature. If you walk on the outside of the foot (supinate), or if your heel leans inward (pronates), look for shoes that are built to correct this imbalance. The following is a brief synopsis of the most important features to look for when purchasing athletic shoes for a particular sport.

● Aerobic dance shoes—Features such as shock absorption materials, good traction from soles, stability, and flexibility are important. For low-impact dance, concentrate more on flexibility and support features. For high-impact, traction and shock absorption are top priorities.

● Basketball shoes—Lots of shock absorption material is critical to cushion feet when jumping. Padding around the ankles and down the tongue of shoe offers more cushion. Firmly built heels are also important.

● Running shoes—Look for plenty of shock absorption material and firm heel support. Running shoes need to have a firm cup built around the heel area (some shoes carry a double cup) to keep the heel rigid and prevent injury. To compensate for high or low arches or for the tendency to supinate

or pronate, special inserts called orthotics can often be purchased along with the shoes.

● Tennis, racquetball, and volleyball shoes—Flexible soft soles (usually made of gum rubber) help provide good traction. Look for shoes that have cushioning in the midfoot area.

● Walking shoes—Good running shoes are suitable for walking, but not all the features of a running shoe, such as the extra shock absorption materials, are necessary for walking. Best features for a walking shoe include a well-cushioned heel, arch support, and a curved sole to encourage heel to toe movement.

To rephrase an old saying, the advice for shoe shoppers should be this: If the shoe fits and it has the features for your sport and foot, wear it.

THAT WAXY SHINE

In an effort to make produce look more appealing and stay fresh longer, manufacturers often apply wax coatings to fresh produce. These coatings, which the FDA recognizes as safe, are brushed, dipped, or sprayed on the produce. The FDA sets limits for the amounts to be used, estimating how much wax consumers will ingest when eating a treated product.

Produce marketers say they apply wax coatings as a replacement for the protective wax coating that is lost when the produce is commercially cleaned with detergents to remove dirt and residues of chemical sprays. Unfortunately, you can't wash off waxes with soapy suds. These substances are immune to cleaning efforts. That's why the FDA approves only substances that are edible.

PRODUCE WITH A DIFFERENCE

Purple green beans and basil, green cauliflower, and yellow watermelon are just a few of the unusual vegetable selections filling produce bins around the country. While they're definitely fun to look at, just what does a purple potato taste like? More important, how does this unusual produce stack up nutritionally?

Nutritionists say the differences are slight. Natural pigments that color a fruit or vegetable do not usually affect nutrient content. This means that a yellow or orange raspberry will carry roughly the same concentration of nutrients as the red variety.

The same story usually holds true for taste. If you close your eyes, you probably won't be able to tell the difference between a purple or a white potato. Highly sharpened taste buds might notice, however, that green peppers have a slightly stronger flavor than the yellow, orange, purple, or red variety. But the differences, again, are very slight. Perhaps the main attraction to unusual colored produce is its visual appeal. The colorful produce may not taste different or offer any unique nutrient contributions, but it certainly will add sparkle to an otherwise ordinary meal.

Different sizes of produce can also add interest to your meal. Baby squash, eggplant, carrots, and corn can be served as side dishes or included in salads or entrées such as a stir-fry or casserole.

1. butter potatoes 2. white potatoes 3. red potatoes 4. new potatoes 5. purple potatoes 6. baby corn 7. purple basil 8. sweet yellow pepper 9. sweet red pepper 10. purple pepper 11. green pepper 12. orange pepper 13. baby green beans 14. cauliflower 15. broccoflower 16. cherry tomatoes 17. yellow cherry tomatoes 18. baby carrots 19. teardrop tomatoes 20. Asian pear 21. dragon snap beans 22. purple wax beans 23. wax beans 24. baby green pattypan squash 25. baby yellow pattypan squash 26. baby zucchini 27. baby yellow zucchini 28. Asian eggplant 29. white eggplant 30. yellow watermelon 31. baby watermelon 32. baby eggplant

Healthy
American
Meals

Celebrate the Fourth of July with family and friends. Everyone will enjoy (from right) Spicy Seafood Boil, Fireworks Coleslaw, and Chile Mayonnaise. (Menu begins on page 74.)

Each menu has been carefully developed for your enjoyment, and each meets the *Cooking Light* guidelines for healthy eating. No more than 50 percent of the total calories of the menu are derived from carbohydrate, 20 percent from protein, and less than 30 percent are contributed by fat. Use this 50-20-30 ratio as a guide when planning your own menus, whatever the occasion.

The four menu chapters reflect the growing interest in nutrition and health along with a desire for freshness and simple elegance. Regional and ethnic flavor adds to the variety. Whether you need ideas for a quick-to-prepare breakfast or for a special occasion to entertain friends, you are sure to find the answer to your menu needs.

Breakfast and Brunch. You'll find plenty of ideas here to help start your day. For a quick breakfast after an early morning workout, prepare Breakfast on the Run, or get the children off to school with School Daze. For more leisurely dining, have a South-of-the-Border Brunch or enjoy your weekend with Elegant Sunday Brunch, complete with French toast and pear turnovers.

Quick and Easy. Making quick, wholesome meals can be a real challenge. But Dinner from the Freezer allows you to prepare two meals at once without any additional work. Place half of the food in the freezer, and you can put an entire meal on the table with little or no preparation beyond thawing and heating. Celebrate with friends with an Oktoberfest Feast, complete with Wiener Schnitzel. Or put the Kids in Charge and take advantage of a family-pleasing menu that they will be proud of and will enjoy.

Microwave It Light. Use the microwave oven to help you put a nutritious meal on the table for family and friends. For a Spring Dinner, enjoy lamb chops and asparagus, two of spring's finest foods. Salads, ideal time savers, can be made ahead of time and chilled until needed for an easy Summer Evening Supper. Complete the meal with Watermelon Sherbet, made from one of the finest attributes of summer.

That's Entertaining! Here's a great way to enjoy entertaining relatives and friends. Invite someone over for a Warming Winter Dinner and prepare Sesame Pork Tenderloin and Gingered Sweet Potatoes, a hearty combination. Italian means more than pasta; instead, savor Turkey alla Osso Buco and Saffron Risotto for a Rustic Italian Dinner. Or enjoy a Fourth of July Celebration with Spicy Seafood Boil and Fireworks Coleslaw.

Bring a lovely brunch to a sweet conclusion with Rum-Raisin Pear Turnovers and Lemon-Mint Tea. (Menu begins on page 43.)

Breakfast & Brunch

Banana-Berry Smoothie and Fruit Granola Bars are energizing ways to start an active day.

Breakfast On The Run

Some days, the morning seems to fly by in an instant. Whether you need a quick breakfast after an early morning workout or you are prone to running late, there is a way for you to have a nutritious breakfast in minutes.

The solution? A hand-held breakfast you can grab on the way out the door. Make the granola bars ahead of time and store them in the refrigerator to simplify your morning schedule.

Banana-Berry Smoothie
Easy Breakfast Sandwiches
Fruit Granola Bars

Serves 3
Total calories per serving: 408

Get the ingredients ready for Easy Breakfast Sandwiches the night before so that, come morning, the sandwiches just need to be assembled. Orange segments

and alfalfa sprouts give a delightfully different twist to the ham and egg variation.

You only have to combine three ingredients for Banana-Berry Smoothie, which is a refreshing eye-opener served over crushed ice.

With this in mind, indulge yourself with a tasty, good-for-you breakfast that doesn't rob anyone of that precious morning commodity—time.

BANANA-BERRY SMOOTHIE

¾ cup cranberry juice cocktail
⅔ cup plain nonfat yogurt
1 medium banana, peeled and sliced
1 cup crushed ice

Combine cranberry juice, yogurt, and sliced banana in container of an electric blender; top with cover, and process until smooth. Add crushed ice, and process until mixture is smooth. Pour beverage into serving glasses, and serve immediately. Yield: 3 cups (106 calories per 1-cup serving).

PROTEIN 3.3 / FAT 0.3 / CARBOHYDRATE 23.7 / CHOLESTEROL 1 / IRON 0.3 / SODIUM 41 / CALCIUM 105

EASY BREAKFAST SANDWICHES

3 (1-ounce) slices lean ham
1½ whole wheat English muffins, split and toasted
2 tablespoons reduced-calorie mayonnaise
2 teaspoons spicy brown mustard
2 hard-cooked eggs, sliced
¼ cup mandarin orange segments in water, drained
3 tablespoons alfalfa sprouts

Place 1 slice ham on each toasted muffin half. Combine mayonnaise and mustard in a small bowl. Spread mixture over ham. Top with equal amounts of eggs, oranges, and sprouts. Yield: 3 servings (183 calories per serving).

PROTEIN 12.9 / FAT 8.1 / CARBOHYDRATE 15.2 / CHOLESTEROL 154 / IRON 0.9 / SODIUM 652 / CALCIUM 23

FRUIT GRANOLA BARS

¼ cup margarine
3 tablespoons light-colored corn syrup
½ cup miniature marshmallows
1½ cups 100% natural cereal
¼ cup dried apricots, coarsely chopped
3 tablespoon currants
Vegetable cooking spray
¼ cup sifted powdered sugar
1 teaspoon unsweetened orange juice
½ teaspoon reduced-calorie margarine, melted
⅛ teaspoon vanilla extract

Combine ¼ cup margarine, corn syrup, and marshmallows in a medium saucepan. Cook over medium heat until melted, stirring constantly. Cook an additional 2 minutes, stirring constantly. Remove from heat; stir in cereal, apricots, and currants, mixing well. Press cereal mixture into an 8-inch square pan coated with cooking spray. Chill 1 hour.

Combine powdered sugar and remaining ingredients; mix well. Drizzle over cereal mixture. Cover and refrigerate at least 8 hours. Cut into 2-inch squares. Store, covered, in refrigerator. Yield: 16 servings (119 calories each).

PROTEIN 1.5 / FAT 5.3 / CARBOHYDRATE 17.4 / CHOLESTEROL 0 / IRON 0.7 / SODIUM 44 / CALCIUM 26

FEEDING CHILDREN LIKE CHILDREN

Skimming the fat, cholesterol, and calories from meals may be safe advice for adults, but it's not always appropriate for growing children, especially those under 2 years of age. Children have high calorie needs, particularly in their first few years. Moreover, their stomach capacity is small. These are good reasons why children need calorie-dense foods, including foods containing fat. All children need some fat and cholesterol, particularly for normal brain and nervous system development.

Research shows that parents who are too strict about fat and calories early in a child's life run the risk of stunting that child's growth. Indeed, there's time enough in later childhood years to fine tune eating habits to make them more in line with adult guidelines. First, let children eat to grow.

School Daze

Cinnamon-Apple Oatmeal
Ham Rollups
Fruitsicles
Chocolate Fizz

Serves 4
Total calories per serving: 341

Children aren't necessarily the only ones in a daze in the morning. But coaxing them to eat a nutritious breakfast before heading off to school may snap you out of yours.

Make the first meal of the day fun for the children and easy on yourself. Feature a childhood favorite—steaming bowls of oatmeal, fortified with raisins and chopped apple.

Ham Rollups are tasty treats in the mornings and are easy to put together the night before.

Keep Fruitsicles on hand in the freezer for a different way to feast on fruit. Everyone will enjoy the novelty, and you'll love the no-mess way the children enjoy their nutritious serving of fruit. For convenience, use either fresh or frozen peaches; both have that "just picked" flavor.

Chocolate and children go hand in hand, so treat them to a Chocolate Fizz. With this menu, it's easy to avoid school daze on school days.

A healthy breakfast of Cinnamon-Apple Oatmeal, Ham Rollups, and Chocolate Fizz helps get the school day off to a good start.

CINNAMON-APPLE OATMEAL

1 cup water
¾ cup unsweetened apple juice
2 tablespoons currants
½ teaspoon ground cinnamon
¾ cup regular oats, uncooked
2½ tablespoons instant nonfat dry milk powder
⅔ cup chopped apple
1½ teaspoons brown sugar

Combine first 4 ingredients in a saucepan; bring to a boil. Add oats and milk powder; cook over medium heat 8 minutes, stirring occasionally. Remove from heat; add apple and brown sugar. Cover; let stand 5 minutes. Yield: 4 servings (131 calories per ½-cup serving).

PROTEIN 4.1 / FAT 1.3 / CARBOHYDRATE 26.8 / CHOLESTEROL 1 / IRON 1.2 / SODIUM 24 / CALCIUM 67

HAM ROLLUPS

2 ounces Neufchâtel cheese, softened
2 teaspoons reduced-calorie mayonnaise
¾ teaspoon prepared mustard
4 (¾-ounce) slices lean ham
⅓ cup alfalfa sprouts

Combine Neufchâtel cheese, mayonnaise, and mustard in a small bowl, stirring well.

Spread mayonnaise mixture evenly over ham slices, and top with alfalfa sprouts.

Carefully roll up ham slices, jellyroll fashion, securing with wooden picks. Cover ham rollups, and chill thoroughly. Yield: 4 servings (71 calories per serving).

PROTEIN 5.7 / FAT 5.1 / CARBOHYDRATE 0.8 / CHOLESTEROL 25 / IRON 0.2 / SODIUM 386 / CALCIUM 14

FRUITSICLES

1⅓ cups peeled, diced peaches
1 cup skim milk
¼ cup water
2 tablespoons sugar
6 (5-ounce) paper cups
2 tablespoons chopped almonds, toasted
6 wooden sticks

Combine first 4 ingredients in container of an electric blender; top with cover, and process until smooth. Pour into paper cups; top each

with 1 teaspoon toasted almonds. Cover tops of cups with aluminum foil, and insert a wooden stick through foil into center of each cup. Freeze until firm.

To serve, let popsicles stand at room temperature 5 minutes; remove foil, and peel paper cups away from popsicles. Yield: 6 servings (63 calories per serving).

PROTEIN 2.2 / FAT 1.3 / CARBOHYDRATE 11.3 / CHOLESTEROL 1 / IRON 0.1 / SODIUM 22 / CALCIUM 59

CHOCOLATE FIZZ

2½ cups 2% low-fat chocolate milk
¾ cup club soda, chilled
1 cup crushed ice

Combine low-fat chocolate milk, club soda, and crushed ice in container of an electric

blender; top with cover, and process until chocolate milk mixture is smooth. Pour into individual serving glasses. Serve immediately. Yield: 4 servings (76 calories per 1¼-cup serving).

PROTEIN 5.1 / FAT 2.9 / CARBOHYDRATE 7.3 / CHOLESTEROL 12 / IRON 0.1 / SODIUM 85 / CALCIUM 188

Hearty Country Breakfast

Hearty Omelet
Potato Medley
Honey-Whole Wheat
Bread
Fruity Jam
Orange Juice

Serves 4
Total calories per serving: 371

Cold mornings and a hearty breakfast that warms you are a perfect match.

Make this tasty omelet, stuffed full of vegetables, turkey, and cheese, to start the day.

To accompany the omelet, serve potatoes made with apples and onions for extra flavor.

Clockwise from top: Honey-Whole Wheat Bread, Fruity Jam, Hearty Omelet, and Potato Medley.

Include ½ cup orange juice, 1 slice of warm whole wheat bread with 1 tablespoon of jam to accompany this meal, and then you will be ready to face the elements.

HEARTY OMELET

Vegetable cooking spray
¾ cup diced tomato
⅔ cup diced cooked turkey breast
½ cup chopped zucchini
¼ cup chopped green pepper
¼ cup chopped sweet red pepper
¼ cup sliced green onions
1 tablespoon chopped fresh parsley
¼ teaspoon hot sauce
1½ cups frozen egg substitute with cheese, thawed
¼ cup skim milk
½ teaspoon minced fresh oregano
¼ teaspoon pepper
¼ cup (1 ounce) shredded 40% less-fat Cheddar cheese, divided

Coat a nonstick skillet with cooking spray; place over medium-high heat until hot. Add tomato and next 7 ingredients; sauté until tender.

Combine egg substitute, milk, oregano, and pepper in a small bowl.

Coat a small nonstick skillet with cooking spray; place over medium heat until hot enough to sizzle a drop of water. Pour half of egg substitute mixture into skillet. As mixture begins to cook, gently lift edges of omelet with a spatula, and tilt pan to allow uncooked portions to flow underneath. When mixture is set, spoon half of vegetable mixture over half of omelet; sprinkle with 2 tablespoons cheese. Loosen omelet with spatula, and carefully fold in half. Carefully slide omelet onto a warm serving platter. Cut omelet into 2 pieces. Repeat procedure with remaining egg mixture and cheese. Yield: 4 servings (112 calories per serving).

PROTEIN 17.0 / FAT 1.7 / CARBOHYDRATE 7.5 / CHOLESTEROL 15 / IRON 2.8 / SODIUM 198 / CALCIUM 115

POTATO MEDLEY

1¾ cups cubed new potato
1½ cups water
1 cup diced cooking apple
1 tablespoon lemon juice
Vegetable cooking spray
2 teaspoons vegetable oil
½ cup chopped onion

Combine potato and water in a medium saucepan. Bring to a boil; cover, reduce heat, and simmer until potato is almost tender (about 10 minutes). Drain well.

Combine apple and lemon juice; toss gently, and set aside.

Coat a large nonstick skillet with cooking spray; add oil. Place over medium-high heat until hot. Add potato and onion; sauté until potato is lightly browned and onion is tender. Add reserved apple; cover and cook 1 minute. Uncover and cook an additional 2 minutes. Yield: 4 servings (105 calories per ½-cup serving).

PROTEIN 2.0 / FAT 2.7 / CARBOHYDRATE 19.3 / CHOLESTEROL 0 / IRON 1.1 / SODIUM 6 / CALCIUM 18

HONEY-WHOLE WHEAT BREAD

1 package dry yeast
2 cups warm water (105° to 115°)
3 tablespoons honey
½ cup instant nonfat dry milk powder
3 tablespoons margarine, melted
½ teaspoon salt
1 cup whole wheat flour
3¾ cups bread flour, divided
1 tablespoon bread flour
Vegetable cooking spray
1 egg white, lightly beaten
1 tablespoon water

Dissolve yeast in warm water in a large bowl; stir in honey, and let stand 5 minutes. Add milk powder, margarine, salt, whole wheat flour, and 2 cups bread flour; beat at medium speed of an electric mixer until well blended. Gradually stir in enough of the remaining 1¾ cups bread flour to make a soft dough.

Sprinkle 1 tablespoon bread flour evenly over work surface. Turn dough out onto floured work surface, and knead until smooth and elastic (about 8 to 10 minutes). Place dough in a large bowl coated with cooking spray, turning to coat top. Cover and let rise in a warm place (85°), free from drafts, 1 hour and 15 minutes or until doubled in bulk.

Punch dough down, and divide in half; shape each portion into a loaf. Place in two 9- x 5- x 3-inch loafpans coated with cooking spray. Cover and let rise in a warm place, free from drafts, 1 hour or until doubled in bulk.

Combine egg white and 1 tablespoon water, stirring well; brush over loaves. Bake at 350° for 40 minutes or until loaves sound hollow when tapped. (Cover with aluminum foil the last 10 minutes of baking to prevent loaves from over-browning, if necessary.) Remove loaves from pans, and let cool on wire racks. Yield: 36 servings (78 calories per ½-inch slice).

PROTEIN 2.7 / FAT 1.2 / CARBOHYDRATE 14.0 / CHOLESTEROL 0 / IRON 0.5 / SODIUM 55 / CALCIUM 25

FRUITY JAM

2 cups peeled, coarsely chopped fresh peaches
1 cup fresh blackberries
⅓ cup sugar
2 teaspoons peeled, grated ginger

Combine all ingredients in a medium-size heavy saucepan. Bring mixture to a boil over medium-high heat, stirring frequently. Reduce heat to medium, and cook 15 minutes or until fruit mixture thickens, stirring frequently. Let jam cool to room temperature. Transfer jam to a jar; cover, and refrigerate up to 10 days. Yield: 1½ cups (20 calories per tablespoon).

PROTEIN 0.1 / FAT 0.0 / CARBOHYDRATE 5.0 / CHOLESTEROL 0 / IRON 0.0 / SODIUM 0 / CALCIUM 2

South-Of-The-Border Brunch

Fiesta Egg Scramble
Fruit Salad with Lime
Bloody Mary Bread
Cinnamon Spice Cake

Serves 4
Total calories per serving: 422

This south-of-the-border menu is a perfect eye opener.

Egg substitute perks up when served with picante sauce. And for a traditional flavor, serve this dish with a fruit salad accented with lime.

Bake the flavor of a Bloody Mary into a loaf bread that is great as is, or toasted. For the finale, feature the popular flavor of cinnamon in the form of a delicious spice cake. (Menu calories have been calculated to include 1 slice bread and 1 serving cake.) Olé!

Fiesta Egg Scramble, Fruit Salad with Lime, and Cinnamon Spice Cake have south-of-the-border flavor.

FIESTA EGG SCRAMBLE

Vegetable cooking spray
⅓ cup chopped sweet red pepper
3 tablespoons chopped green onions
2 tablespoons chopped green chiles, drained
1¼ cups frozen egg substitute with cheese, thawed
3 tablespoons skim milk
¼ cup (1 ounce) shredded reduced-fat Monterey Jack cheese
½ cup low-sodium picante sauce

Coat a large nonstick skillet with cooking spray; place over medium-high heat until hot. Add sweet red pepper, green onions, and chiles; sauté until vegetables are tender. Combine egg substitute and milk; stir well. Pour over pepper mixture in skillet, and cook over medium heat, stirring frequently, until egg substitute mixture is firm but still moist.

Remove from heat. Sprinkle cheese over eggs; cover and let stand 1 minute. Divide eggs evenly among 4 plates. Spoon 2 tablespoons picante sauce over each serving. Yield: 4 servings (123 calories per serving).

PROTEIN 11.8 / FAT 5.5 / CARBOHYDRATE 5.8 / CHOLESTEROL 8 / IRON 0.5 / SODIUM 387 / CALCIUM 79

FRUIT SALAD WITH LIME

2 kiwifruit, peeled and sliced
2 oranges, peeled and sectioned
1 cup sliced fresh strawberries
2 tablespoons lime juice
1 tablespoon plus 1 teaspoon powdered sugar
¼ teaspoon ground cinnamon

Cut kiwifruit slices into quarters. Combine kiwifruit, orange sections, and strawberries in a medium bowl. Pour lime juice over fruit, and toss gently. Cover and chill at least 3 hours.

Combine sugar and cinnamon; add to fruit mixture, and toss well. Yield: 4 servings (71 calories per ½-cup serving).

PROTEIN 1.3 / FAT 0.5 / CARBOHYDRATE 16.6 / CHOLESTEROL 0 / IRON 0.5 / SODIUM 1 / CALCIUM 37

BLOODY MARY BREAD

1 package dry yeast
¼ cup warm water (105° to 115°)
1 (6-ounce) can spicy vegetable juice cocktail
1 tablespoon sugar
2 tablespoons water
1 tablespoon unsalted margarine
1 egg, beaten
½ teaspoon salt
1 cup whole wheat flour
¼ cup wheat germ
1¾ cups all-purpose flour
3 tablespoons all-purpose flour
Vegetable cooking spray

Dissolve yeast in warm water in a large bowl; let stand 5 minutes.

Combine vegetable juice cocktail and next 3 ingredients in a small saucepan; cook over medium heat until margarine melts. Let cool to 105° to 115°. Stir in egg and salt. Add to yeast mixture; stir well. Add whole wheat flour and wheat germ; beat at low speed of an electric mixer until well blended. Beat an additional 3 minutes at high speed. Stir in enough of the 1¾ cups all-purpose flour to make a soft dough.

Sprinkle 3 tablespoons all-purpose flour evenly over work surface. Turn dough out onto floured surface, and knead until smooth and elastic (about 8 to 10 minutes). Place dough in a large

bowl coated with cooking spray, turning to coat top. Cover and let rise in a warm place (85°), free from drafts, 1 hour or until doubled in bulk.

Punch dough down. Roll to a 15- x 8½-inch rectangle. Roll up dough, jellyroll fashion, starting with narrow end; pinch seam and ends to seal. Place loaf, seam side down, in an 8½- x 4½- x 3-inch loafpan coated with cooking spray.

Cover and let rise in a warm place, free from drafts, 45 minutes or until doubled in bulk. Bake at 350° for 35 to 40 minutes or until loaf sounds hollow when tapped. Remove from pan, and let cool completely on wire rack. Yield: 17 servings (94 calories per ½-inch slice).

PROTEIN 3.2 / FAT 1.4 / CARBOHYDRATE 17.2 / CHOLESTEROL 12 / IRON 1.1 / SODIUM 110 / CALCIUM 7

CINNAMON SPICE CAKE

Vegetable cooking spray
¾ cup plus 2 tablespoons cake flour
1 teaspoon baking powder
½ teaspoon ground cinnamon
½ teaspoon ground nutmeg
¼ teaspoon ground cloves
¼ cup margarine, softened
⅓ cup sugar
¼ cup skim milk
1 egg
½ teaspoon vanilla extract
1 tablespoon powdered sugar

Coat an 8-inch square pan with cooking spray; set aside.

Combine cake flour and next 4 ingredients; stir well, and set aside.

Cream margarine; gradually add ⅓ cup sugar, beating well at medium speed of an electric mixer. Add flour mixture, and beat well. Combine milk, egg, and vanilla; add to creamed mixture. Beat at low speed of electric mixer until blended. Continue beating mixture at high speed 2 minutes.

Pour batter into prepared pan. Bake at 350° for 25 to 30 minutes or until wooden pick inserted in center comes out clean. Let cool. Sift powdered sugar over cooled cake. Yield: 9 servings (134 calories per serving).

PROTEIN 2.0 / FAT 5.8 / CARBOHYDRATE 18.5 / CHOLESTEROL 22 / IRON 1.1 / SODIUM 104 / CALCIUM 38

Serve Cheese-Filled French Toast with Rosy Citrus Sauce, Spicy Sausage Links, and Lemon-Mint Tea for a special weekend brunch.

Elegant Sunday Brunch

Company is coming, so make this leisurely Sunday brunch the highlight of the weekend. Get out your good china, and set the table the night before for this nutritious version of a classic brunch.

Treat yourself and guests to cheesy French toast, a classy update to the favorite standby. A mixture of Neufchâtel cheese, orange marmalade, and pecans is sandwiched between high-fiber bread; then the bread is dipped in a cinnamon-egg batter and

Cheese-Filled French Toast
Rosy Citrus Sauce
Spicy Sausage Links
Rum-Raisin Pear Turnovers
Lemon-Mint Tea

Serves 6
Total calories per serving: 579

sautéed. To keep the calories down—and the flavor up—top each serving of French toast with 3 tablespoons of the warm citrus

sauce instead of flooding it with commercial syrup.

The flavorful sausages can be made earlier in the day or the day before for convenience.

Try the flaky turnovers for a special dessert. Pears are baked in phyllo pastry for an elegant ending to your meal. Now refrigerate the flavorful tea in your good crystal pitcher and open up the Sunday paper to enjoy at your leisure, while you wait for your guests to arrive.

CHEESE-FILLED FRENCH TOAST

½ cup Neufchâtel cheese, softened
3 tablespoons low-sugar orange marmalade
2 tablespoons chopped pecans, toasted
12 (¾-ounce) slices light seven-grain sandwich bread
¾ cup frozen egg substitute, thawed
½ cup skim milk
½ teaspoon vanilla extract
¼ teaspoon ground cinnamon
Vegetable cooking spray

Beat cheese at medium speed of an electric mixer until light and fluffy. Stir in marmalade and pecans. Spread cheese mixture on 6 slices

of bread; top with remaining 6 slices of bread, gently pressing slices together. Cut each sandwich in half diagonally to form triangles.

Combine egg substitute and next 3 ingredients in a shallow bowl, beating well. Dip each triangle in egg mixture, coating well.

Coat a large nonstick skillet with cooking spray; place over medium heat until hot. Arrange half the triangles in skillet, and cook 3 minutes on each side or until browned. Repeat procedure with remaining triangles. Yield: 6 servings (185 calories per serving).

PROTEIN 10.3 / FAT 9.4 / CARBOHYDRATE 17.3 / CHOLESTEROL 28 / IRON 2.1 / SODIUM 173 / CALCIUM 99

ROSY CITRUS SAUCE

3 tablespoons sugar
1 tablespoon plus ½ teaspoon cornstarch
½ cup cranberry juice cocktail
¼ cup plus 2 tablespoons unsweetened orange juice
¾ teaspoon reduced-calorie margarine
2 small oranges, peeled, seeded, and sectioned

Combine sugar and cornstarch in a medium saucepan; stir well. Add cranberry juice cocktail

and unsweetened orange juice. Place over medium heat, and cook until cranberry juice mixture is thickened, stirring constantly.

Remove mixture from heat; add margarine, stirring until melted. Gently stir in orange sections. Serve warm over French toast. Yield: 1¼ cups (15 calories per tablespoon).

PROTEIN 0.1 / FAT 0.1 / CARBOHYDRATE 3.7 / CHOLESTEROL 0 / IRON 0.0 / SODIUM 1 / CALCIUM 3

SPICY SAUSAGE LINKS

¾ pound lean ground pork
2 egg whites
2 tablespoons minced onion
2 tablespoons minced fresh parsley
1 teaspoon pepper
1 teaspoon hot sauce
½ teaspoon onion powder
½ teaspoon dried whole oregano
Vegetable cooking spray

Combine first 8 ingredients in a medium bowl; stir well. Shape mixture into 12 links. Cover links, and chill at least 1 hour.

Coat a large nonstick skillet with cooking spray; place over medium-high heat until hot. Place links in skillet, and cook 9 to 10 minutes or until lightly browned, turning frequently. Drain links well on paper towels. Yield: 6 servings (119 calories per serving).

PROTEIN 13.1 / FAT 6.7 / CARBOHYDRATE 0.9 / CHOLESTEROL 40 / IRON 0.7 / SODIUM 55 / CALCIUM 11

RUM-RAISIN PEAR TURNOVERS

3 medium-size ripe pears, peeled, cored, and thinly sliced
2 tablespoons lemon juice
¼ cup diced dried apricot
3 tablespoons raisins
2 tablespoons brown sugar
1 tablespoon dark rum
½ teaspoon ground cinnamon
¼ teaspoon ground nutmeg
6 sheets commercial frozen phyllo pastry, thawed
Butter-flavored vegetable cooking spray

Combine pears and lemon juice in a large bowl; toss gently. Add apricot and next 5 ingredients, stirring gently; set aside.

Place one sheet of phyllo on a damp towel (keep remaining phyllo covered). Lightly coat phyllo with cooking spray. Fold in half lengthwise, and spray again. Place one-sixth of pear mixture at base of phyllo sheet, folding the right bottom corner over filling, making a triangle. Continue folding back and forth into a triangle to end of sheet. Place triangle, seam side down, on a baking sheet coated with cooking spray.

(Keep triangles covered before baking.) Repeat process with remaining phyllo and pear mixture.

Bake at 400° for 15 minutes or until golden. Cool 5 minutes on wire racks; serve warm. Yield: 6 servings (149 calories per serving).

PROTEIN 2.9 / FAT 0.8 / CARBOHYDRATE 34.7 / CHOLESTEROL 0 / IRON 1.3 / SODIUM 4 / CALCIUM 21

LEMON-MINT TEA

4 cups water, divided
4 regular-size tea bags
2 lemons, cut into ½-inch-thick slices
½ cup fresh mint leaves, crushed
2½ cups unsweetened pineapple juice
2 tablespoons sugar
½ teaspoon vanilla extract
½ teaspoon almond extract
Fresh mint sprigs (optional)

Bring 2 cups water to a boil; pour over tea bags. Cover and steep 5 minutes. Add lemon slices and mint leaves; cover and steep 20 minutes. Strain, discarding tea bags, lemon slices, and mint leaves.

Combine tea, remaining 2 cups water, pineapple juice, sugar, and flavorings. Stir well. Serve beverage over ice, and garnish with fresh mint sprigs, if desired. Yield: 6 cups (81 calories per 1-cup serving).

PROTEIN 0.4 / FAT 0.1 / CARBOHYDRATE 19.9 / CHOLESTEROL 0 / IRON 0.4 / SODIUM 1 / CALCIUM 19

Set your table on a sunny porch for Lunch for the Ladies. Tropical Chicken Salad, Miniature Mango Muffins, and Chocolate Malted Coffee will receive rave reviews. (Menu begins on page 48.)

Quick & Easy

The children will enjoy preparing and eating Crispy Drumsticks, The Green Team, Apple Salad with Creamy Maple Dressing, and Strawberry Sodas.

Kids In Charge

Who can resist the children's offer to be in charge of supper! But don't just say yes; give them a menu that will be both successful and fun, to encourage them to offer again very soon.

While your young cooks prepare Crispy Drumsticks, explain to them that most of the fat in chicken is found in the skin and can easily be eliminated by removing the skin.

Part-skim ricotta and reduced-calorie syrup are the base for the

Crispy Drumsticks
The Green Team
Apple Salad with Creamy Maple Dressing
Commercial Dinner Rolls
Strawberry Sodas

Serves 4
Total calories per serving: 576

creamy dressing that is spooned over diced apples. This dressing can also be served as a dip with

other fresh fruits for a healthy and delicious afternoon snack.

Commercial dinner rolls in child-pleasing animal shapes balance the meal. The equivalent of 1 regular-size roll per person is included in the analysis.

And what can top off a meal better for children of any age than ice cream sodas? Use ice milk, and let the entire family join in the fun of making these colorful treats. Just don't forget the straws!

CRISPY DRUMSTICKS

¼ cup fine, dry breadcrumbs
⅛ teaspoon garlic powder
⅛ teaspoon onion powder
⅛ teaspoon dried whole marjoram
⅛ teaspoon dried whole thyme
1 egg white, lightly beaten
1 tablespoon skim milk
8 chicken drumsticks, skinned (about
   1½ pounds)
Vegetable cooking spray

Combine first 5 ingredients in a shallow dish; stir well. Combine egg white and milk in a small bowl. Dip each drumstick in milk mixture; dredge in breadcrumb mixture.

Place drumsticks in a 13- x 9- x 2-inch baking dish coated with cooking spray. Bake, uncovered, at 350° for 40 to 45 minutes or until done. Yield: 4 servings (196 calories per serving).

PROTEIN 28.7 / FAT 5.8 / CARBOHYDRATE 5.0 / CHOLESTEROL 89 / IRON 1.4 / SODIUM 151 / CALCIUM 26

THE GREEN TEAM

1½ cups frozen broccoli flowerets
1 cup frozen English peas
½ cup water
2 tablespoons chopped green onions
1 tablespoon diced pimiento
¼ teaspoon salt
¼ teaspoon dried whole dillweed

Combine first 4 ingredients in a medium saucepan; bring to a boil. Cover, reduce heat, and simmer 4 to 5 minutes or until crisp-tender. Drain. Stir in pimiento, salt, and dillweed. Yield: 4 servings (40 calories per ½-cup serving).

PROTEIN 3.1 / FAT 0.3 / CARBOHYDRATE 7.1 / CHOLESTEROL 0 / IRON 0.9 / SODIUM 191 / CALCIUM 36

APPLE SALAD WITH
CREAMY MAPLE DRESSING

3 tablespoons part-skim ricotta cheese
1 tablespoon plus 1 teaspoon
   reduced-calorie syrup
1 teaspoon skim milk
½ teaspoon vanilla extract
⅛ teaspoon ground cinnamon
4 lettuce leaves
2 cups coarsely chopped apple

Combine first 5 ingredients in container of an electric blender; top with cover, and process until smooth. To serve, line salad plates with lettuce leaves. Spoon ½ cup apple onto each lettuce leaf; top with syrup mixture. Yield: 4 servings (65 calories per ½-cup serving).

PROTEIN 1.8 / FAT 1.2 / CARBOHYDRATE 12.6 / CHOLESTEROL 4 / IRON 0.3 / SODIUM 19 / CALCIUM 44

STRAWBERRY SODAS

2 cups strawberry ice milk
1 cup frozen unsweetened strawberries
½ cup skim milk
1 cup club soda, chilled

Combine strawberry ice milk, unsweetened strawberries, and skim milk in container of an electric blender; top with cover, and process until strawberry mixture is smooth. Add chilled club soda, stirring well to combine. Pour into glasses, and serve immediately. Yield: 4 cups (119 calories per 1-cup serving).

PROTEIN 3.3 / FAT 2.1 / CARBOHYDRATE 23.3 / CHOLESTEROL 1 / IRON 0.4 / SODIUM 85 / CALCIUM 49

Lunch For The Ladies

Green Chile-Corn Dip
Tropical Chicken Salad
Miniature Mango Muffins
Chocolate Malted Coffee

Serves 6
Total calories per serving: 463

This simple menu will delight your friends—it is pretty on the table, tasty to the palate, and light on the calories.

Start with a spicy dip and an arrangement of vegetable crudités, allowing ½ cup of vegetables per serving. Use a pretty platter, and feature the vegetables as a colorful centerpiece.

Your guests will enjoy the miniature mango muffins; three muffins per serving have been included in the analysis.

The dessert coffee can be served iced or warm. Select a chocolate-flavored coffee as a base for a strong coffee flavor with no calories. Combine the remaining ingredients, and serve the coffee in your prettiest mugs as the grand finale.

Begin your ladies' luncheon with Green Chile-Corn Dip and crudités.

GREEN CHILE-CORN DIP

1 (8-ounce) carton 1% low-fat cottage cheese
½ cup frozen whole kernel corn, thawed
2 tablespoons commercial picante sauce
⅛ teaspoon garlic powder
⅛ teaspoon ground cumin
2 tablespoons canned chopped green chiles, drained
1 tablespoon diced sweet red pepper
2 tablespoons frozen whole kernel corn, thawed

Combine first 5 ingredients in container of an electric blender; top with cover, and process until almost smooth. Gently fold in green chiles, sweet red pepper, and 2 tablespoons corn. Cover dip, and chill at least 1 hour. Serve dip with fresh raw vegetables. Yield: 1½ cups (11 calories per tablespoon).

PROTEIN 1.3 / FAT 0.1 / CARBOHYDRATE 1.2 / CHOLESTEROL 0 / IRON 0.1 / SODIUM 49 / CALCIUM 6

TROPICAL CHICKEN SALAD

¼ cup 1% low-fat cottage cheese
1 (8-ounce) can crushed pineapple in juice, drained
2 tablespoons reduced-calorie mayonnaise
1 teaspoon sugar
½ teaspoon grated orange rind
¼ teaspoon grated lime rind
⅛ teaspoon ground ginger
2 teaspoons lemon juice
3 cups chopped cooked chicken breast (skinned before cooking and cooked without salt)
½ cup green grapes
½ cup sliced water chestnuts
1 tablespoon chopped fresh chives
½ cup canned mandarin oranges packed in water, drained
6 cups shredded fresh spinach
1 tablespoon slivered almonds, toasted
Fresh chives (optional)
Orange rind curls (optional)

Position knife blade in food processor bowl. Combine first 8 ingredients in processor bowl; process until smooth.

Combine cottage cheese mixture, chicken, grapes, water chestnuts, and chopped chives in a large bowl, stirring well. Gently fold in oranges. Cover and chill thoroughly.

Place 1 cup spinach on each of 6 individual serving plates; top evenly with chicken mixture. Sprinkle each serving with ½ teaspoon toasted almonds. If desired, garnish with fresh chives and orange curls. Yield: 6 servings (171 calories per serving).

PROTEIN 21.3 / FAT 4.5 / CARBOHYDRATE 11.2 / CHOLESTEROL 53 / IRON 1.7 / SODIUM 146 / CALCIUM 54

CHOCOLATE MALTED COFFEE

4 cups brewed chocolate almond-flavored coffee
1¾ cups skim milk
¼ cup malted milk powder
2 tablespoons chocolate-flavored syrup

Combine all ingredients in container of an electric blender; top with cover, and process until frothy. Serve warm or cold. Yield: 6 cups (68 calories per 1-cup serving).

PROTEIN 3.5 / FAT 0.6 / CARBOHYDRATE 11.9 / CHOLESTEROL 1 / IRON 0.8 / SODIUM 73 / CALCIUM 109

MINIATURE MANGO MUFFINS

½ cup whole wheat flour
½ cup all-purpose flour
2 tablespoons wheat germ
2 tablespoons firmly packed brown sugar
½ teaspoon baking soda
⅛ teaspoon salt
½ cup mashed mango
1½ tablespoons vegetable oil
1 egg, beaten
2¼ teaspoons skim milk
1½ teaspoons dark rum
¼ teaspoon coconut extract
¼ teaspoon almond extract
Vegetable cooking spray

Combine first 6 ingredients in a large bowl; make a well in center of mixture. Combine mango, oil, egg, milk, rum, and flavorings; add liquid mixture to dry ingredients, stirring just until dry ingredients are moistened.

Spoon batter into miniature (1¾-inch) muffin pans coated with cooking spray, filling three-fourths full. Bake at 350° for 10 to 12 minutes or until golden. Remove from pans, and let cool slightly on a wire rack. Yield: 18 muffins (50 calories each).

PROTEIN 1.3 / FAT 1.7 / CARBOHYDRATE 7.8 / CHOLESTEROL 11 / IRON 0.4 / SODIUM 44 / CALCIUM 11

CREEPING WEIGHT GAIN

Between the ages of 25 and 55, the average person gains about 30 pounds. It doesn't happen overnight; it insidiously creeps up, pound by pound. Just a pound a year adds up to that 30-pound gain.

One fitness expert blames this "creeping obesity" more on a decline in physical activity than overeating. People tend to exercise less as they get older. Not only does that equate to weight gain, but also to a higher percentage of body fat. The weight gained by an inactive person is more likely to be pure fat, not muscle. In other words, not only does a person often get heavier, but the percentage of total body fat also increases.

Prevention is the key to putting a stop to this unhealthy trend. So increase your activity level and get moving before those pounds creep up on you.

Vegetarian Supper

Whether a vegetarian diet is your choice for life or just a meal, this simple supper will be intensely satisfying.

A Dutch baby is an easy dish to prepare. Pour a batter of flour, skim milk, and eggs into a pie-plate, and watch it rise to form a golden brown, edible bowl. The filling is a colorful mix of fresh cabbage, carrots, squash, black

**Vegetarian Dutch Baby
Spicy Toast Strips
Peach Meringue Shortcakes**

Serves 4
Total calories per serving: 448

beans and mushrooms. Get a head start—use preshredded slaw mix found in the supermarket's produce section. Also look

for preshredded cheese to trim a few minutes of your time.

Only a tablespoon of reduced-calorie margarine and a few spices are needed to turn pita bread into crisp munchables. Cut each round into strips for an attractive presentation.

Commercial angel food cake gives you a head start on dessert preparation.

Supper takes care of itself with cheese-topped Vegetarian Dutch Baby.

VEGETARIAN DUTCH BABY

Vegetable cooking spray
½ (16-ounce) package commercial slaw mix
1 cup sliced fresh mushrooms
½ cup quartered and thinly sliced yellow squash
½ cup quartered and thinly sliced zucchini
¾ cup canned, cooked black beans, drained and rinsed
½ teaspoon dried whole basil
¼ teaspoon dried whole thyme
¼ teaspoon onion powder
¼ teaspoon garlic powder
⅛ teaspoon salt
⅛ teaspoon pepper
1 tablespoon reduced-calorie margarine
½ cup all-purpose flour
½ cup skim milk
2 eggs, beaten
½ cup (2 ounces) shredded provolone cheese

Coat a large nonstick skillet with cooking spray; place over medium-high heat until hot. Add slaw mix, mushrooms, squash, and zucchini; sauté 5 to 7 minutes or until vegetables are tender, stirring frequently. Stir in black beans and next 6 ingredients. Remove from heat, and keep warm.

Coat a 9-inch pieplate with cooking spray; add margarine. Bake at 425° for 1 minute or until margarine melts. Combine flour, milk, and eggs in a medium bowl; stir well with a wire whisk. Pour mixture into prepared pieplate (do not stir).

Bake at 425° for 15 to 20 minutes or until puffed and browned. Spoon vegetable mixture into shell; sprinkle with cheese. Bake 1 to 2 minutes or until cheese melts. Serve immediately. Yield: 4 servings (240 calories per serving).

PROTEIN 14.0 / FAT 8.9 / CARBOHYDRATE 27.6 / CHOLESTEROL 110 / IRON 2.8 / SODIUM 287 / CALCIUM 208

SPICY TOAST STRIPS

1 (6-inch) whole wheat pita bread round
1 tablespoon reduced-calorie margarine, melted
⅛ teaspoon paprika
⅛ teaspoon ground red pepper
⅛ teaspoon garlic powder

Cut pita in half to form 2 circles. Combine margarine and remaining ingredients; stir well. Brush on inside surface of bread rounds. Cut each round into 8 strips; place strips on an ungreased baking sheet. Bake at 350° for 8 to 10 minutes or until crisp and golden. Yield: 4 servings (66 calories per serving).

PROTEIN 1.0 / FAT 2.2 / CARBOHYDRATE 9.9 / CHOLESTEROL 0 / IRON 0.6 / SODIUM 28 / CALCIUM 16

PEACH MERINGUE SHORTCAKES

4 (1-ounce) slices commercial angel food cake
1 egg white
1 tablespoon sugar
⅛ teaspoon almond extract
2 cups peeled, sliced fresh peaches
1 tablespoon lemon juice
3½ tablespoons water, divided
2 tablespoons peach nectar
1½ teaspoons brown sugar
⅛ teaspoon ground cardamom
1 tablespoon amaretto
1½ teaspoons cornstarch

Place cake slices on an ungreased baking sheet. Bake at 375° for 4 minutes. Turn slices over; bake an additional 4 minutes.

Beat egg white (at room temperature) at high speed of an electric mixer 1 minute. Add 1 tablespoon sugar; beat until stiff peaks form and sugar dissolves. Fold in almond extract.

Cut each cake slice into 2 triangles. Spread meringue over triangles. Place on greased baking sheet. Bake at 400° for 7 minutes or until meringue is lightly browned.

Combine peaches and lemon juice; toss gently. Combine 2 tablespoons water and next 3 ingredients in a large skillet. Cook over medium heat, stirring constantly, until sugar dissolves. Stir in peaches and amaretto. Bring to a boil; reduce heat, and simmer 3 minutes.

Combine remaining 1½ tablespoons water and cornstarch; stir well. Add to peach mixture; cook until thickened, stirring constantly.

Place 2 cake triangles on each individual dessert plate. Top each with peach mixture. Yield: 4 servings (141 calories per serving).

PROTEIN 3.0 / FAT 0.2 / CARBOHYDRATE 33.3 / CHOLESTEROL 0 / IRON 0.2 / SODIUM 55 / CALCIUM 33

Dinner From The Freezer

After a tiring, busy day nothing could be more rewarding than being able to pull an entire meal from your freezer that takes little or no preparation beyond thawing and heating.

This practical menu is actually two in one. Each time-saving recipe makes enough servings for two meals—one for you to cook and eat tonight, the other for you to wrap and freeze for another time. All of the recipes in this menu are simple to prepare and go together well for a balanced and delicious dinner.

Stuffed Peppers
Freezer Slaw
Tortilla Wedges
Easy Mixed Fruit Sherbet

Serves 8
Total calories per serving: 456

Begin with the sherbet, a refreshing icy dessert. Make the sherbet ahead of time and store in the freezer until ready to serve. Before serving, let the sherbet stand at room temperature 15 minutes for easy scooping.

Stuffed Peppers are pretty and can be baked immediately or frozen for later.

Freezer Slaw and Tortilla Wedges will become permanent fixtures in your freezer. The slaw is a slightly sweet version, easy to assemble, and fit for a variety of meals. Tortilla Wedges can be made at the last minute or frozen and reheated.

Either way, these accompaniments will become family favorites. The end result is two great meals in the time it takes to make just one.

STUFFED PEPPERS

4 medium-size green peppers
1¼ pounds ground chuck
3 tablespoons chopped onion
2 tablespoons chopped sweet red pepper
2 tablespoons chopped green pepper
1 (12-ounce) can no-salt-added whole kernel corn
½ cup no-salt-added tomato juice
¼ cup frozen egg substitute, thawed
3 tablespoons unprocessed oat bran
1 tablespoon chili powder
½ teaspoon garlic powder
¼ teaspoon salt
¼ teaspoon pepper
¼ teaspoon hot sauce

Cut peppers in half lengthwise; remove and discard stems and seeds. Cook pepper 5 minutes in boiling water; drain well.

Combine meat and next 3 ingredients in a nonstick skillet. Place over medium heat; cook until meat is browned, stirring to crumble. Drain and pat dry with paper towels. Wipe drippings from skillet with a paper towel. Return mixture to skillet; stir in corn and remaining ingredients. Spoon evenly into pepper halves. Place peppers in a shallow baking dish. Cover and bake at 350° for 30 minutes or until thoroughly heated.

Yield: 8 servings (192 calories per serving). Note: Peppers may be frozen before baking. Thaw; bake, covered, at 350° for 30 minutes or until peppers are thoroughly heated.

PROTEIN 16.7 / FAT 9.6 / CARBOHYDRATE 11.4 / CHOLESTEROL 44 / IRON 3.1 / SODIUM 127 / CALCIUM 19

FREEZER SLAW

½ cup water
½ cup vinegar
¼ cup sugar
¼ teaspoon mustard seeds
¼ teaspoon celery seeds
3 cups shredded cabbage
1½ cups shredded Chinese cabbage
½ cup shredded carrot

Combine first 5 ingredients in a small saucepan; bring to a boil, stirring occasionally. Boil 1 minute. Cool to room temperature.

Combine cabbages and carrot. Add vinegar mixture; toss well. Spoon into two 1-pint freezer containers, leaving ½-inch headspace. Cover and freeze up to 1 month. Thaw to serve. Yield: 4 cups (39 calories per ½-cup serving).

PROTEIN 0.7 / FAT 0.1 / CARBOHYDRATE 9.6 / CHOLESTEROL 0 / IRON 0.4 / SODIUM 16 / CALCIUM 31

Serve scoops of Easy Mixed Fruit Sherbet over ripe cantaloupe for a refreshing dessert.

TORTILLA WEDGES

¼ cup plus 2 tablespoons light process cream
   cheese product
2 tablespoons minced fresh cilantro
2 tablespoons canned chopped green chiles
2 teaspoons skim milk
2 teaspoons commercial picante sauce
8 (6-inch) flour tortillas

Combine light process cream cheese product, cilantro, chiles, milk, and picante sauce in a small bowl; stir well. Spread 2 tablespoons cream cheese mixture onto 4 tortillas; top with remaining tortillas. Cut each into 6 wedges; wrap in aluminum foil, and freeze until firm.

Bake at 350° for 10 minutes or until tortillas are lightly browned. Yield: 24 wedges (47 calories each).

PROTEIN 1.3 / FAT 1.5 / CARBOHYDRATE 7.8 / CHOLESTEROL 2 /
IRON 0.3 / SODIUM 28 / CALCIUM 16

EASY MIXED FRUIT SHERBET

2 (16-ounce) cans mixed fruit in fruit juice,
   undrained
1 small cantaloupe (about 1¾ pounds), seeded
   and cut into 8 wedges
Fresh mint sprigs (optional)

Position knife blade in food processor bowl; add mixed fruit and juice. Process until smooth. Pour into a shallow pan; freeze until almost frozen. Return to processor bowl; process until consistency of soft sherbet; freeze until firm.

Place melon wedges on individual dessert plates. Place one ¼-cup scoop of sherbet on each wedge and place one ¼-cup scoop of sherbet on each plate. Garnish with fresh mint sprigs, if desired. Serve immediately. Yield: 8 servings (85 calories per serving).

PROTEIN 1.4 / FAT 0.3 / CARBOHYDRATE 21.2 / CHOLESTEROL 0 /
IRON 0.4 / SODIUM 13 / CALCIUM 19

Oktoberfest Feast

Wiener Schnitzel
Caraway Noodles
Braised Kale
Winter Fruit Compote
Light Beer

Serves 4
Total calories per serving: 589

This version of a German-style menu has conscientiously trimmed the fat and calories from a meal that is usually heavy on both, while keeping the gusto of the cuisine. Even a 12-ounce mug of light beer has been included.

Start the meal preparation by making the compote. While the fruit simmers, start the kale and noodles. The veal can be made in just minutes. By following the order here, you can have a party-fare meal on the table in record time.

These versions of Wiener Schnitzel, Caraway Noodles, and Braised Kale are lightened German cuisine.

WIENER SCHNITZEL

1 pound veal cutlets (¼-inch thick)
2 tablespoons all-purpose flour
1 teaspoon minced fresh parsley
½ teaspoon pepper
¼ teaspoon paprika
⅛ teaspoon ground cloves
Vegetable cooking spray
1 teaspoon vegetable oil, divided
1½ teaspoons minced fresh parsley
Lemon slices (optional)

Trim fat from cutlets. Place between 2 sheets of heavy-duty plastic wrap; flatten to ⅛-inch thickness, using a meat mallet or rolling pin. Combine flour and next 4 ingredients; stir well.

Dredge cutlets in flour mixture. Coat a large nonstick skillet with cooking spray; add ½ teaspoon oil. Place over medium-high heat until hot. Add half of cutlets; cook 2 to 4 minutes on each side or until lightly browned. Remove from skillet, and keep warm. Wipe drippings from skillet with a paper towel.

Repeat procedure with remaining ½ teaspoon oil and cutlets. Transfer to individual serving plates, and sprinkle with 1½ teaspoons parsley. Garnish with lemon slices, if desired. Yield: 4 servings (154 calories per serving).

PROTEIN 23.3 / FAT 4.7 / CARBOHYDRATE 3.1 / CHOLESTEROL 94 / IRON 1.3 / SODIUM 98 / CALCIUM 20

CARAWAY NOODLES

2 cups cooked medium egg noodles (cooked
    without salt or fat)
¼ cup evaporated skimmed milk
¼ cup Chablis or other dry white wine
2 tablespoons minced fresh parsley
1 tablespoon reduced-calorie margarine, melted
1¼ teaspoons caraway seeds
¼ teaspoon salt

Combine egg noodles, milk, and Chablis in a medium saucepan; toss well. Add parsley, margarine, caraway seeds, and salt; toss well to combine. Place over medium-low heat, and cook just until thoroughly heated. Yield: 4 servings (138 calories per ½-cup serving).

PROTEIN 5.2 / FAT 3.1 / CARBOHYDRATE 22.4 / CHOLESTEROL 27 /
IRON 1.6 / SODIUM 200 / CALCIUM 65

BRAISED KALE

¾ pound kale
½ (14½-ounce) can no-salt-added whole tomatoes,
    undrained and coarsely chopped
Olive oil-flavored vegetable cooking spray
¼ cup diced purple onion
2 cloves garlic, crushed
¼ teaspoon salt
¼ teaspoon dried whole basil
⅛ teaspoon dried whole oregano
1 teaspoon balsamic vinegar
¼ teaspoon freshly ground pepper

Remove tough stems from kale, and wash thoroughly. Drain (do not pat dry). Place kale in a large Dutch oven (do not add water). Cover and cook over medium heat 6 to 8 minutes or until tender. Drain well, and squeeze between paper towels until barely moist. Coarsely chop kale, and set aside.

Drain chopped tomato, reserving 2 tablespoons liquid. Set tomato and liquid aside.

Coat a large nonstick skillet with cooking spray; place over medium-high heat until hot. Add onion, and sauté 3 to 4 minutes or until tender. Add garlic and reserved tomato, stirring well to combine; cook 5 minutes. Add kale, reserved tomato liquid, salt, basil, and oregano, stirring will to combine; cook 5 minutes. Remove mixture from heat; stir in vinegar and pepper. Serve immediately. Yield: 4 servings (46 calories per ½-cup serving).

PROTEIN 2.4 / FAT 0.5 / CARBOHYDRATE 10.0 / CHOLESTEROL 0 /
IRON 2.1 / SODIUM 100 / CALCIUM 96

WINTER FRUIT COMPOTE

1 (16-ounce) can pear halves in light syrup,
    undrained
1 (16-ounce) can apricot halves in light syrup,
    undrained
1 tablespoon grated orange rind
2 tablespoons currants
1½ tablespoons brandy
Fresh mint sprigs (optional)

Drain fruit, reserving syrup. Place syrup in a small saucepan; add orange rind, and bring to a boil over medium-high heat. Reduce heat, and simmer, uncovered, 15 minutes. Add currants, and simmer an additional 10 minutes. Stir in pear and apricot halves and brandy. Cook until thoroughly heated. Spoon fruit evenly into individual compotes, and garnish with fresh mint sprigs, if desired. Yield: 4 servings (152 calories per serving).

PROTEIN 1.1 / FAT 0.3 / CARBOHYDRATE 40.4 / CHOLESTEROL 0 /
IRON 0.8 / SODIUM 9 / CALCIUM 26

Heart-warming, healthy eating includes (clockwise from top right) Saucepan Broccoli-Rice, Deviled Pork Chops, Baked Herbed Tomatoes, dinner rolls, and Sundae Tart.

Down-Home Family Dinner

Becoming nutrition-conscious doesn't mean you have to give up your family's favorite foods. With this menu the foods that your family has loved can still be part of a healthy eating plan.

Pork chops, once considered to be high in fat, are much leaner today, thanks to new breeding and feeding techniques. Enjoy them cooked with the flavorful sauce for a family favorite.

Saucepan Broccoli-Rice is a healthy, lower fat version of the

Deviled Pork Chops
Saucepan Broccoli-Rice
Baked Herbed Tomatoes
Commercial Dinner Rolls
Sundae Tart

Serves 6
Total calories per serving: 619

old-fashioned broccoli-rice casserole. Commercial one-third-less-salt soup and low-fat cheese

lighten the recipe, while instant brown rice adds to the quickness of preparation.

The tomatoes are cut in half, seasoned with Dijon mustard and oregano, and baked just until warm. Add one dinner roll per person to balance the menu.

Everyone in the family will enjoy the tart for dessert. Phyllo makes a unique pastry, and fruit along with a chocolate sauce makes a delicious combination of sundae toppings.

DEVILED PORK CHOPS

⅓ cup reduced-calorie catsup
2 teaspoons prepared horseradish
2 teaspoons reduced-sodium Worcestershire sauce
1 teaspoon prepared mustard
½ teaspoon garlic powder
½ teaspoon chili powder
⅛ teaspoon poultry seasoning
⅛ teaspoon pepper
6 (6-ounce) lean center-cut loin pork chops (½-inch thick)
Vegetable cooking spray
Fresh parsley sprigs (optional)

Combine catsup, horseradish, Worcestershire sauce, mustard, garlic powder, chili powder,

poultry seasoning, and pepper in a small bowl, stirring well until blended. Set aside.

Trim fat from chops. Coat a large nonstick skillet with cooking spray; place over medium-high heat until hot. Add chops, and cook 3 minutes on each side or until browned. Spoon catsup mixture over chops. Bring to a boil; cover, reduce heat, and simmer 45 minutes or until tender. Transfer chops to a serving platter. Spoon sauce over chops. Garnish with fresh parsley sprigs, if desired. Yield: 6 servings (215 calories per serving).

PROTEIN 24.3 / FAT 11.3 / CARBOHYDRATE 1.9 / CHOLESTEROL 77 / IRON 1.0 / SODIUM 83 / CALCIUM 8

SAUCEPAN BROCCOLI-RICE

¾ cup water
¾ cup instant brown rice, uncooked
½ cup chopped onion
½ cup chopped celery
½ (10¾-ounce) can one-third-less-salt cream of mushroom soup, undiluted
1 cup frozen chopped broccoli, thawed
¼ teaspoon salt
⅓ cup (1.3 ounces) shredded 40% less-fat Cheddar cheese

Bring water to a boil in a medium saucepan; add instant brown rice, chopped onion, and chopped celery. Cover, reduce heat, and simmer 5 minutes. Remove pan from heat; stir in soup, chopped broccoli, and salt.

Cover pan, and let stand 5 minutes. Stir in shredded Cheddar cheese. Serve immediately. Yield: 6 servings (91 calories per ½-cup serving).

PROTEIN 3.3 / FAT 2.9 / CARBOHYDRATE 14.7 / CHOLESTEROL 0 / IRON 0.4 / SODIUM 238 / CALCIUM 66

BAKED HERBED TOMATOES

3 medium tomatoes, halved crosswise
1 tablespoon Dijon mustard
½ teaspoon dried whole oregano
3 tablespoons fine, dry breadcrumbs
3 tablespoons minced fresh parsley
1½ tablespoons reduced-calorie margarine, melted

Place tomatoes, cut side up, in an 11- x 7- x 2-inch baking dish. Spread cut sides of tomatoes with mustard; sprinkle with oregano. Combine breadcrumbs and parsley; sprinkle evenly over tomatoes. Drizzle with margarine. Bake at 350° for 12 to 15 minutes or until tomatoes are thoroughly heated. Yield: 6 servings (40 calories per serving).

PROTEIN 1.1 / FAT 1.7 / CARBOHYDRATE 5.8 / CHOLESTEROL 0 /
IRON 0.6 / SODIUM 122 / CALCIUM 13

SUNDAE TART

3 sheets commercial frozen phyllo pastry, thawed
Vegetable cooking spray
1½ teaspoons unflavored gelatin
3 tablespoons cold water
¼ cup unsweetened frozen pineapple juice
  concentrate, thawed
1 cup plain nonfat yogurt
1 tablespoon honey
½ teaspoon vanilla extract
1 medium banana, peeled and sliced
1 (8-ounce) can unsweetened pineapple slices,
  drained
6 strawberry fans
Chocolate Sauce

Place one sheet of phyllo on a damp towel (keep remaining phyllo covered). Lightly coat phyllo with cooking spray. Fold in half lengthwise. Cut phyllo in half crosswise to form 2 rectangles. Place one rectangle in an 8-inch springform pan coated with cooking spray, allowing corners to extend up sides of pan. Place remaining rectangle in pan, crisscrossing over first rectangle. Repeat procedure with remaining sheets of phyllo, crisscrossing layers alternately. Lightly coat top layer with cooking spray. Bake at 350° for 10 to 12 minutes or until golden. Let

cool 15 minutes. Remove sides of pan, and cool completely on a wire rack. Gently transfer tart shell to a serving platter; set aside.

Sprinkle gelatin over cold water in a small saucepan; let stand 1 minute. Cook over low heat, stirring until gelatin dissolves. Remove from heat. Stir in pineapple juice concentrate. Let cool.

Combine cooled gelatin mixture, yogurt, honey, and vanilla. Chill 5 minutes or until mixture mounds from a spoon.

Arrange banana slices in tart shell. Spoon filling over bananas. Cover and chill 1 hour. Arrange pineapple slices and strawberry fans on top of filling. Drizzle Chocolate Sauce over fruit. Yield: 6 servings (149 calories per serving).

Chocolate Sauce:

¼ cup water
1 tablespoon sugar
1 tablespoon unsweetened cocoa
½ teaspoon cornstarch
½ teaspoon vanilla extract

Combine all ingredients in a small saucepan, stirring until smooth. Cook over medium heat, stirring constantly, until smooth and thickened. Let cool to room temperature. Yield: ¼ cup.

PROTEIN 4.6 / FAT 1.0 / CARBOHYDRATE 31.2 / CHOLESTEROL 1 /
IRON 0.8 / SODIUM 34 / CALCIUM 86

For a colorful, delicious, and nutritious meal when company's coming, serve Salmon Steaks with Cucumber-Horseradish Sauce, Rice Pilaf, Sesame Snow Peas, and Spinach Salad with Orange-Poppy Seed Dressing. (Menu begins on page 70.)

Summer Evening Supper

Jalapeño Chicken
Herbed Potato Salad
Garden Broccoli Salad
Commercial Dinner Rolls
Watermelon Sherbet

Serves 4
Total calories per serving: 498

Summer simply is not the time to spend hours over a hot kitchen stove. Streamline the evening's meal by preparing the salads ahead of time.

Make the final table preparations while the chicken cooks. As the chicken stands, warm the rolls, allowing 1 per person.

Scoop ½-cup servings of sherbet into compotes, and freeze the remaining sherbet to enjoy with another meal. With this menu, you'll realize that sensible eating can also be pleasurable.

Watermelon Sherbet, garnished with melon wedges, makes a refreshing addition to warm-weather meals.

JALAPEÑO CHICKEN

2 medium tomatoes, peeled and seeded
3 tablespoons cider vinegar
1 tablespoon plus 2 teaspoons dark molasses
1 tablespoon Dijon mustard
1 small jalapeño pepper, seeded and chopped
3 cloves garlic, pressed
¼ teaspoon salt
4 (4-ounce) skinned, boned chicken breast halves

Place tomatoes in container of electric blender or food processor; top with cover, and process until smooth. Combine pureed tomato and next 6 ingredients in a 2-quart casserole.

Microwave, covered, at HIGH 5 minutes. Set tomato mixture aside.

Place chicken breast halves in an 11- x 7- x 2-inch baking dish with thickest portions towards outside of dish. Spoon tomato mixture over chicken. Cover with wax paper and microwave at HIGH 10 to 12 minutes or until chicken is done, rotating dish a half-turn every 4 minutes. Let stand 3 minutes. Serve warm. Yield: 4 servings (164 calories per serving).

PROTEIN 26.9 / FAT 1.8 / CARBOHYDRATE 9.0 / CHOLESTEROL 66 / IRON 1.6 / SODIUM 337 / CALCIUM 49

HERBED POTATO SALAD

¾ pound small red potatoes
⅓ cup sliced green onions
⅓ cup Chablis or other dry white wine
2 tablespoons white wine vinegar
1 teaspoon olive oil
1 teaspoon Dijon mustard
¼ teaspoon salt
¼ teaspoon freshly ground pepper
2 tablespoons chopped fresh parsley

Wash potatoes; pat potatoes dry, and slice into ¼-inch-thick slices. Arrange potato slices, overlapping slightly in rows, in a 10-inch quiche dish. Sprinkle with green onions, wine, and vinegar. Cover with heavy-duty plastic wrap and microwave at HIGH 10 to 12 minutes or until tender. Let stand, covered, 5 minutes.

Uncover potato slices; drain and reserve liquid. Combine reserved liquid, olive oil and next 3 ingredients; stir with a small wire whisk until well blended. Pour mixture over potato slices, and sprinkle with parsley. Cool. Cover and chill thoroughly. Yield: 4 servings (79 calories per ½-cup serving).

PROTEIN 2.1 / FAT 1.3 / CARBOHYDRATE 15.1 / CHOLESTEROL 0 / IRON 1.5 / SODIUM 193 / CALCIUM 21

GARDEN BROCCOLI SALAD

¾ cup fresh broccoli flowerets
¾ cup fresh cauliflower flowerets
¼ cup water
1 small sweet red pepper, seeded and chopped
1 tablespoon vegetable oil
3 tablespoons white wine vinegar
¼ teaspoon salt
¼ teaspoon freshly ground pepper
⅛ teaspoon garlic powder
Lettuce leaves (optional)

Wash broccoli and cauliflower; combine with water in a 1½-quart casserole. Cover with heavy-duty plastic wrap and microwave at HIGH 4 to 6 minutes or until vegetables are crisp-tender. Drain well. Add sweet red pepper, tossing gently. Set aside.

Combine oil, white wine vinegar, salt, freshly ground pepper, and garlic powder in a jar; cover tightly, and shake vigorously. Pour vinegar mixture over vegetable mixture; toss gently. Cover and chill at least 30 minutes. Serve salad on lettuce leaves, if desired. Yield: 4 servings (50 calories per ½-cup serving).

PROTEIN 1.3 / FAT 3.6 / CARBOHYDRATE 3.7 / CHOLESTEROL 0 / IRON 0.7 / SODIUM 157 / CALCIUM 19

WATERMELON SHERBET

4 cups seeded and cubed watermelon
¼ cup plus 2 tablespoons sugar
¼ cup instant nonfat dry milk powder
2 cups skim milk
2 teaspoons vanilla extract
Watermelon wedges (optional)

Place watermelon in container of an electric blender or food processor; top with cover, and process until smooth. Strain puree, reserving juice; discard pulp.

Combine watermelon juice, sugar, and next 3 ingredients; stir well. Pour mixture into freezer can of a 2-quart hand-turned or electric freezer. Freeze according to manufacturer's instructions. Scoop sherbet into individual dessert compotes. Garnish with watermelon wedges, if desired. Serve immediately. Yield: 5 cups (80 calories per ½-cup serving).

PROTEIN 3.1 / FAT 0.4 / CARBOHYDRATE 16.2 / CHOLESTEROL 2 / IRON 0.1 / SODIUM 43 / CALCIUM 103

Vegetable-Stuffed Turkey Roll, Garlic Mashed Potatoes, Baby Carrots with Horseradish, and Three-Cabbage Salad.

Festive Family Supper

The microwave oven is a great time-saver, especially when it comes to ground turkey. The turkey roll can be made ahead, covered, and refrigerated if last-minute meal preparation time is limited. If it's chilled, you may have to add a minute or two to the cooking time, but the turkey roll will still require only about 10 minutes to cook.

Cook the potatoes first so you'll have time to mash them while the turkey cooks. While the turkey stands, cook the carrots.

Vegetable-Stuffed Turkey Roll
Garlic Mashed Potatoes
Baby Carrots with Horseradish
Three-Cabbage Salad
Cinnamon Apple Dessert

Serves 4
Total calories per serving: 598

Prepare and chill the poppy seed dressing beforehand; then combine the cabbages, carrots, and green onions. Toss the dressing with the salad just before dinner. The poppy seed dressing also would be good served with fruit salads and can be stored, tightly covered, in the refrigerator for up to a week.

For dessert, everyone will enjoy the old-fashioned flavor of the apple dessert, a treat for almost any special evening. Microwave the apples for 5 to 6 minutes; set the dish aside, and keep warm. Then call the family to the table for a festive supper.

VEGETABLE-STUFFED TURKEY ROLL

1 pound raw fresh ground turkey
¼ cup fine, dry breadcrumbs
¼ cup finely chopped onion
2 tablespoons chopped fresh parsley
2 tablespoons reduced-calorie catsup
1 egg
½ teaspoon dried whole thyme
¼ teaspoon dry mustard
¼ teaspoon freshly ground pepper
1 cup chopped fresh broccoli
½ cup chopped fresh mushrooms
¼ cup chopped sweet red pepper
1 clove garlic, minced

Combine first 9 ingredients in a large mixing bowl; mix well. Pat mixture to an 8-inch square on an 11-inch square of plastic wrap; set aside.

Combine broccoli, mushrooms, sweet red pepper, and garlic in a 1-quart casserole. Microwave at HIGH 2 to 3 minutes or until vegetables are crisp-tender; drain.

Spoon vegetable mixture evenly over turkey mixture to within 1 inch of sides. Roll turkey mixture by lifting plastic wrap until turkey begins to roll tightly; peel plastic wrap away as turkey rolls. Place turkey in a 9- x 5- x 3-inch microwave-safe loafpan. Cover with heavy-duty plastic wrap and microwave at HIGH 7 to 9 minutes or until turkey is no longer pink, rotating every 2 minutes. Let stand 5 minutes before serving. Yield: 4 servings (196 calories per serving).

PROTEIN 28.0 / FAT 5.0 / CARBOHYDRATE 8.3 / CHOLESTEROL 124 / IRON 2.9 / SODIUM 149 / CALCIUM 48

GARLIC MASHED POTATOES

2 cups peeled, cubed baking potato
¼ cup water
2 cloves garlic, minced
¼ teaspoon salt
½ cup skim milk
1 tablespoon fresh chives

Combine potato, water, garlic, and salt in a 2-quart casserole. Cover and microwave at HIGH

11 to 13 minutes or until potato is tender, stirring every 5 minutes. Mash potato until smooth.

Add milk to potato. Beat at medium speed of an electric mixer just until mixture is smooth. Add chives, stirring well. Yield: 4 servings (96 calories per ½-cup serving).

PROTEIN 2.9 / FAT 2.9 / CARBOHYDRATE 15.2 / CHOLESTEROL 9 / IRON 0.2 / SODIUM 176 / CALCIUM 73

BABY CARROTS WITH HORSERADISH

1 pound fresh baby carrots with tops
3 tablespoons water
2 teaspoons reduced-calorie margarine
1 teaspoon all-purpose flour
2 tablespoons skim milk
¼ cup low-fat sour cream
1½ teaspoons prepared horseradish
⅛ teaspoon pepper
⅛ teaspoon dry mustard

Scrape baby carrots, leaving ¼ inch of green top, if desired. Combine carrots and water in a 1-quart casserole. Cover carrots with heavy-duty plastic wrap and microwave at HIGH 10 minutes

or until carrots are crisp-tender; drain well, and set carrots aside.

Place margarine in a 1-cup glass measure. Cover and microwave 15 seconds or until margarine melts. Stir in flour; add milk, stirring well. Cover and microwave at HIGH 1 to 2 minutes or until thickened; stir mixture after 1 minute.

Stir in sour cream, horseradish, pepper, and dry mustard. Arrange carrots evenly on individual serving plates, and spoon sauce over carrots. Yield: 4 servings (70 calories per serving).

PROTEIN 1.6 / FAT 3.2 / CARBOHYDRATE 9.6 / CHOLESTEROL 6 / IRON 0.5 / SODIUM 57 / CALCIUM 48

THREE-CABBAGE SALAD

1½ cups finely shredded red cabbage
1 cup finely shredded cabbage
1 cup finely shredded napa cabbage
½ cup finely shredded carrot
2 tablespoons thinly sliced green onions
Apple and Poppy Seed Dressing
4 small red cabbage leaves
Dash of ground white pepper (optional)

Combine shredded cabbages, carrot, and sliced green onions in a medium bowl; toss gently to combine.

Pour Apple and Poppy Seed Dressing over shredded cabbage mixture, and toss gently. Place a small red cabbage leaf on each of 4 individual salad plates.

Spoon 1 cup shredded cabbage mixture onto each cabbage leaf. Sprinkle with pepper, if desired. Yield: 4 servings (77 calories per serving).

Apple and Poppy Seed Dressing:

⅓ cup white wine vinegar
¼ cup water
2 teaspoons cornstarch
3 tablespoons frozen apple juice concentrate, thawed
2 teaspoons vegetable oil
½ teaspoon sugar
½ teaspoon poppy seeds
¼ teaspoon grated orange rind

Combine vinegar, water, and cornstarch in a 2-cup glass measure. Microwave, uncovered, at HIGH 2½ minutes or until thickened; stir once. Add juice and remaining ingredients; stir with a wire whisk. Cover and chill. Yield: ¾ cup.

PROTEIN 1.3 / FAT 2.7 / CARBOHYDRATE 12.5 / CHOLESTEROL 0 / IRON 0.7 / SODIUM 29 / CALCIUM 57

CINNAMON APPLE DESSERT

3½ cups peeled, sliced cooking apple
2 tablespoons unsweetened orange juice
2 tablespoons honey
2 teaspoons lemon juice
½ teaspoon ground cinnamon
3 tablespoons regular oats, uncooked
1 tablespoon brown sugar
1 tablespoon chopped pecans
2 teaspoons reduced-calorie margarine, melted

Combine apple, orange juice, honey, lemon juice, and cinnamon in a large bowl; toss gently. Place apple mixture in an 11- x 7- x 2-inch baking dish. Cover with heavy-duty plastic wrap and microwave apple mixture at HIGH 5 to 6 minutes or until apple is tender.

Combine oats, brown sugar, pecans, and margarine; stir well.

To serve, spoon warm apple mixture evenly into individual dessert dishes, and sprinkle evenly with oat mixture. Yield: 4 servings (159 calories per ½-cup serving).

PROTEIN 1.3 / FAT 3.1 / CARBOHYDRATE 34.5 / CHOLESTEROL 0 / IRON 0.6 / SODIUM 20 / CALCIUM 15

BENEFITS OF BORON

Scientists at one of the USDA's research laboratories have uncovered exciting new findings about boron. The researchers noticed that people whose diets were low in boron experienced minor mental and physical performance problems. Specifically, women whose diets were low in boron performed poorly on tests of alertness and motor dexterity. They could not tap their fingers as fast, follow a target as accurately using a computer joy stick, or locate items in a field of letters as quickly.

In an earlier study, scientists found a link between diets low in boron and increased risk for bone fractures. Researchers suggest that boron may play a role in keeping bones strong, and it may be essential in preventing future problems with osteoporosis.

Luckily, boron is a common component of most fruits, fruit juices, and vegetables; so by eating 6 servings of fruit and vegetables per day (the National Research Council's recommendation), the level of boron in your diet will be more than adequate.

Serve Cider-Glazed Turkey Tenderloins, Carrot-Wild Rice Stuffing, Herbed Green Beans, Mixed Green Salad with Citrus, and Spiced Raspberry Tea for a hearty fall dinner.

Autumn Harvest Dinner

As you look forward to crisp, cool air, bronze-colored trees, and football games in the backyard, you are sure to enjoy this autumn dinner.

The turkey tenderloins are paired with two autumn favorites, apples and apple cider. You can cook the turkey during the standing time for the Carrot-Wild Rice Stuffing. This colorful and hearty dish features time-saving quick-cooking wild rice.

The crisp green salad becomes special when accented with orange slices and topped with a

Cider-Glazed Turkey Tenderloins
Carrot-Wild Rice Stuffing
Herbed Green Beans
Mixed Green Salad with Citrus
Spiced Raspberry Tea
Spicy Pumpkin Pudding

Serves 4
Total Calories per serving: 553

light, flavorful dressing made with balsamic vinegar.

As you start putting the food on the table, treat your guests to Spiced Raspberry Tea, and finish cooking the green beans.

Not forgotten is the dessert—which, of course, in autumn means pumpkin. Make creamy Spicy Pumpkin Pudding early in the day or even the day before to allow it to chill thoroughly before serving.

Try this healthy menu that doesn't skimp on taste or pleasure. Food should be savored, and this autumn meal will let you do just that.

CIDER-GLAZED TURKEY TENDERLOINS

2 (8-ounce) turkey tenderloins
1 small baking apple, cored and sliced
½ cup apple cider
1 tablespoon plus 2 teaspoons cornstarch
2 teaspoons brown sugar
1½ teaspoons Dijon mustard
¼ teaspoon salt
⅛ teaspoon ground nutmeg

Cut each tenderloin in half lengthwise. Place tenderloins between 2 sheets of heavy-duty plastic wrap; flatten to ½-inch thickness, using a meat mallet or rolling pin. Arrange tenderloins around outer edge of a 10-inch glass pieplate, forming a ring and overlapping ends of tenderloins. Arrange apple slices in center of pieplate.

Combine apple cider and remaining ingredients in a small bowl. Pour mixture over tenderloins and apple. Cover tightly with heavy-duty plastic wrap and microwave at HIGH 9 to 10 minutes, rotating a half-turn every 3 minutes. Pierce plastic with a fork to release steam. Let stand 2 to 3 minutes. Remove tenderloins and apple from pieplate with a slotted spoon.

Cut each tenderloin diagonally in 4 pieces. Arrange tenderloin and apple on individual serving plates; spoon sauce evenly over each tenderloin and apple. Yield: 4 servings (197 calories per serving).

PROTEIN 26.8 / FAT 2.1 / CARBOHYDRATE 16.4 / CHOLESTEROL 68 / IRON 1.6 / SODIUM 275 / CALCIUM 22

CARROT-WILD RICE STUFFING

⅔ cup chopped apple
⅔ cup sliced green onions
⅔ cup shredded carrot
¼ cup plus 3 tablespoons quick-cooking wild rice, uncooked
¼ cup plus 3 tablespoons water
2 tablespoons chopped almonds, toasted
2 tablespoons golden raisins
2 tablespoons lemon juice
1 tablespoon reduced-calorie margarine
½ teaspoon ground cardamom
¼ teaspoon salt
¼ teaspoon freshly ground pepper

Combine first 7 ingredients in a 2-quart casserole, stirring well. Add lemon juice, margarine, cardamom, salt, and pepper; stir well. Cover tightly with heavy-duty plastic wrap and microwave at HIGH 5 minutes or until mixture boils, stirring after 2 minutes. Reduce to LOW (10% power) and microwave carrot mixture an additional 2 minutes.

Fold back a small edge of plastic wrap to allow steam to escape; let mixture stand at least 10 minutes. Remove plastic wrap, and stir well. Serve warm. Yield: 4 servings (120 calories per serving).

PROTEIN 3.1 / FAT 5.7 / CARBOHYDRATE 16.2 / CHOLESTEROL 0 / IRON 0.8 / SODIUM 188 / CALCIUM 38

HERBED GREEN BEANS

½ pound fresh green beans
½ cup water
¼ cup chopped sweet green pepper
¼ cup sliced green onions
¾ cup peeled, diced tomato
1 teaspoon minced fresh basil
1 teaspoon lemon juice
¼ teaspoon salt
¼ teaspoon sugar
¼ teaspoon minced fresh rosemary

Wash beans and remove strings. Cut beans into 1½-inch pieces. Combine beans and water in a 1½-quart casserole. Cover with heavy-duty plastic wrap and microwave at HIGH 4 to 5 minutes or until green beans are crisp-tender, stirring after 3 minutes. Let stand, covered, 2 minutes; drain well.

Combine chopped green pepper and sliced green onions in a 1-cup glass measure; stir well. Cover with heavy-duty plastic wrap and microwave at HIGH 1 to 2 minutes or until vegetables are tender.

Add green pepper mixture, tomato, basil, lemon juice, salt, sugar, and rosemary to green beans; stir gently to combine. Cover with heavy-duty plastic wrap and microwave at HIGH 1 minute or until thoroughly heated. Yield: 4 servings (27 calories per ½-cup serving).

PROTEIN 1.4 / FAT 0.2 / CARBOHYDRATE 6.1 / CHOLESTEROL 0 / IRON 1.0 / SODIUM 151 / CALCIUM 32

MIXED GREEN SALAD WITH CITRUS

¼ cup balsamic vinegar
2 tablespoons water
1 small shallot, peeled and chopped
1 teaspoon cornstarch
2 teaspoons olive oil
1 cup torn leaf lettuce
1 cup torn red leaf lettuce
1 cup torn romaine lettuce
1 cup torn curly endive
1 large navel orange, peeled and cut into
  ¼-inch-thick slices
2 tablespoons chopped, toasted pecans

Combine first 5 ingredients in a 2-cup glass measure. Microwave, uncovered, at HIGH 2 to 3 minutes or until mixture boils and is slightly thickened. Stir until smooth, using a wire whisk. Let cool to room temperature.

Combine salad greens in a medium bowl; toss well. Arrange 1 cup mixture on each of 4 individual salad plates. Drizzle each with vinegar mixture. Cut orange slices in half. Arrange slices over salad greens, and sprinkle with pecans. Yield: 4 servings (63 calories per serving).

PROTEIN 0.9 / FAT 4.7 / CARBOHYDRATE 5.5 / CHOLESTEROL 0 / IRON 0.5 / SODIUM 3 / CALCIUM 20

SPICED RASPBERRY TEA

4¼ cups water
1½ tablespoons brown sugar
1 tablespoon grated orange rind
1 teaspoon grated lemon rind
6 whole cloves
2 (3-inch) sticks cinnamon
4 raspberry herb tea bags

Combine first 6 ingredients in a 2-quart glass measure. Cover with heavy-duty plastic wrap and microwave at HIGH 7 to 10 minutes or until water boils. Add tea bags; cover and let stand 5 minutes. Remove tea bags, squeezing gently; discard tea bags. Strain tea mixture; discard rind and spices. Serve warm or cold. Yield: 4 servings (14 calories per 1-cup serving).

PROTEIN 0.1 / FAT 0.0 / CARBOHYDRATE 5.0 / CHOLESTEROL 0 / IRON 0.4 / SODIUM 2 / CALCIUM 20

SPICY PUMPKIN PUDDING

1 cup skim milk
⅓ cup orange juice
2 tablespoons cornstarch
1 egg
¼ cup firmly packed brown sugar
¾ cup cooked, mashed pumpkin
1 teaspoon pumpkin pie spice
Dash of salt

Pour milk into a 1-quart casserole. Microwave, uncovered, at HIGH 3 minutes. Remove from oven. Add orange juice and remaining ingredients; stir with a wire whisk. Cover with heavy-duty plastic wrap and microwave at HIGH 4 minutes. Remove from oven and uncover; stir well. Pour mixture evenly into individual dessert dishes. Chill thoroughly. Yield: 4 servings (132 calories per serving).

PROTEIN 4.3 / FAT 1.5 / CARBOHYDRATE 26.3 / CHOLESTEROL 51 / IRON 1.5 / SODIUM 92 / CALCIUM 110

 TAKE A BREATHER

Deep breathing—pulling in air from the diaphragm, the muscle at the base of your lungs—is an excellent way to relax. It also tends to energize. The reason is simple. The more oxygen you breathe in, the more energy you can generate. During restful, quiet times, most people breathe about 15 times per minute. When activity increases, breathing rate can double. While the mechanism is involuntary, you can train yourself to improve breathing skills.

Most people breathe too shallow. Shallow breathing depletes oxygen stores and is an underlying reason why people yawn. Yawning is an involuntary reflex that draws more oxygen into the blood.

To sharpen your breathing skills, practice inhaling more deeply. Place one hand on your abdomen, and gradually inhale. As your lungs inflate, you should feel your abdomen swelling slightly. Concentrate on the air as it gradually flows out your nose or mouth to your lungs and back again. Don't try to force it; just let the natural in-and-out rhythm take over. That will keep your lungs supplied with plenty of energy-boosting oxygen.

Spring Dinner

Carrot and Potato Soup
Coffee-Glazed Lamb
Chops
Asparagus-Leek Bundles
Commercial Dinner Rolls
Warm Fruit Compote

Serves 4
Total Calories per serving: 492

Welcome the season with a light dinner of spring favorites. The rich creaminess of the soup may come as a surprise since not a drop of cream is used. The smooth consistency results from processing the tender cooked vegetable mixture in an electric blender or food processor.

Espresso powder accents the lamb for just the right flavor combination. Serve the chops with asparagus spears tied together with strands of leek, dinner rolls (allowing 1 roll per person), and an easy fruit dessert.

Flowering herbs such as anise hyssop make a colorful springtime garnish for Carrot and Potato Soup.

CARROT AND POTATO SOUP

1⅔ cups diced onion
1½ cups peeled and diced potato
1 cup peeled and diced celery
⅔ cup scraped and diced parsnip
½ cup scraped and diced carrot
¼ cup chopped shallots
2 cloves garlic, minced
2¼ cups canned no-salt-added chicken broth, divided
¼ teaspoon salt
⅛ teaspoon ground white pepper
Anise hyssop or other flowering herb (optional)

Combine first 7 ingredients in a deep 3-quart casserole; add ½ cup chicken broth. Cover with heavy-duty plastic wrap and microwave at HIGH 15 minutes or until vegetables are tender, stirring every 5 minutes.

Transfer half of mixture to container of an electric blender or food processor; top with cover, and process until smooth. Add half of remaining 1¾ cups chicken broth; process until mixture is combined. Return mixture to casserole. Repeat with remaining potato mixture and chicken broth.

Add salt and pepper, stirring well. Cover and microwave at HIGH 3 to 5 minutes or until thoroughly heated. Ladle soup into individual bowls, and garnish with anise hyssop, if desired. Yield: 4 cups (119 calories per 1-cup serving).

PROTEIN 3.9 / FAT 1.4 / CARBOHYDRATE 23.2 / CHOLESTEROL 0 / IRON 1.2 / SODIUM 262 / CALCIUM 47

COFFEE-GLAZED LAMB CHOPS

4 (6-ounce) lean lamb loin chops (1-inch thick)
1 tablespoon dry sherry
1 teaspoon instant espresso powder
½ teaspoon sugar
⅛ teaspoon salt

Trim fat from chops. Arrange chops in a circle on a microwave roasting rack with thickest portions toward outside of dish.

Combine sherry and remaining ingredients; stir well. Brush chops on both sides with sherry mixture. Microwave at MEDIUM (50% power) 10 to 12 minutes or to desired degree of doneness, turning chops over and rearranging after 5 minutes. Yield: 4 servings (171 calories per serving).

PROTEIN 24.5 / FAT 6.9 / CARBOHYDRATE 0.7 / CHOLESTEROL 77 / IRON 2.3 / SODIUM 153 / CALCIUM 15

ASPARAGUS-LEEK BUNDLES

1 small leek (about ½ pound)
1 pound fresh thin asparagus
¼ cup water
1 tablespoon lemon juice
¼ teaspoon salt
¼ teaspoon pepper

Remove root, tough outer leaves, and tops from leek, leaving 2 inches of dark leaves. Remove one 2-inch-wide leaf. Place in a 13- x 9- x 2-inch baking dish. Cover with heavy-duty plastic wrap, and microwave at HIGH 1 minute. Let stand, covered, 5 minutes or until cool. Cut leek into four ½-inch-wide strips; set aside.

Snap off tough ends of asparagus. Remove scales from spears with a knife or vegetable peeler, if desired. Trim asparagus and remaining leek leaves to the same length. Arrange vegetables in a 13- x 9- x 2-inch baking dish with asparagus stem ends toward outside of dish. Add ¼ cup water. Cover with heavy-duty plastic wrap and microwave at HIGH 6 to 8 minutes or until crisp-tender, rotating a quarter-turn after 4 minutes; drain.

Gather asparagus and leeks into four equal bundles. Carefully tie each bundle with a reserved strip of leek, and snip ends to trim. Brush bundles with lemon juice, and sprinkle with salt and pepper. Yield: 4 servings (39 calories per serving).

PROTEIN 3.3 / FAT 0.3 / CARBOHYDRATE 7.8 / CHOLESTEROL 0 / IRON 1.3 / SODIUM 154 / CALCIUM 39

TAKE A HIKE

Tired of mall walking? Consider a much neglected alternative: hiking. Try hiking on a city park nature trail or in the wide-open country; the choice of location is yours. There are 154 National Forests in 39 states with more than 182 million acres of open space, and that's not counting National or State Parks.

The refreshing change of scenery is an added benefit to the 255 to 300 calories burned per hour on the typical hike. As a bonus, hiking—when it's done on an incline—helps tone muscles in the legs and thighs that regular walking or jogging can't. If you join one of the many hiking clubs, count socializing as another benefit.

WARM FRUIT COMPOTE

2 medium seedless oranges, peeled and sectioned
1 medium banana, peeled, halved lengthwise, and cut into 1 inch pieces
¼ cup seedless green grapes
¼ cup seedless red grapes
¼ cup unsweetened orange juice
1 tablespoon dark rum
¼ teaspoon grated orange rind
2 teaspoons brown sugar

Combine first 4 ingredients in a medium bowl, tossing gently. Combine orange juice, rum, and orange rind in a 1-cup glass measure; stir well. Microwave at HIGH 1 minute or until mixture boils. Pour over fruit mixture, stirring to coat fruit. Spoon fruit mixture evenly into 4 microwave-safe dessert bowls; Sprinkle each with ½ teaspoon brown sugar.

Place bowls on a microwave-safe glass plate. Cover with wax paper, and let stand 10 minutes. Microwave at HIGH 2 minutes or until fruit is warm, rotating after 1 minute. Serve warm. Yield: 4 servings (80 calories per serving).

PROTEIN 1.0 / FAT 0.3 / CARBOHYDRATE 20.0 / CHOLESTEROL 0 / IRON 0.3 / SODIUM 1 / CALCIUM 27

Company's Coming

Salmon Steaks with
Cucumber-Horseradish
Sauce
Rice Pilaf
Sesame Snow Peas
Spinach Salad with
Orange-Poppy Seed
Dressing
Commercial French Bread
Chilled Lemon Soufflés

Serves 6
Total calories per serving: 647

Salmon steaks, a delicious and easy-to-prepare main course, makes an outstanding entrée when accompanied by the colorful pilaf and snow peas.

For a time-saving step, prepare the poppy seed dressing ahead and chill until ready to spoon over the fresh spinach leaves.

For a refreshing dessert that your guests are sure to rave about, serve Chilled Lemon Soufflés. Make the soufflés early in the day or the night before, and add fresh mint and lemon twists just before serving.

For a simple but luscious finale to a meal, serve individual Chilled Lemon Soufflés (page 72) surrounded by lemon slices. Garnished with fresh mint and lemon twists, this dessert will receive rave reviews.

SALMON STEAKS WITH CUCUMBER-HORSERADISH SAUCE

6 (4-ounce) salmon steaks (½-inch thick)
2 tablespoons lemon juice
1 tablespoon reduced-calorie margarine, melted
Cucumber-Horseradish Sauce

Arrange salmon steaks in an 11- x 7- x 2-inch baking dish with thickest portions of steaks toward outside of dish. Combine lemon juice and margarine; drizzle over salmon. Cover with heavy-duty plastic wrap and microwave at HIGH 7 to 8 minutes or until fish flakes easily when tested with a fork, rotating a half-turn after 4 minutes. Transfer salmon steaks to a serving platter, discarding liquid. Serve salmon steaks with Cucumber-Horseradish Sauce. Yield: 6 servings (221 calories per serving).

Cucumber-Horseradish Sauce:

½ cup peeled, seeded, and finely chopped cucumber
¼ cup plus 2 tablespoons low-fat sour cream
1 (2-ounce) jar diced pimiento, drained
1 tablespoon prepared horseradish
1 teaspoon lemon juice
Dash of ground red pepper

Press cucumber between paper towels to remove excess moisture. Combine cucumber and remaining ingredients in a small bowl; stir well. Cover and chill thoroughly. Yield: ¾ cup plus 2 tablespoons.

PROTEIN 23.9 / FAT 12.4 / CARBOHYDRATE 2.3 / CHOLESTEROL 80 / IRON 0.7 / SODIUM 86 / CALCIUM 27

RICE PILAF

1¼ cups instant rice, uncooked
1 cup peeled, seeded, and chopped tomato
½ cup chopped green onions
½ cup chopped green pepper
½ cup chopped sweet yellow pepper
1½ tablespoons chopped fresh basil
2 teaspoons reduced-calorie margarine
½ teaspoon beef-flavored bouillon granules
¼ teaspoon salt
1¼ cups hot water

Combine first 9 ingredients in a 1½-quart casserole. Stir in water. Cover with heavy-duty plastic wrap and microwave at HIGH 7 to 8 minutes or until liquid is absorbed. Let stand, covered, 3 minutes. Serve warm. Yield: 6 servings (96 calories per ½-cup serving).

PROTEIN 2.2 / FAT 1.1 / CARBOHYDRATE 19.4 / CHOLESTEROL 0 / IRON 1.4 / SODIUM 192 / CALCIUM 13

MICROWAVE-SAFE CONTAINERS

It's easy to grab an old margarine tub or a plastic dish that normally holds leftovers and pop it into the microwave oven. But this may not be safe. According to recent research, many plastics leach chemicals into microwave-heated foods. And the new heat susceptors in microwave packaging may not be as safe as scientists initially thought. Manufacturers use these susceptors to make popcorn pop and to brown waffles, french fries, and pizza. Heat susceptors—thin strips or discs of metallicized film that are stuck with adhesive to packages—may get packaging so hot that both the film and particles from the container leach into the food.

While the FDA looks at this problem, avoiding heat-susceptor packaging may be wise. Dual oven-microwave packages and plastic containers specifically labeled "microwave-safe" are safe to use in the microwave. Ceramic mugs are fine as long as they have no metallic glazes.

SESAME SNOW PEAS

¾ pound fresh snow pea pods
1 large sweet red pepper, cut into strips
1½ teaspoons sesame seeds
1½ teaspoons reduced-sodium soy sauce
1½ teaspoons sesame oil

Wash snow peas; trim ends, and remove strings. Combine snow peas and remaining ingredients in a 1-quart casserole, stirring gently. Cover with heavy-duty plastic wrap and microwave at HIGH 5 minutes or until vegetables are crisp-tender, stirring after 2 minutes. Yield: 6 servings (44 calories per ½-cup serving).

PROTEIN 1.9 / FAT 1.7 / CARBOHYDRATE 5.6 / CHOLESTEROL 0 / IRON 1.6 / SODIUM 53 / CALCIUM 32

SPINACH SALAD WITH ORANGE-POPPY SEED DRESSING

2 tablespoons sliced almonds
4 cups torn fresh spinach leaves
½ cup sliced fresh strawberries
Orange-Poppy Seed Dressing

Sprinkle almonds in a glass pieplate. Microwave, uncovered, at HIGH 2 to 3 minutes, or until toasted, stirring after each minute.

Arrange spinach leaves, strawberries, and toasted almonds on individual salad plates. Spoon 2 tablespoons Orange-Poppy Seed Dressing over each salad, and serve immediately. Yield: 6 servings (58 calories per serving).

Orange-Poppy Seed Dressing:

¾ cup plus 2 tablespoons unsweetened orange juice
2¾ teaspoons cornstarch
1 teaspoon vegetable oil
2 teaspoons honey
Dash of ground cardamom
½ teaspoon poppy seeds

Combine first 5 ingredients in a small glass bowl; stir well. Microwave at HIGH 1½ to 2 minutes or until slightly thickened, stirring after 1 minute. Let mixture cool; stir in poppy seeds. Cover and chill. Yield: ¾ cup.

PROTEIN 1.4 / FAT 2.2 / CARBOHYDRATE 9.0 / CHOLESTEROL 0 / IRON 0.7 / SODIUM 15 / CALCIUM 33

CHILLED LEMON SOUFFLÉS

Vegetable cooking spray
⅓ cup water
1 envelope unflavored gelatin
⅓ cup cold water
⅔ cup sugar, divided
⅓ cup lemon juice
5 egg whites
⅓ cup instant nonfat dry milk powder
Fresh mint sprigs (optional)
Lemon twists (optional)

Cut 6 pieces of aluminum foil or wax paper long enough to fit around 6 individual soufflé dishes, allowing a 1-inch overlap; fold foil lengthwise into thirds. Lightly coat one side of foil with cooking spray. Wrap foil around outside of each dish, coated side against dish, allowing it to extend 3 inches above rim to form a collar; secure with string.

Place ⅓ cup water in a small, narrow glass or stainless steel bowl; freeze 25 minutes or until a ⅛-inch-thick layer of ice forms on surface.

Sprinkle gelatin over ⅓ cup cold water in a medium-size microwave-safe bowl; let stand 1 minute. Add ⅓ cup sugar and lemon juice; stir well. Microwave at HIGH 2 minutes or until mixture is smooth and gelatin is dissolved, stirring twice. Cover and chill 30 to 35 minutes or until mixture is consistency of unbeaten egg white, stirring occasionally.

Beat egg whites (at room temperature) in a large glass or stainless steel bowl at medium speed of an electric mixer until soft peaks form. Gradually add remaining ⅓ cup sugar, 1 tablespoon at a time, beating until stiff peaks form. (Do not overbeat.)

Add milk powder to partially frozen water; beat at high speed of electric mixer 5 minutes or until stiff peaks form.

Fold egg white mixture and whipped milk into chilled lemon mixture. Spoon into prepared dishes. Cover and chill 2 hours or until set. Remove collar from each dish. If desired, garnish with fresh mint sprigs and lemon twists. Yield: 6 servings (133 calories per serving).

PROTEIN 6.3 / FAT 0.3 / CARBOHYDRATE 27.1 / CHOLESTEROL 1 / IRON 0.0 / SODIUM 79 / CALCIUM 88

Steamed Salmon Fillets in Cabbage Leaves, Basmati Rice, and Zucchini and Carrot Strands give international flavor to East-West Dinner. (Menu begins on page 85.)

Fourth of July Celebration

Spicy Seafood Boil
Chile Mayonnaise
Fireworks Coleslaw
Commercial French Bread
Pineapple Sorbet with
Fresh Berries

Serves 6
Total calories per serving: 585

Celebrate the Fourth with lots of color and flavor. Spicy Seafood Boil will be a hit among your guests, especially when each serving is accompanied with 1 tablespoon Chile Mayonnaise.

Crushed red pepper accents Fireworks Coleslaw, an attractive side dish for your meal. Menu analysis also includes crusty French bread, 1 slice per person.

And with Pineapple Sorbet in the freezer, you'll have a cool refreshment to end the meal.

Enjoy summer's fresh flavors in Pineapple Sorbet with Fresh Berries.

SPICY SEAFOOD BOIL

2 pounds steamer clams
3 medium ears fresh corn
18 small new potatoes (about 2¼ pounds)
3 large sweet onions, peeled
6 live blue crabs (about 3¼ pounds)
2 (3-ounce) packages crab boil
3 lemons, halved
2 cloves garlic, minced
1 cup vinegar
½ teaspoon freshly ground pepper
1½ pounds unpeeled, medium-size fresh shrimp
Lemon wedges (optional)

Scrub clams. Set aside.
Remove outer dark green husks of each ear of corn; carefully peel back light green husks.

Remove silk and replace husks. Secure husks to corn with string, and set aside.

Fill a 5-gallon pot about two-thirds full of water; bring to a boil. Add potatoes and onions; cover, and cook over high heat 20 minutes. Stir in clams, crabs, and next 5 ingredients; cook an additional 10 minutes. Reduce heat, and add corn; simmer 5 minutes. Remove from heat, and add shrimp; let stand 5 minutes. Drain off water. Cut corn and onions in half. Arrange boiled seafood and vegetables on a large serving platter. Garnish with lemon wedges, if desired. Yield: 6 servings (295 calories per serving).

PROTEIN 23.6 / FAT 2.0 / CARBOHYDRATE 47.6 / CHOLESTEROL 121 / IRON 7.0 / SODIUM 307 / CALCIUM 111

CHILE MAYONNAISE

½ cup reduced-calorie mayonnaise
½ cup soft tofu
1 small jalapeño pepper, seeded and halved
2 teaspoons red wine vinegar
1 teaspoon chili powder
1 teaspoon ground cumin

Position knife blade in food processor bowl; add mayonnaise and tofu. Process until smooth.

Place pepper, skin side up, on a baking sheet. Broil 5½ inches from heat 3 to 4 minutes or until pepper is blistered. Place in ice water, and chill 3 minutes. Remove pepper from water; peel and discard skin.

Add pepper, red wine vinegar, chili powder, and ground cumin to mayonnaise mixture; process 1 minute or until mayonnaise mixture is smooth, scraping sides of processor bowl once. Cover and chill thoroughly. Yield: 1 cup (26 calories per tablespoon).

PROTEIN 0.5 / FAT 2.3 / CARBOHYDRATE 0.8 / CHOLESTEROL 2 / IRON 0.2 / SODIUM 58 / CALCIUM 15

FIREWORKS COLESLAW

2 cups shredded red cabbage
1½ cups shredded Chinese cabbage
¼ cup water
3 tablespoons sugar
1 tablespoon vegetable oil
1 to 2 tablespoons crushed red pepper
1 medium carrot, scraped and cut into julienne strips
1 small sweet red pepper, cut into julienne strips
¼ cup diagonally sliced green onions
3 tablespoons minced fresh parsley
¼ cup rice vinegar
¼ teaspoon salt
¼ teaspoon freshly ground pepper

Combine cabbages in a large bowl; toss well, and set aside.

Combine water, sugar, vegetable oil, and crushed red pepper in a small saucepan; stir well to combine. Bring to a boil, stirring well. Pour mixture over cabbage mixture; toss well.

Add carrot, sweet red pepper, green onions, minced parsley, rice vinegar, salt, and freshly ground pepper, tossing gently to combine. Cover and chill thoroughly. Yield: 6 servings (78 calories per ½-cup serving).

PROTEIN 1.6 / FAT 2.7 / CARBOHYDRATE 13.8 / CHOLESTEROL 0 / IRON 1.1 / SODIUM 128 / CALCIUM 63

PINEAPPLE SORBET WITH FRESH BERRIES

2½ cups unsweetened pineapple juice
2 tablespoons sugar
2 tablespoons lemon juice
1½ cups fresh blueberries
1½ cups fresh raspberries
Fresh strawberries (optional)

Combine pineapple juice and sugar in a medium saucepan; bring to a boil. Reduce heat, and simmer 5 minutes, stirring occasionally. Stir in lemon juice. Pour mixture into a medium bowl; cover and chill 1 hour.

Pour mixture into freezer can of a 2-quart hand-turned or electric freezer. Freeze according to manufacturer's instructions.

Combine blueberries and raspberries in a small bowl. Scoop sorbet into individual dessert bowls, and spoon ½ cup berry mixture evenly over sorbet. Garnish with fresh strawberries, if desired. Serve immediately. Yield: 6 servings (112 calories per serving).

PROTEIN 0.6 / FAT 0.2 / CARBOHYDRATE 23.8 / CHOLESTEROL 0 / IRON 0.4 / SODIUM 3 / CALCIUM 22

Add warm and nourishing excitement to winter meals with Sesame Pork Tenderloin and Salad of Winter Greens.

Warming Winter Dinner

With the ease of this warming dinner, the serenity of a chilly evening is yours. The menu is synchronized for you to move easily from one food to another, culminating in a peaceful repast that delights all the senses.

Start by marinating the pork tenderloin for at least 8 hours, to allow the flavors to absorb into the meat and to help make the meat moist and delicious.

**Sesame Pork Tenderloin
Gingered Sweet Potatoes
Salad of Winter Greens
Banana Soufflé**

Serves 6
Total calories per serving: 470

Gingered Sweet Potatoes offers an unusual combination of sweet potatoes, garlic, and ginger.

Romaine lettuce, Belgian endive, and radicchio are tossed with a vinaigrette dressing made from balsamic vinegar for Salad of Winter Greens. Only a small amount of olive oil is needed in this flavorful dressing.

Put the Banana Soufflé in the oven as you sit down for dinner. By the time you've finished your entrée, the soufflé will be puffed and golden.

SESAME PORK TENDERLOIN

¼ cup reduced-sodium soy sauce
¼ cup unsweetened orange juice
1 tablespoon peeled, minced ginger
2 tablespoons honey
1 clove garlic, minced
2 (¾-pound) pork tenderloins
3 tablespoons sesame seeds
Vegetable cooking spray
¼ cup mirin (Japanese rice wine)
¼ cup canned low-sodium chicken broth, undiluted
2 tablespoons water
2 teaspoons cornstarch
Kumquats (optional)
Fresh rosemary sprigs (optional)

Combine first 5 ingredients in a large zip-top heavy-duty plastic bag. Seal bag; shake well.

Trim fat from pork. Add pork to bag; seal bag and shake until pork is well coated. Marinate in refrigerator 8 hours, shaking bag occasionally.

Remove pork from marinade; drain, reserving marinade. Sprinkle pork evenly with sesame seeds. Coat rack of a roasting pan with cooking spray. Place pork on rack. Insert meat thermometer into thickest part of pork. Bake at 350° for 45 to 55 minutes or until meat thermometer registers 170°. Remove pork from oven, and let stand 15 minutes.

Strain reserved marinade into a medium saucepan. Add mirin and chicken broth, stirring well. Bring mixture to a boil; reduce heat, and simmer 5 minutes.

Combine water and cornstarch; stir until smooth. Add to chicken broth mixture, stirring well. Cook until sauce is slightly thickened, stirring constantly.

Slice pork diagonally into thin slices. Arrange pork on a large serving platter. Spoon sauce evenly over pork. If desired, garnish with kumquats and fresh rosemary sprigs. Yield: 6 servings (168 calories per serving).

PROTEIN 20.4 / FAT 4.7 / CARBOHYDRATE 10.6 / CHOLESTEROL 58 / IRON 2.2 / SODIUM 446 / CALCIUM 57

GINGERED SWEET POTATOES

3 medium-size sweet potatoes, peeled and cut into ¼-inch-thick slices
Vegetable cooking spray
1 tablespoon reduced-calorie margarine
½ cup canned low-sodium chicken broth, undiluted and divided
1 teaspoon cornstarch
¼ cup water
1 clove garlic, minced
1 teaspoon peeled, minced ginger
¼ teaspoon salt
⅛ teaspoon ground white pepper
1 tablespoon minced fresh parsley

Coat a nonstick skillet with cooking spray. Add margarine; place over medium-high heat until hot. Add potatoes and ¼ cup broth. Bring to a boil; cover, reduce heat, and simmer 10 minutes. Uncover; cook an additional 5 minutes, or until tender and browned, turning occasionally.

Combine remaining ¼ cup broth and cornstarch, stirring well. Add cornstarch mixture, water, and remaining ingredients; stir gently. Cover and cook until thoroughly heated. Yield: 6 servings (125 calories per ½-cup serving).

PROTEIN 1.8 / FAT 1.6 / CARBOHYDRATE 26.1 / CHOLESTEROL 0 / IRON 0.7 / SODIUM 130 / CALCIUM 25

DOES SPOT REDUCING WORK?

Spot reducing schemes may be advertised as a way to melt fat from your hips, thighs, or midriff, but that's not biologically possible. In a study of college students, exercises geared toward trimming hips, thighs, and stomachs were no more effective than plain general exercise. While exercise can tone the midsection, the only way to get rid of excess fat is to eat less and exercise more. Fortunately, the areas of greatest fat concentration are often the first to show that loss.

SALAD OF WINTER GREENS

3 cups torn romaine lettuce
2 cups cored, chopped Belgian endive
1 cup torn radicchio
3 tablespoons canned low-sodium chicken broth, undiluted
2 tablespoons balsamic vinegar
2 teaspoons olive oil
¼ teaspoon salt
⅛ teaspoon freshly ground pepper

Combine romaine, endive, and radicchio in a large bowl, and toss well. Combine chicken broth and next 3 ingredients in a small bowl; stir with a wire whisk until blended. Pour over lettuce mixture, and toss well. Sprinkle pepper over salad. Arrange on individual salad plates. Yield: 6 servings (21 calories per 1-cup serving).

PROTEIN 0.6 / FAT 1.6 / CARBOHYDRATE 1.4 / CHOLESTEROL 0 / IRON 0.3 / SODIUM 106 / CALCIUM 8

FITNESS GAINS THAT LAST

A short break in your fitness routine won't put you back at square one when it comes to muscle tone and heart capacity, but if you stop for long periods, chances are you will lose fitness gains. This loss in fitness can be prevented, however, because staying in shape does not call for hard, grueling workouts every day. According to studies at the University of Illinois, far less effort is needed to maintain a certain level of fitness than to get there in the first place.

In these studies, scientists trained athletes to high fitness levels with jogging or exercise bicycle regimens. After 10 weeks of training, participants were divided into 3 groups. Each group lessened either the intensity, frequency, or duration of training. One group worked at two-thirds the intensity as before—they ran at a slower pace or pedaled more slowly. Another group cut back on the length of time they worked out. The last group cut back on the number of workouts.

At the end of 15 weeks, the only group that had lost measurable fitness benefits was the group that lessened workout intensity. Bottom line: once you get in shape, it takes less effort to stay that way. The only hitch is that workouts still need to be intense enough to give the heart a good cardiovascular workout.

BANANA SOUFFLÉ

Vegetable cooking spray
1 tablespoon sugar
1 cup mashed ripe banana
1½ tablespoons fresh lemon juice
¼ cup all-purpose flour
¾ cup skim milk
2 egg yolks
⅓ cup firmly packed brown sugar
5 egg whites
⅛ teaspoon cream of tartar
1 teaspoon ground cinnamon

Cut a piece of aluminum foil long enough to fit around a 1½-quart soufflé dish, allowing a 1-inch overlap; fold foil lengthwise into thirds. Lightly coat one side of foil with cooking spray. Wrap foil around outside of dish, coated side against dish, allowing foil to extend 3 inches above rim of dish to form a collar; secure foil with string.

Coat soufflé dish and collar with cooking spray. Sprinkle with 1 tablespoon sugar, carefully shaking to coat bottom and sides of soufflé dish and collar. Set aside.

Combine banana and lemon juice in a small bowl; stir well.

Combine flour and milk in a medium saucepan. Cook over medium heat, stirring constantly, until mixture comes to a boil. Add banana mixture, stirring well.

Combine egg yolks and brown sugar in a small bowl, beating with a wire whisk. Gradually stir about one-fourth of hot milk mixture into egg yolk mixture; add to remaining hot milk mixture; stirring constantly. Cook 1 minute or until mixture thickens.

Beat egg whites (at room temperature) in a large bowl at high speed of an electric mixer until foamy. Add cream of tartar; beat until stiff peaks form.

Gently fold beaten egg white mixture into banana mixture, and spoon into prepared soufflé dish. Bake at 375° for 35 to 45 minutes or until soufflé is puffed and golden. Remove collar from soufflé dish; sprinkle soufflé with cinnamon. Serve immediately. Yield: 6 servings (156 calories per serving).

PROTEIN 5.7 / FAT 2.3 / CARBOHYDRATE 29.4 / CHOLESTEROL 91 / IRON 1.2 / SODIUM 69 / CALCIUM 68

Rustic Italian Dinner

Low-calorie, but hearty; intensely flavored, yet subtle; that describes this menu which comes from southern Italy.

Before serving the entrée, treat your guests to hearty appetizers. Broiled and then marinated for extra flavor, the eggplant appetizers are sure to whet appetites for the meal to come.

While osso buco is traditionally made with veal, Turkey alla Osso Buco is just as flavorful with herbs and seasonings. Gremolata,

Marinated Eggplant Appetizers
Turkey alla Osso Buco
Saffron Risotto
Commercial Dinner Rolls
Almond Biscotti
Coffee

Serves 6
Total calories per serving: 650

a garnish made of minced parsley, lemon peel and garlic, adds

a fresh, light lemon flavor when sprinkled on top of the turkey.

For risotto, adding broth to the rice ½ cup at a time and stirring the mixture continually until all the liquid is absorbed, allows the rice grains to remain separate and firm. Accompany the risotto with warm dinner rolls, allowing 1 roll per serving.

For dessert, serve each guest 3 Almond Biscotti along with a cup of coffee—a pleasant ending to an Italian meal.

Fresh Italian herbs—basil, oregano, and thyme—accent Marinated Eggplant Appetizers.

MARINATED EGGPLANT APPETIZERS

1 small eggplant (about 10 ounces)
¼ teaspoon salt
Olive oil-flavored vegetable cooking spray
3 tablespoons balsamic vinegar
1 tablespoon minced fresh basil
2 cloves garlic, crushed
1 teaspoon olive oil
2 teaspoons minced fresh thyme
1 teaspoon minced fresh oregano
¼ teaspoon freshly ground pepper
12 (¼-inch-thick) slices French bread
¾ cup peeled, seeded, and chopped tomato
Fresh basil sprigs (optional)

Slice eggplant into 12 slices. Place eggplant in a colander, and sprinkle with salt; let stand 30 minutes. Rinse well and pat dry. Spray both sides of eggplant with cooking spray; place on a rack in a roasting pan. Broil 5½ inches from heat 3 to 4 minutes on each side or until lightly browned and tender. Set aside.

Combine vinegar and next 6 ingredients in a small bowl. Brush mixture on both sides of eggplant, and let stand 1 hour. Spray bread with cooking spray; place on a rack in a roasting pan. Broil 5½ inches from heat until golden. Top each bread slice with an eggplant slice and 1 tablespoon tomato. Garnish with fresh basil sprigs, if desired. Yield: 6 appetizers (67 calories per serving).

PROTEIN 2.0 / FAT 1.8 / CARBOHYDRATE 11.5 / CHOLESTEROL 0 / IRON 0.7 / SODIUM 167 / CALCIUM 31

TURKEY ALLA OSSO BUCO

3 turkey drumsticks, skinned and cut crosswise
    into 2½-inch pieces (about 3½ pounds)
¼ teaspoon salt
¼ teaspoon freshly ground pepper
Olive oil-flavored vegetable cooking spray
1 cup chopped onion
½ cup chopped carrot
½ cup chopped celery
1 (22-ounce) can no-salt-added whole
    tomatoes, crushed
1 cup canned no-salt-added beef broth,
    undiluted
¾ cup Chablis or other dry white wine
3 cloves garlic, crushed
2 bay leaves
2 tablespoons grated orange rind
1 teaspoon chopped fresh oregano
1 teaspoon chopped fresh thyme
¼ teaspoon salt
¼ teaspoon freshly ground pepper
Gremolata

Sprinkle turkey with ¼ teaspoon salt and ¼ teaspoon pepper. Coat a large nonstick skillet with cooking spray; place over medium heat until hot. Add turkey, and cook until browned on all sides, turning frequently. Remove turkey from skillet. Drain and pat dry with paper towels. Wipe turkey drippings from skillet with a paper towel.

Coat skillet with cooking spray, and place over medium-high heat until hot. Add onion, carrot, and celery; sauté 5 minutes or until tender, stirring frequently. Add turkey, tomatoes and next 9 ingredients; stir well. Cover, reduce heat, and simmer 1 hour or until turkey is tender.

Remove and discard bay leaves. Transfer turkey to a large bowl; cover and keep warm. Pour tomato mixture, in batches, into container of an electric blender; top with cover, and process until smooth.

Remove cartilage from turkey. Place turkey on a large serving platter; spoon tomato mixture over turkey. Sprinkle with Gremolata. Yield: 6 servings (219 calories per serving).

Gremolata:

3 tablespoons minced fresh parsley
Zest of 1 lemon, minced
1 large clove garlic, minced

Combine all ingredients in a small bowl; stir well. Yield: ¼ cup.

PROTEIN 28.1 / FAT 6.9 / CARBOHYDRATE 11.5 / CHOLESTEROL 78 / IRON 3.1 / SODIUM 304 / CALCIUM 100

SAFFRON RISOTTO

4 cups canned low-sodium chicken broth, undiluted
Olive oil-flavored vegetable cooking spray
¾ cup finely chopped onion
1 cup arborio rice
⅛ teaspoon powdered saffron
3 tablespoons grated Parmesan cheese
¼ teaspoon salt
⅛ teaspoon freshly ground pepper

Pour broth into a medium saucepan; place over medium heat. Bring to a simmer; cover, reduce heat, and maintain a very low simmer.

Coat a medium skillet with cooking spray; place over medium-high heat until hot. Add onion, and sauté until tender. Add rice, and sauté 2 minutes or until translucent. Add 1 cup simmering broth to rice; stir constantly until most of the liquid has been absorbed. Repeat procedure, adding ½ cup broth at a time, until there is ½ cup broth left (the entire process should take about 15 minutes).

Dissolve saffron in remaining ½ cup chicken broth; add to rice. Cook, stirring rice mixture constantly, until rice is tender and liquid is absorbed. Stir in Parmesan cheese, salt, and pepper. Serve immediately. Yield: 6 servings (150 calories per ½-cup serving).

PROTEIN 3.7 / FAT 1.1 / CARBOHYDRATE 28.7 / CHOLESTEROL 2 / IRON 1.5 / SODIUM 597 / CALCIUM 42

ALMOND BISCOTTI

½ cup sugar
¼ cup margarine, softened
2 eggs
1 teaspoon almond extract
¼ teaspoon anise extract
1¾ cups all-purpose flour, divided
½ cup ground almonds
¼ teaspoon salt
1 teaspoon baking powder
Vegetable cooking spray

Combine first 5 ingredients in a large bowl; beat at medium speed of an electric mixer until well blended. Combine 1½ cups flour, almonds, salt, and baking powder. Add to egg mixture, beating well. Stir in remaining ¼ cup flour to make a soft dough. Cover and chill dough at least 2 hours.

Coat 2 sheets of heavy-duty plastic wrap with cooking spray. Divide dough in half; shape each half into a (12-inch) log on prepared plastic wrap. Transfer logs to a cookie sheet coated with cooking spray; flatten logs to ¾-inch thickness. Bake at 350° for 20 minutes. Transfer logs to a wire rack; let cool.

Slice logs diagonally into ¼-inch slices. Place on cookie sheets, cut sides down. Bake at 300° for 15 minutes; turn cookies over, and bake an additional 15 minutes or until dry. Cool on wire racks. Yield: 4 dozen cookies (42 calories each).

PROTEIN 1.0 / FAT 1.8 / CARBOHYDRATE 5.5 / CHOLESTEROL 8 / IRON 0.3 / SODIUM 32 / CALCIUM 9

SAMPLING SAFFRON

Saffron has been used for years to color and flavor a variety of foods, from breads to main dishes to desserts; the resulting taste is often described as warm and pungent.

Saffron is made from the dried stigmas of a flower belonging to the Iris family. The funnel-shaped flower is light violet, and the stigmas, which extend outside the close-knit petals, are fiery orange-red. It takes thousands of flowers to produce a tiny amount of the spice, and two years are needed to grow one flower crop.

Look for both powdered saffron and saffron threads in specialty food shops or in the spice section of your local supermarket.

Set out tortillas and Faux Guacamole, and guests can assemble their own Turkey Tostadas. Serve the tostadas with Bloody Mary Slushes.

Santa Fe Buffet

Bursting with color and flavor, Tex-Mex cuisine has become a favorite ethnic food. Although it's often avoided because of its high fat content, this menu eliminates that worry.

Start the fiesta with Bloody Mary Slushes, a beverage that can be made ahead and frozen. Shortly before the guests arrive, remove the Bloody Mary mixture from the freezer and let it stand 20 minutes, before processing

Bloody Mary Slushes
Turkey Tostadas with
Roasted Pepper Salsa
Faux Guacamole
Fresh Strawberry Sauce
Commercial Frozen Yogurt

Serves 8
Total calories per serving: 490

the beverage in an electric blender or food processor.

The Roasted Pepper Salsa adds color and flavor to the Turkey Tostadas. Ground turkey, cubed new potatoes, and wine make these tostadas a favorite. And for extra flavor, allow ¼ cup Faux Guacamole per person. It is made from English peas and low-fat sour cream and accented with fresh cilantro.

For dessert, spoon 2 table-spoons Strawberry Sauce over ½ cup frozen low-fat yogurt.

BLOODY MARY SLUSHES

1 small onion, quartered
6½ cups spicy vegetable juice cocktail, divided
2 tablespoons low-sodium Worcestershire sauce
2 tablespoons lemon juice
½ cup vodka
Lime slices (optional)

Combine onion, 3 cups juice, Worcestershire sauce, and lemon juice in container of an electric blender; top with cover, and process until smooth. Pour into a shallow dish; stir in remaining 3½ cups juice. Cover; freeze until firm.

Remove from freezer and let stand 20 minutes. Break mixture into small chunks. Place half of pieces in food processor or electric blender; add ¼ cup vodka, top with cover, and process until smooth. Spoon into glasses. Repeat with remaining vegetable juice mixture and ¼ cup vodka. Garnish each glass with a lime slice, if desired. Serve immediately. Yield: 8 servings (77 calories per 1-cup serving).

PROTEIN 1.3 / FAT 0.0 / CARBOHYDRATE 12.1 / CHOLESTEROL 0 / IRON 0.8 / SODIUM 702 / CALCIUM 3

TURKEY TOSTADAS WITH ROASTED PEPPER SALSA

8 small new potatoes (about ½ pound)
Vegetable cooking spray
1½ pounds fresh raw ground turkey
1½ cups chopped onion
2 cloves garlic, minced
½ cup Chablis or other dry white wine
⅓ cup commercial salsa
½ teaspoon chili powder
¼ teaspoon salt
⅛ teaspoon freshly ground pepper
8 (6-inch) corn tortillas
2 cups shredded romaine lettuce
Roasted Pepper Salsa
½ cup low-fat sour cream

Wash potatoes. Cook in boiling water to cover 15 minutes or until tender; drain and cool. Cut into ¼-inch cubes; set aside.

Coat a large nonstick skillet with cooking spray; place over medium heat until hot. Add turkey, onion, and garlic; cook until turkey is browned, stirring to crumble. Drain turkey mixture, and pat dry with paper towels. Wipe drippings from skillet with a paper towel. Add turkey mixture, wine, salsa, chili powder, and salt to skillet. Bring to a boil; cover, reduce heat, and simmer 10 minutes. Uncover, and increase heat to high. Cook an additional 5 minutes or until most of the liquid has evaporated. Stir in pepper. Set aside, and keep warm.

Place tortillas on baking sheets. Bake at 350°

for 15 to 20 minutes or until crisp. Spoon ¼ cup lettuce onto each tortilla. Top each with ½ cup turkey mixture, potato cubes, ¼ cup Roasted Pepper Salsa, and 1 tablespoon sour cream. Serve immediately. Yield: 8 servings (223 calories per serving).

PROTEIN 22.2 / FAT 6.1 / CARBOHYDRATE 19.4 / CHOLESTEROL 54 / IRON 3.0 / SODIUM 175 / CALCIUM 85

Roasted Pepper Salsa:

1 medium-size sweet red pepper
1 medium-size sweet yellow pepper
1 Anaheim green chile
1½ cups peeled, seeded, and chopped tomato
2 jalapeño peppers, seeded and chopped
1 clove garlic, minced
2 teaspoons red wine vinegar
¼ teaspoon salt

Place sweet peppers and Anaheim chile on a baking sheet; broil 5½ inches from heat, turning often with tongs, until peppers are charred on all sides. Immediately place in a plastic bag; close tightly, and let stand 20 minutes to loosen skins. Peel peppers; remove core and seeds. Cut peppers into small cubes, and place in a medium bowl. Stir in tomato and remaining ingredients. Cover and chill thoroughly. Yield: 2 cups (4 calories per tablespoon).

PROTEIN 0.2 / FAT 0.0 / CARBOHYDRATE 0.8 / CHOLESTEROL 0 / IRON 0.1 / SODIUM 19 / CALCIUM 1

FAUX GUACAMOLE

1 (10-ounce) package frozen English peas
¼ cup low-fat sour cream
1 jalapeño pepper, seeded and minced
1 tablespoon chopped fresh cilantro
1 teaspoon lemon juice
½ teaspoon ground cumin
¼ teaspoon salt
Dash of hot sauce
2 tablespoons diced purple onion
1 cup peeled, seeded, and chopped tomato
Fresh cilantro sprigs (optional)

Cook peas according to package directions, omitting salt. Drain well.

Position knife blade in food processor bowl. Add peas and next 7 ingredients; process until smooth. Transfer pureed mixture to a small bowl. Stir in onion and tomato. Cover and chill thoroughly. Garnish with cilantro, if desired. Serve with Turkey Tostados. Yield: 2 cups (11 calories per tablespoon).

PROTEIN 0.6 / FAT 0.3 / CARBOHYDRATE 1.7 / CHOLESTEROL 1 / IRON 0.2 / SODIUM 27 / CALCIUM 5

FRESH STRAWBERRY SAUCE

1¾ cups fresh strawberries, hulled and divided
2 tablespoons sugar
2 teaspoons cornstarch

Mash 1 cup strawberries. Combine mashed strawberries, sugar and cornstarch in a medium saucepan; stir well. Cook over medium heat 3 to 4 minutes or until mixture is thickened, stirring constantly. Remove strawberry mixture from heat. Slice remaining ¾ cup strawberries, and add to cooked mixture; stir gently. Cool completely. Serve over frozen yogurt. Yield: 1 cup (11 calories per tablespoon).

PROTEIN 0.1 / FAT 0.1 / CARBOHYDRATE 2.7 / CHOLESTEROL 0 / IRON 0.1 / SODIUM 0 / CALCIUM 2

STICKS, TUBS, LIQUIDS, AND SPREADS

Faced with dozens of different selections of margarines, most shoppers can be confused easily. Taste, of course, has to be one consideration. But how do you determine which brand is healthier? Is it better to buy a spread that contains a low level of saturated fat than a stick margarine? Where do tub and liquid or squeezable margarines fit in? These questions are easy to answer once you have some basic definitions of the terms.

By law, anything labeled as margarine must be at least 80 percent fat by weight. Products that carry less fat must either be labeled diet, imitation, or, the newer term, spread. These products are made from the same vegetable oils—corn, sunflower, safflower, soybean—as regular margarines, but less oil is used.

Most companies do print the percentage of oil on the label. Be aware that to achieve this lower amount of fat, manufacturers are mixing vegetable oils with water. In fact, water is often the first item on the ingredient list. In other words, you are getting less fat per tablespoon because that fat is whipped with water.

However, the real difference between margarines and spreads is the type of fat they contain. Since high levels of saturated fat may cause heart problems, look for margarines or spreads with a low level of saturated fat. Vegetable oils start out as unsaturated, but in order to make them into solids, such as stick margarine, hydrogen is added. Hydrogenation of oils makes them more saturated. A general rule of thumb is that stick margarines contain higher levels of saturated fats than tub margarine, which in turn have higher levels than liquid margarine.

Manufacturers often list the amount of polyunsaturated and saturated fat on the nutrient information panel. Nutritionists recommend a ratio of polyunsaturated to saturated fat (P:S) of at least 2 to 1. Margarines that list a liquid oil as their first ingredient are less saturated than those that list a partially hydrogenated oil as the primary ingredient.

Champagne grapes and fresh mint sprigs add a touch of elegance to Sauternes-Poached Pears (page 87).

East-West Dinner

Enjoying flavors from around the world can be an elegant change of pace. Start the meal with an appetizer that is hearty enough to serve as an entrée for two people.

Chinese cabbage leaves are wrapped around salmon and enclose spices and seasonings that give this international dinner flavor appeal.

Basmati rice is a long-grain rice with a fine texture. It can usually be found in Middle Eastern and

Crab-Stuffed Ravioli
Steamed Salmon Fillets in Cabbage Leaves
Zucchini and Carrot Strands
Basmati Rice
Sauternes-Poached Pears
White Wine

Serves 4
Total calories per serving: 675

Indian markets, as well as in most supermarkets. The nutlike

flavor is enhanced with toasted pine nuts in this menu.

Zucchini and carrots can be quickly cut into julienne strips, using a mandoline. This portable piece of equipment has adjustable blades for slicing food and is easily disassembled for cleaning and storing.

Sauternes, a sweet wine from France, adds flavor to the poached pear dessert. Complete the meal with a 6-ounce glass of white wine per person.

CRAB-STUFFED RAVIOLI

⅓ pound fresh lump crabmeat, drained
1 egg, beaten
2 tablespoons minced green onions
1 clove garlic, minced
½ teaspoon sesame oil
¼ teaspoon dry mustard
3 to 4 drops hot sauce
24 fresh or frozen wonton skins, thawed
1 egg white, lightly beaten
Oriental Tomato Sauce
Fresh cilantro sprigs (optional)

Combine first 7 ingredients in a small bowl. Place 1 tablespoon crabmeat mixture in center of each of 12 wonton skins. Brush edges of wonton skins with egg white; top with remaining 12 wonton skins. Press wonton edges together to seal, and trim edges with a fluted pastry wheel. Place wontons on wax paper, and cover with plastic wrap. (Ravioli can be stored in refrigerator up to 3 hours.)

Bring water to a boil in a Dutch oven. Add ravioli, and return water to a boil; reduce heat, and simmer 5 minutes or until ravioli are tender. Remove ravioli with a slotted spoon, and place 3 ravioli on each of 4 individual serving plates.

Spoon Oriental Tomato Sauce evenly over each serving. Garnish with fresh cilantro sprigs, if desired. Yield: 4 servings (99 calories per serving).

Oriental Tomato Sauce:

Vegetable cooking spray
2 tablespoons chopped green onions
2 cloves garlic, minced
1½ teaspoons peeled, minced ginger
¼ cup canned low-sodium chicken broth, undiluted
1 (14½-ounce) can no-salt-added whole tomatoes, drained and chopped
⅛ teaspoon salt
Dash of ground white pepper

Spray a medium saucepan with cooking spray; place over medium-high heat until hot. Add green onions, garlic, and ginger; sauté 1 minute, stirring constantly. Add chicken broth, and cook an additional 2 minutes or until onions are tender. Add tomato, salt, and pepper; cook, uncovered, 5 minutes. Yield: 1 cup.

PROTEIN 11.1 / FAT 2.9 / CARBOHYDRATE 6.7 / CHOLESTEROL 89 / IRON 1.0 / SODIUM 520 / CALCIUM 54

STEAMED SALMON FILLETS IN CABBAGE LEAVES

1 (12-ounce) salmon fillet
2 tablespoons reduced-sodium soy sauce
2 tablespoons dry sherry
1 tablespoon peeled, minced ginger
2 cloves garlic, minced
4 large Chinese cabbage leaves
¼ cup diagonally sliced green onions
1 tablespoon minced fresh cilantro
¼ teaspoon salt
⅛ teaspoon ground white pepper
2 tablespoons lemon juice

Cut fillet into 4 equal pieces, and place in a shallow baking dish. Combine soy sauce, sherry, ginger, and garlic, stirring well; pour over salmon. Cover and marinate in refrigerator 30 minutes.

Blanch cabbage leaves in boiling water 30 seconds. Drain and rinse under cold water until cool; drain again.

Remove salmon from marinade; discard marinade. Combine green onions, cilantro, salt, and pepper in a small bowl. Place one salmon piece at base of a cabbage leaf. Sprinkle with one-fourth of green onion mixture. Fold sides of cabbage over salmon, wrapping salmon like a package. Repeat with remaining salmon, cabbage, and green onion mixture.

Arrange salmon on a steaming rack. Place over boiling water; cover and steam 10 to 12 minutes or until fish flakes easily when tested with a fork. Transfer to a serving platter, and brush with lemon juice. Yield: 4 servings (146 calories per serving).

PROTEIN 20.0 / FAT 5.3 / CARBOHYDRATE 4.4 / CHOLESTEROL 33 / IRON 2.9 / SODIUM 290 / CALCIUM 95

ZUCCHINI AND CARROT STRANDS

Vegetable cooking spray
1 teaspoon olive oil
2 medium carrots, scraped and cut into julienne strips
¼ cup canned low-sodium chicken broth, undiluted
1 medium zucchini, cut into julienne strips
1 clove garlic, minced
¼ teaspoon salt
⅛ teaspoon freshly ground pepper

Coat a large nonstick skillet with cooking spray. Add oil; place over medium heat until hot. Add carrot; sauté 1 minute. Add chicken broth; cook 1 minute, stirring occasionally. Stir in zucchini, garlic, salt, and pepper. Cover and cook 3 minutes or until vegetables are crisp-tender. Yield: 4 servings (36 calories per ½-cup serving).

PROTEIN 1.0 / FAT 1.4 / CARBOHYDRATE 5.4 / CHOLESTEROL 0 / IRON 0.4 / SODIUM 161 / CALCIUM 20

CHEESE LIMITS

Now you can find a variety of new lower fat cheeses, including Cheddar, Monterey Jack, mozzarella, and Swiss. Each contains just a fraction of the fat and cholesterol of regular cheese. Instead of the typical 8 to 10 grams of fat, a ''light'' Cheddar may have only 5 grams. While that can still amount to 50 percent of the calories, it's quite a step down from the higher level.

Attempting to lower fat levels even more, several companies are marketing cheese with 2 grams or less of fat per serving. A recipe from one Wisconsin cheese maker has so little fat that his products can legally be called cholesterol- and fat-free. Texture and taste of these products tend to vary; fat is what gives cheese some of its ''bite.''

Still, given the wide variety of acceptable low-fat products, it's easier for cooks to lighten a traditional recipe by slipping in a lower fat cheese ingredient. None of this means that regular cheese can't be used in the healthful kitchen. Indeed, one of the best ways to take advantage of higher fat cheese is to opt for the stronger flavored varieties and use them sparingly. A sprinkle of Parmesan or a very sharp Cheddar or blue cheese can go a long way flavor-wise; indeed, less is more.

BASMATI RICE

½ cup Basmati rice
1 cup water
¼ teaspoon salt
1½ tablespoons pine nuts, toasted
⅓ cup minced green onions
3 tablespoons minced fresh parsley

Rinse rice in 5 changes of cold water; drain.
Bring 1 cup water to a boil in a small saucepan; add rice and salt. Cover, reduce heat, and simmer for 15 minutes. Remove from heat, and let stand, covered, for 10 minutes. Stir in pine nuts, green onions, and parsley. Yield: 4 servings (106 calories per ½-cup serving).

PROTEIN 2.7 / FAT 2.0 / CARBOHYDRATE 19.7 / CHOLESTEROL 0 / IRON 1.6 / SODIUM 149 / CALCIUM 17

SAUTERNES-POACHED PEARS

4 medium-size fresh pears
1½ cups water
½ cup Sauternes
¼ cup honey
1 tablespoon peeled, chopped ginger
Champagne grapes (optional)
Fresh mint sprigs (optional)

Peel and core pears, leaving stem end intact. Slice pears in half lengthwise, leaving stem intact on 1 side.

Combine water and next 3 ingredients in a large saucepan; bring to a boil. Place pears in pan; baste with water mixture. Cover, reduce heat, and simmer 10 minutes or until tender. Remove pears with a slotted spoon.

Place pears, cut side down, on a cutting surface. Cut thin lengthwise slits in each pear, one-third up from base to stem end. Fan 2 pear halves on each dessert plate. Cover and chill.

Cook remaining liquid over medium-high heat until reduced by half; strain to remove ginger. Cover and chill. To serve, spoon liquid over pears. If desired, garnish with champagne grapes and mint sprigs. Yield: 4 servings (176 calories per serving).

PROTEIN 0.8 / FAT 0.7 / CARBOHYDRATE 45.9 / CHOLESTEROL 0 / IRON 0.7 / SODIUM 4 / CALCIUM 24

Quiet Evening Sonata

Chicken Breasts with
Wild Mushrooms
Saffron Orzo
Roasted Asparagus with
Orange Sauce
Commercial Dinner Rolls
Pink Grapefruit and
Champagne Sorbet
Coffee

Serves 4
Total calories per serving: 573

Sit back and enjoy Pink Grapefruit and Champagne Sorbet, a simple but refreshing dessert.

Although American lifestyles are busier than ever, most people still enjoy sitting down to a quiet home-cooked meal, and this menu is sure to please.

Relax with friends as everyone raves about this meal; it includes favorite comfort foods presented in new, upscale ways.

A porcini mushroom sauce is spooned over chicken breasts for an alternative to fat-laden gravy.

Serve orzo, a grain-shaped pasta, roasted asparagus, and dinner rolls, allowing 1 roll per person, as accompaniments.

CHICKEN BREASTS WITH WILD MUSHROOMS

1 ounce dried porcini mushrooms
4 (4-ounce) skinned, boned chicken breast halves
½ teaspoon pepper
Vegetable cooking spray
1 teaspoon olive oil
½ cup canned low-sodium chicken broth, undiluted
2 cups sliced fresh mushrooms
⅔ cup plain non-fat yogurt

Pour boiling water to cover over dried porcini mushrooms; let stand 30 minutes. Drain mushrooms, reserving ⅔ cup liquid, and coarsely chop; set mushrooms and liquid aside.

Place chicken breasts between 2 sheets of heavy-duty plastic wrap; flatten slightly, using a meat mallet or rolling pin. Sprinkle chicken evenly with pepper.

Coat a large nonstick skillet with cooking spray; add olive oil. Place over medium-high heat until hot. Add chicken, and cook 3½ minutes on each side or until browned. Transfer to a serving platter, and keep warm.

Wipe drippings from skillet with a paper towel. Add chicken broth, reserved porcini liquid, and sliced mushrooms to skillet; cook over high heat until mushrooms are tender, stirring occasionally. Add porcini mushrooms, and cook until all liquid evaporates. Remove from heat; let cool 5 minutes. Stir in yogurt. Cook until thoroughly heated (do not boil). Place chicken breasts on individual serving plates. Spoon sauce evenly over chicken. Yield: 4 servings (211 calories per serving).

PROTEIN 29.6 / FAT 4.5 / CARBOHYDRATE 10.6 / CHOLESTEROL 72 / IRON 1.6 / SODIUM 93 / CALCIUM 91

SAFFRON ORZO

2 quarts water, divided
⅛ teaspoon powdered saffron
¾ cup orzo
1 tablespoon finely shredded fresh basil
1½ teaspoons olive oil
½ teaspoon salt

Bring water to a boil in a large saucepan. Place 2 tablespoons boiling water in a small bowl; add saffron, and stir well. Set saffron mixture aside. Add orzo to remaining boiling water, and allow water to return to a boil. Cook, uncovered, 10 minutes or just until tender; drain.

Combine cooked orzo, reserved saffron mixture, and remaining ingredients in a medium bowl; toss mixture lightly to coat well. Serve immediately. Yield: 4 servings (147 calories per ½-cup serving).

PROTEIN 4.5 / FAT 2.3 / CARBOHYDRATE 26.5 / CHOLESTEROL 0 / IRON 1.4 / SODIUM 295 / CALCIUM 9

ROASTED ASPARAGUS WITH ORANGE SAUCE

1 pound fresh asparagus spears
2 teaspoons olive oil
1 teaspoon grated orange rind
¼ cup fresh orange juice
2 tablespoons lemon juice
¼ cup water
2 teaspoons cornstarch
Orange rind strips (optional)

Snap off tough ends of asparagus. Remove scales from spears with a knife or vegetable peeler, if desired. Arrange spears in a single layer on a baking sheet. Brush spears with olive oil. Bake at 475° for 7 to 9 minutes or until tender, turning every 3 minutes. Transfer to a serving platter, and keep warm.

Combine orange rind, orange juice, and lemon juice in a small saucepan. Bring to a boil over medium heat.

Combine water and cornstarch, stirring until smooth. Slowly add cornstarch mixture to orange juice mixture and cook, stirring constantly, until mixture is thickened. Cook 1 minute. Remove mixture from heat, and spoon orange sauce evenly over asparagus spears. Garnish with orange rind strips, if desired. Yield: 4 servings (49 calories per serving).

PROTEIN 2.3 / FAT 2.4 / CARBOHYDRATE 6.3 / CHOLESTEROL 0 / IRON 0.5 / SODIUM 2 / CALCIUM 18

PINK GRAPEFRUIT AND CHAMPAGNE SORBET

1 large pink grapefruit
1 cup pink grapefruit juice cocktail
2 cups dry champagne
¼ cup sugar
Grapefruit rind curls (optional)

Grate rind from pink grapefruit, and set aside. Carefully peel and section grapefruit, removing white membrane.

Position knife blade in food processor bowl; add grapefruit sections. Process until finely chopped. Add grapefruit juice and grapefruit rind; process until smooth.

Pour grapefruit mixture into freezer can of a 2-quart hand-turned or electric freezer. Add champagne and sugar; stir well. Freeze according to manufacturer's instructions. Let ripen 1 hour, if desired. Scoop sorbet into individual dessert bowls; garnish with grapefruit rind curls, if desired. Serve immediately. Yield: 4½ cups (79 calories per ½-cup serving).

PROTEIN 0.3 / FAT 0.0 / CARBOHYDRATE 10.9 / CHOLESTEROL 0 / IRON 0.3 / SODIUM 4 / CALCIUM 6

Light
Recipes

Fresh from the garden, fruits and vegetables can enhance any meal. Try these light recipes that taste as delicious as they are nutritious: (clockwise from left) Shrimp and Vegetable Salad (page 186), Lemon and Berry Tart (page 243), Apple Mint Juleps (page 101), and Italian Summer Salad (page 178).

In "Light Recipes" you will discover a full range of recipes that capture the best flavors of fresh, wholesome foods. *Cooking Light Cookbook 1991* offers hundreds of recipes from appetizers to main dishes to desserts, so you will have plenty from which to choose. And, best of all, you will find that the light touch in cooking results in foods that are higher in nutrients, fiber, and complex carbohydrates, but lower in fat, cholesterol, sugar, and salt.

When putting together recipes to form menus, remember that of the total calories provided, at least 50 percent of the calories should be from carbohydrate, 20 percent from protein, and no more than 30 percent from fat. And keeping this 50-20-30 ratio in mind, you can create calorie-controlled meals to provide a healthful approach to weight loss.

Most women can safely lose weight while eating 1,200 calories per day; most men can lose while eating 1,600. Once weight is lost, modify the menu plan according to the number of calories needed to maintain your ideal weight. If you are losing weight too slowly, keep in mind that eating fewer calories to speed up weight loss may rob you of the nutrients your body needs to stay healthy. Also, your metabolism may slow down to accommodate a limited food supply. Exercising is the key to speeding up weight loss.

Attention to the principles of sound nutrition, freshness, variety, and presentation will invite success as you plan light meals. But even more important, you will have the satisfaction of serving the healthiest, freshest, and most attractive meals possible.

Whether you are having a backyard picnic, formal dinner, or family celebration, you will find many ideas in the following recipe sections to help you create exciting meals that meet today's high standards for the best in nutrition. And you will be pleased to discover that many of them are as economical and time-efficient as they are appealing and wholesome.

Whether for family or friends, Beef Satay (page 100) and Oriental Shrimp Dip (page 95) will get any meal off to a spectacular start.

Appetizers & Beverages

HOT MEXICAN-STYLE BROCCOLI DIP

1 (10-ounce) package frozen chopped broccoli, thawed
Vegetable cooking spray
½ cup chopped onion
1¼ cups peeled, seeded, and chopped tomato
2 tablespoons chopped jalapeño pepper
1 (8-ounce) package Neufchâtel cheese, cubed and softened
1 cup (4 ounces) shredded reduced-fat Monterey Jack cheese
¾ cup evaporated skimmed milk
⅓ cup sliced ripe olives

Drain broccoli; press between paper towels to remove excess moisture. Place broccoli in container of an electric blender or food processor; top with cover, and process until smooth. Set mixture aside.

Coat a large nonstick skillet with cooking spray; place over medium-high heat until hot. Add onion, and sauté until tender. Add tomato and jalapeño pepper; sauté 2 minutes. Transfer mixture to a large bowl. Stir in reserved broccoli, cheeses, milk, and olives. Spoon into a 1½-quart casserole coated with cooking spray. Bake at 400° for 50 minutes or until bubbly and browned. Serve warm with unsalted tortilla chips or melba rounds. Yield: 4½ cups (18 calories per tablespoon).

PROTEIN 1.1 / FAT 1.2 / CARBOHYDRATE 0.9 / CHOLESTEROL 4 / IRON 0.1 / SODIUM 31 / CALCIUM 14

SPINACH DIP

1 (10-ounce) package frozen chopped spinach, thawed
⅓ cup chopped fresh parsley
⅓ cup 1% low-fat cottage cheese
⅓ cup reduced-calorie mayonnaise
¼ cup chopped green onions
¼ cup nonfat buttermilk
3 tablespoons lemon juice
2 tablespoons grated onion
¼ teaspoon salt
⅛ teaspoon freshly ground pepper
Dash of Worcestershire sauce

Drain spinach; press between paper towels to remove excess moisture. Combine spinach, parsley, cottage cheese, mayonnaise, green onions, buttermilk, lemon juice, onion, salt, pepper, and Worcestershire sauce in container of an electric blender or food processor; top with cover, and process until smooth. Transfer mixture to a small bowl. Cover and chill thoroughly. Serve with fresh raw vegetables or melba rounds. Yield: 2 cups (12 calories per tablespoon).

PROTEIN 0.7 / FAT 0.8 / CARBOHYDRATE 1.6 / CHOLESTEROL 1 / IRON 0.2 / SODIUM 69 / CALCIUM 13

LAYERED MEXICAN DIP

6 ounces lean ground turkey
6 ounces lean ground pork
½ cup chopped onion
1 (16-ounce) can pinto beans, drained and mashed
1 (4-ounce) can chopped green chiles, undrained
½ cup (2 ounces) shredded reduced-fat Monterey Jack cheese
½ cup (2 ounces) shredded 40% less-fat Cheddar cheese
½ cup commercial picante sauce
¼ cup chopped green onions
1 tablespoon sliced ripe olives
½ cup low-fat sour cream

Cook turkey, pork, and onion in a large nonstick skillet over medium heat until browned, stirring to crumble meat. Drain and pat dry with paper towels. Set aside.

Spread pinto beans in an 11- x 7- x 2-inch baking dish; layer reserved meat mixture, chopped green chiles, cheeses, and picante sauce over beans. Bake, uncovered, at 350° for 15 minutes or until cheese melts and mixture is thoroughly heated.

Sprinkle chopped green onions and sliced olives evenly over picante sauce; top with sour cream. Serve with unsalted tortilla chips or melba rounds. Yield: 24 appetizer servings (57 calories per serving).

PROTEIN 4.9 / FAT 2.7 / CARBOHYDRATE 3.4 / CHOLESTEROL 14 / IRON 0.4 / SODIUM 77 / CALCIUM 30

CHILE-CHEESE CORN DIP

1 (11-ounce) can no-salt-added whole kernel corn, drained
¾ cup (3 ounces) shredded 40% less-fat Cheddar cheese
½ cup low-fat sour cream
½ cup plain nonfat yogurt
¼ cup reduced-calorie mayonnaise
3 tablespoons grated Parmesan cheese
1½ tablespoons grated onion
1 tablespoon diced pimiento

Combine corn, Cheddar cheese, sour cream, yogurt, mayonnaise, Parmesan cheese, onion, and pimiento in a medium bowl. Cover and chill thoroughly. Serve with unsalted tortilla chips or melba rounds. Yield: 3 cups (18 calories per tablespoon).

PROTEIN 0.8 / FAT 1.0 / CARBOHYDRATE 1.5 / CHOLESTEROL 3 / IRON 0.0 / SODIUM 28 / CALCIUM 24

ORIENTAL SHRIMP DIP

6 ounces cooked, peeled, and deveined shrimp, finely chopped
¾ cup water chestnuts, drained and minced
⅔ cup low-fat sour cream
¼ cup reduced-calorie mayonnaise
3 tablespoons minced green onions
2 teaspoons low-sodium soy sauce
½ teaspoon grated fresh ginger
Fresh snow pea pods (optional)
Daikon radish strips (optional)
Sweet red pepper pieces (optional)

Combine first 7 ingredients in a medium bowl; mix well. Cover and chill 1 hour. If desired, serve with snow peas, daikon strips, and sweet red pepper pieces. Yield: 2 cups (21 calories per tablespoon).

PROTEIN 1.3 / FAT 1.2 / CARBOHYDRATE 1.2 / CHOLESTEROL 13 / IRON 0.2 / SODIUM 41 / CALCIUM 8

MIDDLE EASTERN DIP

1 (15-ounce) can garbanzo beans
⅓ cup lemon juice, divided
2 tablespoons sesame seeds
2 cloves garlic, minced
2 teaspoons sesame oil
½ teaspoon ground cumin
¼ teaspoon ground red pepper
2 tablespoons minced fresh parsley
¾ cup diced tomato

Drain garbanzo beans, reserving 2 tablespoons liquid; set aside.
Combine reserved liquid, 2 tablespoons lemon juice, sesame seeds, garlic, sesame oil, cumin, and red pepper in container of an electric blender or food processor; top with cover, and process until smooth. Add garbanzo beans, remaining 3 tablespoons plus 1 teaspoon lemon juice, and parsley; process until smooth. Transfer mixture to a medium bowl, and stir in tomato. Cover and chill at least 2 hours. Serve with toasted pita triangles. Yield: 2 cups (23 calories per tablespoon).

PROTEIN 1.0 / FAT 0.8 / CARBOHYDRATE 3.1 / CHOLESTEROL 0 / IRON 0.4 / SODIUM 4 / CALCIUM 12

PESTO SPREAD

½ cup tightly packed fresh basil leaves
½ cup tightly packed fresh spinach leaves
1 tablespoon grated Parmesan cheese
1 tablespoon pine nuts, toasted
1 clove garlic, halved
1 (8-ounce) carton plain nonfat yogurt

Line a colander or sieve with a double layer of cheesecloth that has been rinsed and squeezed dry; allow cheesecloth to extend over outside edges of colander. Set aside.
Position knife blade in food processor bowl; add first 5 ingredients. Process 30 seconds to 1 minute or until smooth.
Stir yogurt until smooth; add yogurt to basil mixture, stirring well. Spoon yogurt mixture into colander and fold edges of cheesecloth over to cover yogurt mixture. Place colander in a large bowl; cover and chill 12 to 24 hours. Remove yogurt mixture from colander and discard liquid. Serve with fresh raw vegetables. Yield: 1 cup (29 calories per tablespoon).

PROTEIN 2.1 / FAT 0.8 / CARBOHYDRATE 4.7 / CHOLESTEROL 1 / IRON 2.5 / SODIUM 23 / CALCIUM 151

SPINACH BOURSIN

1 (10-ounce) package frozen chopped spinach, thawed
1 (8-ounce) package Neufchâtel cheese, cubed and softened
¼ cup minced green onions
2 tablespoons minced fresh parsley
1 teaspoon minced fresh basil
1 teaspoon minced fresh thyme
1 teaspoon lemon juice
½ teaspoon garlic powder
Fresh spinach leaves (optional)

Drain spinach; press between paper towels to remove excess moisture.

Position knife blade in food processor bowl; add spinach and next 7 ingredients. Process 30 seconds or until smooth. Transfer spinach mixture to a small bowl. Cover and chill spinach mixture at least 2 hours.

Spoon spinach mixture into a serving bowl lined with fresh spinach leaves, if desired. Serve with unsalted crackers. Yield: 1¾ cups (24 calories per tablespoon).

PROTEIN 1.1 / FAT 1.9 / CARBOHYDRATE 0.8 / CHOLESTEROL 6 / IRON 0.3 / SODIUM 40 / CALCIUM 19

MARSALA CHICKEN LIVER PÂTÉ

1 tablespoon reduced-calorie margarine
½ cup finely chopped onion
1 pound chicken livers
1 cup chopped fresh mushrooms
2 cloves garlic, minced
¼ cup Marsala wine
½ (8-ounce) package Neufchâtel cheese, softened and cubed
1 tablespoon Dijon mustard
2 tablespoons chopped fresh parsley

Melt margarine in a large nonstick skillet over medium heat. Add onion, livers, mushrooms, and garlic; sauté 5 minutes or until livers are browned. Add wine; cook mixture an additional 5 minutes or until livers are tender and liquid evaporates.

Position knife blade in food processor bowl; add liver mixture, cheese, and mustard. Process 1 minute or until pureed. Stir in parsley. Transfer mixture to a small crock or bowl. Cover and chill thoroughly. Serve pâté with unsalted crackers or party rye bread. Yield: 2 cups (32 calories per tablespoon).

PROTEIN 3.0 / FAT 1.7 / CARBOHYDRATE 1.1 / CHOLESTEROL 65 / IRON 1.3 / SODIUM 43 / CALCIUM 6

SALMON MOUSSE SPREAD

1 envelope unflavored gelatin
¾ cup cold water
1 (6¾-ounce) can smoked salmon, drained and flaked
½ cup reduced-calorie mayonnaise
½ cup plain nonfat yogurt
1 tablespoon lemon juice
1 tablespoon prepared horseradish
Vegetable cooking spray
Red leaf lettuce leaves (optional)

Sprinkle gelatin over cold water in a small saucepan; let stand 1 minute. Cook over low heat, stirring until gelatin dissolves.

Combine salmon and next 4 ingredients in a medium bowl; stir well. Stir in gelatin mixture. Spoon into a 3-cup mold coated with cooking spray. Cover and chill until firm. Unmold onto a lettuce-lined plate, if desired. Serve with unsalted pumpernickel rounds. Yield: 2½ cups (14 calories per tablespoon).

PROTEIN 0.9 / FAT 1.0 / CARBOHYDRATE 0.5 / CHOLESTEROL 2 / IRON 0.0 / SODIUM 50 / CALCIUM 6

HOLIDAY BRIE

1 cup chopped fresh cranberries
½ cup peeled, chopped pear
2 tablespoons honey
1 tablespoon currants
¼ teaspoon pumpkin pie spice
3 tablespoons cranberry juice cocktail
2 tablespoons red wine vinegar
2 teaspoons lemon juice
1 (15-ounce) round fully ripened Brie

Combine first 8 ingredients in a heavy sauce-pan; bring mixture to a boil over medium-high heat. Cover, reduce heat, and simmer 30 minutes, stirring frequently. Uncover and cook an additional 5 minutes or until mixture is thickened, stirring frequently. Cool mixture to room temperature.

Cut circle in top rind of cheese, leaving a ¼-inch border of rind. Carefully remove center circle of rind from cheese, leaving border intact.

Place Brie on an ovenproof serving platter. Spread cranberry mixture over top. Bake at 350° for 12 to 15 minutes or until cheese is bubbly. Serve immediately with melba rounds or sliced apples and pears. Yield: 30 appetizer servings (52 calories per serving).

PROTEIN 2.7 / FAT 3.6 / CARBOHYDRATE 2.5 / CHOLESTEROL 13 / IRON 0.1 / SODIUM 81 / CALCIUM 24

SAFETY TIPS FOR STATIONARY CYCLISTS

Cyclists who push the pedal indoors reap the same aerobic and muscle-toning rewards as those who pedal outside. That is, as long as they cycle the right way. If you're an indoor stationary cyclist, consider these important "rules of the road" for comfort and safety.

• Adjust seat to proper height. A too-low or too-high seat can strain the knees. What's more, leg muscles get an uneven and less-than-optimal workout. The best height is when the pedal drops to the lowest position and the ball of the foot rests comfortably against it. The knee will be slightly bent.

• Wear toe clips. Straps that keep the feet in place are just as important indoors as they are outdoors. Wearing toe clips allows for a push-and-pull movement that works different muscle groups.

• Wear appropriate clothing. Tuck pant legs in your socks or wear pant clips. You don't want any clothes to get caught in the wheel. Also, wear firm, rubber-soled shoes that will not slip off the pedal.

• Keep resistance low. Resist the temptation to turn up the resistance and make it so hard to pedal that you tire quickly. For better results, put the tension level at a more even pace. Pedal at speeds of 60 rpms (novice), but keep it up for a full 30 minutes. This gives you a better aerobic workout and is also a more effective way for you to tone and shape the muscles in your legs and hips.

MINTED WHITE BEANS

1 (19-ounce) can cannellini beans, rinsed and drained
1 cup seeded, diced tomato
¼ cup chopped purple onion
2 tablespoons lemon juice
1½ teaspoons olive oil
2 tablespoons tightly packed fresh parsley
2 tablespoons tightly packed fresh mint leaves
½ teaspoon pepper

Combine beans, tomato, and onion in a medium bowl; set aside.

Combine lemon juice, olive oil, parsley, mint leaves, and pepper in container of an electric blender or food processor. Top with cover, and process 15 seconds or until herbs are finely chopped.

Pour lemon juice mixture over bean mixture. Cover and chill bean mixture at least 4 hours. Serve beans with toasted pita wedges. Yield: 2¾ cups (13 calories per tablespoon).

PROTEIN 0.6 / FAT 0.2 / CARBOHYDRATE 2.1 / CHOLESTEROL 0 / IRON 0.2 / SODIUM 23 / CALCIUM 3

BEER-CHEESE BITES

1 (8-ounce) package 40% less-fat Cheddar cheese, shredded
⅓ cup light beer
¼ cup reduced-calorie mayonnaise
1 teaspoon low-sodium Worcestershire sauce
32 (½-inch) slices zucchini (about 4 small)
½ teaspoon ground red pepper

Combine Cheddar cheese, light beer, mayonnaise, and Worcestershire sauce in container of an electric blender or food processor; top with cover, and process cheese mixture until smooth. Cover and chill cheese mixture at least 2 hours.

Pipe 2¼ teaspoons cheese mixture onto each zucchini slice, using a No. 1 star tip. Sprinkle with red pepper. Yield: 32 appetizers (26 calories each).

PROTEIN 1.5 / FAT 1.5 / CARBOHYDRATE 2.2 / CHOLESTEROL 4 / IRON 0.1 / SODIUM 53 / CALCIUM 51

DILLED BRUSSELS SPROUTS AND CARROTS

1 pound small fresh brussels sprouts
½ pound baby carrots, scraped
1½ cups white wine vinegar
½ cup water
1 clove garlic, split
1 dried red chile
1 tablespoon dried whole dillweed
Fresh dillweed sprigs (optional)

Wash brussels sprouts thoroughly, and remove discolored leaves. Cut off stem ends, and cut a shallow X in bottom of each sprout.

Combine brussels sprouts, baby carrots, vinegar, water, garlic, red chile, and dried whole dillweed in a large saucepan; bring to a boil. Cover, reduce heat, and simmer 15 minutes or until vegetables are crisp-tender.

Transfer mixture to a medium bowl. Cover and marinate in refrigerator 8 hours. Drain well before serving. Discard garlic and red chile. Garnish with fresh dillweed sprigs, if desired. Yield: 16 appetizer servings (15 calories per appetizer serving).

PROTEIN 0.8 / FAT 0.1 / CARBOHYDRATE 2.5 / CHOLESTEROL 0 / IRON 0.3 / SODIUM 12 / CALCIUM 18

SPICY JICAMA CHIPS

1 (1½-pound) jicama, peeled, quartered, and thinly sliced
⅓ cup fresh lime juice
½ teaspoon chili powder
¼ teaspoon ground red pepper

Place jicama in a shallow dish; pour lime juice over jicama. Let stand 1 hour. To serve, arrange jicama slices on serving platter; sprinkle with chili powder and red pepper. Serve immediately. Yield: 32 chips (10 calories each).

PROTEIN 0.3 / FAT 0.1 / CARBOHYDRATE 2.2 / CHOLESTEROL 0 / IRON 0.1 / SODIUM 2 / CALCIUM 4

STUFFED MINIATURE POPOVERS

1½ cups diced cooked chicken breast (skinned before cooking and cooked without salt)
¼ cup plus 2 tablespoons minced fresh mushrooms
¼ cup plus 2 tablespoons reduced-calorie mayonnaise
2 tablespoons chopped fresh parsley
2 tablespoons diced pimiento
1 tablespoon lemon juice
¼ teaspoon salt
½ teaspoon dried whole tarragon
4 drops of hot sauce
1 cup bread flour
1 cup skim milk
2 eggs, beaten
2 tablespoons grated Parmesan cheese
1 tablespoon reduced-calorie margarine
Vegetable cooking spray

Combine first 9 ingredients in a small bowl; stir well. Cover and chill thoroughly.

Combine flour, milk, eggs, Parmesan cheese, and margarine in container of an electric blender; top with cover, and process just until smooth.

Place miniature (1¾-inch) muffin pans coated with cooking spray in a 450° oven for 3 minutes or until a drop of water sizzles when dropped in muffin cup. Remove pans from oven; fill each muffin cup half full with batter. Bake at 450° for 10 minutes; reduce heat to 350°, and bake 5 minutes. Remove popovers from pan, and let cool on a wire rack.

Slice each popover in half to, but not through, other side; fill each with 2 teaspoons chicken mixture. Place on a baking sheet; bake at 400° for 5 minutes or until thoroughly heated. Yield: 32 appetizers (41 calories each).

PROTEIN 2.9 / FAT 1.7 / CARBOHYDRATE 3.4 / CHOLESTEROL 18 / IRON 0.2 / SODIUM 61 / CALCIUM 17

Tarragon, parsley, and lemon juice add flavor to Stuffed Miniature Popovers. Filled with a creamy chicken and mushroom mixture, it's sure to be a favorite appetizer.

APPLE-STUFFED MUSHROOMS

32 large fresh mushrooms (about 1¾ pounds)
Vegetable cooking spray
3 tablespoons finely chopped celery
½ cup minced apple
2 tablespoons finely chopped walnuts, toasted
2 tablespoons fine, dry breadcrumbs
1 tablespoon chopped fresh parsley
1 tablespoon crumbled blue cheese
2 teaspoons lemon juice

Clean mushrooms with damp paper towels. Remove stems; finely chop ⅓ cup stems, reserving remaining stems for another use. Set mushroom caps aside.

Coat a small skillet with cooking spray; place over medium-high heat until hot. Add reserved chopped stems and celery; sauté 2 minutes or until tender.

Combine celery mixture, apple, and next 5 ingredients in a small bowl; stir well. Spoon 1½ teaspoons apple mixture into each reserved mushroom cap. Place mushrooms in a 15- x 10- x 1-inch jellyroll pan; bake at 350° for 15 minutes. Yield: 32 appetizers (13 calories each).

PROTEIN 0.7 / FAT 0.5 / CARBOHYDRATE 1.9 / CHOLESTEROL 0 / IRON 0.3 / SODIUM 8 / CALCIUM 4

FETA-STUFFED MUSHROOMS

⅔ cup 1% low-fat cottage cheese
2 ounces feta cheese, crumbled
1½ tablespoons chopped fresh dillweed
1 teaspoon lemon juice
½ teaspoon olive oil
¼ teaspoon dried whole oregano
30 medium-size fresh mushrooms (about 1 pound)
Fresh dillweed sprigs (optional)

Combine first 6 ingredients in a small bowl; stir well.

Clean mushrooms with damp paper towels. Remove stems, reserving stems for another use. Spoon 1 teaspoon cheese mixture into each mushroom cap. Garnish with fresh dillweed sprigs, if desired. Yield: 30 appetizers (12 calories each).

PROTEIN 1.1 / FAT 0.6 / CARBOHYDRATE 0.7 / CHOLESTEROL 2 / IRON 0.2 / SODIUM 42 / CALCIUM 14

POTATO SKINS

7 medium-size baking potatoes (about 2¾ pounds)
1½ tablespoons reduced-calorie margarine, melted
3 tablespoons grated Parmesan cheese
1 teaspoon garlic powder
¼ teaspoon onion powder
¼ teaspoon black pepper
⅛ teaspoon ground red pepper

Scrub potatoes; prick several times with a fork. Bake at 400° for 45 minutes to 1 hour or until done. Let potatoes cool to touch.

Cut potatoes in half lengthwise and carefully scoop out potato pulp, leaving ¼-inch-thick shells. Reserve pulp for another use. Cut each potato shell lengthwise into 2 equal strips; cut strips in half crosswise.

Place potato skins, skin side down, in a 15- x 10- x 1-inch jellyroll pan. Brush potato skins lightly with melted margarine. Combine Parmesan cheese and remaining ingredients in a small bowl; sprinkle mixture over potato skins. Bake at 450° for 20 minutes or until crisp. Yield: 56 appetizers (13 calories each).

PROTEIN 0.3 / FAT 0.3 / CARBOHYDRATE 2.2 / CHOLESTEROL 0 / IRON 0.0 / SODIUM 8 / CALCIUM 4

SPICY CRAB WONTONS

1 (8-ounce) package Neufchâtel cheese, softened
1 (6-ounce) can lump crabmeat, drained and flaked
2 tablespoons minced fresh chives
2 teaspoons minced jalapeño pepper
32 fresh or frozen wonton skins, thawed

Beat cheese in a bowl at medium speed of an electric mixer until light and fluffy. Stir in crabmeat, chives, and pepper.

Spoon 2 teaspoons cheese mixture in center of each wonton. Lightly brush edges of wonton with water. Gently bring wonton corners together at top, twisting to enclose crab mixture. Repeat procedure with remaining wonton skins and crab mixture.

Place wontons in a single layer in a steamer rack over boiling water. Cover and steam 5 minutes. Repeat procedure with remaining wontons. Serve wontons immediately with salsa or Chinese hot mustard. Yield: 32 appetizers (31 calories each).

PROTEIN 1.8 / FAT 1.9 / CARBOHYDRATE 1.6 / CHOLESTEROL 16 / IRON 0.1 / SODIUM 59 / CALCIUM 10

BEEF SATAY

1 pound lean round steak
⅓ cup lime juice
3 tablespoons reduced-sodium soy sauce
2 tablespoons creamy no-salt-added peanut butter, melted
1 tablespoon rice wine vinegar
1 teaspoon chili oil
Vegetable cooking spray
Lime wedges (optional)

Partially freeze steak; trim fat from steak. Slice steak diagonally across grain into ¼-inch strips. Place strips in a large shallow dish. Add lime juice; cover and chill 4 hours.

Combine soy sauce and next 3 ingredients in container of an electric blender; top with cover, and process until smooth. Set aside.

Remove steak from marinade, discarding marinade. Thread steak on 12 (6-inch) wooden skewers. Place skewers on rack of a broiler pan coated with cooking spray. Broil 5½ inches from heat 2 to 3 minutes on each side. Serve warm with reserved soy sauce mixture. Arrange skewers on a serving plate, and garnish with lime wedges, if desired. Yield: 12 appetizers (77 calories per beef strip and 1½ teaspoons sauce).

PROTEIN 8.8 / FAT 4.0 / CARBOHYDRATE 1.4 / CHOLESTEROL 22 / IRON 0.9 / SODIUM 168 / CALCIUM 4

These beverages take on the flavor and flair of freshness: (from left) Apricot-Melon Freeze, Amaretto Smoothie (page 103), and Sparkling Pineapple Punch (page 102).

APPLE MINT JULEPS

3½ cups unsweetened apple juice
3 cups water
2 regular-size tea bags
1 cup fresh mint leaves
½ cup bourbon
Fresh mint sprigs (optional)

Combine apple juice and water in a saucepan; bring to a boil. Pour mixture over tea bags; cover and steep 5 minutes. Remove and discard tea bags. Add fresh mint leaves and bourbon; stir well. Chill thoroughly. Strain mixture, and serve over crushed ice. Garnish with fresh mint sprigs, if desired. Yield: 7 cups (98 calories per 1-cup serving).

PROTEIN 0.1 / FAT 0.1 / CARBOHYDRATE 14.7 / CHOLESTEROL 0 / IRON 0.6 / SODIUM 5 / CALCIUM 11

APRICOT-MELON FREEZE

1 (16-ounce) package frozen cantaloupe and honeydew melon balls
1 (12-ounce) can apricot nectar
1 (10-ounce) bottle club soda, chilled
1 cup ice cubes
¼ teaspoon rum extract

Combine frozen cantaloupe and honeydew melon balls and apricot nectar in container of an electric blender; top with cover, and process melon mixture until smooth. Add chilled club soda, ice cubes, and rum extract to melon mixture; process until smooth. Pour beverage into glasses, and serve immediately. Yield: 6 cups (81 calories per 1-cup serving).

PROTEIN 0.7 / FAT 0.1 / CARBOHYDRATE 20.3 / CHOLESTEROL 0 / IRON 0.4 / SODIUM 19 / CALCIUM 14

SPARKLING PINEAPPLE PUNCH

3 cups chopped fresh pineapple (about
  1½ pounds)
2 cups unsweetened pineapple-orange-banana juice
4 cups lime-flavored sparkling mineral water,
  chilled
2 cups Chablis or other dry white wine, chilled

Combine pineapple and juice in container of an electric blender; top with cover, and process until smooth. Pour mixture into a 13- x 9- x 2-inch pan. Cover and freeze until firm.

To serve, partially thaw fruit mixture; break into chunks, and place into a small punch bowl. Add mineral water and wine; stir until slushy. Yield: 12 cups (77 calories per 1-cup serving).

PROTEIN 0.3 / FAT 0.3 / CARBOHYDRATE 13.0 / CHOLESTEROL 0 /
IRON 0.4 / SODIUM 21 / CALCIUM 7

PINK GRAPEFRUIT MOCKTAIL

2 cups lemon-lime-flavored sparkling mineral water,
  chilled
2 cups pink grapefruit juice cocktail, chilled
2 tablespoons fresh lime juice
¼ teaspoon aromatic bitters
Fresh lime wedges (optional)

Combine first 4 ingredients in a small pitcher, stirring gently. Serve over ice. Garnish each glass with a lime wedge, if desired. Yield: 4 cups (55 calories per 1-cup serving).

PROTEIN 0.0 / FAT 0.0 / CARBOHYDRATE 14.1 / CHOLESTEROL 0 /
IRON 0.0 / SODIUM 35 / CALCIUM 1

FRUIT AND GINGER SPRITZER

2 cups unsweetened orange juice
1½ cups unsweetened frozen strawberries
1 teaspoon minced fresh ginger
½ cup sparkling mineral water, chilled

Combine orange juice, strawberries, and minced ginger in container of an electric blender or food processor; top with cover, and process until smooth. Pour into a pitcher and stir in mineral water. Serve immediately. Yield: 4 cups (76 calories per 1-cup serving).

PROTEIN 1.1 / FAT 0.1 / CARBOHYDRATE 18.5 / CHOLESTEROL 0 /
IRON 0.6 / SODIUM 9 / CALCIUM 20

TASTY TOMATO COCKTAIL

3½ cups no-salt-added tomato juice
¼ cup water
¼ cup fresh orange juice
1 tablespoon lime juice
1 teaspoon chicken-flavored bouillon granules
½ teaspoon garlic powder
½ teaspoon dried whole rosemary, crushed
½ teaspoon aromatic bitters
¼ teaspoon hot sauce

Combine all ingredients in a medium saucepan. Cook over medium heat until thoroughly heated, stirring constantly. Pour beverage into mugs. Serve warm. Yield: 4 cups (55 calories per 1-cup serving).

PROTEIN 2.4 / FAT 0.3 / CARBOHYDRATE 13.1 / CHOLESTEROL 0 /
IRON 0.1 / SODIUM 230 / CALCIUM 4

 DEVELOPING SPORTING SAVVY

A common mistake that many newly motivated exercisers make when they decide to "shape-up" is to choose a sport—any sport—and start playing. After all, activity is the name of the game when it comes to fitness, right? Not necessarily. Experts caution that taking up a sport out of the blue can be dangerous, particularly as people get older. The reason: bodies need to be in shape before playing ball, tennis, or squash. Otherwise, the risk for major or minor injury is greatly increased. If you have been inactive for the past few months, jumping into action at the company softball game is more likely to result in pulled muscles rather than toned muscles. The best way to shape up is to ease into sports. Stretching, walking briskly, and doing aerobic exercises can build and tone your muscles. Once you are in shape, choose a sport—any sport—to help you stay that way.

BANANA FRUIT SHAKE

1 cup peeled, sliced banana
1 cup skim milk
½ cup cranberry juice cocktail, chilled
½ cup fresh orange juice, chilled
Orange slices (optional)

Wrap banana slices in heavy-duty plastic wrap, and freeze until firm.

Combine frozen banana, skim milk, cranberry juice, and orange juice in container of an electric blender; top with cover, and process until smooth. Pour into glasses, and garnish with orange slices, if desired. Serve immediately. Yield: 3 cups (124 calories per 1-cup serving).

PROTEIN 3.6 / FAT 0.4 / CARBOHYDRATE 28.1 / CHOLESTEROL 2 / IRON 0.3 / SODIUM 45 / CALCIUM 109

AMARETTO SMOOTHIE

3 cups strawberry ice milk, softened
1 cup skim milk
⅓ cup amaretto
Whole fresh strawberries (optional)

Combine first 3 ingredients in container of an electric blender; top with cover, and process until smooth. Pour into champagne glasses, and garnish with whole strawberries, if desired. Serve immediately. Yield: 4 cups (145 calories per ⅔-cup serving).

PROTEIN 3.4 / FAT 2.1 / CARBOHYDRATE 22.7 / CHOLESTEROL 1 / IRON 0.0 / SODIUM 76 / CALCIUM 50

TROPICAL MILK SHAKE

1 (20-ounce) can crushed pineapple in juice, undrained
3¼ cups skim milk
1 teaspoon vanilla extract
½ teaspoon rum extract
Freshly grated nutmeg

Drain pineapple, reserving juice. Spread pineapple in a thin layer in an 8- x 8-inch baking pan. Freeze until firm.

Combine reserved juice, frozen pineapple, milk, and flavorings in container of an electric blender; top with cover, and process until smooth. Pour into tall frosted glasses. Sprinkle with nutmeg. Serve immediately. Yield: 6 cups (107 calories per 1-cup serving).

PROTEIN 4.9 / FAT 0.3 / CARBOHYDRATE 21.5 / CHOLESTEROL 3 / IRON 0.3 / SODIUM 70 / CALCIUM 177

CIDER MILK PUNCH

1 cup unsweetened apple cider
1 tablespoon brown sugar
1 (3-inch) stick cinnamon
½ teaspoon whole cloves
½ teaspoon whole allspice
3 cups warm skim milk
2 tablespoons nonfat dry milk powder
¾ teaspoon vanilla extract

Combine first 5 ingredients in a medium saucepan; bring cider mixture to a boil. Cover, reduce heat, and simmer 30 minutes. Strain liquid, discarding spices. Stir in milk, milk powder, and vanilla. Cook just until heated. Serve immediately. Yield: 4 cups (123 calories per 1-cup serving).

PROTEIN 7.6 / FAT 0.4 / CARBOHYDRATE 21.7 / CHOLESTEROL 4 / IRON 0.4 / SODIUM 119 / CALCIUM 280

PEAR AND SPICE TEA

3 cups water
4 whole cardamom pods
3 thin slices ginger
4 Darjeeling tea bags
2½ cups pear nectar

Place water in a medium saucepan. Peel one side of cardamom pods, exposing seeds. Place pods and sliced ginger in water; bring to a boil over high heat. Reduce heat, and simmer 5 minutes. Remove from heat. Add tea bags; cover and steep 5 minutes. Remove and discard tea bags and spices. Stir in pear nectar. Reheat to serve warm or chill thoroughly and serve over ice. Yield: 5 cups (64 calories per 1-cup serving).

PROTEIN 0.4 / FAT 0.2 / CARBOHYDRATE 16.1 / CHOLESTEROL 0 / IRON 0.1 / SODIUM 1 / CALCIUM 4

COFFEE-COCOA COOLER

2 cups strong cold coffee
½ cup water
¼ cup firmly packed dark brown sugar
¼ cup cocoa
3 (1-inch) sticks cinnamon
3 cups skim milk
1 teaspoon vanilla extract
Ground cinnamon (optional)

Pour coffee into 2 ice cube trays; freeze 3 to 4 hours or until firm. Combine water and next 3 ingredients in a medium saucepan. Bring mixture to a boil, stirring constantly. Reduce heat; slowly stir in milk and vanilla. Cook until thoroughly heated, stirring constantly. Remove from heat; chill thoroughly.

Remove and discard cinnamon sticks. Pour milk mixture into container of an electric blender; add frozen coffee cubes. Top with cover, and process until smooth. Pour into individual glasses, and sprinkle with cinnamon, if desired. Serve immediately. Yield: 7 cups (83 calories per 1-cup serving).

PROTEIN 4.5 / FAT 0.6 / CARBOHYDRATE 14.7 / CHOLESTEROL 2 / IRON 1.1 / SODIUM 59 / CALCIUM 142

KONA COOLER

½ cup plus 2 tablespoons whole Kona coffee beans
4½ cups water
3 cups vanilla ice milk, softened
2 cups unsweetened pineapple juice, chilled

Place whole coffee beans in coffee grinder; process to a coarse grind.

Place ground coffee beans in coffee filter or filter basket of a drip coffee maker. Add water to coffee maker, and brew according to manufacturer's instructions. Chill thoroughly.

Combine chilled coffee, ice milk, and pineapple juice in a large bowl. Beat at low speed of an electric mixer until smooth and frothy. Serve immediately. Yield: 9 cups (94 calories per 1-cup serving).

PROTEIN 1.9 / FAT 1.9 / CARBOHYDRATE 17.3 / CHOLESTEROL 6 / IRON 0.2 / SODIUM 36 / CALCIUM 68

ANISE-SCENTED COFFEE

½ cup ground coffee
½ teaspoon anise seeds, crushed
2 teaspoons ground cinnamon
½ teaspoon ground cloves
4½ cups water

Combine ground coffee, anise seeds, ground cinnamon, and cloves in a medium bowl.

Place coffee mixture in basket of an electric percolator. Add water to percolator, and brew according to manufacturer's instructions. To serve, pour into individual mugs. Serve warm. Yield: 4½ cups (5 calories per ¾-cup serving).

PROTEIN 0.1 / FAT 0.1 / CARBOHYDRATE 0.8 / CHOLESTEROL 0 / IRON 0.4 / SODIUM 1 / CALCIUM 12

(Clockwise from top left): Italian Dinner Rolls (page 110), Cardamom Yeast Braid (page 113), Honey-Potato Batter Bread (page 110), Glazed Lemon-Poppy Seed Bread (page 109), and Country Rosemary and Thyme Wheat Bread (page 114) are favorite breads that have been made light.

Breads, Grains & Pastas

JELLY BISCUITS

1 cup all-purpose flour
1 tablespoon sugar
2 teaspoons baking powder
¼ teaspoon ground cinnamon
2 tablespoons margarine, chilled
¼ cup plus 2 tablespoons skim milk
1 tablespoon all-purpose flour
Vegetable cooking spray
1 tablespoon plus 1 teaspoon no-sugar-added
    strawberry spread

Combine first 4 ingredients in a medium bowl; cut in margarine with a pastry blender until mixture resembles coarse meal. Add milk, stirring just until dry ingredients are moistened.

Sprinkle 1 tablespoon flour evenly over work surface. Turn dough out onto floured surface; knead 4 to 5 times. Roll dough to ½-inch thickness; cut with a 2-inch biscuit cutter. Transfer rounds to a baking sheet coated with cooking spray. Press thumb into top of each round, leaving a deep indentation. Place ½ teaspoon strawberry spread in each indentation. Bake at 425° for 10 minutes or until golden. Yield: 8 biscuits (95 calories each).

PROTEIN 2.0 / FAT 3.1 / CARBOHYDRATE 14.5 / CHOLESTEROL 0 / IRON 0.5 / SODIUM 115 / CALCIUM 66

WHOLE WHEAT BISCUITS

¾ cup whole wheat flour
⅔ cup all-purpose flour
2½ teaspoons baking powder
¼ teaspoon salt
3 tablespoons margarine, chilled
½ cup plus 1 tablespoon skim milk, divided
1 tablespoon all-purpose flour
Vegetable cooking spray
1 teaspoon poppy seeds
1 tablespoon untoasted wheat germ

Combine first 4 ingredients in a medium bowl; cut in margarine with a pastry blender until mixture resembles coarse meal. Add ½ cup milk, stirring just until dry ingredients are moistened.

Sprinkle 1 tablespoon flour over work surface. Turn dough out onto floured surface; knead 3 to 4 times. Roll dough to ¾-inch thickness; cut with

a 2-inch biscuit cutter. Transfer to a baking sheet coated with cooking spray; brush with remaining 1 tablespoon milk. Combine poppy seeds and wheat germ; sprinkle over rounds. Bake at 400° for 12 minutes or until golden. Yield: 9 biscuits (112 calories each).

PROTEIN 3.2 / FAT 4.4 / CARBOHYDRATE 15.6 / CHOLESTEROL 0 / IRON 0.7 / SODIUM 202 / CALCIUM 84

SOUR CREAM BISCUIT MUFFINS

1½ cups all-purpose flour
2 teaspoons baking powder
½ teaspoon baking soda
¼ teaspoon salt
1 cup low-fat sour cream
1 egg, beaten
1 tablespoon vegetable oil
Vegetable cooking spray

Combine first 4 ingredients in a medium bowl; make a well in center of mixture. Combine sour cream, egg, and oil; add to dry ingredients, stirring until moistened. Spoon batter into muffin pans coated with cooking spray, filling two-thirds full. Bake at 400° for 15 minutes or until lightly browned. Remove from pans immediately. Yield: 1 dozen (98 calories each).

PROTEIN 2.6 / FAT 4.3 / CARBOHYDRATE 12.0 / CHOLESTEROL 24 / IRON 0.5 / SODIUM 147 / CALCIUM 64

CARROT BRAN MUFFINS

1 cup bran flakes cereal
1 cup skim milk
1 cup whole wheat flour
½ cup all-purpose flour
1 teaspoon baking powder
½ teaspoon baking soda
¼ teaspoon salt
2 tablespoons brown sugar
½ teaspoon ground cinnamon
1 egg, lightly beaten
2 tablespoons vegetable oil
1 tablespoon lemon juice
1 cup grated carrot
3 tablespoons currants
Vegetable cooking spray

Combine cereal and milk in a small bowl; let stand 5 minutes.

Combine whole wheat flour, all-purpose flour, baking powder, baking soda, salt, cinnamon, and brown sugar in a bowl; make a well in center of mixture. Combine cereal mixture, egg, oil, and lemon juice; add to dry ingredients, stirring just until moistened. Stir in grated carrot and currants.

Spoon batter into muffin pans coated with cooking spray, filling two-thirds full. Bake at 400° for 15 to 20 minutes or until lightly browned. Remove from pans immediately. Yield: 1 dozen (114 calories each).

PROTEIN 3.7 / FAT 3.3 / CARBOHYDRATE 18.7 / CHOLESTEROL 17 / IRON 1.7 / SODIUM 162 / CALCIUM 64

WILD RICE PANCAKES

1¼ cups all-purpose flour
1 teaspoon baking powder
½ teaspoon baking soda
¼ teaspoon salt
1 teaspoon sugar
1¼ cups nonfat buttermilk
2 eggs, separated
1 cup cooked wild rice (cooked without salt or fat)
2 tablespoons reduced-calorie margarine, melted
3 egg whites
Vegetable cooking spray

Combine flour, baking powder, baking soda, salt, and sugar in a medium bowl; make a well in center of mixture. Combine buttermilk and egg yolks; add to dry ingredients, stirring just until moistened. Stir in wild rice and melted margarine.

Beat 5 egg whites (at room temperature) in a large bowl at high speed of an electric mixer until stiff peaks form; gently fold beaten egg whites into batter.

For each pancake, pour ¼ cup batter onto a hot griddle or skillet coated with cooking spray. Turn pancakes when tops are covered with bubbles and edges look cooked. Yield: 20 (4-inch) pancakes (58 calories each).

PROTEIN 2.7 / FAT 1.6 / CARBOHYDRATE 8.2 / CHOLESTEROL 20 / IRON 0.4 / SODIUM 107 / CALCIUM 19

BANANA-OAT BRAN PANCAKES

⅔ cup unprocessed oat bran
⅔ cup all-purpose flour
1 teaspoon baking powder
1 teaspoon baking soda
1 tablespoon sugar
1 (8-ounce) carton plain nonfat yogurt
⅓ cup mashed ripe banana
1 tablespoon vegetable oil
2 teaspoons vanilla extract
3 egg whites
Vegetable cooking spray

Combine first 5 ingredients in a medium bowl; make a well in center of mixture. Combine yogurt, banana, oil, and vanilla; add to dry ingredients, stirring until moistened.

Beat egg whites (at room temperature) in a medium bowl at high speed of an electric mixer until stiff peaks form; gently fold into batter.

For each pancake, pour ¼ cup batter onto a hot griddle or skillet coated with cooking spray. Turn pancakes when tops are covered with bubbles and edges look cooked. Yield: 12 (4-inch) pancakes (84 calories each).

PROTEIN 3.8 / FAT 1.8 / CARBOHYDRATE 12.7 / CHOLESTEROL 0 / IRON 0.6 / SODIUM 121 / CALCIUM 75

 THAT PSYLLIUM PSTUFF

Psyllium, an obscure grain from India, has yet to capture the hearts and stomachs of the American public. But because it boasts 8 times more cholesterol-reducing soluble fiber than oat bran, that day may soon come. On the plus side for this grain, scientific studies already confirm that psyllium fiber—derived from the ipaghula plant—does indeed have the ability to lower blood cholesterol levels. Research scientists are now placing the grain in a class with other water-soluble fibers as a definite cholesterol-lowering agent.

Currently, government officials are worried about the safety of using psyllium, which in part explains why it is found in so few foods. This grain is an uncommon ingredient in American foods, so officials would like to have a better idea of how much is too much when it comes to adding psyllium to foods. For years, psyllium has been the main ingredient in at least two over-the-counter laxatives.

Perfect for breakfast or brunch, Belgian Waffles are delicious topped with fresh strawberries and sprinkled with powdered sugar.

BELGIAN WAFFLES

2 cups all-purpose flour
1 tablespoon plus 1 teaspoon baking powder
1 tablespoon sugar
½ teaspoon salt
2 eggs, beaten
1½ cups skim milk
¼ cup reduced-calorie margarine, melted
Vegetable cooking spray
Powdered sugar (optional)
Fresh sliced strawberries (optional)
Fresh mint sprigs (optional)

Combine first 4 ingredients in a medium bowl. Combine eggs, milk, and margarine; add to dry ingredients, beating well at medium speed of an electric mixer.

Coat a Belgian waffle iron with cooking spray; allow waffle iron to preheat. For each waffle, spoon ¼ cup batter onto hot waffle iron, spreading batter to edges. Bake 4 to 5 minutes or until steaming stops. Repeat procedure with remaining batter. If desired, sift powdered sugar over waffles, serve with sliced strawberries, and garnish with mint sprigs. Yield: 12 (4-inch) waffles (119 calories each).

PROTEIN 4.1 / FAT 3.7 / CARBOHYDRATE 17.4 / CHOLESTEROL 34 / IRON 0.7 / SODIUM 261 / CALCIUM 109

CHILE-CHEESE CORNBREAD

1 cup yellow cornmeal
1 cup all-purpose flour
1 tablespoon plus 1 teaspoon baking powder
¼ teaspoon salt
¼ cup nonfat dry milk powder
1 tablespoon sugar
1 cup water
½ cup frozen egg substitute, thawed
2 tablespoons vegetable oil
¾ cup (3 ounces) shredded 40% less-fat Cheddar cheese
1 (4-ounce) can chopped green chiles, drained
Vegetable cooking spray

Combine cornmeal, flour, baking powder, salt, milk powder, and sugar in a medium bowl; make a well in center of cornmeal mixture. Combine water, egg substitute, and vegetable oil; add to dry ingredients, stirring just until moistened. Stir in shredded Cheddar cheese and chopped green chiles.

Pour batter into an 8-inch square baking pan coated with cooking spray. Bake at 375° for 30 to 35 minutes or until golden. Yield: 16 servings (99 calories per serving).

PROTEIN 3.9 / FAT 2.7 / CARBOHYDRATE 14.9 / CHOLESTEROL 0 / IRON 0.6 / SODIUM 133 / CALCIUM 112

CRANBERRY-ORANGE BREAD

2 cups whole wheat flour
½ cup sugar
¼ cup instant nonfat dry milk powder
1 teaspoon baking powder
1 teaspoon baking soda
¼ teaspoon salt
¼ cup margarine, melted
2 eggs
1 cup unsweetened orange juice
¼ cup chopped walnuts
1½ cups fresh cranberries, coarsely chopped
Vegetable cooking spray

Combine first 6 ingredients in a large bowl; make a well in center of mixture. Whisk together margarine, eggs, and orange juice; add to dry ingredients, stirring just until moistened. Stir in walnuts and cranberries.

Spoon batter into a 9- x 5- x 3-inch loafpan coated with cooking spray. Bake at 350° for 1 hour or until a wooden pick inserted in center comes out clean. Let cool in pan 10 minutes; remove from pan, and let cool on a wire rack. Yield: 18 servings (125 calories per ½-inch slice).

PROTEIN 3.7 / FAT 4.4 / CARBOHYDRATE 19.1 / CHOLESTEROL 23 / IRON 0.7 / SODIUM 142 / CALCIUM 52

GLAZED LEMON-POPPY SEED BREAD

1¾ cups all-purpose flour
1½ teaspoons baking powder
Dash of salt
½ cup sugar
1 tablespoon poppy seeds
1 tablespoon grated lemon rind
¾ cup skim milk
¼ cup vegetable oil
1 egg, beaten
1 tablespoon lemon juice
Vegetable cooking spray
½ cup sifted powdered sugar
1½ teaspoons lemon juice

Combine flour, baking powder, salt, sugar, poppy seeds, and lemon rind in a large bowl; make a well in center of flour mixture. Combine skim milk, vegetable oil, egg, and 1 tablespoon lemon juice; add mixture to dry ingredients, stirring just until moistened.

Pour batter into an 8½- x 4½- x 3-inch loafpan coated with cooking spray. Bake at 400° for 30 to 35 minutes or until a wooden pick inserted in center comes out clean. Let cool in pan 10 minutes; remove from pan, and let cool on a wire rack.

Combine powdered sugar and 1½ teaspoons lemon juice; drizzle glaze over bread. Yield: 16 servings (127 calories per ½-inch slice).

PROTEIN 2.2 / FAT 4.1 / CARBOHYDRATE 20.5 / CHOLESTEROL 13 / IRON 0.5 / SODIUM 48 / CALCIUM 44

HONEY-POTATO BATTER BREAD

1 package dry yeast
½ cup warm water (105° to 115°)
3 tablespoons honey
1 (12-ounce) can evaporated skimmed milk
½ cup instant mashed potatoes
2 tablespoons margarine, melted
½ teaspoon salt
4 cups all-purpose flour, divided
Vegetable cooking spray

Dissolve yeast in warm water in a large bowl; add honey, and let stand 15 minutes. Stir in milk and next 3 ingredients. Gradually add 3 cups flour, 1 cup at a time, beating well after each addition. Stir in enough of the remaining 1 cup flour to make a soft dough.

Place dough in a 10-inch tube pan coated with cooking spray. Cover and let rise in a warm place (85°), free from drafts, 1 hour or until doubled in bulk. Bake at 350° for 45 to 50 minutes or until loaf sounds hollow when tapped. Cool in pan 10 minutes; remove from pan, and let cool on a wire rack. Yield: 24 servings (102 calories per slice).

PROTEIN 3.3 / FAT 1.2 / CARBOHYDRATE 19.3 / CHOLESTEROL 1 / IRON 0.7 / SODIUM 79 / CALCIUM 47

BASIC WHITE BREAD

1 package dry yeast
1 cup warm water (105° to 115°)
3 tablespoons instant nonfat dry milk powder
1 tablespoon vegetable oil
1 teaspoon sugar
1 teaspoon salt
2¼ cups bread flour
2 tablespoons bread flour, divided
Vegetable cooking spray

Dissolve yeast in warm water in a large bowl; let stand 5 minutes. Add milk powder and next 3 ingredients; beat at medium speed of an electric mixer until well blended. Gradually stir in enough of the 2¼ cups flour to make a soft dough. Cover and let rest 15 minutes.

Sprinkle 1 tablespoon flour evenly over work surface. Turn dough out onto floured surface, and knead until smooth and elastic (about 8 to 10 minutes). Place in a large bowl coated with cooking spray, turning to coat top. Cover and let rise in a warm place (85°), free from drafts, 1 hour or until doubled in bulk.

Punch dough down; sprinkle remaining 1 tablespoon flour evenly over work surface. Roll dough to a 10- x 6-inch rectangle. Roll up dough, starting at short side, pressing firmly to eliminate air pockets; pinch ends to seal. Place dough, seam side down, in an 8½- x 4½- x 3-inch loafpan coated with cooking spray.

Cover and let rise in a warm place, free from drafts, 45 minutes or until doubled in bulk. Bake at 375° for 25 minutes or until loaf sounds hollow when tapped. Remove from pan, and let cool on a wire rack. Yield: 17 servings (73 calories per ½-inch slice).

PROTEIN 2.5 / FAT 1.0 / CARBOHYDRATE 13.1 / CHOLESTEROL 0 / IRON 0.5 / SODIUM 145 / CALCIUM 20

ITALIAN DINNER ROLLS

2 packages dry yeast
2 tablespoons sugar
2 cups warm water (105° to 115°)
4½ cups bread flour
½ cup grated Parmesan cheese
1 teaspoon dried Italian seasoning
½ teaspoon salt
3 tablespoons bread flour, divided
1 teaspoon cornmeal

Dissolve yeast and sugar in warm water in a large bowl; let stand 5 minutes.

Combine 4½ cups flour, cheese, Italian seasoning, and salt in a medium bowl; stir well. Add 3 cups flour mixture to yeast mixture, beating at medium speed of an electric mixer until well blended. Gradually stir in enough of the remaining 1½ cups flour mixture to make a soft dough. Cover and let rest 15 minutes.

Sprinkle 2 tablespoons flour evenly over work surface. Turn dough out onto floured surface, and knead until smooth and elastic (about 8 to 10 minutes), using remaining 1 tablespoon flour for kneading, if necessary.

Divide dough into 20 equal portions; shape each portion into a ball. Place on an ungreased baking sheet sprinkled with 1 teaspoon cornmeal. Gently cut a ¼-inch-deep slit across top of each ball with a razor blade or sharp knife.

Cover and let rise in a warm place (85°), free from drafts, 35 minutes or until doubled in bulk. Place a 13- x 9- x 2-inch pan of boiling water on lower rack of oven. Place baking sheet on middle rack of oven. Bake at 400° for 15 minutes or until rolls are golden. Remove from baking sheet, and cool on wire racks. Yield: 20 rolls (115 calories each).

PROTEIN 4.3 / FAT 0.9 / CARBOHYDRATE 21.8 / CHOLESTEROL 2 / IRON 1.0 / SODIUM 97 / CALCIUM 35

HERBED PARMESAN WEDGES

1 package dry yeast
1½ cups warm water (105° to 115°)
2 teaspoons dried Italian seasoning
½ teaspoon sugar
½ teaspoon salt
3 cups plus 2 tablespoons bread flour
1 tablespoon all-purpose flour
Vegetable cooking spray
1 tablespoon olive oil
½ cup grated Parmesan cheese

Dissolve yeast in warm water in a large bowl; let stand 5 minutes. Add seasoning, sugar, and salt, stirring well. Gradually stir in enough of the bread flour to make a soft dough.

Sprinkle all-purpose flour evenly over work surface. Turn dough out onto floured surface, and knead until smooth and elastic (about 8 to 10 minutes). Place in a large bowl coated with cooking spray, turning to coat top. Cover and let rise in a warm place (85°), free from drafts, 1½ hours or until doubled in bulk.

Punch dough down, and divide in half. Coat 2 large baking sheets with cooking spray. Place one portion of dough on each baking sheet. Roll each to a 12-inch circle.

Cover and let rise in a warm place, free from drafts, 30 minutes or until doubled in bulk. Prick dough generously with a fork. Drizzle each circle with 1½ teaspoons olive oil, and sprinkle each with ¼ cup Parmesan cheese. Bake at 400° for 25 minutes or until golden. Cut into wedges. Serve immediately. Yield: 24 servings (71 calories per wedge).

PROTEIN 2.6 / FAT 1.3 / CARBOHYDRATE 11.8 / CHOLESTEROL 1 / IRON 0.6 / SODIUM 80 / CALCIUM 29

OLD-FASHIONED OATMEAL BREAD

2 cups water
⅔ cup regular oats, uncooked
1 teaspoon salt
1 package dry yeast
½ cup warm water (105° to 115°)
2 tablespoons vegetable oil
2 tablespoons light molasses
6 cups plus 1 tablespoon all-purpose flour, divided
3 tablespoons all-purpose flour
Vegetable cooking spray
1 tablespoon plus 1 teaspoon regular oats, uncooked

Combine first 3 ingredients in a medium saucepan. Place over medium heat, and cook until mixture comes to a boil; stir well. Remove from heat, and cool to room temperature.

Dissolve yeast in warm water in a large bowl; let stand 5 minutes. Stir in vegetable oil, molasses, and cooled oatmeal mixture. Add 3 cups flour; beat at medium speed of an electric mixer until well blended. Gradually stir in enough of the remaining 3 cups plus 1 tablespoon flour to make a soft dough.

Sprinkle 3 tablespoons flour evenly over work surface. Turn dough out onto floured surface, and knead until smooth and elastic (about 8 to 10 minutes). Place in a large bowl coated with cooking spray, turning to coat top. Cover and let rise in a warm place (85°), free from drafts, 1 hour or until doubled in bulk.

Punch dough down, and divide in half. Roll each portion to a 15- x 8½-inch rectangle. Roll up dough, starting at short side, pressing firmly to eliminate air pockets; pinch ends to seal. Place dough, seam side down, in two 8½- x 4½- x 3-inch loafpans coated with cooking spray. Brush loaves lightly with water, and sprinkle each loaf with 2 teaspoons oats.

Cover and let rise in a warm place, free from drafts, 45 minutes or until doubled in bulk. Bake at 375° for 25 minutes or until loaves sound hollow when tapped. (Cover loaves with aluminum foil the last 10 minutes of baking to prevent over-browning, if necessary.) Remove from pans, and let cool on wire racks. Yield: 34 servings (95 calories per ½-inch slice).

PROTEIN 2.6 / FAT 1.2 / CARBOHYDRATE 18.1 / CHOLESTEROL 0 / IRON 0.8 / SODIUM 70 / CALCIUM 7

FINNISH RYE BREAD

1 package dry yeast
1 cup warm water (105° to 115°)
¾ cup rye flour
1 tablespoon brown sugar
1 tablespoon margarine, melted
½ teaspoon salt
1¾ cups plus 2 tablespoons all-purpose flour
2 tablespoons all-purpose flour, divided
Vegetable cooking spray

Dissolve yeast in warm water in a large bowl; let stand 5 minutes. Add rye flour and next 3 ingredients; beat at medium speed of an electric mixer until well blended. Gradually stir in enough of the 1¾ cups plus 2 tablespoons all-purpose flour to make a soft dough. Cover and let rest 15 minutes.

Sprinkle 1 tablespoon all-purpose flour evenly over work surface. Turn dough out onto floured surface, and knead until smooth and elastic (about 8 to 10 minutes). Place in a large bowl coated with cooking spray, turning to coat top. Cover and let rise in a warm place (85°), free from drafts, 1 hour or until doubled in bulk.

Punch dough down; sprinkle remaining 1 tablespoon flour evenly over work surface. Turn dough out onto work surface, and roll dough to a 6-inch circle. Place on a baking sheet coated with cooking spray. Prick dough generously with a fork.

Cover and let rise in a warm place, free from drafts, 30 minutes or until dough is doubled in bulk. Bake at 375° for 25 to 30 minutes or until loaf sounds hollow when tapped. Remove bread from baking sheet, and let cool on a wire rack. Cut bread into wedges. Yield: 16 servings (78 calories per wedge).

PROTEIN 2.1 / FAT 0.9 / CARBOHYDRATE 15.1 / CHOLESTEROL 0 / IRON 0.6 / SODIUM 82 / CALCIUM 5

THREE-GRAIN BREAD

2¼ cups boiling water
¾ cup bulgur wheat
1 cup quick-cooking oats, uncooked
1 cup rye flour
½ cup instant nonfat dry milk powder
3 tablespoons honey
1 tablespoon caraway seeds
½ teaspoon salt
2 packages dry yeast
½ cup warm water (105° to 115°)
3¼ cups bread flour
2 tablespoons bread flour
Vegetable cooking spray
1 tablespoon skim milk
2 tablespoons sesame seeds, toasted

Pour boiling water over bulgur wheat; cool to room temperature. Add oats, rye flour, milk powder, honey, caraway seeds, and salt, stirring well to combine.

Dissolve yeast in warm water in a large bowl; let stand 5 minutes. Add oat mixture; beat at medium speed of an electric mixer until well blended. Gradually stir in enough of the 3¼ cups flour to make a soft dough. Cover bread dough and let rest 15 minutes.

Sprinkle 2 tablespoons flour evenly over work surface. Turn dough out onto floured surface, and knead until smooth and elastic (about 8 to 10 minutes). Place in a large bowl coated with cooking spray, turning to coat top. Cover and let rise in a warm place (85°), free from drafts, 1 hour or until doubled in bulk.

Punch dough down, and divide in half; shape each portion into a loaf. Place each loaf of dough in an 8½- x 4½- x 3-inch loafpan coated with cooking spray.

Cover and let rise in a warm place, free from drafts, 45 minutes or until doubled in bulk. Brush loaves with milk, and sprinkle evenly with sesame seeds. Gently cut a ⅛-inch-deep slit lengthwise down loaves with a razor blade or sharp knife. Bake at 350° for 40 minutes or until loaves sound hollow when tapped. Remove from pans, and let cool on wire racks. Yield: 34 servings (103 calories per ½-inch slice).

PROTEIN 3.7 / FAT 1.0 / CARBOHYDRATE 19.8 / CHOLESTEROL 0 / IRON 0.9 / SODIUM 45 / CALCIUM 36

HEARTY WHOLE WHEAT BREAD

2 packages dry yeast
3 cups warm water (105° to 115°)
2 tablespoons dark molasses
3 cups whole wheat flour
½ cup soy flour
½ cup instant nonfat dry milk powder
¼ cup untoasted wheat germ
1 teaspoon salt
2 tablespoons vegetable oil
4 cups bread flour
1 tablespoon all-purpose flour
Vegetable cooking spray

Combine yeast, water, and molasses in a large bowl; stir gently. Let stand 5 minutes. Add whole wheat flour; beat at low speed of an electric mixer until well blended. Add soy flour and next 4 ingredients, beating well. Add enough of the bread flour, 1 cup at a time, to make a soft dough.

Sprinkle all-purpose flour evenly over work surface. Turn dough out onto floured surface, and knead until smooth and elastic (about 8 to 10 minutes). Place dough in a large bowl coated with cooking spray, turning to coat top. Cover and let rise in a warm place (85°), free from drafts, 1 hour or until doubled in bulk.

Punch dough down, and divide in half. Shape each portion into a loaf. Place each loaf of dough in an 8½- x 4½- x 3-inch loafpan coated with cooking spray.

Cover and let rise in a warm place, free from drafts, 45 minutes or until doubled in bulk. Bake at 350° for 40 to 45 minutes or until loaves sound hollow when tapped. Remove from pans, and let cool completely on wire racks. Yield: 34 servings (111 calories per ½-inch slice).

PROTEIN 4.8 / FAT 1.4 / CARBOHYDRATE 20.5 / CHOLESTEROL 0 / IRON 1.1 / SODIUM 80 / CALCIUM 37

CARDAMOM YEAST BRAID

2 packages dry yeast
1¼ cups warm water (105° to 115°)
3 eggs
¼ cup sugar
¼ cup margarine, melted
1 teaspoon crushed cardamom seeds
½ teaspoon salt
4½ cups all-purpose flour, divided
Vegetable cooking spray
¼ cup all-purpose flour, divided
1 egg white, beaten
¼ cup sliced almonds

Dissolve yeast in warm water in a large bowl; let stand 5 minutes. Add eggs, sugar, margarine, cardamom, salt, and 2½ cups flour; beat at medium speed of an electric mixer until well blended. Gradually stir in enough of the remaining 2 cups flour to make a soft dough. (Dough will be sticky.)

Place dough in a large bowl coated with cooking spray, turning to coat top. Cover tightly, and refrigerate 2 hours.

Sprinkle 1 tablespoon flour evenly over top of dough. Divide dough into 6 equal portions. Shape each portion into an 18-inch rope, using remaining 3 tablespoons flour. Place 3 ropes, side by side, on a baking sheet coated with cooking spray or lined with parchment paper; braid ropes. Tuck ends under to seal. Repeat with remaining 3 ropes.

Cover and let rise in a warm place (85°), free from drafts, 45 minutes or until doubled in bulk. Brush loaves with egg white, and sprinkle with almonds. Bake at 375° for 20 to 25 minutes or until golden. Yield: 36 servings (84 calories per ½-inch slice).

PROTEIN 2.5 / FAT 2.2 / CARBOHYDRATE 13.3 / CHOLESTEROL 17 / IRON 0.6 / SODIUM 55 / CALCIUM 7

FOCUS ON FIBER

Food scientists realize that different types of fiber have different health benefits. Soluble fiber, as found in oats, barley, dried beans, apples, prunes, and melons, appears to help lower blood cholesterol. Insoluble fiber, the predominant type found in foods such as wheat bran, whole wheat breads, bran cereal, brown rice, asparagus, and brussels sprouts, works other wonders. Insoluble fiber helps prevent constipation, and it may also protect against certain types of cancer.

COUNTRY ROSEMARY AND THYME WHEAT BREAD

2 packages dry yeast
2 cups warm water (105° to 115°)
1 tablespoon dried whole rosemary, crushed
1 tablespoon dried whole thyme, crushed
2 cloves garlic, crushed
1 teaspoon olive oil
½ teaspoon salt
2 cups whole wheat flour
2 cups bread flour
2 tablespoons bread flour
Vegetable cooking spray
2 teaspoons bread flour

Dissolve yeast in warm water in a large bowl; let stand 5 minutes. Add rosemary and next 4 ingredients; beat at medium speed of an electric mixer until well blended. Add whole wheat flour and enough of the 2 cups bread flour to make a soft dough.

Sprinkle 2 tablespoons bread flour evenly over work surface. Turn dough out onto floured surface, and knead until smooth and elastic (about 8 to 10 minutes). Place dough in a large bowl coated with cooking spray, turning to coat top of dough. Cover and let rise in a warm place (85°), free from drafts, 1½ hours or until doubled in bulk.

Coat a 9-inch round, closely woven, wicker basket (about 3 inches deep) with cooking spray. Dust with 2 teaspoons bread flour.

Punch dough down, and shape into a ball, gently smoothing surface of dough. Place ball of dough, smooth side down, in prepared wicker basket.

Cover and let rise in a warm place, free from drafts, 30 minutes or until doubled in bulk. Place unglazed tiles on middle rack of oven to cover about 16 inches square.

Heat tiles at 400° until hot. Place a pan of boiling water on lower rack. Gently invert dough onto hot tiles, and remove wicker basket. Bake at 400° for 35 minutes or until loaf sounds hollow when tapped.

Remove loaf from oven, and let cool on a wire rack. Cut into wedges. Yield: 20 servings (92 calories per wedge).

PROTEIN 3.4 / FAT 0.8 / CARBOHYDRATE 18.4 / CHOLESTEROL 0 / IRON 1.2 / SODIUM 60 / CALCIUM 14

MINIATURE HERB BREADS

1 package dry yeast
1 cup warm water (105° to 115°)
⅓ cup instant nonfat dry milk powder
1 egg, beaten
1 tablespoon sugar
1 tablespoon margarine, softened
1 teaspoon salt
1 teaspoon dried whole basil
1 teaspoon dried whole thyme
½ teaspoon dried whole dillweed
½ teaspoon ground savory
3¼ cups all-purpose flour
2 tablespoons all-purpose flour, divided
Vegetable cooking spray

Dissolve yeast in warm water in a large bowl; let stand 5 minutes. Add milk powder and next 8 ingredients, and beat at medium speed of an electric mixer until yeast mixture is well blended. Stir in enough of the 3¼ cups flour to make a soft dough.

Sprinkle 1 tablespoon flour evenly over work surface. Turn dough out onto floured surface, and knead until dough is smooth and elastic (about 8 to 10 minutes). Place dough in a large bowl coated with cooking spray, turning to coat top of dough. Cover and let rise in a warm place (85°), free from drafts, 1 hour or until dough is doubled in bulk.

Punch dough down, and divide into 3 equal portions. Sprinkle 1 teaspoon all-purpose flour evenly over work surface. Roll one portion of dough on floured surface to a 10- x 6-inch rectangle. Roll up dough, starting at short side, pressing firmly to eliminate air pockets; pinch ends of dough to seal.

Place dough, seam side down, in a 5- x 2½- x 2½-inch loafpan coated with cooking spray. Repeat procedure with remaining 2 teaspoons flour and dough.

Cover and let rise in a warm place, free from drafts, 1 hour or until doubled in bulk. Bake at 375° for 15 minutes or until loaves sound hollow when tapped.

Remove bread from pans immediately, and let cool on wire racks. Yield: 30 servings (61 calories per ½-inch slice).

PROTEIN 2.2 / FAT 0.7 / CARBOHYDRATE 11.1 / CHOLESTEROL 7 / IRON 0.5 / SODIUM 92 / CALCIUM 23

Warm Orange Twists, drizzled with an orange glaze, will turn an ordinary breakfast into a special occasion.

ORANGE TWISTS

1 package dry yeast
¾ cup warm water (105° to 115°)
3 tablespoons sugar
1 egg
2 tablespoons instant nonfat dry milk powder
2 tablespoons margarine, melted
½ teaspoon salt
3¼ cups all-purpose flour, divided
1 tablespoon all-purpose flour
Vegetable cooking spray
3 tablespoons sugar
3 tablespoons grated orange rind
½ cup sifted powdered sugar
1 tablespoon unsweetened orange juice

Dissolve yeast in warm water in a large bowl; let stand 5 minutes. Add 3 tablespoons sugar, egg, milk powder, melted margarine, salt, and 2 cups flour; beat at medium speed of an electric mixer until well blended. Gradually stir in enough of the remaining 1¼ cups flour to make a soft dough.

Sprinkle 1 tablespoon flour evenly over work surface. Turn dough out onto floured surface, and knead until smooth and elastic (about 8 to 10 minutes). Place dough in a large bowl coated with cooking spray, turning to coat top. Cover and let rise in a warm place (85°), free from drafts, 1½ hours or until doubled in bulk.

Punch dough down, and roll into a 14- x 12-inch rectangle. Combine 3 tablespoons sugar and orange rind; stir well, and sprinkle over dough. Fold dough in half lengthwise; cut into 18 (¾-inch) strips. Twist each strip twice, and place 2 inches apart on baking sheets coated with cooking spray.

Cover and let rise in a warm place, free from drafts, 1 hour or until doubled in bulk. Bake at 375° for 12 minutes or until golden. Combine powdered sugar and juice; drizzle over twists. Yield: 1½ dozen (127 calories each).

PROTEIN 3.0 / FAT 1.9 / CARBOHYDRATE 24.5 / CHOLESTEROL 11 / IRON 0.7 / SODIUM 89 / CALCIUM 18

COFFEE-GLAZED CINNAMON ROLLS

2 packages dry yeast
1¼ cups warm water (105° to 115°)
2 eggs
⅓ cup instant nonfat dry milk powder
2 tablespoons reduced-calorie margarine, melted
2 tablespoons sugar
½ teaspoon salt
4¼ cups plus 2 tablespoons all-purpose flour, divided
Vegetable cooking spray
1 tablespoon all-purpose flour
2 tablespoons reduced-calorie margarine, melted
¼ cup firmly packed brown sugar
1 teaspoon ground cinnamon
½ teaspoon instant coffee granules
2 tablespoons boiling water
⅔ cup sifted powdered sugar

Dissolve yeast in warm water in a large bowl; let stand 5 minutes. Add eggs, milk powder, 2 tablespoons margarine, 2 tablespoons sugar, salt, and 2¼ cups flour; beat at medium speed of an electric mixer until well blended. Stir in enough of the remaining 2 cups plus 2 tablespoons flour to make a soft dough. Place dough in a large bowl coated with cooking spray, turning to coat top. Cover and refrigerate 2 hours.

Punch dough down; sprinkle 1 tablespoon flour evenly over work surface. Turn dough out onto floured surface, and roll to an 18-inch square. Brush dough with 2 tablespoons melted margarine. Combine brown sugar and cinnamon; sprinkle over dough. Roll up dough, jellyroll fashion, starting with long side; pinch seam to seal. Cut roll into 24 slices. Place slices, cut side down, in two 9-inch square pans coated with cooking spray. Cover and let rise in a warm place (85°), free from drafts, 1 hour or until doubled in bulk. Bake at 375° for 15 to 20 minutes or until golden.

Combine coffee granules and boiling water; stir until granules dissolve. Add powdered sugar; stir well. Brush glaze over hot rolls. Serve warm. Yield: 2 dozen (127 calories each).

PROTEIN 3.6 / FAT 1.9 / CARBOHYDRATE 23.9 / CHOLESTEROL 17 / IRON 0.9 / SODIUM 83 / CALCIUM 30

CINNAMON-RAISIN SWIRL BREAD

1 package dry yeast
2 cups warm water (105° to 115°)
1 tablespoon sugar
½ teaspoon salt
2 tablespoons vegetable oil
4¾ cups bread flour, divided
2 tablespoons bread flour, divided
Vegetable cooking spray
3 tablespoons sugar
1½ teaspoons ground cinnamon
¼ cup plus 2 tablespoons raisins, divided

Dissolve yeast in warm water in a large bowl; stir in 1 tablespoon sugar, and let stand 5 minutes. Add salt, oil, and 2 cups flour; beat at medium speed of an electric mixer until well blended. Gradually stir in enough of the remaining 2¾ cups flour to make a soft dough.

Sprinkle 1 tablespoon flour evenly over work surface. Turn dough out onto floured surface, and knead until smooth and elastic (about 8 to 10 minutes). Place dough in a large bowl coated with cooking spray, turning to coat top. Cover and let rise in a warm place (85°), free from drafts, 1½ hours or until doubled in bulk.

Punch dough down, and divide in half; sprinkle remaining 1 tablespoon flour evenly over work surface. Turn dough out onto floured surface, and roll each portion to a 14- x 8-inch rectangle. Combine 3 tablespoons sugar and cinnamon; stir well. Sprinkle half of sugar mixture over each rectangle. Sprinkle each with 3 tablespoons raisins. Roll up each rectangle, jellyroll fashion, starting with short side; pinch ends and seam to seal. Place loaves, seam side down, in two 8½- x 4½- x 3-inch loafpans coated with cooking spray.

Cover and let rise in a warm place, free from drafts, 1 hour or until doubled in bulk. Bake at 375° for 25 to 30 minutes or until golden. Yield: 34 servings (79 calories per ½-inch slice).

PROTEIN 2.1 / FAT 1.0 / CARBOHYDRATE 15.2 / CHOLESTEROL 0 / IRON 0.6 / SODIUM 35 / CALCIUM 5

SOUTHERN-STYLE BARLEY

Vegetable cooking spray
½ cup chopped green onions
2½ cups water
1½ cups frozen sliced okra, thawed
1 cup pearl barley
1 cup frozen whole kernel corn, thawed
1 cup chopped tomato
1½ teaspoons chicken-flavored bouillon granules
½ teaspoon hot sauce
2 tablespoons diced pimiento

Coat a large nonstick skillet with cooking spray; place over medium-high heat until hot. Add onions, and sauté until tender. Stir in water and next 6 ingredients; bring to a boil. Cover, reduce heat, and simmer 20 minutes or until barley is tender and liquid is absorbed. Stir in pimiento. Yield: 10 servings (104 calories per ½-cup serving).

PROTEIN 3.1 / FAT 0.5 / CARBOHYDRATE 23.6 / CHOLESTEROL 0 / IRON 0.8 / SODIUM 130 / CALCIUM 25

APPLE COUSCOUS

¾ cup unsweetened apple juice
¾ cup water
1 cup uncooked couscous
1⅓ cups peeled, chopped cooking apple
2 tablespoons raisins
2 tablespoons diced unsweetened dates
¼ teaspoon apple pie spice

Combine apple juice and water in a medium saucepan; bring to a boil. Remove from heat. Add couscous, chopped apple, raisins, unsweetened dates, and apple pie spice; cover and let stand 5 minutes or until couscous is tender and liquid is absorbed.

Fluff couscous with a fork, and transfer to a large serving bowl. Yield: 8 servings (118 calories per ½-cup serving).

PROTEIN 2.9 / FAT 0.1 / CARBOHYDRATE 26.9 / CHOLESTEROL 0 / IRON 0.6 / SODIUM 1 / CALCIUM 13

BROWN RICE SCORES HIGH RATING

For a good source of fiber and nutrients, select brown rice. Brown rice maintains its brown color because it still contains the tough, darker outer layer of the rice kernel. Concentrated in that bran coating are many vitamins and minerals: vitamin E, phosphorus, riboflavin, and calcium.

Although most white rice is enriched to replace some of the nutrients lost in processing, the fiber content of brown rice is triple that of white.

What's more, new studies suggest that the oil found in rice bran (brown rice is 10 percent rice bran) appears to help lower blood cholesterol. But health benefits aside, taste is one of the best reasons to try this whole grain. The nutty flavor and chewy texture of brown rice offer a delightful change of pace. Try substituting brown rice for white rice in casseroles and side dishes.

Brown rice takes twice as long to cook as white rice, so if time is a factor, try quick-cooking brown rice, a new product available in most supermarkets.

MIDDLE EASTERN PILAF

Vegetable cooking spray
1⅓ cups sliced fresh mushrooms
½ cup chopped green onions
2½ cups water
1½ teaspoons chicken-flavored bouillon granules
1 teaspoon grated lemon rind
½ teaspoon dried whole thyme
1 cup brown rice, uncooked
1 cup shredded carrots
2 tablespoons raisins, chopped

Coat a large nonstick skillet with cooking spray; place over medium-high heat until hot. Add mushrooms and onions; sauté 5 minutes or until tender. Set aside.

Combine water and next 3 ingredients in a large saucepan; bring to a boil. Add rice and remove from heat. Stir in reserved mushroom mixture, carrot, and raisins. Pour mixture into a 1½-quart baking dish coated with cooking spray. Cover and bake at 350° for 1 hour or until rice is tender and liquid is absorbed. Yield: 8 servings (104 calories per ½-cup serving).

PROTEIN 2.4 / FAT 0.9 / CARBOHYDRATE 22.2 / CHOLESTEROL 0 / IRON 0.9 / SODIUM 162 / CALCIUM 19

BROWN RICE-VEGETABLE SAUTÉ

Vegetable cooking spray
1 teaspoon margarine
2 medium carrots, scraped and chopped
½ cup chopped green onions
2 cloves garlic, minced
1 cup brown rice, uncooked
2 cups water
¼ cup dry sherry
¼ cup chopped fresh parsley
1 teaspoon beef-flavored bouillon granules
¼ teaspoon pepper
1 cup sliced fresh mushrooms
2 tablespoons grated Parmesan cheese

Coat a large nonstick skillet with cooking spray; add margarine. Place over medium heat until margarine melts. Add carrot, green onions, and garlic; sauté until tender. Add rice; cook over low heat 1 minute, stirring constantly. Add water and next 4 ingredients; bring to a boil. Cover, reduce heat, and simmer 45 minutes or until rice is tender and liquid is absorbed. Transfer mixture to a medium bowl. Set aside, and keep warm.

Coat skillet with cooking spray, and place over medium-high heat until hot. Add mushrooms, and sauté until tender. Add rice mixture to skillet; cook until thoroughly heated. Remove from heat, and sprinkle with cheese. Yield: 8 servings (116 calories per ½-cup serving).

PROTEIN 2.8 / FAT 1.6 / CARBOHYDRATE 20.7 / CHOLESTEROL 1 /
IRON 0.9 / SODIUM 156 / CALCIUM 37

ZESTY DILLED RICE

Vegetable cooking spray
½ cup chopped onion
1 clove garlic, minced
2⅔ cups water
¾ teaspoon chicken-flavored bouillon granules
1 tablespoon lemon juice
1 tablespoon chopped fresh dillweed or ¾ teaspoon dried whole dillweed
¼ teaspoon grated lemon rind
¼ teaspoon salt
¼ teaspoon pepper
1 cup long-grain rice, uncooked
Fresh dillweed sprigs (optional)

Coat a small nonstick skillet with cooking spray; place over medium heat until hot. Add onion and garlic; sauté until tender. Set aside.

Combine water and next 6 ingredients in a medium saucepan; bring to a boil. Add rice; cover and cook over medium heat 20 minutes or until rice is tender and liquid is absorbed. Remove from heat, and stir in sautéed onion and garlic. Transfer mixture to a serving dish, and garnish with fresh dillweed sprigs, if desired. Serve warm. Yield: 6 servings (121 calories per ½-cup serving).

PROTEIN 2.3 / FAT 0.4 / CARBOHYDRATE 26.4 / CHOLESTEROL 0 /
IRON 1.0 / SODIUM 202 / CALCIUM 15

GREEK PILAF

Vegetable cooking spray
2 teaspoons vegetable oil
½ cup chopped onion
1 cup long-grain rice, uncooked
3 tablespoons sliced ripe olives
2 cups water
2 teaspoons beef-flavored bouillon granules
½ teaspoon dried whole thyme
¼ teaspoon dried whole oregano
1¼ cups peeled, diced cucumber
⅓ cup crumbled feta cheese
1 tablespoon diced pimiento
Fresh oregano sprigs (optional)

Coat a large nonstick skillet with cooking spray; add oil. Place over medium-high heat until hot. Add onion, and sauté until tender. Add rice; reduce heat, and cook, uncovered, over low heat until rice mixture is lightly browned, stirring frequently. Transfer rice mixture to a 1½-quart baking dish coated with cooking spray. Sprinkle with sliced olives.

Combine water, bouillon granules, thyme, and oregano in a small saucepan; bring to a boil. Remove from heat, and pour over rice mixture. Cover and bake at 350° for 25 to 30 minutes or until rice is tender and liquid is absorbed. Remove from oven, and stir in cucumber, feta cheese, and pimiento. Garnish with fresh oregano sprigs, if desired. Serve immediately. Yield: 10 servings (104 calories per ½-cup serving).

PROTEIN 2.3 / FAT 3.0 / CARBOHYDRATE 16.9 / CHOLESTEROL 5 /
IRON 1.0 / SODIUM 292 / CALCIUM 44

Ground cumin and red pepper give Mexican Black Beans 'n' Rice authentic south-of-the-border flavor.

MEXICAN BLACK BEANS 'N' RICE

2 teaspoons olive oil
1 cup chopped onion
½ cup chopped green pepper
2 cups cooked long-grain rice (cooked without salt or fat)
½ teaspoon ground cumin
¼ teaspoon ground red pepper
⅛ teaspoon dried coriander
1 (15-ounce) can black beans, rinsed and drained
¾ cup chopped tomato

Heat olive oil in a large nonstick skillet over medium-high heat until hot. Add onion and green pepper; sauté until tender. Stir in rice and next 3 ingredients; sauté 3 minutes. Add beans and chopped tomato; sauté 3 minutes or until thoroughly heated. Yield: 8 servings (123 calories per ½-cup serving).

PROTEIN 3.8 / FAT 1.5 / CARBOHYDRATE 23.7 / CHOLESTEROL 0 /
IRON 1.4 / SODIUM 3 / CALCIUM 19

CONFETTI RICE

⅔ cup water
½ cup long-grain rice, uncooked
½ cup commercial oil-free Italian dressing
¾ cup shredded zucchini
½ cup finely chopped broccoli
⅓ cup shredded carrot
¼ cup chopped fresh parsley
2 teaspoons lemon juice

Combine water, rice, and Italian dressing in a medium saucepan; place over medium-high heat. Bring to a boil; cover, reduce heat, and simmer 25 minutes or until rice is tender and liquid is absorbed.

Stir in zucchini, broccoli, carrot, fresh parsley, and lemon juice. Cover and let stand 10 minutes. Yield: 6 servings (73 calories per ½-cup serving).

PROTEIN 1.6 / FAT 0.1 / CARBOHYDRATE 16.2 / CHOLESTEROL 0 /
IRON 0.8 / SODIUM 187 / CALCIUM 16

PIZZA RICE

Vegetable cooking spray
½ cup chopped green pepper
1 clove garlic, minced
1 (14½-ounce) can no-salt-added whole
   tomatoes, undrained and chopped
1¼ cups water
1 (.7-ounce) envelope Italian dressing mix
1 cup long-grain rice, uncooked
3 tablespoons sliced ripe olives
2 tablespoons chopped fresh parsley
1 tablespoon grated Parmesan cheese
Freshly ground pepper (optional)

Coat a large nonstick skillet with cooking spray; place over medium-high heat until hot. Add green pepper and garlic; sauté 5 minutes or until tender. Add tomato, water, and dressing mix; bring to a boil. Add rice; return to a boil. Cover, reduce heat, and simmer 20 minutes or until rice is tender and liquid is absorbed. Stir in olives and parsley. Sprinkle with Parmesan cheese and pepper, if desired. Yield: 8 servings (112 calories per ½-cup serving).

PROTEIN 2.6 / FAT 1.0 / CARBOHYDRATE 23.1 / CHOLESTEROL 0 / IRON 1.2 / SODIUM 379 / CALCIUM 38

EASY RICE PRIMAVERA

2 cups water
½ cup Chablis or other dry white wine
1 cup long-grain rice, uncooked
Vegetable cooking spray
1 cup broccoli flowerets
1 cup diced zucchini
¼ cup chopped green pepper
2 cloves garlic, minced
½ cup diced tomato
2 tablespoons chopped fresh parsley
1½ tablespoons grated Parmesan cheese
Freshly ground pepper

Bring water and wine to a boil. Add rice; cover, reduce heat, and simmer 20 minutes or until rice is tender and liquid is absorbed.

Coat a nonstick skillet with cooking spray; place over medium heat until hot. Add broccoli, and next 3 ingredients; sauté 5 minutes or until crisp-tender. Add broccoli mixture, tomato, and parsley to rice; stir well. Transfer to a serving bowl. Sprinkle with cheese and pepper. Yield: 10 servings (82 calories per ½-cup serving).

PROTEIN 2.3 / FAT 0.5 / CARBOHYDRATE 17.1 / CHOLESTEROL 1 / IRON 0.9 / SODIUM 21 / CALCIUM 27

FRIED RICE AND PASTA

Vegetable cooking spray
¼ cup thinly sliced celery
¼ cup thinly sliced green onions
1 tablespoon reduced-calorie margarine
½ cup long-grain rice, uncooked
2 ounces vermicelli, uncooked and broken into
   ½-inch pieces
2 cups hot water
1 tablespoon chopped fresh parsley
½ teaspoon chicken-flavored bouillon granules
¼ teaspoon salt
¼ teaspoon garlic powder

Coat a large nonstick skillet with cooking spray; place over medium-high heat until hot.

Add celery and onions; sauté until tender. Transfer to a serving bowl, and set aside.

Coat skillet with cooking spray; add margarine, and place over medium heat until margarine melts. Stir in rice and vermicelli; cook over medium heat until vermicelli is lightly browned, stirring frequently. Add water, sautéed celery and onions, and remaining ingredients to rice mixture. Cover, reduce heat, and simmer 15 to 20 minutes or until rice is tender and liquid is absorbed. Stir before serving. Yield: 7 servings (91 calories per ½-cup serving).

PROTEIN 2.0 / FAT 1.4 / CARBOHYDRATE 17.2 / CHOLESTEROL 0 / IRON 0.7 / SODIUM 163 / CALCIUM 10

ORZO MILANESE

Vegetable cooking spray
2 teaspoons reduced-calorie margarine
1½ cups chopped onion
½ cup chopped green pepper
½ cup chopped celery
1 (10½-ounce) can low-sodium chicken broth, undiluted
1 cup orzo
Dash of powdered saffron
¼ teaspoon salt
⅛ teaspoon pepper
3 tablespoons freshly grated Parmesan cheese

Coat a 1½-quart ceramic heatproof dish with cooking spray; add margarine. Place over low heat until margarine melts. Add onion, green pepper, and celery; sauté until tender. Add chicken broth; bring to a boil. Add orzo, saffron, salt, and pepper; stir well. Cover and bake at 350° for 25 minutes or until liquid is absorbed. Sprinkle with Parmesan cheese, and serve immediately. Yield: 8 servings (125 calories per ½-cup serving).

PROTEIN 4.6 / FAT 1.8 / CARBOHYDRATE 22.1 / CHOLESTEROL 2 / IRON 1.0 / SODIUM 134 / CALCIUM 50

NOODLES ROMANOFF

Vegetable cooking spray
1½ cups sliced fresh mushrooms
2 cloves garlic, minced
2 cups cooked medium egg noodles (cooked without salt or fat)
½ cup low-fat sour cream
2 tablespoons chopped green onions
2 tablespoons chopped fresh parsley
¼ teaspoon salt
¼ teaspoon pepper
2 tablespoons grated Parmesan cheese

Coat a large nonstick skillet with vegetable cooking spray; place skillet over medium-high heat until hot. Add sliced mushrooms and minced garlic; sauté 3 minutes or until mushrooms are tender. Add noodles, sour cream, chopped green onions, chopped fresh parsley, salt, and pepper to skillet, stirring gently.

Transfer noodle mixture to a 1-quart casserole coated with cooking spray. Top with Parmesan cheese. Bake, covered, at 350° for 20 minutes; uncover and bake an additional 5 minutes or until cheese is lightly browned. Yield: 6 servings (110 calories per ½-cup serving).

PROTEIN 3.9 / FAT 4.0 / CARBOHYDRATE 14.7 / CHOLESTEROL 25 / IRON 0.8 / SODIUM 139 / CALCIUM 56

PASTA WITH RED PEPPER SAUCE

Olive oil-flavored vegetable cooking spray
2 teaspoons olive oil
2 cups chopped onion
2 cloves garlic, minced
4¾ cups chopped sweet red peppers (about 4 large)
½ cup canned no-salt-added chicken broth, undiluted
1 tablespoon white wine vinegar
½ teaspoon salt
¼ teaspoon ground white pepper
Dash of crushed red pepper
10 ounces linguine, uncooked
Fresh basil sprigs (optional)

Coat a large Dutch oven with cooking spray; add oil. Place over medium-high heat until hot. Add chopped onion and garlic; sauté until tender. Add sweet red pepper and chicken broth; bring to a boil. Cover, reduce heat, and simmer 15 minutes or until pepper is tender. Remove from heat.

Transfer pepper mixture, in batches, to container of an electric blender or food processor; top with cover, and process until smooth. Return pureed mixture to Dutch oven. Add white wine vinegar, salt, white pepper, and crushed red pepper. Cook over medium-low heat until thoroughly heated.

Cook linguine according to package directions, omitting salt and fat; drain. Place linguine in a large serving bowl. Add red pepper sauce, tossing well. Garnish with fresh basil sprigs, if desired. Yield: 12 servings (104 calories per ½-cup serving).

PROTEIN 3.4 / FAT 1.8 / CARBOHYDRATE 18.7 / CHOLESTEROL 10 / IRON 1.5 / SODIUM 163 / CALCIUM 26

Lots of fresh vegetables, herbs, and cheese make Pasta Primavera a flavorful dish.

PASTA PRIMAVERA

¼ pound fresh asparagus spears, diagonally
  sliced into 1-inch pieces
½ cup broccoli flowerets
½ cup fresh snow pea pods, trimmed and
  diagonally sliced into 1-inch pieces
½ cup sliced yellow squash
½ cup sliced zucchini
Vegetable cooking spray
¼ pound fresh mushrooms, sliced
1 clove garlic, minced
1 tablespoon chopped fresh chives
1 tablespoon water
8 ounces fresh linguine, uncooked
¼ cup hot water
2 tablespoons Chablis or other dry
  white wine
¼ teaspoon chicken-flavored bouillon
  granules
¾ cup skim milk
1 tablespoon all-purpose flour
¼ cup plus 1 tablespoon grated Parmesan
  cheese, divided
1 tablespoon chopped fresh parsley
1½ teaspoons chopped fresh basil
⅛ teaspoon salt
⅛ teaspoon pepper

Arrange asparagus spears, broccoli flowerets, snow peas, yellow squash, and zucchini in a vegetable steamer over boiling water. Cover and steam 15 to 20 minutes or until vegetables are crisp-tender. Set aside.

Coat a large nonstick skillet with cooking spray; place over medium-high heat until hot. Add mushrooms and garlic; sauté 5 minutes or until mushrooms are tender. Add reserved vegetables, chives, and 1 tablespoon water; reduce heat and simmer, uncovered, 5 minutes. Set vegetable mixture aside.

Cook linguine according to package directions, omitting salt and fat. Drain and set aside.

Combine ¼ cup hot water, wine, and bouillon granules in a small saucepan. Bring mixture to a boil; cook until mixture is reduced to 2 tablespoons.

Combine milk and flour in a small bowl; stir well. Gradually add flour mixture to wine mixture, stirring constantly. Cook over medium heat, stirring constantly, 5 minutes or until thickened and bubbly.

Pour sauce over linguine, and toss gently. Add ¼ cup Parmesan cheese, chopped parsley, chopped basil, salt, and pepper; toss gently.

Transfer linguine mixture to a large serving platter, and top with reserved vegetable mixture; sprinkle with remaining 1 tablespoon cheese. Yield: 6 servings (162 calories per 1-cup serving).

PROTEIN 8.3 / FAT 2.5 / CARBOHYDRATE 26.6 / CHOLESTEROL 20 /
IRON 1.7 / SODIUM 273 / CALCIUM 134

ROMA TOMATOES AND PASTA

2 teaspoons olive oil
3 cloves garlic, minced
2 pounds ripe plum tomatoes, peeled,
  seeded, and cut into quarters
3 tablespoons minced fresh parsley
3 tablespoons minced fresh basil
½ teaspoon salt
¼ teaspoon freshly ground pepper
2 tablespoons canned low-sodium chicken
  broth, undiluted
4 ounces thin spaghetti or vermicelli,
  uncooked
Fresh basil leaves (optional)

Place olive oil in a large nonstick skillet over medium heat until hot; add garlic, and sauté 2 minutes. Add tomato and next 5 ingredients; cook until thoroughly heated, stirring occasionally. Set aside, and keep warm.

Cook pasta according to package directions, omitting salt and fat; drain well. Combine pasta and tomato mixture, tossing gently. Garnish with fresh basil leaves, if desired. Serve warm or at room temperature. Yield: 4 servings (170 calories per 1-cup serving).

PROTEIN 5.9 / FAT 3.0 / CARBOHYDRATE 30.8 / CHOLESTEROL 0 /
IRON 2.1 / SODIUM 302 / CALCIUM 44

THREE-MUSHROOM SAUCE WITH WHOLE WHEAT PASTA

2 cups boiling water
1 ounce dried shiitake mushrooms
½ ounce dried porcini mushrooms
4 ounces part-skim ricotta cheese
1½ tablespoons plain nonfat yogurt
Olive oil-flavored vegetable cooking spray
2 tablespoons minced shallots
1½ pounds fresh mushrooms, thinly sliced
¼ cup Chablis or other dry white wine
1 cup canned low-sodium chicken broth, undiluted
1 teaspoon dried whole rosemary
¼ teaspoon salt
⅛ teaspoon freshly ground pepper
4 ounces whole wheat spaghetti or fettuccine, uncooked
¼ cup grated Parmesan cheese
2 tablespoons chopped fresh parsley

Pour boiling water over dried shiitake and porcini mushrooms; let stand 30 minutes. Drain mushrooms, reserving ½ cup liquid; coarsely chop mushrooms. Set aside.

Combine ricotta cheese and yogurt in container of an electric blender or food processor; top with cover, and process until smooth, scraping sides of container occasionally. Set aside.

Coat a large nonstick skillet with cooking spray; place over medium-high heat until hot. Add minced shallots, and sauté until tender. Add reserved chopped mushrooms and sliced fresh mushrooms; sauté 8 to 10 minutes or until mushrooms are lightly browned. Stir in wine, and cook mushroom mixture 3 to 5 minutes or until liquid evaporates.

Combine chicken broth and reserved mushroom liquid; add to mixture, and cook 8 to 10 minutes or until liquid is reduced by half. Add reserved ricotta cheese mixture, rosemary, salt, and freshly ground pepper; stir well. Remove from heat, and keep warm.

Cook pasta according to package directions, omitting salt and fat; drain well. Combine pasta and mushroom mixture in a large bowl; top with Parmesan cheese and parsley. Serve immediately. Yield: 10 servings (105 calories per ½-cup serving).

PROTEIN 5.7 / FAT 2.4 / CARBOHYDRATE 15.9 / CHOLESTEROL 5 / IRON 1.5 / SODIUM 117 / CALCIUM 76

CILANTRO PESTO WITH PASTA

¾ cup plain nonfat yogurt
½ cup fresh cilantro leaves
½ cup fresh parsley
¼ cup grated Parmesan cheese
2 tablespoons pine nuts, lightly toasted
3 cloves garlic
2 teaspoons olive oil
¼ teaspoon salt
⅛ teaspoon freshly ground pepper
12 ounces tomato-basil pasta

Combine all ingredients except pasta in container of an electric blender or food processor; top with cover, and process 1 minute or until smooth, scraping sides of container occasionally.

Cook pasta according to package directions, omitting salt and fat; drain. Place pasta in a large bowl; add cilantro mixture, tossing gently. Serve immediately. Yield: 11 servings (154 calories per ½-cup serving).

PROTEIN 5.9 / FAT 3.3 / CARBOHYDRATE 25.3 / CHOLESTEROL 2 / IRON 1.1 / SODIUM 102 / CALCIUM 68

For an entrée appealing to both eye and palate, serve Orange Roughy with Carambola Salsa (page 128) garnished with fresh cilantro.

BAKED BASS WITH FENNEL

1 pound fennel
Vegetable cooking spray
1 cup Chablis or other dry white wine, divided
¼ cup water
1 teaspoon lemon juice
½ teaspoon lemon-pepper seasoning
6 (4-ounce) bass fillets
½ cup chopped fresh mushrooms
½ cup finely chopped green pepper
½ cup finely chopped sweet red pepper

Wash fennel; trim off and mince leaves, reserving 2 tablespoons. Discard remaining fennel leaves. Trim off tough outer stalks and discard. Cut bulb in half lengthwise; remove core. Cut crosswise into ¼-inch slices.

Coat a large nonstick skillet with cooking spray; place over medium-high heat until hot. Add fennel slices, ½ cup wine, and water; cook 8 to 10 minutes or until fennel is tender, stirring frequently.

Transfer fennel slices to a 13- x 9- x 2-inch baking dish. Sprinkle with lemon juice and lemon-pepper seasoning. Arrange fillets over fennel. Combine reserved fennel leaves, mushrooms, and peppers; spoon evenly over fillets. Pour remaining ½ cup wine over vegetable mixture. Bake, uncovered, at 350° for 30 minutes or until fish flakes easily when tested with a fork. Yield: 6 servings (157 calories per serving).

PROTEIN 23.3 / FAT 4.7 / CARBOHYDRATE 5.1 / CHOLESTEROL 77 / IRON 3.7 / SODIUM 117 / CALCIUM 151

CHEESE-TOPPED CATFISH

2 tablespoons reduced-calorie mayonnaise
2 teaspoons skim milk
1 teaspoon honey
⅛ teaspoon ground red pepper
1 egg white
½ cup (2 ounces) shredded 40% less-fat Cheddar cheese
6 (4-ounce) farm-raised catfish fillets
Vegetable cooking spray

Combine first 4 ingredients in a small bowl; stir well. Beat egg white (at room temperature) in a small bowl at high speed of an electric mixer until stiff peaks form. Fold egg white into mayonnaise mixture; fold in cheese.

Place fillets on rack of a broiler pan coated with cooking spray. Broil 5½ inches from heat 12 minutes or until fish flakes easily when tested with a fork. Spread egg white mixture over fillets, and broil 3 minutes or until lightly browned. Yield: 6 servings (171 calories per serving).

PROTEIN 22.1 / FAT 7.4 / CARBOHYDRATE 3.5 / CHOLESTEROL 70 / IRON 1.1 / SODIUM 165 / CALCIUM 110

CATFISH FINGERS WITH PARSLEY MAYONNAISE

½ cup corn flake crumbs
¼ teaspoon ground cumin
¼ teaspoon salt
⅛ teaspoon ground red pepper
4 (4-ounce) farm-raised catfish fillets
2 egg whites, lightly beaten
Butter-flavored vegetable cooking spray
Parsley Mayonnaise

Combine corn flake crumbs, cumin, salt, and red pepper in a small bowl; stir well. Cut fillets into 2- x ¾-inch strips. Dip catfish strips into egg white; dredge in crumb mixture.

Place catfish strips on a baking sheet coated with cooking spray. Bake, uncovered, at 500° for 8 minutes or until fish flakes easily when tested with a fork. Serve with 2 tablespoons Parsley Mayonnaise per serving. Yield: 4 servings (247 calories per serving).

Parsley Mayonnaise:

¼ cup reduced-calorie mayonnaise
¼ cup plain nonfat yogurt
1½ tablespoons minced fresh parsley
1½ tablespoons minced fresh cilantro
1 tablespoon minced green onions
⅛ teaspoon dried whole oregano
⅛ teaspoon garlic powder

Combine all ingredients in container of an electric blender; top with cover, and process until smooth. Cover and chill. Yield: ½ cup.

PROTEIN 24.4 / FAT 9.2 / CARBOHYDRATE 15.2 / CHOLESTEROL 71 / IRON 2.3 / SODIUM 505 / CALCIUM 83

A marinade of tangerine juice, vermouth, rosemary, and thyme provides extra flavor to Grilled Grouper Tangerine. Even your pickiest eater will want to try this colorful entrée.

GRILLED GROUPER TANGERINE

3 (8-ounce) grouper fillets
¼ cup unsweetened tangerine concentrate, thawed and undiluted
2 tablespoons dry vermouth
2 teaspoons vegetable oil
½ teaspoon dried whole rosemary
¼ teaspoon dried whole thyme
¼ teaspoon pepper
Vegetable cooking spray
2 tablespoons thinly sliced green onions
2 tablespoons finely chopped sweet red pepper
Fresh rosemary and thyme sprigs (optional)

Place fillets in a 13- x 9- x 2-inch baking dish. Combine tangerine concentrate, vermouth, vegetable oil, rosemary, thyme, and pepper in a small bowl; stir well. Pour tangerine mixture over fillets; cover and marinate in refrigerator 2 hours, turning once.

Remove fillets from marinade, reserving marinade. Bring marinade to a boil in a small saucepan; boil 2 minutes. Set aside.

Coat grill rack with cooking spray; place on grill over medium-hot coals. Place fillets on rack, and cook 5 minutes on each side or until fish flakes easily when tested with a fork, basting frequently with marinade. Transfer fillets to a serving platter. Combine onions and red pepper; spoon mixture evenly over fillets. If desired, garnish with fresh rosemary and thyme. Yield: 6 servings (121 calories per serving).

PROTEIN 18.3 / FAT 2.6 / CARBOHYDRATE 5.1 / CHOLESTEROL 34 / IRON 1.1 / SODIUM 39 / CALCIUM 23

ORANGE ROUGHY WITH CARAMBOLA SALSA

2 medium carambola (starfruit), thinly sliced
1 cup fresh strawberries, hulled and sliced
½ cup finely chopped onion
1 tablespoon chopped jalapeño pepper
1 tablespoon minced fresh cilantro
1 teaspoon grated lime rind
1 tablespoon lime juice
¼ teaspoon ground coriander
⅛ teaspoon ground red pepper
2 tablespoons lime juice
2 teaspoons reduced-calorie margarine, melted
6 (4-ounce) orange roughy fillets
Vegetable cooking spray
Fresh cilantro sprigs (optional)

Combine first 9 ingredients in a medium bowl. Cover and chill salsa 2 hours.

Combine 2 tablespoons lime juice and margarine; stir well. Place fillets on rack of a broiler pan coated with cooking spray, and brush with lime mixture. Broil 5½ inches from heat 10 minutes or until fish flakes easily when tested with a fork. To serve, spoon salsa over fillets. Garnish with cilantro sprigs, if desired. Yield: 6 servings (229 calories per serving).

PROTEIN 21.0 / FAT 11.8 / CARBOHYDRATE 9.9 / CHOLESTEROL 54 / IRON 1.0 / SODIUM 79 / CALCIUM 52

POACHED SALMON STEAKS ROSÉ

1 cup rosé wine
½ cup water
1 teaspoon grated lemon rind
1 bay leaf
½ teaspoon black peppercorns
¼ teaspoon dried whole thyme
⅓ cup sliced carrot
4 (4-ounce) salmon steaks (½-inch thick)
½ cup sliced celery
½ cup sliced green onions
¼ cup chopped fresh parsley
Lemon wedges (optional)
Fresh parsley sprigs (optional)

Combine first 6 ingredients in a large nonstick skillet; stir well. Bring to a boil; cover, reduce heat, and simmer 8 minutes. Add carrot; cover and simmer an additional 2 minutes.

Place salmon steaks in wine mixture; arrange celery, green onions, and chopped parsley around steaks. Bring to a boil; cover, reduce heat, and simmer 8 minutes or until fish flakes easily when tested with a fork. Transfer fish and vegetables to a serving platter, using a slotted spoon. Remove and discard bay leaf. If desired, garnish with lemon wedges and parsley sprigs. Yield: 4 servings (208 calories per serving).

PROTEIN 24.9 / FAT 9.8 / CARBOHYDRATE 4.2 / CHOLESTEROL 70 / IRON 1.5 / SODIUM 79 / CALCIUM 37

SHARK STEAK KABOBS

2 pounds shark steaks (¾-inch thick)
3 tablespoons reduced-sodium soy sauce
2 tablespoons lemon juice
1 tablespoon dry sherry
2 teaspoons brown sugar
¼ teaspoon ground ginger
¼ teaspoon dry mustard
⅛ teaspoon garlic powder
2 small zucchini, cut into 8 (1-inch) slices
2 small yellow squash, cut into 8 (1-inch) slices
8 cherry tomatoes
8 medium-size fresh mushrooms
Vegetable cooking spray

Cut shark steaks into 1¼-inch pieces, and place in a shallow dish. Combine soy sauce and next 6 ingredients in a small bowl; stir well, and pour over steak pieces. Cover and marinate in refrigerator 1 hour.

Remove steak pieces from marinade, reserving marinade. Bring marinade to a boil in a small saucepan; boil 2 minutes. Set aside.

Arrange steak pieces, zucchini, yellow squash, tomatoes, and mushrooms alternately on 8 (12-inch) skewers.

Coat grill rack with cooking spray; place on grill over medium-hot coals. Place kabobs on rack, and grill 10 minutes or until fish flakes easily when tested with a fork, turning and basting occasionally with reserved marinade. Yield: 8 servings (140 calories per serving).

PROTEIN 19.9 / FAT 4.3 / CARBOHYDRATE 4.7 / CHOLESTEROL 45 / IRON 1.4 / SODIUM 299 / CALCIUM 42

SOLE FILLETS ATHENIAN

Vegetable cooking spray
¼ cup chopped onion
¼ cup diced sweet red pepper
1 clove garlic, minced
1 (10-ounce) package frozen chopped spinach,
    thawed and well drained
½ cup crumbled feta cheese
2 tablespoons sliced ripe olives
1 teaspoon grated lemon rind
½ teaspoon dried whole basil
¼ teaspoon dried whole oregano
⅛ teaspoon ground white pepper
8 (4-ounce) sole fillets
¼ teaspoon paprika

Coat a small nonstick skillet with cooking spray; place over medium-high heat until hot. Add onion, sweet red pepper, and garlic; sauté until tender. Remove from heat. Combine onion mixture, spinach, and next 6 ingredients in a medium bowl; stir well.

Spoon 3 tablespoons spinach mixture in center of each fillet; roll up jellyroll fashion, beginning at narrow end. Secure with a wooden pick. Sprinkle rolls with paprika.

Place rolls, seam side down, in a 13- x 9- x 2-inch baking dish coated with cooking spray. Bake, uncovered, at 350° for 20 to 25 minutes or until fish flakes easily when tested with a fork. Transfer rolls to a serving platter, and remove wooden picks. Yield: 8 servings (149 calories per serving).

PROTEIN 24.1 / FAT 4.3 / CARBOHYDRATE 3.0 / CHOLESTEROL 64 / IRON 1.5 / SODIUM 268 / CALCIUM 120

PEPPERED SOLE

4 (4-ounce) sole fillets
Vegetable cooking spray
½ teaspoon pepper mélange, coarsely ground
¼ cup unsweetened pineapple juice
1 tablespoon reduced-calorie margarine, melted

Arrange fillets in a 13- x 9- x 2-inch baking dish coated with cooking spray; sprinkle pepper mélange evenly over fillets. Combine pineapple juice and melted margarine; pour over fillets.

Bake, uncovered, at 400° for 15 to 18 minutes or until fish flakes easily when tested with a fork. Transfer to a serving platter. Yield: 4 servings (129 calories per serving).

PROTEIN 21.4 / FAT 3.3 / CARBOHYDRATE 2.3 / CHOLESTEROL 54 / IRON 0.5 / SODIUM 120 / CALCIUM 24

MORE HEALTHY BENEFITS

Research has shown that omega-3 fatty acids found in fish oils can lower blood pressure, keep arteries open after coronary artery surgery, and perhaps interfere with the process of inflammation that leads to arthritis and psoriasis.

However, research on fish oils is still incomplete, and adverse reactions and long-term effects of fish oil supplements are still not known. Nutritionists advise that for now, add omega-3 fatty acids to your diet by including cold-water fish such as salmon, tuna, herring, mackerel, and lake trout rather than fish oil supplements.

SWORDFISH CALCUTTA

2 tablespoons unsweetened orange juice
1 tablespoon lemon juice
½ teaspoon ground coriander
½ teaspoon ground cumin
¼ teaspoon ground cardamom
¼ teaspoon ground cinnamon
¼ teaspoon ground nutmeg
⅛ teaspoon ground cloves
⅛ teaspoon pepper
4 (4-ounce) swordfish steaks (¾-inch thick)
Vegetable cooking spray

Combine first 9 ingredients in a small bowl; stir well. Place swordfish steaks in a shallow baking dish. Brush orange juice mixture over steaks; cover and marinate in refrigerator 8 hours.

Remove steaks from marinade; discard marinade. Place steaks on rack of a broiler pan coated with cooking spray. Broil 5½ inches from heat 10 to 12 minutes or until fish flakes easily when tested with a fork. Yield: 4 servings (155 calories per serving).

PROTEIN 24.4 / FAT 5.3 / CARBOHYDRATE 0.9 / CHOLESTEROL 48 / IRON 1.1 / SODIUM 111 / CALCIUM 10

Chopped mango and papaya bring tropical freshness to grilled Island Swordfish.

ISLAND SWORDFISH

½ cup chopped ripe mango
¼ cup peeled, seeded, and chopped papaya
2 tablespoons finely chopped celery
1 tablespoon minced fresh parsley
1 tablespoon lime juice
2 teaspoons finely chopped purple onion
1 teaspoon grated fresh ginger
1 teaspoon seeded, minced jalapeño pepper
2 tablespoons rice vinegar
2 tablespoons Dijon mustard
1 tablespoon plus 1 teaspoon low-sodium soy sauce
4 (4-ounce) swordfish steaks (¾-inch thick)
Vegetable cooking spray
Fresh parsley sprigs (optional)

Combine first 8 ingredients in a small bowl. Combine rice vinegar, mustard, and soy sauce in a small bowl; stir with a wire whisk until well blended. Brush vinegar mixture over steaks.

Coat grill rack with cooking spray; place on grill over medium-hot coals. Place steaks on rack, and grill 5 minutes on each side or until fish flakes easily when tested with a fork. Transfer steaks to individual plates and serve with ¼ cup mango mixture. Garnish with parsley sprigs, if desired. Serve immediately. Yield: 4 servings (178 calories per serving).

PROTEIN 22.8 / FAT 5.3 / CARBOHYDRATE 8.2 / CHOLESTEROL 44 / IRON 1.1 / SODIUM 459 / CALCIUM 15

LEMON-HERB BAKED TROUT

1 cup soft breadcrumbs
3 tablespoons grated Parmesan cheese
2 teaspoons grated lemon rind
1 clove garlic, minced
½ teaspoon dried whole thyme
½ teaspoon dried whole basil
¼ teaspoon dried whole tarragon
¼ teaspoon pepper
3 tablespoons chopped fresh parsley
6 (4-ounce) trout fillets
Vegetable cooking spray
1½ tablespoons reduced-calorie margarine, melted
1 tablespoon lemon juice
Lemon twists (optional)

Combine first 8 ingredients in container of an electric blender; top with cover, and process until well blended. Combine breadcrumb mixture and parsley; stir well.

Dredge fillets in breadcrumb mixture. Arrange fillets in a single layer in a 13- x 9- x 2-inch baking dish coated with cooking spray. Combine melted margarine and lemon juice in a small bowl; drizzle over coated fillets. Cover and bake at 500° for 10 minutes; uncover and bake an additional 5 minutes or until fish flakes easily when tested with a fork. Transfer fillets to a serving platter. Garnish with lemon twists, if desired. Yield: 6 servings (224 calories per serving).

PROTEIN 25.5 / FAT 10.5 / CARBOHYDRATE 5.7 / CHOLESTEROL 68 / IRON 2.3 / SODIUM 182 / CALCIUM 99

TUNA-STUFFED PEPPERS

6 small sweet red peppers
2 (6½-ounce) cans white tuna in spring water, drained
½ cup cooked long-grain rice (cooked without salt or fat)
½ cup finely chopped onion
½ cup thinly sliced celery
¼ cup reduced-calorie mayonnaise
2 tablespoons chopped fresh parsley
1 tablespoon lemon juice
¼ teaspoon lemon-pepper seasoning
¼ cup (1 ounce) shredded 40% less-fat Cheddar cheese

Cut tops off peppers; reserve tops. Remove and discard seeds. Cook peppers and tops in boiling water 5 minutes; drain. Set aside.

Combine tuna and next 7 ingredients in a medium bowl; stir well. Spoon tuna mixture evenly into peppers; sprinkle cheese evenly over mixture. Top with reserved pepper tops. Place peppers in a shallow baking dish. Bake at 350° for 20 minutes or until thoroughly heated. Yield: 6 servings (170 calories per serving).

PROTEIN 16.0 / FAT 5.2 / CARBOHYDRATE 15.5 / CHOLESTEROL 27 / IRON 2.3 / SODIUM 322 / CALCIUM 51

CRAB CAKES WITH TARRAGON TARTAR SAUCE

1 pound fresh lump crabmeat, drained
½ cup fine, dry breadcrumbs
¼ cup finely chopped onion
2 tablespoons chopped celery
2 tablespoons chopped green pepper
1 egg, beaten
¼ cup skim milk
1 teaspoon dry mustard
1 teaspoon low-sodium Worcestershire sauce
Vegetable cooking spray
2 teaspoons reduced-calorie margarine
Tarragon Tartar Sauce

Combine first 9 ingredients in a large bowl; stir well. Shape into 6 patties.

Coat a large nonstick skillet with cooking spray; add margarine. Place over medium heat until margarine melts. Add patties; cook 5 minutes on each side or until golden. Serve with 1 tablespoon Tarragon Tartar Sauce per serving. Yield: 6 servings (158 calories per serving).

Tarragon Tartar Sauce:

¼ cup plain nonfat yogurt
2 tablespoons reduced-calorie mayonnaise
1½ tablespoons sweet pickle relish
1 teaspoon lemon juice
½ teaspoon dried whole tarragon

Combine all ingredients in a small bowl; stir well. Cover and chill thoroughly. Yield: ¼ cup plus 2 tablespoons.

PROTEIN 17.8 / FAT 4.9 / CARBOHYDRATE 10.0 / CHOLESTEROL 108 / IRON 1.1 / SODIUM 368 / CALCIUM 125

CRUSTLESS CRAB AND BROCCOLI QUICHE

1 cup chopped fresh broccoli
½ cup finely chopped sweet red pepper
¼ cup finely chopped onion
¼ cup water
1 (8-ounce) carton frozen egg substitute, thawed
1 (6-ounce) can lump crabmeat, drained
½ cup (2 ounces) shredded reduced-fat Swiss cheese
½ cup skim milk
½ teaspoon salt
¼ teaspoon dry mustard
¼ teaspoon ground red pepper
Vegetable cooking spray

Combine broccoli, sweet red pepper, onion, and water in a medium saucepan. Cover and cook over medium heat 3 to 5 minutes or until vegetables are crisp-tender. Drain well.

Combine vegetable mixture, egg substitute, and next 6 ingredients in a large bowl, stirring well. Pour mixture into a 9-inch quiche dish coated with cooking spray. Bake at 350° for 35 to 40 minutes or until set. Let stand 10 minutes before slicing into wedges. Yield: 6 servings (87 calories per serving).

PROTEIN 12.4 / FAT 2.2 / CARBOHYDRATE 3.8 / CHOLESTEROL 26 / IRON 1.2 / SODIUM 356 / CALCIUM 69

LOBSTER TAILS ORIENTAL

3 tablespoons sake (rice wine)
3 tablespoons low-sodium soy sauce
2 tablespoons finely chopped onion
2 teaspoons vegetable oil
1 clove garlic, minced
½ teaspoon ground ginger
¼ teaspoon dry mustard
⅛ teaspoon ground red pepper
4 (6-ounce) frozen lobster tails, partially thawed
Vegetable cooking spray

Combine first 8 ingredients in container of an electric blender; top with cover, and process until mixture is smooth. Set sake mixture aside.

Split lobster tails lengthwise; cut through upper hard shell and three-fourths of the way through meat with an electric knife. Do not cut through bottom shell. Lift lobster meat through split shell to rest on outside of shell, leaving meat attached to far end of lobster shell.

Place lobster tails on a broiler rack coated with cooking spray. Brush sake mixture over lobster tails. Broil lobster 5½ inches from heat 12 to 15 minutes, basting frequently with remaining sake mixture. Yield: 4 servings (122 calories per serving).

PROTEIN 18.8 / FAT 3.1 / CARBOHYDRATE 2.4 / CHOLESTEROL 65 / IRON 0.4 / SODIUM 638 / CALCIUM 59

BAY SCALLOPS MONTEREY

1 pound fresh bay scallops
Vegetable cooking spray
1 tablespoon unsalted margarine
2 tablespoons all-purpose flour
¾ cup skim milk
⅓ cup (1⅓ ounces) shredded reduced-fat Monterey Jack cheese
2 teaspoons grated Parmesan cheese
1 jalapeño pepper, seeded and chopped

Place scallops in a vegetable steamer over boiling water. Cover and steam 3 to 5 minutes.

Transfer scallops to 4 individual baking dishes coated with cooking spray; set aside.

Melt margarine in saucepan over low heat; add flour, stirring until smooth. Cook 1 minute, stirring constantly. Gradually add milk; cook over medium heat, stirring constantly, until mixture is thickened and bubbly. Stir in shredded cheese.

Pour cheese sauce over scallops. Sprinkle with Parmesan cheese and jalapeño. Broil scallops 5½ inches from heat until lightly browned. Yield: 4 servings (157 calories per serving).

PROTEIN 18.2 / FAT 6.0 / CARBOHYDRATE 7.1 / CHOLESTEROL 34 / IRON 0.4 / SODIUM 220 / CALCIUM 88

TROPICAL SCALLOP COMBO

2 medium oranges
Vegetable cooking spray
2 teaspoons vegetable oil
1½ pounds fresh bay scallops
1 small green pepper, cut into strips
1 small sweet red pepper, cut into strips
½ cup chopped onion
1 clove garlic, minced
1 cup unsweetened orange juice
1 tablespoon cornstarch
½ teaspoon ground ginger
¼ teaspoon dry mustard
¼ teaspoon ground red pepper
1½ cups cubed fresh pineapple

Peel oranges; cut oranges crosswise into ¼-inch-thick slices. Cut slices in half, and set aside.

Coat a large nonstick skillet with cooking spray; add oil. Place over medium-high heat until hot. Add scallops, and sauté 2 to 3 minutes; add pepper strips, onion, and garlic; sauté 4 minutes. Remove scallop mixture from skillet, using a slotted spoon; drain on paper towels, and set aside. Discard liquid, and wipe drippings from skillet with a paper towel.

Combine orange juice and next 4 ingredients in skillet; stir well. Cook over medium heat until thickened, stirring constantly. Add reserved scallop mixture, orange slices, and cubed pineapple to skillet; stir well. Cook 3 minutes or until thoroughly heated. Serve warm. Yield: 7 servings (171 calories per serving).

PROTEIN 17.6 / FAT 2.5 / CARBOHYDRATE 20.0 / CHOLESTEROL 32 / IRON 0.9 / SODIUM 158 / CALCIUM 54

SMILE POWER

Smiling can do more than just increase your face value. New studies from the University of Michigan and the University of California Medical School at San Francisco have found that simply lifting the corners of the mouth can cause positive changes in heart rate, breath rate, and even blood temperature. The reason is partly physiological. Exercising "smile" muscles triggers a cool-down in blood temperature. This, in turn, signals a release of endorphins, chemicals that act as the body's natural painkillers. Frown, and the mood will change.

SEAFOOD PHYLLO PIES

Vegetable cooking spray
¼ cup sliced green onions
1 cup sliced fresh mushrooms
3 tablespoons all-purpose flour
1 teaspoon chicken-flavored bouillon
 granules
1 cup skim milk
2 tablespoons dry sherry
⅛ teaspoon ground white pepper
¼ pound medium-size fresh shrimp,
 cooked, peeled, and deveined
¼ pound fresh lump crabmeat, drained
¼ pound fresh bay scallops
1 cup frozen broccoli flowerets, thawed
½ cup frozen sliced carrot, thawed
3 (12- x 18½-inch) sheets commercial
 frozen phyllo pastry, thawed
2 tablespoons unsalted margarine,
 melted

Coat a large nonstick skillet with cooking spray; place over medium-high heat until hot. Add green onions and mushrooms; sauté until tender, stirring constantly.

Combine flour, bouillon granules, skim milk, sherry, and pepper in a small bowl; stir well. Add to mushroom mixture; bring to a boil, stirring constantly. Reduce heat, and simmer 3 minutes or until thickened. Add shrimp, crabmeat, scallops, broccoli flowerets, and carrot slices; stir well. Spoon seafood mixture evenly into four 6-ounce custard cups coated with cooking spray. Set aside.

Brush one sheet of phyllo with 2 teaspoons margarine (keep remaining phyllo pastry covered). Top with second sheet, and brush with 2 teaspoons margarine. Repeat with remaining phyllo sheet and margarine. Cut phyllo in half lengthwise; place one half on top of the other, forming 6 layers. Cut phyllo layers into four 3½-inch circles.

Carefully place phyllo circles on top of seafood mixture, pressing gently but firmly to edges of custard cups. Bake at 350° for 30 to 40 minutes or until phyllo pastry is puffed and golden. Serve warm. Yield: 4 servings (220 calories per serving).

PROTEIN 18.7 / FAT 7.4 / CARBOHYDRATE 20.2 / CHOLESTEROL 52 / IRON 1.8 / SODIUM 616 / CALCIUM 141

Spicy Shrimp and Vegetable Stir-Fry served over a Chinese Noodle Pancake makes a filling entrée.

SPICY SHRIMP AND VEGETABLE STIR-FRY

1 tablespoon dry sherry
1 teaspoon cornstarch
1 egg white
1½ pounds medium-size fresh shrimp, peeled and deveined
Vegetable cooking spray
1 tablespoon safflower oil
2 cloves garlic, minced
2 tablespoons minced fresh ginger
½ teaspoon crushed red pepper
¼ cup cider vinegar
3 tablespoons reduced-sodium soy sauce
2 tablespoons sugar
2 teaspoons cornstarch
6 ounces snow pea pods, trimmed
1 large carrot, scraped and sliced diagonally into thin slices
1 stalk celery, sliced diagonally into thin slices
1 (8-ounce) can bamboo shoots, drained
Chinese Noodle Pancake

Combine sherry, 1 teaspoon cornstarch, and egg white in a small bowl; beat lightly with a wire whisk. Place shrimp in a medium bowl. Drizzle egg white mixture over shrimp; toss well. Cover and marinate in refrigerator 30 minutes.

Coat a wok or large nonstick skillet with cooking spray; add oil. Place over medium-high heat until hot. Add garlic, ginger, and red pepper; stir-fry 10 seconds. Add marinated shrimp, and stir-fry 3 minutes. Remove shrimp, and drain on paper towels.

Combine vinegar, soy sauce, sugar, and 2 teaspoons cornstarch in a small bowl; stir well with a wire whisk. Set aside.

Add snow peas, carrot, and celery to wok; stir-fry 1 minute. Add shrimp and reserved soy sauce mixture to vegetables; cook, stirring constantly, until slightly thickened. Stir in bamboo shoots. Serve over Chinese Noodle Pancake. Yield: 8 servings (233 calories per serving).

Chinese Noodle Pancake:

8 ounces fresh angel hair pasta, uncooked
1 teaspoon sesame oil
¼ teaspoon salt
Vegetable cooking spray
2 teaspoons safflower oil

Cook pasta according to package directions, omitting salt and fat; drain well. Place pasta in a large bowl; add sesame oil and salt; toss well.

Coat a 12-inch nonstick skillet with cooking spray; add safflower oil. Place over medium-high heat until hot. Add cooked pasta, and press firmly with a spatula to an even thickness. Cook, uncovered, 6 to 8 minutes; carefully turn pancake. Cook an additional 6 to 8 minutes or until pancake is golden. Cut into 8 wedges, and top with stir-fry. Yield: 8 servings.

PROTEIN 15.6 / FAT 5.0 / CARBOHYDRATE 30.6 / CHOLESTEROL 77 / IRON 2.8 / SODIUM 393 / CALCIUM 55

FETTUCCINE WITH SHRIMP AND GREEN ONION SAUCE

Vegetable cooking spray
1 tablespoon reduced-calorie margarine
1 pound medium-size fresh shrimp, peeled and deveined
1½ cups sliced green onions
½ cup canned low-sodium chicken broth, undiluted
½ cup skim milk
½ cup grated Parmesan cheese
2 tablespoons Chablis or other dry white wine
½ teaspoon ground white pepper
¼ teaspoon ground nutmeg
2 teaspoons cornstarch
2 teaspoons water
8 ounces spinach fettuccine, uncooked

Coat a large nonstick skillet with cooking spray; add margarine. Place over medium heat until margarine melts. Add shrimp, and sauté 5 minutes or until pink. Remove shrimp from skillet with a slotted spoon, and drain on paper towels; set aside.

Add green onions to skillet; sauté until tender. Add chicken broth and next 5 ingredients to skillet; stir well. Combine cornstarch and water,

and add to broth mixture; bring mixture to a boil over medium heat. Reduce heat, and simmer 5 minutes or until cheese melts and sauce is slightly thickened, stirring occasionally. Add reserved shrimp, and cook mixture until thoroughly heated.

Cook fettuccine according to package directions, omitting salt and fat; drain. Combine fettuccine and shrimp mixture; toss well. Serve immediately. Yield: 5 servings (289 calories per 1-cup serving).

PROTEIN 21.6 / FAT 7.1 / CARBOHYDRATE 36.5 / CHOLESTEROL 89 / IRON 3.5 / SODIUM 267 / CALCIUM 206

SHRIMP AND SUMMER SQUASH SAUTÉ

Vegetable cooking spray
1 teaspoon vegetable oil
2 cups sliced zucchini
2 cups sliced yellow squash
¾ cup chopped sweet red pepper
3 cloves garlic, minced
1½ pounds medium-size fresh shrimp, peeled and deveined
¼ cup Chablis or other dry white wine
2 tablespoons chopped fresh parsley
2 tablespoons lemon juice
2 teaspoons chopped fresh basil
½ teaspoon chopped fresh thyme
¼ teaspoon pepper
3 cups cooked spinach noodles (cooked without salt or fat)
3 tablespoons freshly grated Parmesan cheese

Coat a large nonstick skillet with cooking spray; add oil. Place over medium-high heat until hot. Add zucchini, yellow squash, sweet red pepper, and garlic; sauté until crisp-tender. Stir in shrimp and next 6 ingredients. Reduce heat to medium, and simmer 5 minutes or until shrimp turn pink.

To serve, place ½ cup noodles on each individual serving plate; spoon 1 cup shrimp mixture over each serving, using a slotted spoon. Sprinkle 1½ teaspoons cheese evenly over each serving. Yield: 6 servings (234 calories per serving).

PROTEIN 23.2 / FAT 4.5 / CARBOHYDRATE 25.2 / CHOLESTEROL 128 / IRON 4.7 / SODIUM 206 / CALCIUM 155

SHRIMP CREOLE

Vegetable cooking spray
½ cup chopped green pepper
½ cup chopped onion
½ cup chopped celery
2 cloves garlic, minced
2 (14½-ounce) cans no-salt-added whole tomatoes, undrained and chopped
1 (8-ounce) can no-salt-added tomato sauce
1 teaspoon sugar
½ teaspoon salt
½ teaspoon chili powder
1 tablespoon low-sodium Worcestershire sauce
½ teaspoon hot sauce
2 teaspoons cornstarch
1 tablespoon water
1½ pounds medium-size fresh shrimp, peeled and deveined
3 cups cooked long-grain rice (cooked without salt or fat)

Coat a Dutch oven with cooking spray; place over medium-high heat until hot. Add green pepper, onion, celery, and garlic; sauté 5 minutes or until vegetables are tender. Add tomato, tomato sauce, sugar, salt, chili powder, Worcestershire sauce, and hot sauce; stir well to combine. Cook, uncovered, over medium heat 15 minutes, stirring occasionally. Cover, reduce heat, and simmer 45 minutes.

Combine cornstarch and water in a small bowl, blending well; add to tomato mixture, stirring constantly. Add shrimp to mixture; simmer 5 minutes or until shrimp are done.

To serve, place ½ cup cooked rice in each individual serving bowl; spoon ¾ cup shrimp mixture over each serving. Yield: 6 servings (291 calories per serving).

PROTEIN 22.1 / FAT 1.9 / CARBOHYDRATE 45.1 / CHOLESTEROL 133 / IRON 4.0 / SODIUM 376 / CALCIUM 112

SHRIMP AND RICE BAKE

1½ pounds medium-size fresh shrimp, cooked, peeled, and deveined
Vegetable cooking spray
2 cups sliced fresh mushrooms
½ cup chopped onion
½ cup chopped green onions
3 cups cooked long-grain rice (cooked without salt or fat)
¾ cup low-fat sour cream
2 tablespoons reduced-calorie mayonnaise
2 teaspoons prepared mustard
1 cup (4 ounces) shredded 40% less-fat Cheddar cheese
1 tablespoon chopped fresh parsley

Cut shrimp in half lengthwise. Set aside. Coat a large nonstick skillet with cooking spray; place over medium-high heat until hot. Add mushrooms, onion, and green onion; sauté until tender. Set vegetables aside.

Place cooked long-grain rice in a 2-quart baking dish coated with cooking spray; arrange shrimp over rice.

Combine sour cream, mayonnaise, and mustard in a small bowl; spoon sour cream mixture over shrimp. Top with reserved mushroom mixture. Sprinkle Cheddar cheese evenly over top. Cover and bake at 350° for 30 minutes or until shrimp and rice mixture is thoroughly heated. Top with chopped parsley. Yield: 8 servings (245 calories per serving).

PROTEIN 16.0 / FAT 7.0 / CARBOHYDRATE 29.7 / CHOLESTEROL 87 / IRON 2.5 / SODIUM 130 / CALCIUM 162

Brown rice and cheese form a unique crust for Brown Rice Pizza (page 143). Sautéed garden-fresh vegetables and additional cheese adorn the top.

ANYTIME BREAKFAST BAGEL

1 cup small broccoli flowerets
½ cup frozen egg substitute with cheese, thawed
¼ cup 1% low-fat cottage cheese
¼ teaspoon pepper
Vegetable cooking spray
¼ cup (1 ounce) shredded 40% less-fat Cheddar cheese
2 (2-ounce) frozen bagels, thawed, split, and toasted

Cook broccoli in boiling water 2 to 3 minutes or until crisp-tender. Drain; rinse with cold water, and drain again. Set aside.

Combine egg substitute, cottage cheese, and pepper in a small bowl; beat well with a wire whisk. Stir in broccoli.

Coat a medium nonstick skillet with cooking spray; place over medium-high heat until hot. Pour egg mixture into skillet; sprinkle with cheese. Cook, stirring gently, until egg mixture is set. Spoon egg mixture evenly over 2 bagel halves. Top with remaining bagel halves. Serve immediately. Yield: 2 servings (299 calories per serving).

PROTEIN 20.2 / FAT 7.3 / CARBOHYDRATE 38.8 / CHOLESTEROL 11 / IRON 2.0 / SODIUM 622 / CALCIUM 155

THREE-PEPPER BURRITOS

Vegetable cooking spray
½ cup chopped onion
1 clove garlic, minced
1 cup chopped sweet red peppers
1 cup chopped sweet yellow peppers
1 jalapeño pepper, seeded and diced
1 (15-ounce) can kidney beans, rinsed and drained
½ teaspoon ground cumin
6 (6-inch) flour tortillas
1 cup chopped tomato
¾ cup (3 ounces) shredded reduced-fat Monterey Jack cheese
6 cups shredded iceberg lettuce
¼ cup plus 2 tablespoons low-fat sour cream

Coat a large nonstick skillet with cooking spray; place over medium-high heat until hot.

Add onion, garlic, and peppers; sauté until tender. Set aside.

Mash kidney beans with a potato masher; stir in cumin. Spread kidney bean mixture evenly over tortillas. Top evenly with reserved pepper mixture. Sprinkle chopped tomato over pepper mixture; top each tortilla with 2 tablespoons cheese. Roll up tortillas, and secure with wooden picks; place seam side up in an 8-inch square baking dish coated with cooking spray. Cover and bake at 350° for 20 minutes.

To serve, remove wooden picks from burritos. Place 1 cup shredded lettuce on each serving plate; place burritos on lettuce. Dollop each burrito with 1 tablespoon sour cream. Yield: 6 servings (232 calories per serving).

PROTEIN 11.3 / FAT 7.4 / CARBOHYDRATE 33.6 / CHOLESTEROL 16 / IRON 2.8 / SODIUM 94 / CALCIUM 66

CHILE-CHEESE CASSEROLE

4 (1-ounce) slices thinly sliced white bread
Vegetable cooking spray
1 cup (4 ounces) shredded reduced-fat Monterey Jack cheese
¾ cup (3 ounces) shredded 40% less-fat Cheddar cheese
2 (4-ounce) cans chopped green chiles, undrained
1½ cups frozen egg substitute, thawed
1½ cups skim milk
1 teaspoon ground oregano
1 teaspoon paprika
½ teaspoon garlic powder
½ teaspoon pepper
¼ teaspoon dry mustard

Arrange bread slices in an 8-inch square baking dish coated with cooking spray. Sprinkle cheeses evenly over bread slices. Arrange chiles on cheese layer.

Combine egg substitute and remaining ingredients in a medium bowl; beat at medium speed of an electric mixer until well blended. Slowly pour egg mixture over chiles. Cover and refrigerate 8 hours. Bake, uncovered, at 325° for 1½ hours or until top is golden and eggs are set. Yield: 6 servings (205 calories per serving).

PROTEIN 18.1 / FAT 7.0 / CARBOHYDRATE 19.5 / CHOLESTEROL 23 / IRON 2.1 / SODIUM 400 / CALCIUM 213

GREEN CHILE QUICHE

2 (4-ounce) cans whole green chiles, drained
Vegetable cooking spray
1 cup (4 ounces) shredded reduced-fat Monterey Jack cheese
1 medium-size sweet red pepper, seeded and cut into thin strips
1½ cups frozen egg substitute with cheese, thawed
1 teaspoon low-sodium Worcestershire sauce

Cut chiles down one side; remove and discard seeds, and open chiles out flat. Coat a 9-inch pieplate with cooking spray; line with green chiles to form a crust. Sprinkle cheese over chiles. Arrange pepper strips over cheese.

Combine egg substitute and Worcestershire sauce; gently pour over pepper strips. Bake at 325° for 40 minutes or until set. Let stand 10 minutes before serving. Yield: 6 servings (130 calories per serving).

PROTEIN 12.5 / FAT 7.2 / CARBOHYDRATE 3.6 / CHOLESTEROL 16 / IRON 0.3 / SODIUM 357 / CALCIUM 1

RICE CUSTARD QUICHE

4 small zucchini (about ¾ pound)
2 tablespoons water
Vegetable cooking spray
2 cups sliced fresh mushrooms
½ cup sliced green onions
½ cup minced sweet red pepper
2 cups cooked brown rice (cooked without salt or fat)
1 cup (4 ounces) shredded 40% less-fat Cheddar cheese
¾ cup frozen egg substitute, thawed
¾ cup skim milk
¼ teaspoon dried whole rosemary, crushed
¼ teaspoon salt
1 medium-size tomato, sliced

Cut zucchini into ¼-inch-thick slices. Combine zucchini and water in a medium saucepan. Bring to a boil over medium heat; cover, reduce heat, and simmer 10 minutes or until tender. Let cool 10 minutes. Drain well. Arrange zucchini slices on bottom and around sides of a 9-inch pieplate coated with cooking spray.

Coat a large nonstick skillet with cooking spray; place over medium-high heat until hot. Add mushrooms, onions, and red pepper; sauté until tender. Drain on paper towels.

Combine mushroom mixture, rice, and next 5 ingredients, stirring well; gently pour into prepared pieplate. Bake at 325° for 40 to 45 minutes or until set. Remove from oven, and arrange tomato slices on top of quiche. Let stand 10 minutes before serving. Yield: 6 servings (168 calories per serving).

PROTEIN 10.4 / FAT 3.7 / CARBOHYDRATE 26.0 / CHOLESTEROL 11 / IRON 1.9 / SODIUM 266 / CALCIUM 200

EXTRA EGGS

In 1989, the American Heart Association (AHA) upped its allowance for eggs to four per week; old standards placed the limit at three. The reason for this change is that more precise techniques have been developed for determining the cholesterol content of foods. This advanced technology has led researchers to the discovery that an egg, or more specifically the egg yolk, has 213 milligrams of cholesterol. Previous figures put that number at 274 milligrams.

Granted, 213 milligrams of cholesterol is still high when you consider that the AHA recommends no more than 300 milligrams of cholesterol per day. But there are ways to stretch that allowance. In omelets or recipes that call for two eggs, try substituting one whole egg plus two egg whites. Or use a commercial egg substitute. Although a bit higher in sodium, these substitutes for real eggs use egg whites as their main ingredient, making them low in fat and virtually cholesterol-free.

Flaky phyllo pastry encases Cheesy Broccoli-Corn Strudel, a rich-tasting meatless entrée.

CHEESY BROCCOLI-CORN STRUDEL

1 cup part-skim ricotta cheese
3 ounces Neufchâtel cheese, softened
1 (10-ounce) package frozen chopped broccoli, thawed and drained
1 cup whole kernel corn
½ cup (2 ounces) shredded fontina cheese
½ cup frozen egg substitute, thawed
¼ cup sliced green onions
1 (2-ounce) jar diced pimiento, drained
½ teaspoon dried whole basil
¼ teaspoon pepper
12 sheets commercial frozen phyllo pastry, thawed
Butter-flavored vegetable cooking spray
¼ cup toasted wheat germ
1 teaspoon reduced-calorie margarine, melted

Combine cheeses; mix well. Add broccoli and next 7 ingredients; mix well.

Place 4 sheets of phyllo pastry on wax paper (keep remaining phyllo pastry covered). Coat phyllo with cooking spray, and sprinkle with 2 tablespoons wheat germ. Top with 4 more sheets; coat with cooking spray, and sprinkle with remaining 2 tablespoons wheat germ. Top with remaining 4 phyllo sheets; coat with cooking spray.

Spoon cheese mixture lengthwise down half of phyllo stack, leaving a 1-inch margin on long side and a 1½-inch margin on short sides. Roll phyllo jellyroll fashion, starting with longest side. Tuck ends under, and place diagonally, seam side down, on a 15- x 10- x 1-inch jellyroll pan coated with cooking spray. Brush with melted margarine. Make diagonal slits about ¼-inch deep, 2 inches apart, across top of pastry, using a sharp knife. Bake at 375° for 30 minutes. Let stand 10 minutes before serving. Yield: 7 servings (279 calories per serving).

PROTEIN 15.8 / FAT 10.2 / CARBOHYDRATE 33.6 / CHOLESTEROL 30 / IRON 2.3 / SODIUM 138 / CALCIUM 185

SPAGHETTI SQUASH FLORENTINE

1 (10-ounce) package frozen chopped spinach, thawed
1 (4-pound) spaghetti squash
Vegetable cooking spray
1 cup part-skim ricotta cheese
2 eggs, beaten
½ teaspoon dried Italian seasoning
¼ teaspoon salt
2 (8-ounce) cans no-salt-added tomato sauce
¾ cup (3 ounces) shredded part-skim mozzarella cheese

Drain spinach; press between paper towels to remove excess moisture. Set aside.

Wash squash; cut in half lengthwise. Remove and discard seeds. Place squash, cut side down, in a Dutch oven; add water to Dutch oven to a depth of 2 inches. Bring to a boil; cover, reduce heat, and simmer 20 to 25 minutes or until tender. Drain squash and cool. Using a fork, remove spaghetti-like strands from squash; discard shells. Place squash strands in a 13- x 9- x 2-inch baking dish coated with cooking spray.

Combine spinach, ricotta cheese, and next 3 ingredients. Beat at medium speed of an electric mixer until blended; spread over squash. Top with tomato sauce; sprinkle with mozzarella cheese. Cover and bake at 350° for 30 minutes. Yield: 6 servings (198 calories per serving).

PROTEIN 13.4 / FAT 7.7 / CARBOHYDRATE 20.5 / CHOLESTEROL 87 / IRON 1.8 / SODIUM 319 / CALCIUM 314

CHEESY NOODLES AMANDINE

Vegetable cooking spray
½ cup chopped sweet red pepper
½ cup sliced celery
¼ cup sliced green onions
1½ cups 1% low-fat cottage cheese
½ cup skim milk
1 egg
½ teaspoon garlic powder
¼ teaspoon salt
¼ teaspoon ground white pepper
3 cups cooked medium egg noodles (cooked without salt or fat)
¼ cup freshly grated Parmesan cheese
2 tablespoons sliced almonds, toasted

Coat a nonstick skillet with cooking spray; place over medium-high heat until hot. Add red pepper, celery, and onions; sauté until tender.

Combine cottage cheese and next 5 ingredients in container of an electric blender; top with cover, and process until smooth. Combine reserved vegetables, cottage cheese mixture, and noodles. Place mixture in an 8-inch square baking dish coated with cooking spray; top with Parmesan cheese and almonds. Bake at 350° for 20 minutes or until thoroughly heated. Yield: 6 servings (201 calories per serving).

PROTEIN 14.4 / FAT 5.3 / CARBOHYDRATE 23.3 / CHOLESTEROL 64 / IRON 1.3 / SODIUM 435 / CALCIUM 142

CHEESY PASTA AND LENTILS

1½ cups dried lentils
4 (8-ounce) cans no-salt-added tomato sauce
½ cup water
1 cup chopped onion
2 cloves garlic, minced
½ teaspoon salt
¼ teaspoon pepper
1 teaspoon ground bay leaves
¼ teaspoon dried whole thyme
¼ teaspoon dried whole marjoram
1 cup thinly sliced carrot
1 cup thinly sliced celery
1 cup chopped green pepper
½ cup water
3 cups cooked gemelli pasta (cooked without salt or fat)
3 tablespoons chopped fresh parsley, divided
1 cup (4 ounces) shredded 40% less-fat Cheddar cheese

Combine first 10 ingredients in a large Dutch oven; stir well. Bring to a boil; cover, reduce heat, and cook 40 minutes. Add carrot, celery, green pepper, and ½ cup water; stir well. Cover and cook 20 to 25 minutes or until vegetables are tender. Stir in pasta and 2 tablespoons parsley. Spoon 1 cup mixture into each of 8 individual serving dishes. Sprinkle each with 2 tablespoons cheese. Sprinkle remaining 1 tablespoon parsley evenly over dishes. Yield: 8 servings (285 calories per serving).

PROTEIN 16.7 / FAT 2.8 / CARBOHYDRATE 50.9 / CHOLESTEROL 8 / IRON 4.4 / SODIUM 264 / CALCIUM 139

ITALIAN MACARONI AND CHEESE

Vegetable cooking spray
1 cup diced zucchini
½ cup chopped fresh mushrooms
¼ cup chopped onion
2 tablespoons reduced-calorie margarine
1 tablespoon all-purpose flour
1¼ cups no-salt-added tomato juice
½ teaspoon dried whole basil
½ teaspoon dried whole oregano
¼ teaspoon salt
3 cups cooked elbow macaroni (cooked without salt or fat)
1½ cups (6 ounces) shredded part-skim mozzarella cheese
1½ tablespoons grated Parmesan cheese
2 tablespoons untoasted wheat germ

Coat a small nonstick skillet with cooking spray; place over medium-high heat until hot. Add zucchini, mushrooms, and onion; sauté until tender. Remove from heat, and set aside.

Melt margarine in a small, heavy saucepan over medium heat; add flour, stirring until smooth. Cook 1 minute, stirring constantly with a wire whisk. Gradually add tomato juice, stirring constantly. Cook, stirring constantly, an additional 10 minutes or until mixture is thickened and bubbly. Stir in basil, oregano, and salt.

Combine reserved tomato juice mixture, vegetables, and macaroni; stir well. Add mozzarella cheese, and toss to combine. Pour mixture into a 2-quart casserole coated with cooking spray. Combine Parmesan cheese and wheat germ; sprinkle over macaroni mixture. Cover and bake at 350° for 20 minutes; uncover and bake an additional 10 minutes. Yield: 4 servings (280 calories per serving).

PROTEIN 16.5 / FAT 12.2 / CARBOHYDRATE 28.2 / CHOLESTEROL 26 / IRON 1.5 / SODIUM 446 / CALCIUM 324

VEGETARIAN STROGANOFF

1 cup dried lentils
3¾ cups water, divided
2 teaspoons vegetable oil
2½ cups sliced fresh mushrooms
1 cup chopped onion
3 tablespoons all-purpose flour, divided
2 teaspoons dry mustard
¼ cup Chablis or other dry white wine
1 (8-ounce) carton plain nonfat yogurt
3 cups cooked medium egg noodles (cooked without salt or fat)
¼ cup plus 2 tablespoons low-fat sour cream
1 tablespoon chopped fresh parsley

Combine lentils and 3 cups water in a Dutch oven. Bring to a boil; cover, reduce heat, and simmer 30 to 35 minutes or until tender. Drain. Set aside, and keep warm.

Heat vegetable oil in a large nonstick skillet over medium-high heat until hot. Add mushrooms and onion; sauté until tender. Combine 2 tablespoons flour and mustard; add to mushroom mixture, stirring until smooth. Cook 1 minute, stirring constantly. Gradually add remaining ¾ cup water and wine, stirring constantly. Cook over medium heat, stirring constantly, until mixture is thickened and bubbly.

Combine remaining tablespoon flour and yogurt; stir well. Add reserved lentils and yogurt mixture to mushroom mixture, stirring gently. Cook over low heat until thoroughly heated (do not boil). To serve, place ½ cup cooked noodles on each of 6 individual serving plates. Spoon ¾ cup lentil mixture over each serving. Top each serving with 1 tablespoon sour cream; sprinkle each with ½ teaspoon chopped parsley. Yield: 6 servings (296 calories per serving).

PROTEIN 16.2 / FAT 5.3 / CARBOHYDRATE 46.6 / CHOLESTEROL 31 / IRON 4.2 / SODIUM 42 / CALCIUM 127

NATURAL HIGH FROM EXERCISE

The natural "high" experienced during an intense workout may be due to biochemical changes. Endorphins, the body's natural pain killers, provide part of the clue. It is speculated that exercise "highs" may result from a chain of reactions that makes the body even more sensitive to its own natural mood changes. The downside to these findings is that during the exercise euphoria state people may become "intoxicated" with feelings of invincibility, which could lead to injury.

MEXICAN STUFFED PEPPERS

6 medium-size green peppers
1 cup cooked long-grain rice (cooked without salt or
    fat)
1 cup cooked lentils
¾ cup spicy hot vegetable juice cocktail
½ cup frozen whole kernel corn, thawed
2 tablespoons diced pimiento
½ teaspoon ground cumin
1 cup (4 ounces) shredded reduced-fat Monterey
    Jack cheese with jalapeño peppers, divided

Cut tops off peppers, and remove seeds. Cook peppers in boiling water 5 minutes. Drain and set peppers aside.

Combine rice and next 5 ingredients in a medium bowl; stir well. Stir in ½ cup cheese.

Spoon rice mixture evenly into peppers; place peppers in an 11- x 7- x 2-inch baking dish. Add hot water to pan to a depth of ½ inch. Cover and bake at 350° for 25 minutes. Sprinkle remaining ½ cup cheese over peppers; bake, uncovered, an additional 5 minutes or until cheese melts. Serve warm. Yield: 6 servings (191 calories per serving).

PROTEIN 10.9 / FAT 4.8 / CARBOHYDRATE 28.5 / CHOLESTEROL 13 / IRON 3.3 / SODIUM 218 / CALCIUM 19

HERBED BROWN RICE AND BEANS

Vegetable cooking spray
1 clove garlic, minced
2½ cups water
1 cup long-grain brown rice, uncooked
½ cup plus 1 tablespoon sliced green onions,
    divided
¼ teaspoon salt
¼ teaspoon pepper
1 (15-ounce) can black beans, rinsed and drained
1 cup chopped, seeded tomato
2 jalapeño peppers, seeded and minced
3 tablespoons chopped fresh cilantro
½ cup (2 ounces) shredded reduced-fat Monterey
    Jack cheese, divided
¼ cup plus 1 tablespoon low-fat sour cream

Coat a medium saucepan with cooking spray; place pan over medium-high heat until hot. Add garlic, and sauté 2 minutes. Add water, rice, ¼ cup green onions, salt, and pepper; stir well. Bring to a boil over medium heat; cover, reduce heat, and simmer 50 minutes or until rice is tender and liquid is absorbed.

Add beans, tomato, jalapeño pepper, cilantro, and ¼ cup plus 3 tablespoons cheese to rice. Cook over medium heat until thoroughly heated. Spoon 1 cup mixture onto each individual serving plate. Top each serving with 1 tablespoon green onions and sour cream. Sprinkle remaining 1 tablespoon cheese over servings. Yield: 5 servings (276 calories per serving).

PROTEIN 12.1 / FAT 5.8 / CARBOHYDRATE 45.3 / CHOLESTEROL 14 / IRON 2.3 / SODIUM 195 / CALCIUM 54

BROWN RICE PIZZA

1½ cups cooked brown rice (cooked without salt or
    fat)
1½ cups (6 ounces) shredded part-skim mozzarella
    cheese, divided
1 egg, beaten
1 teaspoon dried whole oregano, divided
Vegetable cooking spray
1 cup broccoli flowerets
1 cup sliced zucchini
1 cup sliced fresh mushrooms
1 small onion, sliced
1 (8-ounce) can no-salt-added tomato sauce

Combine rice, ½ cup cheese, egg, and ½ teaspoon oregano in a medium bowl; stir well. Press mixture evenly into a 12-inch pizza pan coated with cooking spray. Bake at 400° for 25 minutes.

Coat a large nonstick skillet with cooking spray; place over medium-high heat until hot. Add broccoli, zucchini, mushrooms, and onion; sauté until tender.

Combine tomato sauce and remaining ½ teaspoon oregano; spread evenly over baked crust. Top with sautéed vegetable mixture. Sprinkle with remaining 1 cup cheese. Bake at 400° for 10 minutes or until pizza is thoroughly heated and cheese is melted. Yield: 4 servings (255 calories per serving).

PROTEIN 16.0 / FAT 9.3 / CARBOHYDRATE 28.1 / CHOLESTEROL 75 / IRON 1.5 / SODIUM 238 / CALCIUM 321

TOFU PARMIGIANA

1 (10½-ounce) package firm tofu
¼ cup grated Parmesan cheese
¼ cup untoasted wheat germ
1 tablespoon plus 1 teaspoon olive oil, divided
2 (8-ounce) cans no-salt-added tomato sauce
2 teaspoons dried Italian seasoning
½ teaspoon garlic powder
1 cup (4 ounces) shredded part-skim mozzarella cheese

Wrap tofu in several layers of cheesecloth or paper towels; press lightly to remove excess moisture. Remove cheesecloth; cut tofu into ¼-inch-thick slices.

Combine Parmesan cheese and wheat germ in a shallow bowl. Dip tofu slices in Parmesan cheese mixture, pressing lightly to coat tofu.

Pour 2 teaspoons oil into a large nonstick skillet; place over medium-high heat until hot. Add tofu slices, and cook until lightly browned. Drizzle remaining 2 teaspoons oil over slices; turn and cook until lightly browned. Drain tofu slices on paper towels.

Combine tomato sauce, Italian seasoning, and garlic powder in a medium bowl. Spoon ½ cup tomato sauce mixture into a 13- x 9- x 2-inch baking pan. Arrange tofu slices over tomato sauce. Top with remaining tomato sauce, and sprinkle with shredded mozzarella cheese. Bake at 400° for 20 minutes. Serve warm. Yield: 4 servings (249 calories per serving).

PROTEIN 17.7 / FAT 14.6 / CARBOHYDRATE 15.0 / CHOLESTEROL 20 / IRON 5.0 / SODIUM 255 / CALCIUM 346

PESTO-STUFFED SHELLS

Vegetable cooking spray
1¾ cups finely chopped sweet red peppers (about 2 medium)
½ cup chopped onion
2 cloves garlic, minced
1 (14½-ounce) can no-salt-added whole tomatoes, undrained
1 (8-ounce) can no-salt-added tomato sauce
½ teaspoon dried Italian seasoning
¼ teaspoon salt
¼ teaspoon ground white pepper
12 jumbo pasta shells (4½ ounces), uncooked
½ pound firm tofu
1¼ cups part-skim ricotta cheese
¼ cup grated Parmesan cheese
½ cup minced fresh basil
½ cup minced fresh parsley

Coat a large nonstick skillet with cooking spray; place over medium-high heat until hot. Add sweet red pepper, onion, and garlic; sauté until tender.

Place sautéed vegetables and whole tomatoes in container of an electric blender or food processor; top with cover, and process until smooth. Pour mixture into a medium saucepan. Add tomato sauce, Italian seasoning, salt, and white pepper; stir well. Bring mixture to a boil; reduce heat, and simmer, uncovered, 20 minutes. Spread ½ cup tomato sauce mixture into an 11- x 7- x 2-inch baking dish coated with cooking spray; set aside. Reserve remaining tomato sauce mixture.

Cook pasta shells according to package directions, omitting salt and fat; drain and set aside.

Wrap tofu in several layers of cheesecloth or paper towels; press lightly to remove excess moisture. Remove cheesecloth; crumble tofu.

Position knife blade in food processor bowl; add tofu and remaining ingredients. Process 1 minute or until smooth. Spoon tofu mixture evenly into pasta shells, and place filled shells in prepared baking dish. Top shells evenly with remaining tomato sauce mixture. Cover and bake at 400° for 40 minutes. Yield: 6 servings (232 calories per serving).

PROTEIN 13.8 / FAT 7.1 / CARBOHYDRATE 28.8 / CHOLESTEROL 17 / IRON 3.6 / SODIUM 244 / CALCIUM 256

Pesto and a creamy double-cheese filling are combined to make Pesto-Stuffed Shells a hearty dish. Sautéed sweet red pepper, onion, garlic, and Italian seasoning add flavor to the simmered sauce.

SPICY CHILI MAC

Vegetable cooking spray
1½ cups finely chopped onion
1⅓ cups finely chopped green peppers
2 cloves garlic, minced
1 tablespoon chili powder
1 teaspoon ground cumin
½ teaspoon garlic powder
½ teaspoon crushed red pepper
1 (28-ounce) can crushed tomatoes with puree, undrained
½ pound firm tofu, drained and crumbled
2 (15-ounce) cans red kidney beans, drained
7 ounces wagon wheel pasta, uncooked
¼ cup plus 3 tablespoons (1¾ ounces) shredded 40% less-fat Cheddar cheese

Coat a Dutch oven with cooking spray; place over medium-high heat until hot. Add onion, green pepper, and garlic, and sauté vegetable mixture until tender.

Add chili powder, cumin, garlic powder, and crushed red pepper; sauté 1 minute, stirring constantly. Stir in tomato and tofu. Bring mixture to a boil; reduce heat, and simmer, uncovered, 15 minutes. Add kidney beans, and cook an additional 10 minutes or until bean mixture is thoroughly heated.

Cook pasta according to package directions, omitting salt and fat; drain.

To serve, place ½ cup pasta in each of 7 individual serving bowls, and spoon 1 cup chili over pasta. Top each serving of pasta with 1 tablespoon cheese. Yield: 7 servings (310 calories per serving).

PROTEIN 18.1 / FAT 5.4 / CARBOHYDRATE 50.5 / CHOLESTEROL 4 / IRON 7.8 / SODIUM 205 / CALCIUM 196

 GRADUAL VEGETARIAN

You don't have to love alfalfa sprouts and wheat germ to reap the health benefits of a vegetarian eating style. Meatless meals have come a long way since the crunchy granola days of the sixties and seventies. Now you can choose foods such as pasta primavera, red beans and rice, and vegetable chowder. All are tasty meals based solely on vegetables and grains—meals that glean high marks from nutritionists.

Indeed, with the focus on diet and disease, the healthful attributes of fruits, vegetables, and whole grains are becoming more apparent to scientists and nutritionists everyday. That's because these foods are naturally low in fat, high in fiber, and are rich sources of vitamins and minerals, all characteristics that health professionals recommend for healthy food choices.

Evidence is growing that people who eat more fruits, vegetables, and whole grains may be less likely to fall victim to chronic illnesses such as cancer, coronary heart disease, diabetes, high blood pressure, and obesity. The evidence is so compelling, in fact, that the National Academy of Sciences recently began advising Americans just how many fruits, vegetables, and whole grains to eat daily. The academy recommends 5 servings of fruits and vegetables and 6 servings of grains per day.

If you begin gravitating toward vegetable-rich meals, keep this point in mind. When substituting cheese and milk products for meat, stick to the low-fat varieties of these dairy foods. Heavy cheese toppings or rich creamy sauces add large amounts of saturated fat to a vegetarian meal, sometimes reducing the benefits of those vegetables.

Company Veal Roast (page 157) relies on a rolled boneless veal roast for pleasing shape and easy preparation. Served with tender cooked fruits and garnished with fresh sage, this roast makes an impressive entrée.

BROCCOLI-BEEF LASAGNA

Vegetable cooking spray
¾ pound ground chuck
1 cup chopped onion
3 cloves garlic, minced
1 (14½-ounce) can no-salt-added whole tomatoes, undrained and chopped
1 (8-ounce) can no-salt-added tomato sauce
1 (6-ounce) can no-salt-added tomato paste
1 cup thinly sliced fresh mushrooms
¼ cup chopped fresh parsley
1 tablespoon red wine vinegar
1 teaspoon dried whole oregano
1 teaspoon dried whole basil
1 bay leaf
½ teaspoon salt
½ teaspoon crushed red pepper
1½ cups part-skim ricotta cheese
1 cup (4 ounces) shredded part-skim mozzarella cheese, divided
6 cooked lasagna noodles (cooked without salt or fat)
3 cups cooked chopped broccoli, well drained
1 tablespoon grated Parmesan cheese

Coat a Dutch oven with cooking spray; place over medium-high heat until hot. Add ground chuck, chopped onion, and minced garlic; cook until meat is browned and onion is tender, stirring to crumble. Drain and pat meat mixture dry with paper towels. Wipe drippings from Dutch oven with a paper towel.

Return meat mixture to Dutch oven. Add tomatoes and next 10 ingredients. Bring to a boil; cover, reduce heat, and simmer 30 minutes, stirring occasionally. Remove and discard bay leaf. Set meat sauce aside.

Combine ricotta cheese and ½ cup mozzarella cheese in a small bowl; stir well, and set cheese mixture aside.

Coat an 11- x 7- x 2-inch baking dish with cooking spray. Place 2 lasagna noodles in bottom of dish. Top with 1 cup chopped broccoli, one-third of the meat sauce, and one-third of the cheese mixture. Repeat layers twice. Cover and bake at 350° for 25 minutes. Uncover and sprinkle with remaining ½ cup mozzarella cheese and Parmesan cheese. Bake, uncovered, an additional 10 minutes or until cheese melts. Let stand 10 minutes before serving. Yield: 8 servings (308 calories per serving).

PROTEIN 22.7 / FAT 11.8 / CARBOHYDRATE 29.2 / CHOLESTEROL 49 / IRON 2.9 / SODIUM 331 / CALCIUM 291

MEATBALLS WITH BERRY BARBECUE SAUCE

1¼ pounds ground chuck
¼ cup fine, dry breadcrumbs
1 egg, beaten
3 tablespoons minced onion
3 tablespoons minced celery
2 teaspoons prepared horseradish
¼ teaspoon salt
⅛ teaspoon pepper
Vegetable cooking spray
Berry Barbecue Sauce

Combine first 8 ingredients in a medium bowl; stir well. Shape mixture into 48 meatballs, using 1 tablespoon mixture for each meatball.

Coat a large nonstick skillet with cooking spray; place over medium-high heat until hot. Add meatballs; cook, turning occasionally, until browned. Drain and pat dry with paper towels. Wipe drippings from skillet with a paper towel.

Return meatballs to skillet; pour Berry Barbecue Sauce over meatballs. Bring to a boil; cover, reduce heat, and simmer 20 minutes. Yield: 6 servings (246 calories per serving).

Berry Barbecue Sauce:

1 (6-ounce) can no-salt-added tomato paste
½ cup cranberry juice cocktail
¼ cup water
1 tablespoon low-sodium Worcestershire sauce
1 teaspoon grated lemon rind
1 tablespoon lemon juice
⅛ teaspoon ground cloves

Combine all ingredients in a small bowl; stir well with a wire whisk. Yield: 1¼ cups.

PROTEIN 21.4 / FAT 12.6 / CARBOHYDRATE 13.0 / CHOLESTEROL 92 / IRON 2.6 / SODIUM 202 / CALCIUM 29

BEEF-STUFFED PAPAYAS

1 pound ground chuck
½ cup chopped onion
1 clove garlic, minced
½ cup shredded carrot
¼ cup finely chopped celery
2 tablespoons no-salt-added tomato sauce
¼ teaspoon salt
¼ teaspoon ground ginger
¼ teaspoon ground cumin
3 medium papayas (about 2½ pounds)
2 tablespoons grated Parmesan cheese

Combine ground chuck, onion, and garlic in a large nonstick skillet; cook over medium heat until browned, stirring to crumble. Drain and pat dry with paper towels.

Combine meat mixture, carrot, and next 5 ingredients in a medium bowl; stir well, and set mixture aside.

Cut papayas in half lengthwise; scoop out and discard seeds. (Cut a thin slice from bottom of each papaya half, if necessary, so that it will sit flat.) Spoon meat mixture evenly into papaya halves; sprinkle evenly with cheese. Arrange filled papaya halves in a 13- x 9- x 2-inch baking dish; add hot water to dish to a depth of 1 inch. Bake at 350° for 30 minutes. Serve warm. Yield: 6 servings (226 calories per serving).

PROTEIN 16.4 / FAT 10.1 / CARBOHYDRATE 18.1 / CHOLESTEROL 49 / IRON 1.5 / SODIUM 186 / CALCIUM 76

DEVILED MEAT LOAF

2 (¾-ounce) slices light oatmeal bread, cubed
¼ cup reduced-calorie catsup
1 egg, beaten
1 pound ground chuck
3 tablespoons minced onion
1 tablespoon low-sodium Worcestershire sauce
2 teaspoons prepared mustard
2 teaspoons prepared horseradish
½ teaspoon pepper
½ teaspoon garlic powder
½ teaspoon chili powder
⅛ teaspoon poultry seasoning
Vegetable cooking spray

Combine bread cubes, catsup, and egg in a large bowl; let stand 5 minutes. Add ground chuck, onion, Worcestershire sauce, mustard, horseradish, pepper, garlic powder, chili powder, and poultry seasoning; mix well. Shape into a 7- x 4- x 2-inch loaf, and place on a rack in a roasting pan coated with cooking spray. Bake at 350° for 45 to 50 minutes or until done. Let stand 5 minutes before slicing. Yield: 6 servings (183 calories per serving).

PROTEIN 16.9 / FAT 10.2 / CARBOHYDRATE 5.5 / CHOLESTEROL 80 / IRON 1.8 / SODIUM 108 / CALCIUM 14

SAUERBRATEN MEAT LOAF WITH GINGER SAUCE

1 pound ground chuck
¾ cup soft breadcrumbs
1 egg, beaten
½ cup finely chopped onion
½ cup finely chopped carrot
¼ cup water
3 tablespoons gingersnap crumbs
2 tablespoons lemon juice
¼ teaspoon salt
¼ teaspoon pepper
Vegetable cooking spray
1 cup water
2 tablespoons lemon juice
¼ cup gingersnap crumbs
2 tablespoons brown sugar
2 tablespoons raisins
1 teaspoon beef-flavored bouillon granules

Combine first 10 ingredients in a medium bowl; stir well to combine. Shape mixture into an 8- x 4-inch loaf; place on a rack in a roasting pan coated with cooking spray. Bake at 350° for 1 hour. Transfer meat loaf to a serving platter, and keep warm.

Combine 1 cup water, 2 tablespoons lemon juice, ¼ cup gingersnap crumbs, brown sugar, raisins, and bouillon granules in a small saucepan; stir well. Cook over medium heat 10 minutes or until thickened, stirring occasionally. Spoon evenly over meat loaf. Serve warm. Yield: 6 servings (268 calories per serving).

PROTEIN 18.0 / FAT 12.2 / CARBOHYDRATE 22.1 / CHOLESTEROL 84 / IRON 2.7 / SODIUM 371 / CALCIUM 46

Curried Steak and Baby Vegetable Stir-Fry takes advantage of the simplicity and speed of wok cooking for a unique approach to a beef and vegetable dish.

CURRIED STEAK AND BABY VEGETABLE STIR-FRY

1 (1-pound) lean flank steak
¼ cup dry sherry
2 tablespoons reduced-sodium soy sauce
1 teaspoon grated fresh ginger
½ teaspoon curry powder
¼ teaspoon ground coriander
¼ teaspoon dry mustard
Vegetable cooking spray
1 teaspoon vegetable oil
2 cloves garlic, minced
1 small onion, sliced
1 (8-ounce) package frozen baby corn, thawed
9 baby zucchini, halved lengthwise
3 cups cooked long-grain rice (cooked without salt or fat)
¼ cup finely chopped sweet red pepper

Partially freeze steak; trim fat from steak. Slice steak diagonally across grain into ¼-inch strips.

Combine sherry and next 5 ingredients in a small bowl; stir well, and set aside.

Coat a wok or large nonstick skillet with cooking spray; add oil. Heat at medium-high (375°) until hot. Add steak strips and garlic; stir-fry 5 minutes. Remove steak strips from wok, and set aside. Add onion, corn, and zucchini to wok; stir-fry 1 minute. Add steak strips and reserved sherry mixture; cook, stirring constantly, 4 minutes. Serve over cooked rice, and sprinkle with chopped sweet red pepper. Yield: 6 servings (310 calories per serving).

PROTEIN 20.3 / FAT 8.7 / CARBOHYDRATE 37.4 / CHOLESTEROL 38 / IRON 3.1 / SODIUM 266 / CALCIUM 25

SPINACH-STUFFED FLANK STEAK

1 (1½-pound) lean flank steak
1 (10-ounce) package frozen chopped spinach,
 thawed and drained
½ cup finely chopped carrot
¼ cup finely chopped onion
2 tablespoons fine, dry breadcrumbs
¼ teaspoon salt
¼ teaspoon ground white pepper
¼ teaspoon ground mace
⅛ teaspoon garlic powder
Vegetable cooking spray
1 teaspoon vegetable oil
½ cup water
½ cup Burgundy or other dry red wine
1 bay leaf, crumbled
½ teaspoon dried whole basil

Trim fat from steak. Cut steak lengthwise to within ½ inch of outer edge, leaving 1 long side connected; flip cut piece over to enlarge steak.

Combine spinach and next 7 ingredients in a medium bowl; stir well. Spread spinach mixture in center of meat to within 1 inch of sides. Roll up steak, jellyroll fashion, starting with long side. Secure at 2-inch intervals with string.

Coat a Dutch oven with cooking spray; add oil. Place over medium-high heat until hot. Add steak roll; cook until browned on all sides. Drain and pat dry with paper towels. Wipe drippings from pan with a paper towel.

Return steak to pan. Combine water, wine, bay leaf, and basil; pour over steak. Bring to a boil; cover, reduce heat, and simmer 1 hour to 1 hour and 15 minutes or until steak is tender. Yield: 8 servings (187 calories per serving).

PROTEIN 18.1 / FAT 10.7 / CARBOHYDRATE 4.1 / CHOLESTEROL 46 / IRON 2.7 / SODIUM 169 / CALCIUM 53

MOROCCAN BEEF

1½ pounds lean round steak
½ teaspoon ground coriander
½ teaspoon ground cumin
¼ teaspoon ground ginger
¼ teaspoon pepper
⅛ teaspoon saffron threads, crushed
Olive oil-flavored vegetable cooking spray
2 cups sliced carrot
1 medium onion, sliced
½ cup water
¼ cup lemon juice
2 tablespoons chopped fresh parsley
1 tablespoon chopped fresh mint
½ teaspoon chicken-flavored bouillon granules
2 cups cooked couscous (cooked without salt
 or fat)
Grated lemon rind (optional)
Chopped fresh parsley (optional)

Trim fat from steak; cut steak into 1-inch pieces, and place in a large shallow dish. Combine ground coriander, cumin, ginger, pepper, and crushed saffron threads in a small bowl; stir well. Sprinkle mixture evenly over steak. Cover and refrigerate 8 hours.

Coat a Dutch oven with cooking spray; place over medium-high heat until hot. Add steak and cook until browned, stirring often. Add carrot and next 6 ingredients. Bring to a boil; cover, reduce heat, and simmer 1 hour or until meat is tender. Place couscous on a serving platter. Spoon beef mixture over couscous with a slotted spoon. If desired, garnish with lemon rind and chopped fresh parsley. Yield: 6 servings (255 calories per serving).

PROTEIN 28.2 / FAT 6.0 / CARBOHYDRATE 21.0 / CHOLESTEROL 66 / IRON 3.3 / SODIUM 148 / CALCIUM 34

 ## LOOKING FOR LEAN

Now that fat is a major health issue, supermarket meat cases are filled with packages of extra-lean. When it comes to whole meats—roasts, chops, steaks—the USDA says that any meat labeled as lean must contain no more than 10 percent fat. The term extra-lean is reserved for meat with no more than 5 percent fat. However, a label saying lean or extra-lean on a package of ground meat equates to 22½ percent fat or less. This means that ground meat may contain twice as much fat as whole meat and still be called lean. Keep in mind, too, that 22½ percent fat by weight for a hamburger is 60 percent fat by calories.

Luckily, there are ways to trim the fat from ground meat. Purchase a lean cut such as top round or eye of round, and have your butcher grind it.

GARDEN BEEF ROLLS

½ pound fresh green beans, cut in half
2 medium carrots, sliced diagonally
1½ pounds lean round steak
½ teaspoon dried whole dillweed
¼ teaspoon dry mustard
¼ teaspoon salt
¼ teaspoon pepper
6 green onions, cut into 3-inch pieces
Vegetable cooking spray
1 teaspoon vegetable oil
½ cup water
2 tablespoons reduced-sodium soy sauce
1 teaspoon grated lemon rind
2 teaspoons lemon juice
Green onion fans (optional)
Carrot curls (optional)

Cook green beans and carrot in boiling water to cover 10 minutes or until crisp-tender; drain and set aside.

Trim fat from steak. Place steak between 2 sheets of heavy-duty plastic wrap, and flatten to ⅛-inch thickness, using a meat mallet or rolling pin. Cut steak into 6 equal pieces. Combine dillweed, mustard, salt, and pepper in a small bowl, stirring well; sprinkle mixture evenly over steak pieces.

Divide reserved vegetables and green onion pieces into 6 equal portions; place along short side of steak pieces. Carefully roll steak pieces, jellyroll fashion, starting at short side. Secure with wooden picks.

Coat a large nonstick skillet with cooking spray; add oil. Place over medium-high heat until hot. Add steak rolls, and brown evenly on all sides. Remove steak rolls from skillet. Drain and pat dry with paper towels. Wipe drippings from skillet with a paper towel.

Return steak rolls to skillet. Combine water, soy sauce, lemon rind, and lemon juice in a small bowl, stirring well to combine. Pour mixture over steak rolls. Bring to a boil; cover, reduce heat, and simmer 25 to 30 minutes or until meat is tender. Transfer steak rolls to a large serving platter. If desired, garnish with green onion fans and carrot curls. Yield: 6 servings (203 calories per serving).

PROTEIN 26.0 / FAT 8.0 / CARBOHYDRATE 6.3 / CHOLESTEROL 71 / IRON 3.2 / SODIUM 363 / CALCIUM 36

PEPPERY STEAK CUTLETS

1 pound lean round steak
1 teaspoon green peppercorns, crushed
Vegetable cooking spray
1 small sweet red pepper, seeded and cut into strips
1 small sweet yellow pepper, seeded and cut into strips
⅓ cup sliced green onions
½ cup canned no-salt-added beef broth, undiluted
1 jalapeño pepper, seeded and minced
2 teaspoons spicy hot brown mustard
1 tablespoon chopped fresh cilantro

Trim fat from steak; cut steak into 4 equal pieces. Place steak between 2 sheets of heavy-duty plastic wrap, and flatten to ¼-inch thickness, using a meat mallet or rolling pin. Sprinkle steak with crushed peppercorns.

Coat a large nonstick skillet with cooking spray; place over medium-high heat until hot. Add steak, and cook 1 minute on each side or until browned. Remove steak from skillet. Drain and pat dry with paper towels. Wipe drippings from skillet with a paper towel.

Coat skillet with cooking spray, and place over medium-high heat until hot. Add pepper strips and green onions; sauté until crisp-tender. Stir in broth, jalapeño pepper, and mustard. Return steak to skillet; cover, reduce heat, and simmer 6 minutes. Transfer to a serving platter, using a slotted spoon; sprinkle with cilantro. Yield: 4 servings (183 calories per serving).

PROTEIN 24.1 / FAT 7.3 / CARBOHYDRATE 3.9 / CHOLESTEROL 67 / IRON 3.1 / SODIUM 80 / CALCIUM 14

BEEF LIVER STROGANOFF

1 pound thinly sliced beef liver
Vegetable cooking spray
1 medium onion, thinly sliced
1 cup sliced fresh mushrooms
½ cup chopped sweet red pepper
½ cup water
2 tablespoons dry sherry
½ teaspoon beef-flavored bouillon granules
½ cup plain nonfat yogurt
1 tablespoon all-purpose flour
2 cups cooked medium egg noodles (cooked without salt or fat)

Partially freeze liver; cut into ½-inch strips. Coat a large nonstick skillet with cooking spray; place over medium-high heat until hot. Add liver strips; cook 2 minutes on each side or until browned. Remove liver from skillet. Drain and pat dry with paper towels. Set liver aside. Wipe drippings from skillet with a paper towel.

Coat skillet with cooking spray, and place over medium-high heat until hot. Add onion, mushrooms, and red pepper; sauté until tender. Combine water, sherry, and bouillon granules; stirring until granules dissolve. Pour over vegetables. Return liver to skillet; cover and simmer 5 minutes. Remove from heat.

Combine yogurt and flour; pour over liver mixture. Cook over low heat 1 minute, stirring constantly. Serve over cooked noodles. Yield: 4 servings (284 calories per serving).

PROTEIN 26.5 / FAT 6.0 / CARBOHYDRATE 29.8 / CHOLESTEROL 352 / IRON 7.1 / SODIUM 203 / CALCIUM 82

SPICY HOT GRILLED SIRLOIN

1 (1-pound) lean boneless beef sirloin steak
½ cup finely chopped onion
¼ cup chopped fresh cilantro
1 tablespoon sugar
½ cup unsweetened pineapple juice
½ cup lime juice
2 tablespoons reduced-sodium soy sauce
3 serrano chiles, seeded and sliced
3 cloves garlic, minced
Vegetable cooking spray

Trim fat from steak. Place in a large shallow dish. Combine onion and next 7 ingredients in container of an electric blender; top with cover, and process until smooth. Reserve ½ cup juice mixture; cover and chill. Pour remaining juice mixture over steak; cover and marinate in refrigerator 8 hours, turning occasionally.

Remove steak from marinade; discard marinade. Coat grill rack with cooking spray; place on grill over medium-hot coals. Place steak on rack, and cook 6 to 7 minutes on each side or to desired degree of doneness, basting frequently with reserved ½ cup juice mixture. Slice steak diagonally across grain into thin slices. Yield: 4 servings (217 calories per serving).

PROTEIN 26.7 / FAT 7.7 / CARBOHYDRATE 9.6 / CHOLESTEROL 76 / IRON 3.4 / SODIUM 260 / CALCIUM 26

ROAST BEEF WITH FRESH HERB SAUCE

1 (3-pound) beef eye-of-round roast
½ teaspoon dried whole marjoram
¼ teaspoon dried whole thyme
¼ teaspoon pepper
⅛ teaspoon garlic powder
Vegetable cooking spray
2 cups water
1 teaspoon vegetable oil
½ cup finely chopped onion
½ cup finely chopped celery
2 cloves garlic, minced
1 (4-ounce) jar sliced pimiento, undrained
¼ cup red wine vinegar
¼ cup chopped fresh chives
3 tablespoons chopped fresh parsley
1 tablespoon chopped fresh sage
¼ teaspoon salt
¼ teaspoon pepper
Fresh parsley sprigs (optional)
Fresh sage sprigs (optional)

Trim fat from roast. Combine marjoram, thyme, ¼ teaspoon pepper, and garlic powder in a small bowl; rub mixture over entire surface of roast.

Place roast on rack of a broiler pan coated with cooking spray. Insert meat thermometer into thickest part of roast, if desired. Pour water into broiler pan. Cover roast with aluminum foil, and bake at 450° for 20 minutes. Uncover roast, and bake an additional 1 to 1½ hours or until meat thermometer registers 140° (rare) or 160° (medium).

Let roast stand 15 minutes; slice diagonally across grain into thin slices. Transfer roast to a large serving platter, and keep warm.

Heat vegetable oil in a small saucepan over medium-high heat until hot. Add chopped onion, chopped celery, and minced garlic; sauté until tender. Add pimiento, vinegar, chopped chives, chopped parsley, and sage, stirring well to combine. Add salt and pepper; stir well. Cook 2 to 3 minutes or until thoroughly heated.

Spoon herb sauce evenly over each serving of roast. If desired, garnish roast with fresh parsley sprigs and fresh sage sprigs. Yield: 12 servings (162 calories per serving).

PROTEIN 24.0 / FAT 5.9 / CARBOHYDRATE 1.6 / CHOLESTEROL 56 / IRON 2.0 / SODIUM 108 / CALCIUM 14

SANTA FE POT ROAST

2 medium onions, cut into ¼-inch slices
1 tablespoon chili powder
1 teaspoon sugar
1 teaspoon ground cumin
½ teaspoon salt
¼ teaspoon ground red pepper
1 (4-pound) lean boneless round roast
Vegetable cooking spray
¾ cup water
¼ cup Burgundy or other dry red wine
3 tablespoons chopped fresh parsley
2½ cups peeled, seeded, and chopped tomato

Place onion slices in a small bowl. Combine chili powder and next 4 ingredients; sprinkle over onion slices, and toss to coat evenly. Let stand 30 minutes.

Trim fat from roast. Coat a Dutch oven with cooking spray; place over medium-high heat until hot. Add roast; cook until browned on all sides. Combine water, wine, and parsley; stir well. Pour over roast. Cover, reduce heat, and simmer 2 to 2½ hours or until roast is tender. Add chopped tomato, and cook an additional 15 minutes. Yield: 16 servings (149 calories per serving).

PROTEIN 23.5 / FAT 4.3 / CARBOHYDRATE 2.8 / CHOLESTEROL 58 / IRON 2.5 / SODIUM 132 / CALCIUM 14

RATATOUILLE-TOPPED VEAL PATTIES

2 pounds ground veal
¾ teaspoon dried whole oregano
¼ teaspoon pepper
¼ teaspoon dried whole thyme
Vegetable cooking spray
2 teaspoons olive oil
5½ cups cubed eggplant (about 1 medium)
2 medium zucchini, cut into ½-inch slices
2 cups peeled, chopped tomato
1 medium-size yellow squash, cut into ½-inch slices
1 medium-size green pepper, seeded and cut into strips
1 small onion, sliced
¼ cup minced fresh parsley
½ teaspoon dried whole basil
¼ teaspoon salt
¼ teaspoon pepper

Combine veal, oregano, ¼ teaspoon pepper, and thyme in a medium bowl; stir well. Shape mixture into 8 (¾-inch-thick) patties.

Coat a large nonstick skillet with cooking spray; place over medium-high heat until hot. Add patties; cook 5 minutes on each side or to desired degree of doneness. Remove patties from skillet. Drain and pat dry with paper towels. Set aside, and keep warm. Wipe drippings from skillet with a paper towel.

Add oil to skillet; place over medium-high heat until hot. Add eggplant and remaining ingredients; cover, reduce heat, and simmer 20 minutes, stirring occasionally. Uncover and cook an additional 5 minutes. Transfer veal patties to a serving platter, and spoon vegetable mixture evenly over patties. Yield: 8 servings (216 calories per serving).

PROTEIN 29.1 / FAT 7.2 / CARBOHYDRATE 8.7 / CHOLESTEROL 100 / IRON 2.2 / SODIUM 155 / CALCIUM 63

SAVORY HERBED VEAL

1 pound lean boneless veal
Vegetable cooking spray
1 small onion, sliced
½ cup diced carrot
1 clove garlic, minced
½ cup water
¼ cup Chablis or other dry white wine
1 teaspoon grated lemon rind
2 tablespoons lemon juice
1 teaspoon fennel seeds
1 teaspoon dried whole rosemary
½ teaspoon dried whole thyme
½ teaspoon chicken-flavored bouillon granules
¼ teaspoon ground white pepper

Trim fat from veal; cut into ½-inch cubes. Coat a large nonstick skillet with cooking spray; place over medium-high heat until hot. Add veal, and sauté until browned, stirring often. Remove veal from skillet with a slotted spoon. Drain and pat dry with paper towels. Wipe drippings from skillet with a paper towel.

Coat skillet with cooking spray, and place over medium-high heat until hot. Add onion, carrot, and garlic; sauté until crisp-tender.

Return veal to skillet. Add water and remaining ingredients, stirring well. Bring to a boil;

cover, reduce heat, and simmer 15 minutes or until veal is tender. Yield: 4 servings (164 calories per serving).

PROTEIN 20.8 / FAT 6.4 / CARBOHYDRATE 5.4 / CHOLESTEROL 90 / IRON 1.4 / SODIUM 186 / CALCIUM 37

GARLIC POINTERS

No matter whether it's sliced, chopped, minced, or mashed, garlic adds a distinct flavor to foods. The strength and flavor depends on how it's used and prepared. Garlic yields the most intense flavor when the cloves are pressed or minced, because juice and flavoring oils are allowed to escape. If the cloves are left whole or are cut into large pieces, the flavor will be milder. According to the Fresh Garlic Association, whole cloves cooked for a long time (baked with chicken or roasts or simmered in stews) develop a sweet, nut-like flavor.

VEAL CUTLETS MONTEREY

1 pound veal cutlets (¼-inch thick)
2 tablespoons all-purpose flour
¼ teaspoon salt
¼ teaspoon lemon-pepper seasoning
Vegetable cooking spray
1 teaspoon vegetable oil
3 tablespoons lemon juice
1 tablespoon water
1 teaspoon sugar
½ teaspoon grated lemon rind
¼ medium avocado, peeled
1 small tomato, cut into 4 slices
¼ cup (2 ounces) shredded reduced-fat Monterey
   Jack cheese with jalapeño pepper

Trim fat from cutlets. Place between 2 sheets of heavy-duty plastic wrap, and flatten to ⅛-inch thickness, using a meat mallet or rolling pin. Combine flour, salt, and lemon-pepper seasoning; stir well. Dredge cutlets in flour mixture.

Coat a large nonstick skillet with cooking spray; add oil. Place over medium-high heat until hot. Add cutlets; cook 2 minutes on each side or until browned. Remove cutlets from skillet. Drain and pat dry with paper towels. Wipe drippings from skillet with a paper towel.

Return cutlets to skillet. Combine lemon juice and next 3 ingredients, stirring well. Pour lemon juice mixture over cutlets. Cover and simmer 5 minutes. Cut avocado into 8 thin slices; top each cutlet with 1 tomato slice, 2 avocado slices, and 1 tablespoon cheese. Cover and cook until thoroughly heated and cheese is melted. Yield: 4 servings (281 calories per serving).

PROTEIN 26.0 / FAT 16.7 / CARBOHYDRATE 7.0 / CHOLESTEROL 98 / IRON 1.2 / SODIUM 331 / CALCIUM 22

VEAL WITH SPIKED APPLE WEDGES

1 pound veal cutlets (¼-inch thick)
3 tablespoons all-purpose flour, divided
¼ teaspoon rubbed sage
¼ teaspoon pepper
Vegetable cooking spray
2 teaspoons reduced-calorie margarine
¼ cup water
¼ cup canned no-salt-added chicken broth,
   undiluted
¼ cup applejack
1 small onion, sliced
1 teaspoon grated lemon rind
1 teaspoon minced fresh thyme
1 small apple, cut into thin wedges
Fresh thyme sprigs (optional)

Trim fat from cutlets. Place between 2 sheets of heavy-duty plastic wrap, and flatten to ⅛-inch thickness, using a meat mallet or rolling pin. Combine 2 tablespoons flour, sage, and pepper; stir well. Dredge cutlets in flour mixture.

Coat a large nonstick skillet with cooking spray; add margarine. Place over medium heat until margarine melts. Add cutlets; cook 4 minutes on each side or until browned. Remove cutlets from skillet. Drain and pat dry with paper towels. Set aside, and keep warm. Wipe drippings from skillet with a paper towel.

Combine remaining 1 tablespoon flour, water, and next 5 ingredients in skillet, stirring well; cook over medium heat until thickened, stirring constantly. Add veal and apple wedges; cover and cook until thoroughly heated. Garnish with fresh thyme sprigs, if desired. Yield: 4 servings (245 calories per serving).

PROTEIN 22.0 / FAT 12.3 / CARBOHYDRATE 10.6 / CHOLESTEROL 88 / IRON 1.3 / SODIUM 107 / CALCIUM 27

Hearty Veal Shanks à la Française has a robust flavor. Tomatoes, ripe olives, orange rind, and tarragon complement this entrée.

VEAL SHANKS À LA FRANÇAISE

4 (5-ounce) veal shanks
Vegetable cooking spray
1 (14½-ounce) can no-salt-added whole tomatoes, undrained and chopped
¼ cup Chablis or other dry white wine
¼ cup sliced ripe olives
1 tablespoon grated orange rind
2 teaspoons dried whole tarragon
¼ teaspoon salt
¼ teaspoon pepper
Minced fresh parsley (optional)

Trim fat from shanks. Coat a large nonstick skillet with cooking spray; place over medium-high heat until hot. Add shanks, and cook 3 minutes on each side or until browned. Transfer shanks to an ungreased 2-quart casserole. Combine tomato and next 6 ingredients in a medium bowl; pour over shanks. Cover and bake at 325° for 1½ hours or until shanks are tender. Transfer to a serving platter with a slotted spoon. Garnish with minced fresh parsley, if desired. Yield: 4 servings (175 calories per serving).

PROTEIN 22.1 / FAT 7.0 / CARBOHYDRATE 5.9 / CHOLESTEROL 94 / IRON 1.6 / SODIUM 302 / CALCIUM 58

VEAL CHOPS VERMOUTH

4 (6-ounce) loin veal chops (¾-inch thick)
¼ teaspoon garlic powder
¼ teaspoon dried whole dillweed
¼ teaspoon pepper
Vegetable cooking spray
1 teaspoon vegetable oil
1 small onion, sliced
1 small green pepper, seeded and cut into strips
¼ cup dry vermouth
1 tablespoon water
1 tablespoon lemon juice

Trim fat from veal chops. Combine garlic powder, dillweed, and pepper in a small bowl; sprinkle mixture over veal chops.

Coat a large nonstick skillet with cooking spray; add oil. Place over medium-high heat until hot. Add veal chops, and cook 3 to 4 minutes on each side or until browned. Remove veal chops from skillet. Drain veal chops and pat dry with paper towels. Wipe drippings from skillet with a paper towel.

Return veal chops to skillet; add onion and green pepper. Combine vermouth and remaining ingredients; pour over veal chops. Bring to a boil; cover, reduce heat, and simmer 20 to 25 minutes or until veal is tender. Yield: 4 servings (208 calories per serving).

PROTEIN 26.8 / FAT 8.6 / CARBOHYDRATE 4.7 / CHOLESTEROL 97 / IRON 1.5 / SODIUM 69 / CALCIUM 36

 ### BEING A DIET BUDDY

Helping a friend or family member lose weight can be tricky. Every dieter wants some encouragement and support, but there is a fine line between being a nag and being helpful. Follow these tips to ensure that you are on the right track to being a weight loss buddy.
• Make sure the dieter knows that you care about him or her, whether fat or thin. Don't base respect and friendship on weight loss.
• Give praise for any accomplishment, no matter how minuscule. Positive reinforcement keeps the dieter going in the right direction.
• Share activities with the dieter that don't revolve around food: walking, gardening, or going to the theater, for example.

COMPANY VEAL ROAST

1 (3½-pound) boneless rolled veal rump roast
8 fresh sage leaves, minced
¼ teaspoon garlic powder
¼ teaspoon ground white pepper
¼ teaspoon dried whole thyme
Vegetable cooking spray
½ cup pitted dried prunes
½ cup dried apricots
¾ cup tawny port
¼ cup water
2 teaspoons grated orange rind
Fresh sage sprigs (optional)
Orange zest (optional)

Unroll roast, and trim excess fat from roast. Combine sage and next 3 ingredients; sprinkle sage mixture over roast. Reroll roast, and tie securely with string.

Coat a large ovenproof Dutch oven with cooking spray; place over medium-high heat until hot. Add roast, and cook until browned on all sides, turning occasionally. Arrange prunes and apricots around roast.

Combine port, water, and 2 teaspoons orange rind; pour over roast. Cover and bake at 325° for 1 hour and 15 minutes, basting frequently with pan juices. Remove roast from oven; let stand 5 minutes. Transfer roast to a serving platter, and remove string; arrange fruit around roast. If desired, garnish veal roast with fresh sage sprigs and orange zest. Yield: 14 servings (134 calories per serving).

PROTEIN 18.3 / FAT 2.9 / CARBOHYDRATE 8.4 / CHOLESTEROL 66 / IRON 1.2 / SODIUM 59 / CALCIUM 13

GRECIAN LAMB CASSEROLE

1 pound lean ground lamb
1 cup chopped onion
1 clove garlic, minced
Olive oil-flavored vegetable cooking spray
5 medium zucchini, sliced into ¼-inch-thick slices
1 egg, beaten
¼ cup no-salt-added tomato sauce
½ teaspoon dried whole oregano
½ teaspoon dried whole marjoram
¼ teaspoon dried whole basil
¼ teaspoon pepper
2½ cups seeded, chopped tomato (about 3 medium)
1 cup soft breadcrumbs
¼ cup grated Parmesan cheese

Combine lamb, onion, and garlic in a large nonstick skillet; cook over medium heat until browned, stirring to crumble. Drain and pat dry with paper towels. Wipe drippings from skillet with a paper towel.

Coat skillet with cooking spray, and place over medium-high heat until hot. Add zucchini, and sauté until crisp-tender; set aside.

Combine lamb mixture, egg, and next 5 ingredients; stir well. Spoon half of zucchini into a 13- x 9- x 2-inch baking dish; top with lamb mixture, chopped tomato, and remaining zucchini. Combine breadcrumbs and Parmesan cheese, stirring well; sprinkle breadcrumb mixture over zucchini. Bake at 350° for 35 to 45 minutes or until lightly browned. Yield: 7 servings (181 calories per serving).

PROTEIN 19.0 / FAT 6.9 / CARBOHYDRATE 11.0 / CHOLESTEROL 77 / IRON 2.0 / SODIUM 153 / CALCIUM 81

Savory Lamb Ragout may be low in fat, but it's not lacking in flavor.

SAVORY LAMB RAGOUT

1½ pounds lean boneless lamb
Vegetable cooking spray
1 large onion, sliced
2 cloves garlic, minced
1 (14½-ounce) can no-salt-added whole tomatoes, undrained and chopped
1 cup thinly sliced carrot
⅓ cup Chablis or other dry white wine
1 teaspoon minced fresh rosemary
1 bay leaf
½ teaspoon dried whole thyme
½ teaspoon chicken-flavored bouillon granules
2 cups cubed yellow squash (about 2 medium)
1 (9-ounce) package frozen artichoke hearts, thawed
1 cup sliced fresh mushrooms
4 cups cooked medium egg noodles (cooked without salt or fat)
Chopped fresh parsley (optional)
Fresh rosemary sprigs (optional)

Cut lamb into ½-inch cubes. Coat a Dutch oven with cooking spray; place over medium-high heat until hot. Add lamb, onion, and garlic; cook 8 minutes or until lamb is lightly browned on all sides. Drain and pat dry with paper towels. Wipe drippings from Dutch oven with a paper towel.

Return lamb mixture to Dutch oven. Add tomato and next 6 ingredients. Bring mixture to a boil over medium heat; cover, reduce heat, and simmer 20 minutes or until lamb is tender.

Stir in yellow squash, artichoke hearts, and sliced mushrooms; cook 10 to 12 minutes or until vegetables are tender. Remove and discard bay leaf. Serve lamb ragout over cooked noodles. If desired, garnish with chopped fresh parsley and fresh rosemary sprigs. Yield: 8 servings (292 calories per serving).

PROTEIN 25.2 / FAT 7.8 / CARBOHYDRATE 30.2 / CHOLESTEROL 87 / IRON 3.5 / SODIUM 140 / CALCIUM 66

GRILLED LAMB CHOPS PROVENCE

6 (6-ounce) lean lamb loin chops (1-inch thick)
2 cloves garlic, crushed
1 teaspoon dried whole rosemary, crushed
1 teaspoon dried whole thyme
1 teaspoon dried whole basil
½ teaspoon pepper
Vegetable cooking spray

Trim fat from chops. Combine garlic and next 4 ingredients; stir well. Rub chops with garlic mixture; place chops in a shallow dish. Cover and refrigerate 1 hour.

Coat grill rack with cooking spray; place on grill over medium-hot coals. Place chops on rack, and cook 7 minutes on each side or to desired degree of doneness. Yield: 6 servings (188 calories per serving).

PROTEIN 25.6 / FAT 8.4 / CARBOHYDRATE 0.8 / CHOLESTEROL 81 / IRON 2.2 / SODIUM 72 / CALCIUM 29

LAMB CHOPS WITH SWEET PEPPER SAUCE

4 (6-ounce) lean lamb loin chops (1-inch thick)
Vegetable cooking spray
½ teaspoon dried whole basil
¼ teaspoon salt
¼ teaspoon pepper
⅛ teaspoon garlic powder
¼ cup chopped sweet red pepper
¼ cup chopped sweet yellow pepper
2 tablespoons sliced ripe olives
¼ cup plain nonfat yogurt
¼ cup low-fat sour cream
Sweet red pepper rings (optional)
Sweet yellow pepper rings (optional)

Trim fat from chops. Coat a large nonstick skillet with cooking spray; place over medium-high heat until hot. Add chops, and cook 4 minutes on each side or until browned. Combine basil and next 3 ingredients; sprinkle basil mixture over chops. Reduce heat to medium-low; cook, uncovered, 5 minutes on each side or to desired degree of doneness. Transfer chops to a serving platter, and keep warm. Wipe drippings from skillet with a paper towel.

Coat skillet with cooking spray, and place over medium-high heat until hot. Add chopped red and yellow peppers; sauté until crisp-tender. Stir in olives, and remove mixture from heat.

Combine yogurt and sour cream in a small bowl; add pepper mixture, and stir well. Spoon pepper sauce over chops. If desired, garnish with red and yellow pepper rings. Yield: 4 servings (229 calories per serving).

PROTEIN 27.0 / FAT 11.3 / CARBOHYDRATE 3.4 / CHOLESTEROL 87 / IRON 2.3 / SODIUM 297 / CALCIUM 72

LAMB CHOPS WITH HERBED CITRUS SAUCE

6 (6-ounce) lean lamb loin chops (1-inch thick)
½ cup dry vermouth
¼ cup chopped fresh parsley
1 tablespoon chopped fresh basil
2 teaspoons grated lemon rind
1 teaspoon grated orange rind
¼ teaspoon ground white pepper
⅛ teaspoon garlic powder
Vegetable cooking spray
Lemon or orange wedges (optional)
Fresh basil sprigs (optional)

Trim fat from chops. Place chops in a large shallow dish. Combine vermouth and next 6 ingredients; stir well. Pour vermouth mixture over chops. Cover and marinate in refrigerator 8 hours, turning occasionally.

Remove chops from marinade, reserving marinade. Coat a large nonstick skillet with cooking spray; place over medium-high heat until hot. Add chops, and cook 4 minutes on each side or until browned. Remove chops from skillet. Drain and pat dry with paper towels. Wipe drippings from skillet with a paper towel.

Return chops to skillet; pour reserved marinade over chops. Bring mixture to a boil over medium heat; cover, reduce heat, and simmer 20 minutes or until chops are tender. Transfer chops to a serving platter with a slotted spoon. If desired, garnish with lemon or orange wedges and fresh basil sprigs. Yield: 6 servings (190 calories per serving).

PROTEIN 25.6 / FAT 8.4 / CARBOHYDRATE 1.3 / CHOLESTEROL 81 / IRON 2.0 / SODIUM 75 / CALCIUM 24

ROAST LAMB WITH FRUITED RICE STUFFING

1 (3½-pound) lean boneless leg of lamb
½ teaspoon ground cinnamon
½ teaspoon ground coriander
¼ teaspoon ground red pepper
2 cups cooked long-grain rice (cooked without salt or fat)
1 cup pitted whole dates, chopped
½ cup finely chopped green onions
½ cup unsweetened orange juice
¼ cup chopped pecans, toasted
1 tablespoon honey
2 teaspoons grated orange rind
1 teaspoon grated lemon rind
Vegetable cooking spray
½ cup water

Trim fat from lamb; place lamb on heavy-duty plastic wrap with boned side of lamb facing up. Starting from center, slice horizontally through thickest part of lamb almost to, but not through, the outer edge. Flip cut piece over to enlarge leg. Place lamb between 2 sheets of heavy-duty plastic wrap, and flatten to an even thickness, using a meat mallet or rolling pin. Combine cinnamon, coriander, and red pepper. Rub spice mixture over entire surface of lamb.

Combine rice, chopped dates, green onions, orange juice, and pecans in a medium bowl; stir well. Add honey, orange rind, and lemon rind, stirring well. Spread rice mixture over lamb to within 2 inches of sides; roll up lamb, jellyroll fashion, starting with short end. Secure at 2-inch intervals with heavy string. Place seam side down on a rack in a shallow roasting pan coated with cooking spray. Insert meat thermometer into thickest part of lamb, if desired. Pour water into pan. Bake at 325° for 2 hours or until meat thermometer registers 140° (rare) or 160° (medium). Transfer lamb to a serving platter. Let stand 15 minutes; remove string, and slice into ½-inch-thick slices. Yield: 14 servings (230 calories per serving).

PROTEIN 22.4 / FAT 7.2 / CARBOHYDRATE 18.3 / CHOLESTEROL 66 / IRON 2.2 / SODIUM 52 / CALCIUM 18

PORK AND VEGETABLE STIR-FRY

1 pound lean boneless pork loin
½ teaspoon dried whole tarragon
½ teaspoon lemon-pepper seasoning
¼ teaspoon salt
⅛ teaspoon garlic powder
1½ teaspoons cornstarch
¼ cup water
¼ cup Chablis or other dry white wine
3 tablespoons lemon juice
1 teaspoon sugar
Vegetable cooking spray
1½ cups sliced carrot
1¼ cups cubed turnips
1 leek, cut into ½-inch pieces
1¼ cups sliced celery
3 cups cooked long-grain rice (cooked without salt or fat)

Partially freeze pork; trim fat, and slice pork diagonally across grain into 2- x ¼-inch strips.
Combine tarragon, lemon-pepper seasoning, salt, and garlic powder; sprinkle mixture evenly over pork strips, tossing gently to coat. Set pork strips aside.

Combine cornstarch, water, Chablis, lemon juice, and sugar in a small bowl; stir well. Set mixture aside.

Coat a large nonstick skillet or wok with cooking spray; place over medium-high heat until hot. Add pork; stir-fry 5 to 7 minutes or until browned. Remove pork from skillet. Drain and pat dry with paper towels; set aside. Wipe drippings from skillet with a paper towel.

Coat skillet with cooking spray. Add sliced carrot and turnips; stir-fry 5 to 7 minutes or until vegetables are crisp-tender. Add leek and celery; stir-fry 3 minutes. Add pork and reserved cornstarch mixture to skillet; bring mixture to a boil. Cook, stirring constantly, until thickened. Serve over cooked rice. Yield: 6 servings (277 calories per serving).

PROTEIN 18.1 / FAT 2.9 / CARBOHYDRATE 43.6 / CHOLESTEROL 46 / IRON 2.9 / SODIUM 221 / CALCIUM 61

PORK AND GINGERED VEGETABLES

1½ pounds lean boneless pork loin
Vegetable cooking spray
2 cups sliced carrot
1 cup unsweetened orange juice
½ cup water
2 cups sliced celery
1 medium onion, sliced
2 tablespoons chopped fresh mint
2 teaspoons minced fresh ginger
¼ teaspoon salt
¼ teaspoon ground white pepper
1½ teaspoons cornstarch
2 tablespoons water

Trim fat from pork; cut pork into ½-inch cubes. Coat a large nonstick skillet with cooking spray; place over medium-high heat until hot. Add pork cubes, and cook 10 minutes or until pork is browned, stirring frequently. Remove pork cubes from skillet. Drain pork cubes, and pat dry with paper towels. Wipe drippings from skillet with a paper towel.

Combine carrot, orange juice, and ½ cup water in skillet; cook over medium-high heat 5 minutes. Add pork, celery, and next 5 ingredients; stir well. Bring to a boil; cover, reduce heat, and simmer 30 to 35 minutes or until pork and vegetables are tender.

Transfer pork and vegetables to a serving platter with a slotted spoon; reserve orange juice mixture. Combine cornstarch and 2 tablespoons water, stirring until blended; add to orange juice mixture. Cook, stirring constantly, until slightly thickened. Spoon over pork and vegetables. Yield: 6 servings (164 calories per serving).

PROTEIN 19.2 / FAT 3.3 / CARBOHYDRATE 14.1 / CHOLESTEROL 57 / IRON 1.6 / SODIUM 195 / CALCIUM 50

GRILLED PORK CHOPS WITH SWEET AND TANGY TOPPING

4 (6-ounce) lean center-cut loin pork chops (½-inch thick)
¼ teaspoon ground coriander
¼ teaspoon pepper
⅛ teaspoon garlic powder
Vegetable cooking spray
¼ cup finely chopped onion
¼ cup commercial reduced-calorie Catalina dressing
¼ cup low-fat sour cream
1 tablespoon no-sugar-added apricot spread
1 teaspoon low-sugar orange marmalade
1 teaspoon grated lime rind

Trim fat from pork chops. Combine coriander, pepper, and garlic powder in a small bowl; sprinkle mixture evenly over pork chops. Coat grill rack with cooking spray, and place on grill over medium-hot coals. Place pork chops on rack, and cook 15 to 20 minutes or until tender, turning pork chops frequently.

Coat a small saucepan with cooking spray; place over medium heat until hot. Add onion, and sauté until tender. Add Catalina dressing and remaining ingredients; stir well. Reduce heat, and cook until thoroughly heated. Spoon 3 tablespoons dressing mixture over each chop. Yield: 4 servings (259 calories per serving).

PROTEIN 24.7 / FAT 13.6 / CARBOHYDRATE 8.1 / CHOLESTEROL 83 / IRON 1.0 / SODIUM 190 / CALCIUM 26

POSITIVE ABOUT PORK

Over the past few years, new feeding and breeding methods have changed the fat content of pork. While some cuts of meat are still high in fat (spareribs, Boston blade, and loin blade roast, for example), others are now considered lean.

Pork tenderloin compares nutritionally with a skinned chicken breast. A 3-ounce serving of pork tenderloin contains just 141 calories, less than 5 grams of fat, and only 79 milligrams of cholesterol.

On a comparable level with lean beef are center loin and rump roast cuts. However, when shopping for pork, follow the same rules as when shopping for other meats: choose lean cuts, keep marbling to a minimum, and trim excess fat.

A ribbon of colorful vegetables and herbs runs through Confetti-Stuffed Pork Roast.

TROPICAL CURRIED PORK CHOPS

4 (6-ounce) lean center-cut loin pork chops (½-inch thick)
½ teaspoon curry powder
¼ teaspoon ground ginger
⅛ teaspoon garlic powder
Vegetable cooking spray
1 small onion, sliced
¼ cup lime juice
2 tablespoons Dijon mustard
1 tablespoon honey
1 cup peeled, cubed mango

Trim fat from chops. Combine curry powder, ginger, and garlic powder; rub chops with curry mixture.

Coat a large nonstick skillet with cooking spray; place over medium-high heat until hot. Add chops, and cook 3 minutes on each side or until browned. Remove chops from skillet. Drain and pat dry with paper towels. Wipe drippings from skillet with a paper towel.

Return chops to skillet; add onion slices. Combine lime juice, mustard, and honey; pour lime juice mixture over chops. Bring to a boil; cover, reduce heat, and simmer 15 to 20 minutes or until pork chops are tender. Add mango, and cook until heated. Serve immediately. Yield: 4 servings (266 calories per serving).

PROTEIN 24.7 / FAT 11.9 / CARBOHYDRATE 14.3 / CHOLESTEROL 77 / IRON 1.2 / SODIUM 283 / CALCIUM 18

CONFETTI-STUFFED PORK ROAST

Vegetable cooking spray
½ cup shredded carrot
½ cup shredded zucchini
½ cup diced sweet red pepper
¼ cup finely chopped onion
1 clove garlic, minced
2 tablespoons chopped fresh parsley
2 tablespoons Chablis or other dry white wine
1 (2½-pound) lean boneless double pork loin roast, tied
½ teaspoon dried whole basil
¼ teaspoon dried whole thyme
¼ teaspoon pepper
Fresh basil sprigs (optional)

Coat a medium nonstick skillet with cooking spray; place over medium-high heat until hot. Add carrot and next 4 ingredients; sauté until tender. Stir in parsley and wine. Cook, uncovered, until liquid is absorbed.

Untie roast, and trim fat. Spread vegetable mixture over inside of roast. Retie roast. Combine ½ teaspoon basil, thyme, and pepper; rub mixture over surface of roast. Place roast on a rack in a roasting pan coated with cooking spray. Insert meat thermometer into thickest part of roast, if desired. Bake, uncovered, at 325° for 2 hours or until meat thermometer registers 170°.

Let roast stand 10 minutes. Remove string; slice roast diagonally across grain into ¼-inch slices, and arrange on a large serving platter. Garnish with fresh basil sprigs, if desired. Yield: 10 servings (197 calories per serving).

PROTEIN 26.4 / FAT 8.7 / CARBOHYDRATE 1.7 / CHOLESTEROL 80 / IRON 1.0 / SODIUM 67 / CALCIUM 12

 LIFESTYLE CHANGES LOWER HEART RISK

People who adopt healthy lifestyle habits—those who control the amount of fat they eat, keep blood pressure in control, and do not smoke—reduce their chances of dying from a heart attack by as much as 24 percent. At least that's the word from scientists involved in one of the largest studies of heart disease—the Multiple Risk Factor Intervention Trial (MR FIT). This study was conducted at 22 centers around the country and included nearly 13,000 male participants. The men already had at least two risk factors for heart disease (family history, high blood pressure, excess weight, or elevated blood cholesterol). Scientists then followed the group for more than a decade.

Half of the men were treated with regular medical care. That is, they were given medications as needed and were observed and followed as normal medical care dictated. The other half received preventive care. These men learned how to trim the fat from their diet, keep their blood pressure low, and quit smoking. In other words, they learned how to make healthy changes in how they ate and lived. After 10 years, the men who took steps to eat better and develop a healthier lifestyle showed major improvements in their overall health, and their risk of heart disease was much lower.

SAGE-SEASONED PORK TENDERLOINS

½ cup Zinfandel or other dry red wine
3 tablespoons minced green onions
2 tablespoons minced fresh sage leaves
1 tablespoon minced fresh parsley
½ teaspoon dried whole thyme
½ teaspoon pepper
2 (¾-pound) pork tenderloins
Vegetable cooking spray
Fresh sage sprigs (optional)
Fresh parsley sprigs (optional)

Combine first 6 ingredients in a large zip-top heavy-duty plastic bag; seal bag, and shake well. Trim fat from pork. Add pork to bag; seal bag, and shake until pork is well coated. Marinate pork in refrigerator 8 hours, turning bag occasionally.

Remove pork from marinade. Place marinade in a small saucepan. Bring to a boil, and cook 5 minutes. Place pork on a rack in a roasting pan coated with cooking spray. Insert meat thermometer into thickest part of tenderloin, if desired. Bake at 400° for 45 minutes or until meat thermometer registers 170°, basting frequently with marinade.

Transfer tenderloins to a serving platter. Let stand 10 minutes; slice diagonally across grain into thin slices. If desired, garnish with fresh sage and fresh parsley sprigs. Yield: 6 servings (141 calories per serving).

PROTEIN 23.9 / FAT 4.1 / CARBOHYDRATE 0.7 / CHOLESTEROL 77 / IRON 1.7 / SODIUM 58 / CALCIUM 15

PORK ROAST WITH SUMMER FRUIT RELISH

1 cup chopped fresh plums
1 cup peeled, chopped fresh peaches
¼ cup finely chopped onion
1 tablespoon unsweetened orange juice
1½ teaspoons grated fresh ginger
1½ teaspoons grated orange rind
¼ teaspoon ground allspice
1 (2½-pound) lean boneless pork loin roast, rolled and tied
Vegetable cooking spray
2 cloves garlic, minced
½ teaspoon dry mustard
¼ teaspoon ground red pepper

Combine first 7 ingredients in a medium bowl; stir well. Cover fruit relish and chill.

Untie roast, and trim fat. Retie roast, and place on a rack in a roasting pan coated with cooking spray. Combine garlic, mustard, and pepper; stir well. Rub garlic mixture over entire surface of roast. Insert meat thermometer into thickest part of roast, if desired. Place roast in a 450° oven. Reduce heat to 350°, and bake 1 hour and 45 minutes or until meat thermometer registers 170°.

Let roast stand 10 minutes. Remove string; slice roast diagonally across grain into ½-inch slices. Serve with fruit relish. Yield: 10 servings (190 calories per serving).

PROTEIN 24.0 / FAT 8.0 / CARBOHYDRATE 4.6 / CHOLESTEROL 72 / IRON 0.7 / SODIUM 58 / CALCIUM 8

When sliced, Turkey Tenderloin with Mole Sauce (page 174) can be arranged to show off this spectacular entrée.

STIR-FRIED CHICKEN AND VEGETABLES

½ pound fresh asparagus spears
1 cup canned low-sodium chicken broth, undiluted
¼ cup reduced-sodium soy sauce
2 tablespoons cornstarch
1 tablespoon peeled, grated ginger
1 clove garlic, crushed
⅛ teaspoon crushed red pepper
⅛ teaspoon Szechwan peppercorns
Vegetable cooking spray
2 teaspoons dark sesame oil, divided
4 (4-ounce) skinned, boned chicken breast halves, cut into thin strips
3½ cups sliced bok choy (about 2 pounds)
1 cup sliced fresh mushrooms
5 green onions, cut diagonally into 1-inch slices (about 1 cup)
1 (8-ounce) can sliced water chestnuts, drained
3½ cups cooked long-grain rice (cooked without salt or fat)

Snap off tough ends of asparagus. Remove scales from stalks with a knife or vegetable peeler, if desired. Cut asparagus diagonally into 1-inch slices. Set aside.

Combine chicken broth, soy sauce, cornstarch, grated ginger, crushed garlic, crushed red pepper, and peppercorns in a small bowl; stir well. Set aside.

Coat a wok or large nonstick skillet with cooking spray; add 1 teaspoon sesame oil. Place over medium-high heat (375°) until hot. Add chicken, and stir-fry 3 minutes or until lightly browned. Remove chicken from wok. Drain and pat dry with paper towels. Wipe drippings from wok with a paper towel.

Add remaining 1 teaspoon sesame oil to wok; place over medium-high heat until hot. Add reserved asparagus, bok choy, mushrooms, and green onions; stir-fry 3 to 4 minutes or until crisp-tender. Add reserved chicken broth mixture and water chestnuts; stir well. Return chicken to wok. Cook, stirring constantly, until mixture is thickened and thoroughly heated. Serve chicken mixture over cooked rice. Yield: 7 servings (283 calories per serving).

PROTEIN 19.7 / FAT 3.5 / CARBOHYDRATE 41.8 / CHOLESTEROL 40 / IRON 2.7 / SODIUM 389 / CALCIUM 58

COUNTRY CAPTAIN STIR-FRY

Vegetable cooking spray
2 teaspoons vegetable oil, divided
4 (4-ounce) skinned, boned chicken breast halves, cut into ½-inch-wide strips
1 medium-size sweet onion, thinly sliced
1 clove garlic, minced
1½ teaspoons curry powder
½ teaspoon salt
½ teaspoon dried whole thyme, crushed
⅛ teaspoon ground red pepper
⅛ teaspoon sugar
1 large green pepper, seeded and cut into thin strips
1 large sweet red pepper, seeded and cut into thin strips
1 pound tomatoes, peeled, seeded, and cut into 1-inch strips
½ cup canned low-sodium chicken broth, undiluted
¼ cup raisins
2 cups cooked long-grained rice (cooked without salt or fat)
2 tablespoons slivered almonds, toasted
2 tablespoons chopped fresh parsley

Coat a wok or large nonstick skillet with cooking spray; add 1 teaspoon vegetable oil. Place over medium-high heat (375°) until hot. Add chicken, and stir-fry 3 minutes or until lightly browned.

Remove chicken from wok. Drain chicken and pat dry with paper towels. Wipe drippings from wok with a paper towel.

Add remaining 1 teaspoon vegetable oil to wok; place over medium-high heat until hot. Add onion and garlic; stir-fry 3 minutes or until tender. Add curry powder and next 4 ingredients; stir well. Add pepper strips, and stir-fry 1 minute. Add tomato, chicken broth, and raisins, stirring well; bring tomato mixture to a boil. Stir-fry mixture 3 minutes or until liquid is reduced by half, stirring constantly.

Return chicken to wok. Cook, stirring constantly, until thoroughly heated. Spoon chicken mixture over cooked rice, and sprinkle with almonds and parsley. Yield: 6 servings (268 calories per serving).

PROTEIN 20.9 / FAT 5.6 / CARBOHYDRATE 33.2 / CHOLESTEROL 47 / IRON 2.8 / SODIUM 243 / CALCIUM 48

The spicy, hot flavors of jalapeño pepper and cilantro are tempered with the mild flavor of chicken in Jalapeño Chicken and Pasta.

JALAPEÑO CHICKEN AND PASTA

Olive oil-flavored vegetable cooking spray
3 (4-ounce) skinned, boned chicken breast halves, cut into 1-inch cubes
2 medium-size sweet red peppers, seeded and cut into 1-inch cubes
2 medium-size sweet yellow peppers, seeded and cut into 1-inch cubes
10 ounces fresh shiitake mushrooms, sliced
2 cloves garlic, minced
1 jalapeño pepper, seeded and chopped
3 tablespoons Chablis or other dry white wine
½ cup canned low-sodium chicken broth, undiluted
6 ounces rigatoni, uncooked
1 tablespoon olive oil
¼ cup diagonally sliced green onions
¼ cup freshly grated Parmesan cheese
¼ teaspoon salt
⅛ teaspoon freshly ground pepper
¼ cup chopped fresh cilantro

Coat a large nonstick skillet with cooking spray; place over medium-high heat until hot. Add chicken, pepper cubes, mushrooms, minced garlic, and jalapeño pepper; sauté 4 minutes or until chicken is lightly browned. Add wine, and sauté 2 minutes or until wine evaporates. Add chicken broth; reduce heat to medium, and simmer, uncovered, 2 minutes. Remove chicken mixture from heat, and set aside.

Cook rigatoni according to package directions, omitting salt and fat. Drain well. Place rigatoni in a large bowl; add olive oil, and toss well. Add chicken mixture, and stir well. Add sliced green onions, Parmesan cheese, salt, pepper, and chopped cilantro, tossing chicken mixture gently to combine. Yield: 6 servings (250 calories per serving).

PROTEIN 21.5 / FAT 5.9 / CARBOHYDRATE 39.6 / CHOLESTEROL 35 / IRON 4.2 / SODIUM 207 / CALCIUM 71

Chicken Burritos prove that traditional Mexican cuisine can be healthy.

CHICKEN BURRITOS

4 (4-ounce) skinned, boned chicken breast halves
2 teaspoons lemon juice
¼ teaspoon salt
¼ teaspoon pepper
4 (8-inch) flour tortillas
2 teaspoons vegetable oil, divided
2 green onions, cut into ¼-inch slices
½ cup low-fat sour cream, divided
¼ cup plain nonfat yogurt
Tomato Salsa
3 cups shredded iceberg lettuce
Fresh cilantro sprigs (optional)

Place chicken in a shallow dish. Combine lemon juice, salt, and pepper in a small bowl; pour over chicken. Cover and chill 30 minutes.

Wrap tortillas in aluminum foil, and bake at 325° for 15 minutes or until thoroughly heated.

Heat 1 teaspoon oil in a large nonstick skillet over medium-high heat until hot. Add chicken, and cook 5 to 8 minutes on each side or until chicken is done. Remove chicken from skillet. Drain and pat dry with paper towels. Wipe drippings from skillet with a paper towel. Cut chicken into ½-inch cubes; set aside.

Heat remaining 1 teaspoon oil in skillet over medium-high heat until hot. Add green onions, and cook 1 minute or until tender. Return chicken to skillet; cook until thoroughly heated. Remove from heat, and stir in ¼ cup sour cream and yogurt; keep warm.

Spoon chicken mixture evenly onto tortillas; top evenly with Tomato Salsa. Roll up tortillas, and serve each tortilla on ¾ cup shredded lettuce; top each with 1 tablespoon sour cream. Garnish with fresh cilantro sprigs, if desired. Yield: 4 servings (249 calories per serving).

Tomato Salsa:
2 cups seeded, chopped tomato
¼ cup sliced green onions
3 cloves garlic, minced
2 tablespoons chopped fresh cilantro
1 tablespoon chopped green chiles
2 tablespoons lime juice
¼ teaspoon salt

Combine all ingredients in a medium bowl; stir well. Yield: 2 cups.

PROTEIN 29.2 / FAT 9.4 / CARBOHYDRATE 11.8 / CHOLESTEROL 82 / IRON 1.9 / SODIUM 392 / CALCIUM 105

SANTA FE-STYLE GRILLED CHICKEN BREASTS

4 (4-ounce) skinned, boned chicken breast halves
¼ teaspoon salt
¼ teaspoon pepper
⅓ cup lime juice
2 teaspoons olive oil
1¾ cups diced plum tomato (about ¾ pound)
⅓ cup chopped onion
3 tablespoons minced fresh cilantro
2 tablespoons red wine vinegar
1 tablespoon seeded, minced jalapeño pepper
Vegetable cooking spray

Place chicken between 2 sheets of heavy-duty plastic wrap, and flatten to ½-inch thickness, using a meat mallet or rolling pin. Make ⅛-inch-deep diagonal slits in each chicken breast, forming a diamond pattern. Sprinkle chicken with salt and pepper; place in a shallow dish.

Combine lime juice and olive oil in a small bowl; stir well, and pour over chicken. Cover

chicken, and marinate in refrigerator 3 hours, turning occasionally.

Combine tomato and next 4 ingredients in a small bowl; stir well. Cover and chill thoroughly.

Remove chicken from marinade, discarding marinade. Coat grill rack with cooking spray; place on grill over medium-hot coals. Place chicken on rack, and cook 5 to 6 minutes on each side or until done. Cut chicken into thin slices. Serve with chilled tomato mixture. Yield: 4 servings (168 calories per serving).

PROTEIN 26.7 / FAT 3.9 / CARBOHYDRATE 5.5 / CHOLESTEROL 70 / IRON 1.5 / SODIUM 217 / CALCIUM 29

CHICKEN BREASTS WITH FRESH TOMATO SAUCE

4 (4-ounce) skinned, boned chicken breast halves
2 teaspoons lemon juice
¼ teaspoon salt
¼ teaspoon pepper
2 teaspoons olive oil, divided
1 clove garlic, minced
1 small shallot, minced
2¼ cups seeded, diced tomato
1 tablespoon chopped fresh basil
Fresh basil sprigs (optional)

Place chicken in a large shallow dish; sprinkle with lemon juice, salt, and pepper. Cover and set aside.

Heat 1 teaspoon olive oil in a large nonstick skillet over medium heat until hot. Add garlic and shallot; sauté 2 minutes or until tender. Add tomato and chopped basil; reduce heat, and simmer 5 minutes. Pour mixture into container of an electric blender; top with cover, and process until smooth.

Heat remaining 1 teaspoon olive oil in skillet over medium heat until hot. Add chicken, and cook 5 to 10 minutes or until browned, turning often. Pour tomato mixture over chicken, and cook until thoroughly heated.

Spoon tomato sauce onto a serving platter; arrange chicken on top of sauce. Garnish with fresh basil sprigs, if desired. Yield: 4 servings (164 calories per serving).

PROTEIN 27.0 / FAT 3.8 / CARBOHYDRATE 4.6 / CHOLESTEROL 66 / IRON 1.3 / SODIUM 227 / CALCIUM 24

WINE COUNTRY CHICKEN

1 tablespoon all-purpose flour
¼ teaspoon dried whole basil
¼ teaspoon dried whole tarragon
¼ teaspoon paprika
¼ teaspoon salt
¼ teaspoon freshly ground pepper
4 (4-ounce) skinned, boned chicken breast halves
Olive oil-flavored vegetable cooking spray
2 cloves garlic, minced
½ cup Chablis or other dry white wine
1 cup seedless red grapes, halved
½ cup canned low-sodium chicken broth, undiluted
1 teaspoon lemon juice
1 tablespoon chopped fresh parsley

Combine first 6 ingredients; stir well. Dredge chicken in flour mixture.

Coat a large nonstick skillet with cooking spray; place over medium-high heat until hot. Add chicken and garlic; cook 4 minutes on each side or until chicken is browned. Add wine; cover and cook 3 minutes or until chicken is tender. Add grapes, chicken broth, and lemon juice; cook until thoroughly heated. Transfer chicken and grapes to a serving platter, using a slotted spoon. Cook broth mixture over high heat 5 minutes or until reduced to a glaze; spoon over chicken. Sprinkle with chopped fresh parsley. Serve warm. Yield: 4 servings (166 calories per serving).

PROTEIN 26.9 / FAT 1.8 / CARBOHYDRATE 9.2 / CHOLESTEROL 66 / IRON 1.3 / SODIUM 225 / CALCIUM 27

CRISPY BROILED CHICKEN

2 tablespoons yellow cornmeal
2 cloves garlic, crushed
1 teaspoon dried whole rosemary
½ teaspoon freshly ground black pepper
¼ teaspoon salt
¼ teaspoon ground red pepper
3 tablespoons lemon juice
2 teaspoons vegetable oil
6 (6-ounce) skinned chicken breast halves
Vegetable cooking spray

Combine first 8 ingredients in a small bowl; stir well until thoroughly mixed.

Place chicken in a 13- x 9- x 2-inch baking dish coated with cooking spray. Spread cornmeal mixture evenly over chicken breasts. Cover and refrigerate 1 hour.

Place chicken, skinned side down, on rack of a broiler pan coated with cooking spray. Broil 8 inches from heat 25 minutes. Turn chicken; broil an additional 15 minutes or until tender. Yield: 6 servings (179 calories per serving).

PROTEIN 28.9 / FAT 5.0 / CARBOHYDRATE 2.7 / CHOLESTEROL 78 / IRON 1.1 / SODIUM 166 / CALCIUM 21

GRILLED CHICKEN TERIYAKI

½ cup low-sodium soy sauce
¼ cup Chablis or other dry white wine
2 tablespoons honey
2 cloves garlic, minced
½ teaspoon ground ginger
6 (6-ounce) skinned chicken breast halves
Vegetable cooking spray

Combine first 5 ingredients in a small bowl; stir well. Place chicken in a shallow dish; pour soy sauce mixture over chicken. Cover and marinate in refrigerator 8 hours, turning occasionally.

Remove chicken from marinade; place marinade in a small saucepan. Bring to a boil; reduce heat, and simmer 5 minutes.

Coat grill rack with cooking spray; place on grill over medium-hot coals. Place chicken on rack, and cook 20 to 25 minutes or until chicken is tender, turning and basting frequently with reserved marinade. Yield: 6 servings (185 calories per serving).

PROTEIN 28.7 / FAT 3.4 / CARBOHYDRATE 6.4 / CHOLESTEROL 78 / IRON 1.0 / SODIUM 589 / CALCIUM 17

HONEY-BAKED CHICKEN

1 (3-pound) broiler-fryer, cut up and skinned
¼ cup water
3 tablespoons finely chopped onion
3 tablespoons reduced-sodium soy sauce
2 tablespoons honey
2 cloves garlic, minced
1 tablespoon peeled, grated ginger
Vegetable cooking spray
¾ cup thinly sliced green onions

Trim excess fat from chicken. Rinse chicken under cold, running water, and pat dry. Place chicken in a 13- x 9- x 2-inch baking dish.

Combine water, onion, soy sauce, honey, garlic, and ginger; stir well. Pour mixture over chicken; cover and marinate in refrigerator 1 hour, turning once.

Remove chicken from marinade; place marinade in a small saucepan. Bring to a boil; reduce heat, and simmer 5 minutes.

Place chicken on a rack in a roasting pan coated with cooking spray. Bake at 400° for 35 minutes, turning and basting occasionally with reserved marinade. Sprinkle sliced green onions over chicken. Bake an additional 10 minutes or until chicken is tender. Serve warm. Yield: 6 servings (188 calories per serving).

PROTEIN 24.3 / FAT 6.2 / CARBOHYDRATE 7.7 / CHOLESTEROL 73 / IRON 1.3 / SODIUM 371 / CALCIUM 20

SPICY GRILLED CHICKEN

1 (3-pound) broiler-fryer, cut up and skinned
1 (6-ounce) can no-salt-added tomato paste
⅓ cup Burgundy or other dry red wine
⅓ cup water
¼ cup red wine vinegar
1 tablespoon olive oil
1 teaspoon creole seasoning
½ teaspoon salt
½ teaspoon freshly ground black pepper
½ teaspoon ground red pepper
½ teaspoon crushed red pepper
Vegetable cooking spray

Trim excess fat from chicken. Rinse chicken under cold, running water, and pat dry. Place chicken in a large shallow dish. Combine tomato paste and next 9 ingredients in a large bowl; stir well. Pour tomato paste mixture over chicken. Cover and marinate chicken in refrigerator 8 hours.

Remove chicken from marinade; place marinade in a small saucepan. Bring to a boil; reduce heat, and simmer 5 minutes.

Coat grill rack with cooking spray; place rack on grill over hot coals. Place chicken on rack, and cook 10 minutes; turn chicken and baste with marinade. Grill chicken an additional 10 to

15 minutes or until done, basting frequently with marinade. Yield: 6 servings (201 calories per serving).

PROTEIN 24.7 / FAT 8.5 / CARBOHYDRATE 5.6 / CHOLESTEROL 73 / IRON 1.6 / SODIUM 476 / CALCIUM 25

BLACKENED CORNISH GAME HENS WITH ROASTED SPICES

2 tablespoons sesame seeds
¼ teaspoon coriander seeds
¼ teaspoon black peppercorns
3 whole cloves
1 (¼-inch) stick cinnamon
¼ bay leaf
2 tablespoons freshly ground espresso powder
1 teaspoon sugar
¼ teaspoon salt
3 (1-pound) Cornish hens, skinned
Vegetable cooking spray
2 teaspoons olive oil
Fresh coriander sprigs (optional)

Place first 6 ingredients in separate piles on a baking sheet. Bake at 300° for 25 minutes or until sesame seeds are golden. Reserve 1 tablespoon toasted sesame seeds. Combine remaining spices, and crush until pulverized, using a mortar and pestle. Transfer spice mixture to a small bowl; add espresso powder, sugar, and salt. Stir well, and set aside.

Remove giblets from hens; reserve for another use. Rinse hens under cold, running water, and pat dry. Split each hen in half lengthwise using an electric knife. Rub spice mixture over entire surface of hens, and place in a 13- x 9- x 2-inch baking dish. Cover and refrigerate 8 hours.

Coat a large nonstick skillet with cooking spray; add olive oil. Place over medium-high heat until hot. Add hens, skinned side down, and sauté 5 minutes; turn hens. Reduce heat to medium; cover and cook 20 to 30 minutes or until hens are done. Sprinkle with reserved toasted sesame seeds, and garnish with fresh coriander sprigs, if desired. Yield: 6 servings (183 calories per serving).

PROTEIN 26.7 / FAT 7.1 / CARBOHYDRATE 1.5 / CHOLESTEROL 84 / IRON 1.5 / SODIUM 193 / CALCIUM 27

MARGARITA GRILLED CORNISH HENS

4 (1-pound) Cornish hens, skinned
½ cup lime juice
¼ cup golden tequila
2 tablespoons Triple Sec or other orange-flavored liqueur
2 teaspoons olive oil
2 cloves garlic, minced
¼ teaspoon salt
⅛ teaspoon freshly ground pepper
Vegetable cooking spray

Remove giblets from hens; reserve for another use. Rinse hens under cold, running water, and pat dry. Split each hen in half lengthwise using an electric knife, and place in a shallow dish.

Combine lime juice, tequila, Triple Sec, olive oil, and garlic in a small bowl; stir well, and pour over hens. Cover and marinate in refrigerator 8 hours.

Remove hens from marinade, reserving marinade. Sprinkle hens with salt and pepper, and place cut side down in a shallow baking dish. Bake, uncovered, at 400° for 15 minutes.

Place reserved marinade in a small saucepan. Bring marinade to a boil; reduce heat, and simmer 5 minutes.

Coat grill rack with cooking spray; place on grill over medium-hot coals. Place hens on rack, and cook 10 to 15 minutes or until done, turning and basting frequently with marinade. Yield: 8 servings (192 calories per serving).

PROTEIN 25.8 / FAT 7.8 / CARBOHYDRATE 3.4 / CHOLESTEROL 79 / IRON 1.1 / SODIUM 150 / CALCIUM 17

TURKEY MEAT LOAF

1 (14½-ounce) can no-added-salt whole tomatoes, undrained and chopped
2 (1-ounce) slices white bread, torn into pieces
2 pounds freshly ground raw turkey
1 cup chopped onion (about 1 medium)
2 eggs, slightly beaten
1½ teaspoons dry mustard
1 teaspoon chili powder
¼ teaspoon salt
¼ teaspoon freshly ground pepper
Vegetable cooking spray

Drain tomatoes, reserving ¼ cup liquid. Combine tomato, reserved liquid, bread pieces, and next 7 ingredients in a large bowl; stir well to combine.

Place mixture in a 13- x 9- x 2-inch baking dish coated with cooking spray, and shape into a slightly rounded loaf. (Mixture will be soft.) Bake at 350° for 1½ hours. Yield: 10 servings (154 calories per serving).

PROTEIN 22.1 / FAT 4.0 / CARBOHYDRATE 6.3 / CHOLESTEROL 99 / IRON 1.9 / SODIUM 172 / CALCIUM 41

DILLED TURKEY BREAST AND VEGETABLES

½ pound fresh asparagus spears
3 tablespoons all-purpose flour
1 teaspoon grated lemon rind
½ teaspoon coarsely ground pepper
1 pound boneless fresh turkey breast slices
Vegetable cooking spray
2 teaspoons olive oil
1 medium-size sweet red pepper, cut into 1-inch pieces
1¼ cups sliced fresh mushrooms
½ cup canned low-sodium chicken broth, undiluted
1 teaspoon dried whole dillweed

Snap off tough ends of asparagus. Carefully remove scales with a knife or vegetable peeler, if desired. Cut asparagus into 2-inch pieces. Set asparagus pieces aside.

Combine flour, lemon rind, and pepper. Dredge turkey breast slices in flour mixture.

Coat a nonstick skillet with cooking spray; add oil. Place over medium heat until hot. Add turkey; cook until lightly browned on both sides. Add asparagus, pepper, mushrooms, chicken broth, and dillweed. Cover and simmer 10 minutes or until turkey is done and vegetables are crisp-tender. Yield: 6 servings (133 calories per serving).

PROTEIN 19.7 / FAT 3.0 / CARBOHYDRATE 6.2 / CHOLESTEROL 45 / IRON 1.8 / SODIUM 50 / CALCIUM 23

Variegated sage and lemon slices enhance juicy Lemon Turkey Cutlets.

LEMON TURKEY CUTLETS

8 (2-ounce) turkey breast cutlets
2½ tablespoons all-purpose flour
2 teaspoons olive oil
¼ teaspoon salt
¼ teaspoon freshly ground pepper
2 tablespoons lemon juice
1 lemon, sliced (optional)
Fresh sage sprigs (optional)

Place turkey cutlets between 2 sheets of heavy-duty plastic wrap, and flatten to ⅛-inch thickness, using a meat mallet or rolling pin. Dredge cutlets in flour.

Heat oil in a large nonstick skillet over high heat until hot. Add cutlets, and cook 2 minutes on each side or until browned. Transfer cutlets to a serving platter; sprinkle with salt, pepper, and lemon juice. If desired, garnish with lemon slices and fresh sage sprigs. Serve warm. Yield: 4 servings (177 calories per serving).

PROTEIN 26.8 / FAT 5.1 / CARBOHYDRATE 4.2 / CHOLESTEROL 61 / IRON 1.5 / SODIUM 203 / CALCIUM 20

TURKEY TENDERLOIN WITH
MOLE SAUCE

4 (8-ounce) turkey tenderloins
2 teaspoons chili powder
¼ teaspoon pepper
2 teaspoons corn oil, divided
1⅓ cups chopped onion
1 clove garlic, minced
⅛ teaspoon anise seeds, crushed
⅛ teaspoon ground coriander
⅛ teaspoon ground cumin
⅛ teaspoon ground cloves
3 tablespoons chili powder
2 tablespoons unsweetened cocoa
2 tablespoons raisins
1 tablespoon creamy peanut butter
2 teaspoons sesame seeds, toasted
1 teaspoon sugar
¼ cup canned no-salt-added tomato sauce
2 cups canned no-salt-added chicken broth,
  undiluted
Fresh Tomato Salsa
Corn Salsa
Fresh cilantro sprigs (optional)

Cut each turkey tenderloin in half lengthwise along tendon; remove tendons. (This will prevent the meat from curling while cooking.) Rub chili powder and pepper over entire surface of tenderloins. Cover and set aside.

Heat 1 teaspoon oil in a large nonstick skillet over medium heat until hot. Add chopped onion and minced garlic; sauté 2 minutes or until tender. Remove from heat, and place onion mixture in container of an electric blender. Add crushed anise seeds and next 10 ingredients; top with cover, and process until smooth. With blender running, add chicken broth in a slow, steady stream to make a smooth sauce. Set sauce aside.

Heat remaining 1 teaspoon oil in skillet. Add turkey tenderloins, and sauté over medium heat

5 minutes, turning frequently. Add reserved sauce, and cook, uncovered, 10 minutes or until turkey is tender.

Divide sauce evenly among serving plates. Diagonally slice turkey into ¼-inch pieces, and arrange over sauce. Spoon 3 tablespoons Fresh Tomato Salsa and 2 tablespoons Corn Salsa evenly over each serving of turkey. Garnish tenderloin with fresh cilantro sprigs, if desired. Yield: 8 servings (199 calories per serving).

Fresh Tomato Salsa:

1½ cups seeded, chopped tomato (about 2
  medium)
⅓ cup sliced green onions
⅓ cup chopped green pepper
1½ tablespoons fresh lime juice
1 tablespoon chopped fresh cilantro
1½ teaspoons seeded, chopped jalapeño
  pepper
1 clove garlic, minced
¼ teaspoon salt

Combine all ingredients in a small bowl; stir well. Cover and chill thoroughly. Yield: 1½ cups.

Corn Salsa:

¾ cup frozen whole kernel corn, thawed
1½ tablespoons sliced green onions
1½ tablespoons chopped green pepper
1 tablespoon chopped green chiles
¾ teaspoon seeded, finely chopped jalapeño
  pepper
1 tablespoon white wine vinegar

Combine all ingredients in a small bowl; stir well. Cover and chill thoroughly. Yield: 1 cup.

PROTEIN 27.1 / FAT 4.6 / CARBOHYDRATE 12.7 / CHOLESTEROL 66 / IRON 2.6 / SODIUM 199 / CALCIUM 44

To show off this Raspberry-Peach Salad (page 177), arrange orchard-fresh peaches on plates lined with lettuce, and top with raspberry sauce.

Salads & Salad Dressings

TANGY WALDORF SALAD

¼ cup plain nonfat yogurt
2 tablespoons reduced-calorie mayonnaise
1½ tablespoons lemon juice
1 teaspoon Dijon mustard
1 cup chopped Granny Smith apple
1 cup chopped Red Delicious apple
1 cup chopped celery
Red leaf lettuce leaves (optional)
1 tablespoon chopped pecans

Combine yogurt, mayonnaise, lemon juice, and mustard in a large bowl; stir well. Add chopped apples and celery; toss gently to combine. To serve, spoon salad onto individual lettuce-lined salad plates, if desired. Sprinkle each salad with ½ teaspoon pecans. Yield: 6 servings (52 calories per ½-cup serving).

PROTEIN 0.9 / FAT 2.4 / CARBOHYDRATE 7.4 / CHOLESTEROL 2 / IRON 0.2 / SODIUM 87 / CALCIUM 30

APPLE AND FENNEL SALAD

¾ pound fennel
1 small Red Delicious apple, cored, and coarsely chopped
½ cup seedless red grapes, halved
2 tablespoons chopped fresh parsley
3 tablespoons unsweetened orange juice
1 tablespoon vegetable oil
1 tablespoon sugar
½ teaspoon celery seeds
½ teaspoon dry mustard
⅛ teaspoon pepper

Wash fennel. Trim off leaves and tough outer stalks; discard. Cut bulb in half lengthwise; remove core, and coarsely chop fennel. Combine fennel, apple, grapes, and parsley.

Combine orange juice and remaining ingredients in a saucepan. Cook over medium heat 3 minutes or until thoroughly heated. Pour over fennel mixture; toss gently. Cover and chill. Yield: 4 servings (120 calories per 1-cup serving).

PROTEIN 2.2 / FAT 4.2 / CARBOHYDRATE 21.2 / CHOLESTEROL 0 / IRON 2.2 / SODIUM 8 / CALCIUM 80

CITRUS MOUSSE RING

¼ cup unsweetened orange juice
1 envelope unflavored gelatin
½ cup cold water
¼ cup sugar
2 teaspoons grated orange rind
1 tablespoon chopped crystallized ginger
1 (8-ounce) carton vanilla low-fat yogurt
1 (8-ounce) can crushed pineapple in juice, drained
2 egg whites
2 tablespoons sugar
¼ cup instant nonfat dry milk powder
2 medium navel oranges, peeled and sectioned

Place orange juice in a small, narrow glass or stainless steel bowl; freeze 25 minutes or until a ⅛-inch-thick layer of ice forms on surface.

Sprinkle gelatin over cold water in a small saucepan; let stand 1 minute. Add ¼ cup sugar; cook over low heat, stirring until gelatin and

sugar dissolve. Remove from heat; stir in orange rind and ginger. Cool.

Combine gelatin mixture, yogurt, and pineapple, stirring until smooth. Chill 20 to 30 minutes or until mixture mounds from a spoon.

Beat egg whites (at room temperature) at high speed of an electric mixer until foamy. Gradually add 2 tablespoons sugar, 1 tablespoon at a time, beating until stiff peaks form. Fold egg whites into gelatin mixture.

Add milk powder to partially frozen orange juice; beat at high speed of electric mixer 5 minutes or until stiff peaks form. Gently fold into egg white mixture. Spoon mixture into a 6-cup mold. Chill until firm. Unmold onto a serving platter; top with orange sections. Yield: 8 servings (103 calories per serving).

PROTEIN 4.7 / FAT 0.5 / CARBOHYDRATE 20.9 / CHOLESTEROL 2 / IRON 0.1 / SODIUM 53 / CALCIUM 109

BLUSH-MELON SALAD

1 tablespoon unflavored gelatin
1½ cups white Zinfandel or other blush wine
1 cup raspberry-flavored sparkling water, chilled
1 cup small cantaloupe balls
1 cup small honeydew balls
1 cup small seedless green grapes, halved
Vegetable cooking spray
8 lettuce leaves
Fresh mint sprigs (optional)

Sprinkle gelatin over wine in a small saucepan; let stand 1 minute. Cook over low heat, stirring until gelatin dissolves. Combine gelatin mixture and sparkling water in a medium bowl. Chill gelatin mixture until the consistency of unbeaten egg white.

Gently fold melon balls and grapes into chilled gelatin mixture. Spoon mixture into eight ¾-cup molds coated with cooking spray. Chill until set. Unmold onto lettuce-lined salad plates. Garnish with fresh mint sprigs, if desired. Yield: 8 servings (40 calories per serving).

PROTEIN 1.7 / FAT 0.5 / CARBOHYDRATE 8.4 / CHOLESTEROL 0 /
IRON 0.4 / SODIUM 17 / CALCIUM 13

RASPBERRY-PEACH SALAD

1 (10-ounce) package frozen raspberries in light
   syrup, thawed
1 tablespoon raspberry vinegar
8 medium-size ripe peaches
3 tablespoons lemon juice
Curly leaf lettuce (optional)
¼ cup sliced almonds, toasted
½ cup fresh raspberries (optional)

Place raspberries in container of an electric blender or food processor; top with cover, and process until smooth. Press puree through a sieve to remove seeds. Discard seeds. Add vinegar to puree; stir well, and set aside.

Cut peaches in half lengthwise; remove pits. Slice halves lengthwise into ¼-inch-thick slices, leaving slices attached ½-inch from stem end. Brush peaches with lemon juice.

Arrange leaf lettuce on 8 individual salad plates, if desired. Arrange peaches over lettuce, letting slices fan out slightly.

Drizzle each salad with 2 tablespoons raspberry mixture, and sprinkle evenly with toasted almonds. Garnish with fresh raspberries, if desired. Serve immediately. Yield: 8 servings (118 calories per serving).

PROTEIN 2.1 / FAT 2.0 / CARBOHYDRATE 25.8 / CHOLESTEROL 0 /
IRON 0.5 / SODIUM 1 / CALCIUM 22

SPICY BROCCOLI AND CAULIFLOWER
SALAD

¾ pound fresh broccoli flowerets
¾ pound fresh cauliflower flowerets
¼ cup canned low-sodium chicken broth, undiluted
¼ cup water
1 tablespoon grated lemon rind
2 tablespoons lemon juice
2 cloves garlic, minced
2 teaspoons crushed red pepper
2 teaspoons olive oil
1 teaspoon Dijon mustard
½ teaspoon salt
¼ teaspoon freshly ground pepper
⅛ teaspoon paprika
2 tablespoons chopped fresh parsley

Arrange broccoli and cauliflower in a vegetable steamer over boiling water. Cover and steam 5 minutes or until vegetables are crisp-tender. Transfer vegetables to a large bowl, and set aside.

Combine chicken broth and next 10 ingredients in a jar. Cover tightly, and shake vigorously to combine. Pour chicken broth mixture over vegetable mixture, and toss gently to coat vegetables. Sprinkle evenly with fresh parsley before serving. Yield: 6 servings (50 calories per 1-cup serving).

PROTEIN 3.1 / FAT 1.9 / CARBOHYDRATE 7.4 / CHOLESTEROL 0 /
IRON 1.0 / SODIUM 247 / CALCIUM 51

ITALIAN SUMMER SALAD

24 (¼-inch-thick) slices roma tomato (about 4 large)
8 ounces part-skim mozzarella cheese
12 fresh basil leaves
3 tablespoons balsamic vinegar
1 tablespoon olive oil
2 tablespoons chopped fresh basil
¼ teaspoon salt
⅛ teaspoon freshly ground pepper

Arrange tomato slices on a serving platter in a circular design, overlapping slices.

Slice cheese into 24 thin rectangular-shaped slices. Place a cheese slice between each tomato slice. Place a basil leaf on alternating cheese slices.

Combine vinegar and remaining ingredients in a small bowl; stir with a wire whisk until well blended. Drizzle dressing over salad, and serve immediately. Yield: 8 servings (104 calories per serving).

PROTEIN 7.8 / FAT 6.4 / CARBOHYDRATE 4.8 / CHOLESTEROL 16 /
IRON 1.8 / SODIUM 210 / CALCIUM 263

ROASTED POTATO SALAD WITH BLUE CHEESE

1½ pounds small new potatoes
Olive oil-flavored vegetable cooking spray
¼ teaspoon salt
⅛ teaspoon pepper
½ cup sliced green onions
¼ cup minced fresh parsley
¼ cup 1% low-fat cottage cheese
¼ cup plain nonfat yogurt
2 ounces crumbled blue cheese
1 clove garlic, minced
½ teaspoon dried whole thyme
¼ teaspoon salt
¼ teaspoon freshly ground pepper

Wash potatoes. Cut into quarters, and place in a 13- x 9- x 2-inch baking dish coated with cooking spray. Lightly coat potatoes with cooking spray; sprinkle with ¼ teaspoon salt and ⅛ teaspoon pepper. Bake at 400° for 30 minutes; turn every 10 minutes. Cool 20 minutes. Transfer potatoes to a bowl. Add green onions and parsley.

Position knife blade in food processor bowl; add cottage cheese and yogurt. Process until

smooth. Stir in blue cheese and remaining ingredients. Pour over salad and toss gently. Yield: 8 servings (102 calories per ½-cup serving).

PROTEIN 4.8 / FAT 2.4 / CARBOHYDRATE 15.7 / CHOLESTEROL 6 /
IRON 1.5 / SODIUM 287 / CALCIUM 76

CUCUMBER AND RADISH SALAD

4 cups coarsely chopped English cucumber
¾ cup thinly sliced radishes
½ cup plain nonfat yogurt
⅓ cup peeled, seeded, and diced tomato
¼ cup diced purple onion
¼ cup low-fat sour cream
1 tablespoon chopped fresh mint
⅛ teaspoon ground white pepper
Dash of ground red pepper
Fresh mint sprigs (optional)

Combine first 9 ingredients in a large bowl; toss well. Garnish with mint, if desired. Yield: 10 servings (29 calories per ½-cup serving).

PROTEIN 1.4 / FAT 0.9 / CARBOHYDRATE 4.3 / CHOLESTEROL 3 /
IRON 0.3 / SODIUM 17 / CALCIUM 44

CHOPPED VEGETABLE SALAD

2½ cups seeded, chopped tomato
2 cups chopped English cucumber
1 cup chopped sweet red pepper
1¼ cups chopped avocado
¾ cup chopped purple onion
3 tablespoons minced fresh parsley
¼ cup red wine vinegar
2 tablespoons canned low-sodium chicken broth, undiluted
1 tablespoon fresh lemon juice
2 teaspoons olive oil
1 clove garlic, minced
¼ teaspoon salt
⅛ teaspoon freshly ground pepper

Combine first 6 ingredients in a medium bowl; toss gently.

Combine vinegar and remaining ingredients, stirring well with a wire whisk. Pour over vegetable mixture, and toss gently. Yield: 14 servings (41 calories per ½-cup serving).

PROTEIN 0.9 / FAT 2.7 / CARBOHYDRATE 4.4 / CHOLESTEROL 0 /
IRON 0.5 / SODIUM 47 / CALCIUM 11

PICNIC SALAD

¼ pound snow pea pods
½ medium-size sweet red pepper
½ medium-size sweet yellow pepper
¼ daikon radish, scraped
3 cups finely shredded purple cabbage
½ cup water
3 tablespoons lime juice
1 tablespoon reduced-sodium soy sauce
2 teaspoons dark sesame oil
1 teaspoon cornstarch
2 teaspoons peeled, grated ginger
1 tablespoon sesame seeds, toasted

Cut snow peas, peppers, and daikon radish into julienne strips. Place julienne strips in a large bowl. Add shredded cabbage, and toss gently. Set mixture aside.

Combine water, lime juice, soy sauce, sesame oil, and cornstarch in a small saucepan, stirring until smooth. Bring to a boil over medium heat; cook until slightly thickened, stirring frequently. Stir in grated ginger. Remove from heat, and let cool 15 minutes.

Pour mixture over vegetables, and toss gently to coat. Sprinkle vegetable mixture with sesame seeds. Cover tightly, and chill at least 1 hour before serving. Yield: 6 servings (47 calories per 1-cup serving).

PROTEIN 1.5 / FAT 2.2 / CARBOHYDRATE 6.2 / CHOLESTEROL 0 / IRON 1.9 / SODIUM 103 / CALCIUM 37

Colorful Picnic Salad is the ideal vegetable salad to accompany a festive dinner, indoors or out.

POTATO AND MUSSEL SALAD

3 pounds fresh mussels
½ cup cornmeal
3 cups water
½ cup Chablis or other dry white wine
2 bay leaves
1½ pounds small new potatoes
Tarragon Vinaigrette
1¾ cups sliced celery
½ (14-ounce) jar roasted red peppers, drained and diced
1 cup diced purple onion
¼ cup chopped fresh parsley
Radicchio or green leaf lettuce leaves (optional)

Remove beards on mussels; scrub shells with a brush. Discard open or cracked mussels or heavy ones (they're filled with sand). Place mussels in a large bowl; cover with cold water. Sprinkle with cornmeal; let stand 30 minutes. Drain and rinse mussels.

Combine 3 cups water, wine, and bay leaves in a large Dutch oven. Add mussels; cover and simmer 5 minutes or until shells open, shaking pan several times. Transfer mussels to a bowl with a slotted spoon; discard liquid in pan. Let mussels cool. Remove mussels from shells, and place in a bowl; discard shells.

Wash potatoes. Cook in boiling water to cover 15 minutes or until tender; drain and cool slightly. Cut potatoes into quarters; place in a large bowl. Pour half of vinaigrette over potatoes. Add celery, diced pepper, onion, and parsley, stirring gently. Stir in mussels and remaining vinaigrette. Cover and chill 1 hour, stirring twice. Serve on radicchio- or lettuce-lined salad plates, if desired. Yield: 10 servings (90 calories per 1-cup serving).

Tarragon Vinaigrette:

2 teaspoons tarragon vinegar
2 teaspoons lemon juice
1 teaspoon Dijon mustard
¼ teaspoon salt
⅛ teaspoon freshly ground pepper
¼ cup canned low-sodium chicken broth, undiluted
1 tablespoon water
1 teaspoon olive oil

Combine first 5 ingredients in a small bowl; stir with a wire whisk until well blended. Add chicken broth, water, and oil; stir with a wire whisk until well blended. Yield: ½ cup.

PROTEIN 5.0 / FAT 1.3 / CARBOHYDRATE 15.1 / CHOLESTEROL 7 / IRON 2.2 / SODIUM 171 / CALCIUM 31

WHITE BEAN SALAD

½ pound dried Great Northern beans
3 cups canned no-salt-added chicken broth, undiluted
1 bay leaf
1½ teaspoons mustard seeds
3 tablespoons lemon juice
1½ tablespoons onion broth
1 tablespoon Dijon mustard
1½ teaspoons olive oil
¼ teaspoon salt
⅛ teaspoon ground white pepper
1 cup diced celery
½ cup chopped sweet red pepper
½ cup chopped, seeded cucumber
¼ cup thinly sliced green onions
2 cloves garlic, crushed
2 tablespoons white wine vinegar
1 tablespoon minced fresh parsley

Sort and wash beans; place in a large Dutch oven. Cover with water to a depth of 3 inches above beans. Bring to a boil; boil 5 minutes. Remove from heat. Cover and let stand 1 hour. Drain beans, and return to pan. Add chicken broth, bay leaf, and mustard seeds to beans; stir well. Bring to a boil; cover, reduce heat, and simmer 1 hour or until beans are tender. Drain beans, and discard bay leaf. Place beans in a large bowl.

Combine lemon juice, onion broth, mustard, olive oil, salt, and white pepper in a small bowl; stir with a wire whisk until well blended. Pour over bean mixture, and toss gently. Let beans cool completely.

Combine bean mixture, celery, and next 5 ingredients; stir well. Sprinkle with minced fresh parsley. Yield: 10 servings (105 calories per ½-cup serving).

PROTEIN 6.0 / FAT 1.8 / CARBOHYDRATE 16.3 / CHOLESTEROL 0 / IRON 1.5 / SODIUM 161 / CALCIUM 53

Salsa and cilantro add lots of flavor to Black and White Bean Salad. Served over romaine lettuce, it's sure to be a crowd pleaser.

BLACK AND WHITE BEAN SALAD

1 (15.8-ounce) can Great Northern beans, rinsed and drained

1 (15-ounce) can black beans, rinsed and drained

1¼ cups peeled, seeded, and chopped tomato

¾ cup diced sweet red pepper

¾ cup diced sweet yellow pepper

¾ cup thinly sliced green onions

½ cup commercial salsa

¼ cup red wine vinegar

2 tablespoons chopped fresh cilantro

¼ teaspoon salt

⅛ teaspoon freshly ground pepper

10 cups finely shredded romaine lettuce (about 1 head)

Combine Great Northern beans, black beans, and chopped tomato in a large bowl, stirring gently. Add sweet red pepper, yellow pepper, and sliced green onions; stir gently to combine. Set bean mixture aside.

Combine salsa, vinegar, cilantro, salt, and pepper in a small bowl; stir with a wire whisk until well blended. Pour over bean mixture, and toss gently. Line a large serving bowl with shredded lettuce; top with bean mixture. Divide bean mixture evenly among serving plates. Yield: 10 servings (76 calories per serving).

PROTEIN 4.9 / FAT 0.5 / CARBOHYDRATE 13.9 / CHOLESTEROL 0 / IRON 2.1 / SODIUM 67 / CALCIUM 50

BLACK-EYED PEAS AND GREENS SALAD

1½ cups dried black-eyed peas
5 cups water
1 bay leaf
4 cups baby dandelion or beet greens (about ½ pound)
1 (¾-pound) slice lean cooked ham, cubed
¾ cup thinly sliced green onions
1¾ cups peeled, seeded, and chopped tomato
1 cup diced purple onion
¼ cup minced fresh parsley
4 cloves garlic, minced
1 teaspoon fresh rosemary
¾ cup canned low-sodium chicken broth, undiluted
¼ cup red wine vinegar
2 teaspoons olive oil
¼ teaspoon salt
¼ teaspoon freshly ground pepper

Sort and wash black-eyed peas; place peas in a large Dutch oven. Cover peas with water to a depth of 3 inches above peas; let peas soak at least 8 hours.

Drain peas, and return to Dutch oven. Add 5 cups water and bay leaf to peas. Bring to a boil over medium heat; cover, reduce heat, and simmer 45 minutes or until tender. Drain peas, and discard bay leaf. Place peas in a large bowl. Add dandelion greens, ham, sliced green onions, chopped tomato, and purple onion; toss gently to combine. Add parsley, garlic, and rosemary; toss gently. Stir well, and set aside.

Combine chicken broth and remaining ingredients in a small bowl, stirring well with a wire whisk until blended. Pour over pea mixture, and toss gently. Divide salad evenly among individual serving plates. Yield: 12 servings (86 calories per 1-cup serving).

PROTEIN 8.1 / FAT 2.5 / CARBOHYDRATE 8.3 / CHOLESTEROL 17 / IRON 1.3 / SODIUM 464 / CALCIUM 55

BEETS AND BITTER GREENS SALAD

6 small beets (about 1¼ pounds)
1 head Belgian endive
4½ cups torn curly endive
1 small head radicchio, torn into bite-size pieces
¼ cup canned low-sodium chicken broth, undiluted
3 tablespoons red wine vinegar
3 tablespoons balsamic vinegar
2 tablespoons water
2 teaspoons walnut oil
1 teaspoon coarse-grained mustard
¼ teaspoon salt
1 tablespoon minced fresh parsley
1 tablespoon chopped fresh chives
¼ teaspoon freshly ground pepper

Leave root and 1 inch of stem on beets; scrub with a vegetable brush. Place beets in a saucepan; add water to cover. Bring to a boil; cover, reduce heat, and simmer 35 to 40 minutes or until beets are tender. Drain; pour cold water over beets, and drain. Trim off stems and roots, and rub off skins; cut beets into ½-inch cubes, and set aside.

Peel leaves from core of Belgian endive. Wash leaves, and pat dry with paper towels. Slice diagonally into ½-inch pieces. Combine Belgian endive, curly endive, and radicchio in a large bowl; set aside.

Combine chicken broth, red wine vinegar, balsamic vinegar, water, walnut oil, mustard, and salt in a small bowl; stir well with a wire whisk. Pour ½ cup broth mixture over endive mixture, and toss gently.

Combine reserved beets with remaining broth mixture; toss gently.

Arrange endive mixture evenly on individual salad plates. Top each with beet mixture, dividing evenly. Combine minced parsley, chopped chives, and freshly ground pepper; sprinkle evenly over salads. Serve immediately. Yield: 8 servings (35 calories per serving).

PROTEIN 1.0 / FAT 1.5 / CARBOHYDRATE 5.0 / CHOLESTEROL 0 / IRON 0.7 / SODIUM 123 / CALCIUM 13

FRESH SPRINGTIME SALAD

1 pound fresh asparagus spears
4 cups torn fresh spinach
2 cups torn red leaf lettuce
2 cups torn leaf lettuce
Warm Seasoned Dressing

Snap off tough ends of asparagus. Remove scales with a knife or vegetable peeler, if desired. Cut asparagus into 2-inch pieces. Arrange asparagus in a vegetable steamer over boiling water. Cover and steam 4 to 5 minutes or until crisp-tender.

Combine asparagus and next 3 ingredients in a large bowl, tossing gently. Pour dressing over salad; toss gently. Serve immediately. Yield: 9 servings (30 calories per 1-cup serving).

Warm Seasoned Dressing:

¼ cup plus 3 tablespoons canned low-sodium chicken broth, undiluted
¼ cup lemon juice
¼ cup balsamic vinegar
1 teaspoon dried whole thyme
2 teaspoons olive oil
2 cloves garlic, minced
1½ tablespoons Dijon mustard

Combine first 6 ingredients in a small saucepan; cook over medium heat 3 to 4 minutes or until thoroughly heated. Add mustard; stir with a wire whisk until well blended. Serve warm. Yield: 1 cup.

PROTEIN 1.8 / FAT 1.3 / CARBOHYDRATE 3.5 / CHOLESTEROL 0 / IRON 1.0 / SODIUM 87 / CALCIUM 32

SPINACH SALAD WITH CHUTNEY DRESSING

4 cups fresh spinach
¼ cup mango chutney
¼ cup canned low-sodium chicken broth, undiluted
1 tablespoon safflower oil
2 teaspoons lemon juice
½ teaspoon curry powder
¼ teaspoon salt
3 cups chopped Red Delicious apples
1 large fresh navel orange, peeled and sectioned
¾ cup diagonally sliced green onions
¼ cup sliced almonds, toasted

Remove stems from spinach; discard stems. Wash leaves thoroughly, and pat dry with paper towels. Set spinach aside.

Combine chutney and next 5 ingredients in container of an electric blender or food processor; top with cover, and process 30 seconds or until combined, scraping sides of container.

Combine spinach, apple, orange sections, green onions, and almonds in a large bowl. Pour chutney mixture over salad; toss gently. Serve immediately. Yield: 8 servings (90 calories per 1-cup serving).

PROTEIN 1.4 / FAT 3.5 / CARBOHYDRATE 14.9 / CHOLESTEROL 0 / IRON 0.8 / SODIUM 101 / CALCIUM 37

SAVOR THE FLAVOR

When using fresh herbs, keep in mind that fresh herbs are milder in flavor than dried herbs. As a rule of thumb, add three times the amount of a fresh herb to a recipe to match the intensity of flavor of the dried variety. For instance, if a recipe calls for ¼ teaspoon dried whole thyme, substitute ¾ teaspoon minced fresh thyme to achieve a similar flavor in the recipe.

GARDEN COUSCOUS SALAD

⅔ cup water
¼ teaspoon dried whole thyme
⅓ cup uncooked couscous
½ cup chopped green pepper
½ cup peeled, seeded, and chopped tomato
3 tablespoons commercial reduced-calorie creamy cucumber dressing
2 tablespoons raisins, chopped
1 tablespoon minced fresh chives
1 tablespoon chopped, roasted unsalted peanuts

Combine water and thyme in a small saucepan, and bring to a boil. Remove from heat. Add couscous; cover, and let stand 5 minutes or until couscous is tender and liquid is absorbed. Add green pepper and next 4 ingredients, stirring well. Transfer mixture to a serving bowl; cover and chill thoroughly. Stir in peanuts just before serving. Yield: 4 servings (118 calories per ½-cup serving).

PROTEIN 3.3 / FAT 3.4 / CARBOHYDRATE 19.1 / CHOLESTEROL 0 / IRON 0.9 / SODIUM 168 / CALCIUM 18

GRILLED PAILLARD OF BEEF SALAD

1 (¾-pound) lean flank steak
¾ teaspoon freshly ground pepper, divided
¼ teaspoon salt
¼ cup canned low-sodium beef broth,
   undiluted
2 tablespoons lemon juice
Vegetable cooking spray
¼ cup reduced-calorie mayonnaise
2 tablespoons Dijon mustard
2 tablespoons canned low-sodium beef broth,
   undiluted
1 tablespoon lemon juice
2 bunches fresh arugula
¼ cup freshly grated Parmesan cheese
¼ cup julienned fresh basil

Trim fat from flank steak. Sprinkle steak with ½ teaspoon pepper and salt. Place steak in a large shallow dish.

Combine ¼ cup beef broth and 2 tablespoons lemon juice; pour broth mixture over steak.

Cover and marinate steak in refrigerator 3 hours, turning occasionally.

Remove steak from marinade, discarding marinade. Coat grill rack with cooking spray; place on grill over medium-hot coals. Place steak on rack, and cook 6 to 7 minutes on each side or to desired degree of doneness. Slice steak diagonally across grain into ¼-inch-thick slices. Set aside, and keep warm.

Combine mayonnaise and next 3 ingredients in a small bowl; stir well with a wire whisk.

Remove stems from arugula, and arrange leaves on individual serving plates. Arrange steak slices evenly over arugula. Drizzle each salad with 2 tablespoons mayonnaise mixture, and sprinkle with Parmesan cheese, basil, and remaining ¼ teaspoon pepper. Yield: 4 servings (262 calories per serving).

PROTEIN 21.3 / FAT 17.4 / CARBOHYDRATE 4.0 / CHOLESTEROL 59 / IRON 2.7 / SODIUM 657 / CALCIUM 148

WARM SZECHWAN CHICKEN SALAD

2 tablespoons Szechwan peppercorns
Vegetable cooking spray
4 (4-ounce) skinned, boned chicken breast halves
3 stalks celery, sliced into 1½- x ¼- x ¼-inch strips
2 small carrots, scraped and sliced into 1½- x ¼- x ¼-inch strips
1 large cucumber, peeled, seeded, and sliced into 1½- x ¼- x ¼-inch strips
¼ teaspoon salt
¼ cup canned low-sodium chicken broth, undiluted
2½ tablespoons low-sodium soy sauce
2 teaspoons chili oil
2 teaspoons vinegar
1 teaspoon dark sesame oil
½ teaspoon sugar
¼ teaspoon ground white pepper
3¾ cups finely shredded lettuce
4 green onions, diagonally sliced into 1-inch pieces

Place heavy skillet over medium-high heat until hot; add peppercorns, and cook 3 minutes, stirring frequently. Crush peppercorns using a mortar and pestle; set aside.

Coat a large nonstick skillet with cooking spray; place over medium heat until hot. Add chicken, and cook 4 minutes on each side or until browned. Remove chicken from skillet. Drain and pat dry with paper towels. Shred chicken into bite-size pieces, and place in a large bowl. Keep warm. Wipe drippings from skillet with a paper towel.

Coat skillet with cooking spray, and place over medium-high heat until hot. Add celery and carrot strips; sauté until crisp-tender. Add sautéed celery and carrot strips, cucumber, and salt to shredded chicken.

Combine chicken broth and next 6 ingredients in a small bowl, stirring well with a wire whisk. Pour over chicken mixture, and toss well. Place lettuce on a large serving platter, and top with chicken mixture. Sprinkle with reserved crushed peppercorns and green onions. Serve immediately. Yield: 5 servings (166 calories per 1-cup serving).

PROTEIN 21.6 / FAT 5.4 / CARBOHYDRATE 6.4 / CHOLESTEROL 56 / IRON 1.6 / SODIUM 390 / CALCIUM 45

Luncheon or dinner guests are sure to enjoy colorful Citrus Lobster Salad.

CITRUS LOBSTER SALAD

3 (8-ounce) fresh or frozen lobster tails,
  thawed
1 medium-size pink grapefruit, peeled and
  sectioned
1 medium-size orange, peeled and
  sectioned
¼ cup orange low-fat yogurt
3 tablespoons orange juice
1 tablespoon fresh lemon juice
1 teaspoon grated orange rind
1 teaspoon grated lime rind
⅛ teaspoon ground white pepper
4 cups torn fresh spinach
2 teaspoons chopped fresh chives
Orange rind curls (optional)

Cook lobster tails in boiling water 6 to 8 minutes or until done; drain. Rinse with cold water. Split and clean tails. Cut lobster tail meat into bite-size pieces. Combine lobster, grapefruit sections, and orange sections.

Combine yogurt and next 5 ingredients in a small bowl; stir with a wire whisk until well blended. Pour over lobster mixture; toss well.

Arrange spinach on individual serving plates. Top each serving with 1 cup lobster mixture. Sprinkle ½ teaspoon chives over each serving. Garnish with orange rind curls, if desired. Yield: 4 servings (153 calories per serving).

PROTEIN 24.3 / FAT 1.0 / CARBOHYDRATE 11.6 / CHOLESTEROL 80 /
IRON 1.2 / SODIUM 444 / CALCIUM 124

WARM SCALLOP SALAD

¼ cup white wine vinegar
3 tablespoons canned no-salt-added chicken broth, undiluted
2 teaspoons olive oil
1 clove garlic, crushed
¼ teaspoon salt
⅛ teaspoon freshly ground pepper
Olive oil-flavored vegetable cooking spray
1½ pounds fresh bay scallops
½ pound fresh mushrooms, quartered
3 cups torn Bibb lettuce
2 cups torn chicory
2 cups torn curly endive
1 cup torn radicchio
¾ cup peeled, seeded, and chopped tomato
¼ cup chopped green onions
3 tablespoons chopped fresh parsley
Fresh enoki mushrooms (optional)

Combine first 6 ingredients in a small saucepan; cook over medium heat until thoroughly heated. Set aside, and keep warm.

Coat a large nonstick skillet with cooking spray; place over medium-high heat until hot. Add scallops and mushrooms; sauté 3 to 4 minutes or until scallops are opaque. Set aside, and keep warm.

Combine Bibb lettuce, chicory, endive, radicchio, tomato, and green onions in a large bowl; toss well. Pour warm broth mixture over greens; toss well. Arrange 1 cup mixed greens on each of 8 individual serving plates. Spoon scallop mixture evenly over greens; sprinkle with parsley. Garnish with enoki mushrooms, if desired. Yield: 8 servings (108 calories per serving).

PROTEIN 15.9 / FAT 2.2 / CARBOHYDRATE 6.2 / CHOLESTEROL 28 / IRON 1.2 / SODIUM 227 / CALCIUM 50

SHRIMP AND VEGETABLE SALAD

⅔ cup water
½ cup chopped onion
⅓ cup Chablis or other dry white wine
¼ teaspoon crushed red pepper
1½ pounds medium-size fresh shrimp, peeled and deveined
Olive oil-flavored vegetable cooking spray
3 carrots, scraped and cut into julienne strips
1 clove garlic, minced
½ pound snow pea pods, trimmed
1 small sweet red pepper, seeded and cut into julienne strips
1 small sweet yellow pepper, seeded and cut into julienne strips
1 small green pepper, seeded and cut into julienne strips
1 small zucchini, cut into julienne strips
1 small yellow squash, cut into julienne strips
¾ cup plain nonfat yogurt
¼ cup reduced-calorie mayonnaise
2 tablespoons chopped fresh dillweed
1 tablespoon lemon juice
¼ teaspoon salt
¼ teaspoon freshly ground black pepper
Dash of ground red pepper
7½ cups shredded romaine lettuce

Combine water, onion, wine, and crushed red pepper in a medium nonstick skillet; bring to a boil. Boil 5 minutes. Add shrimp; cook 3 to 5 minutes. Remove shrimp with a slotted spoon, reserving liquid in skillet. Rinse shrimp with cold water, and drain well. Place shrimp in a large bowl. Set aside.

Boil reserved liquid 3 minutes or until reduced by half. Set aside 2 tablespoons reduced liquid; discard remaining liquid.

Coat a large nonstick skillet with cooking spray; place over medium-high heat until hot. Add carrot and garlic; sauté 2 minutes. Add snow peas, pepper strips, zucchini, and squash; sauté 3 to 4 minutes or until vegetables are crisp-tender. Add vegetables to shrimp.

Combine reserved 2 tablespoons liquid, yogurt, and next 6 ingredients in a small bowl; stir with a wire whisk until blended. Pour yogurt mixture over shrimp mixture; toss gently. Place ¾ cup shredded lettuce on each of 10 individual serving plates; spoon shrimp mixture over lettuce. Serve warm. Yield: 10 servings (114 calories per serving).

PROTEIN 12.8 / FAT 2.9 / CARBOHYDRATE 9.5 / CHOLESTEROL 76 / IRON 2.7 / SODIUM 200 / CALCIUM 97

GRILLED CORN AND SHRIMP SALAD

4 ears fresh corn
36 large fresh shrimp, peeled and deveined (about 1¼ pounds)
Olive oil-flavored vegetable cooking spray
1¼ cups diced sweet red pepper
¾ cup diced purple onion
1 cup seeded, diced tomato
3 tablespoons cider vinegar
3 tablespoons lime juice
¼ teaspoon salt
⅛ teaspoon freshly ground black pepper
⅛ teaspoon ground red pepper
¼ cup fresh cilantro leaves
⅓ cup canned low-sodium chicken broth, undiluted
2 teaspoons olive oil
1 head romaine lettuce, torn into bite-size pieces
Fresh cilantro sprigs (optional)

Remove husks and silks from corn.
Thread shrimp on 6 (12-inch) skewers.
Coat grill rack with cooking spray; place on grill over medium-hot coals. Place corn on rack, and cook 20 minutes or until corn is tender and slightly charred, turning frequently. Remove corn, and set aside. Place skewers of shrimp on rack, and cook 6 to 8 minutes or until shrimp are done, turning frequently.

Remove shrimp from skewers. Cut corn from cobs, and place in a medium bowl. Add shrimp, sweet red pepper, onion, and tomato; toss gently to combine.

Combine vinegar and next 4 ingredients in container of an electric blender or food processor; top with cover, and process 3 seconds. Add cilantro leaves, and process until pureed. With blender running, gradually add chicken broth and olive oil in a slow steady stream; process until well blended. Pour chicken broth mixture over shrimp mixture; toss gently.

Arrange torn lettuce on individual serving plates, and top evenly with shrimp mixture. Garnish with fresh cilantro sprigs, if desired. Yield: 6 servings (150 calories per serving).

PROTEIN 15.3 / FAT 3.6 / CARBOHYDRATE 15.9 / CHOLESTEROL 96 / IRON 2.8 / SODIUM 205 / CALCIUM 55

THAI SHRIMP AND CALAMARI SALAD

½ pound fresh spinach
1 medium-size sweet yellow pepper, seeded and cut into julienne strips
1⅓ cups diagonally sliced celery
¼ cup diagonally sliced green onions
3 cups water
½ pound small fresh shrimp, peeled and deveined
½ pound cleaned, skinned calamari (squid)
¼ cup fresh lime juice
3 tablespoons water
2 tablespoons brown sugar
1 tablespoon minced fresh cilantro
1 tablespoon reduced-sodium soy sauce
1 clove garlic, minced
2 teaspoons olive oil
¼ teaspoon crushed red pepper
Fresh cilantro sprigs (optional)

Remove stems from spinach. Wash leaves thoroughly; pat dry with paper towels. Combine spinach, sweet yellow pepper, celery, and green onions in a large bowl; set aside.

Bring 3 cups water to a boil; add shrimp, and cook 3 to 5 minutes. Drain well; rinse with cold water, and drain again.

Slice calamari into ½-inch rings. Drop into boiling water for 30 to 40 seconds or until calamari begins to curl around edges. Drain well; rinse with cold water, and drain again.

Combine reserved spinach mixture, shrimp, and calamari in a large bowl. Combine lime juice and next 7 ingredients in a small bowl, stirring with a wire whisk until well blended; pour over shrimp mixture, tossing well. Garnish with fresh cilantro sprigs, if desired. Serve immediately. Yield: 7 servings (131 calories per 1-cup serving).

PROTEIN 14.1 / FAT 3.4 / CARBOHYDRATE 12.1 / CHOLESTEROL 140 / IRON 3.3 / SODIUM 305 / CALCIUM 90

SMOKED TURKEY AND FRUIT SALAD

8 green leaf lettuce leaves
½ pound smoked turkey breast, cut into ¾-inch pieces
1 medium-size fresh pear, thinly sliced
1 small mango, peeled, seeded, and thinly sliced
1 cup fresh raspberries
1 cup cubed fresh pineapple
1 cup sliced carambola (starfruit)
Honey-Poppy Seed Dressing

Place lettuce leaves on a large serving platter. Arrange turkey and next 5 ingredients on lettuce in an attractive design. Drizzle Honey-Poppy Seed Dressing over salad. Yield: 8 servings (143 calories per serving).

Honey-Poppy Seed Dressing:

¾ cup plain nonfat yogurt
3 tablespoons honey
2 teaspoons lemon juice
1 teaspoon poppy seeds

Combine all ingredients in a small bowl; stir well. Cover and chill. Yield: ¾ cup.

PROTEIN 9.0 / FAT 2.3 / CARBOHYDRATE 23.8 / CHOLESTEROL 16 / IRON 1.3 / SODIUM 216 / CALCIUM 68

DILLED TUNA AND PASTA SALAD

8 ounces tri-colored fusilli, uncooked
2 (6½-ounce) cans 60% less-salt tuna in water, well drained
½ cup diced purple onion
½ cup plain nonfat yogurt
¼ cup reduced-calorie mayonnaise
1 tablespoon dried whole dillweed
2 tablespoons white wine vinegar
1 tablespoon lemon juice
¼ teaspoon salt
⅛ teaspoon freshly ground pepper

Cook pasta according to package directions, omitting salt and fat; drain and rinse with cold water. Set aside.
Combine tuna and onion in a large bowl; add pasta, and toss gently.
Combine yogurt and remaining ingredients in a small bowl; stir with a wire whisk until well blended. Pour dressing over pasta mixture, and toss well. Cover and chill thoroughly. Yield: 6 servings (240 calories per 1-cup serving).

PROTEIN 18.8 / FAT 3.4 / CARBOHYDRATE 32.1 / CHOLESTEROL 4 / IRON 2.8 / SODIUM 210 / CALCIUM 67

FRESH BASIL DRESSING

⅓ cup minced fresh basil
⅓ cup red wine vinegar
1½ tablespoons lemon juice
1 tablespoon olive oil
1 tablespoon water
2 cloves garlic, crushed
¼ teaspoon pepper

Combine all ingredients in a small bowl; stir well. Cover and chill at least 1 hour. Serve over sliced tomatoes or with salad greens. Yield: ½ cup (19 calories per tablespoon).

PROTEIN 0.1 / FAT 1.7 / CARBOHYDRATE 0.7 / CHOLESTEROL 0 / IRON 0.2 / SODIUM 2 / CALCIUM 5

SUN-DRIED TOMATO DRESSING

½ cup sun-dried tomatoes (without salt or oil)
½ cup water
2 teaspoons olive oil
½ cup canned low-sodium chicken broth, undiluted
3 tablespoons red wine vinegar
2 teaspoons Dijon mustard
2 shallots
1 clove garlic, crushed
¼ teaspoon salt
⅛ teaspoon freshly ground pepper

Combine tomatoes, water, and oil in a small bowl; let stand 1½ hours. Position knife blade in food processor bowl; add tomato mixture, and process mixture until finely chopped. Add chicken broth and remaining ingredients; process mixture until smooth. Serve with salad greens or cold cooked pasta. Yield: 1⅓ cups (9 calories per tablespoon).

PROTEIN 0.3 / FAT 0.6 / CARBOHYDRATE 1.2 / CHOLESTEROL 0 / IRON 0.0 / SODIUM 63 / CALCIUM 3

CURRY VINAIGRETTE DRESSING

½ teaspoon unflavored gelatin
1 tablespoon cold water
¼ teaspoon ground ginger
1 teaspoon curry powder
2 tablespoons minced fresh parsley
⅛ teaspoon hot sauce
1 teaspoon honey
2 tablespoons finely chopped chutney
⅓ cup lemon juice
⅔ cup unsweetened apple juice

Sprinkle gelatin over cold water in a small bowl; let stand 1 minute. Combine ginger and remaining ingredients in a nonaluminum saucepan; bring to a boil. Remove from heat. Add reserved gelatin mixture; stir until gelatin dissolves. Cover and chill. Stir with a wire whisk before serving. Serve with salad greens. Yield: 1¼ cups (11 calories per tablespoon).

PROTEIN 0.1 / FAT 0.0 / CARBOHYDRATE 2.8 / CHOLESTEROL 0 / IRON 0.1 / SODIUM 4 / CALCIUM 2

CLUB DRESSING

½ cup reduced-calorie mayonnaise
¼ cup plus 2 tablespoons red wine vinegar
¼ cup plain nonfat yogurt
2 tablespoons minced fresh parsley
2 tablespoons Dijon mustard
1 tablespoon prepared horseradish
2 cloves garlic, crushed
¼ teaspoon salt
½ teaspoon paprika

Combine mayonnaise, vinegar, and yogurt in container of an electric blender or food processor; top with cover, and process until smooth. Add parsley and remaining ingredients; process mayonnaise mixture until smooth. Cover and chill. Serve dressing with salad greens. Yield: 1½ cups (17 calories per tablespoon).

PROTEIN 0.2 / FAT 1.4 / CARBOHYDRATE 0.8 / CHOLESTEROL 2 / IRON 0.0 / SODIUM 101 / CALCIUM 6

GORGONZOLA-YOGURT DRESSING

½ cup plain nonfat yogurt
4 ounces Gorgonzola cheese, crumbled
½ cup Neufchâtel cheese, softened
1 tablespoon chopped fresh chives
2 tablespoons skim milk
1½ tablespoons lemon juice
⅛ teaspoon ground white pepper

Combine all ingredients in container of an electric blender or food processor; top with cover, and process until smooth. Cover and chill thoroughly. Serve with salad greens. Yield: 1⅓ cups (36 calories per tablespoon).

PROTEIN 2.1 / FAT 2.7 / CARBOHYDRATE 0.9 / CHOLESTEROL 9 / IRON 0 / SODIUM 99 / CALCIUM 45

SESAME-TOFU DRESSING

½ cup plain nonfat yogurt
4 ounces firm tofu, drained
2 tablespoons lemon juice
1 tablespoon minced green onions
2 teaspoons sesame seeds
1½ teaspoons honey
½ teaspoon peeled, grated ginger

Combine all ingredients in container of an electric blender or food processor; top with cover, and process until smooth. Cover and chill thoroughly. Serve with salad greens or fresh fruit. Yield: 1¼ cups (15 calories per tablespoon).

PROTEIN 1.3 / FAT 0.7 / CARBOHYDRATE 1.4 / CHOLESTEROL 0 / IRON 0.7 / SODIUM 5 / CALCIUM 27

ROUILLE (RED PEPPER MAYONNAISE)

2 cloves garlic
½ cup reduced-calorie mayonnaise
½ cup soft tofu
1 (2-ounce) jar diced pimiento, drained
12 fresh basil leaves
1 tablespoon olive oil
¼ teaspoon salt
⅛ teaspoon ground red pepper

Position knife blade in food processor bowl; add garlic, and process until minced. Add mayonnaise, tofu, pimiento, basil, olive oil, salt, and ground red pepper; process until smooth. Cover and chill thoroughly. Serve with Mexican or chicken salad. Yield: 1¼ cups (27 calories per tablespoon).

PROTEIN 0.4 / FAT 2.5 / CARBOHYDRATE 0.8 / CHOLESTEROL 2 / IRON 0.2 / SODIUM 74 / CALCIUM 14

MUSTARDY MAYONNAISE

⅔ cup reduced-calorie mayonnaise
3¼ cups plus 2 tablespoons sherry wine vinegar
2 tablespoons stone-ground mustard
1 tablespoon Dijon mustard
½ teaspoon dried whole tarragon
¼ teaspoon salt
¼ teaspoon ground white pepper

Combine mayonnaise, vinegar, and mustards in a small bowl; stir well with a wire whisk until blended. Add tarragon, salt, and pepper; stir well. Cover and chill thoroughly. Serve with bitter greens such as radicchio or endive, or with chicken, seafood, or ham. Yield: 1¼ cups (29 calories per tablespoon).

PROTEIN 0.2 / FAT 2.3 / CARBOHYDRATE 0.9 / CHOLESTEROL 3 / IRON 0.0 / SODIUM 158 / CALCIUM 2

GUACAMOLE DRESSING

1 medium avocado, peeled and coarsely chopped
2 tablespoons lemon juice
1 cup nonfat buttermilk
½ cup low-fat sour cream
½ cup canned low-sodium chicken broth, undiluted
2 tablespoons minced onion
2 tablespoons chopped fresh cilantro
1 tablespoon cider vinegar
1 clove garlic, minced
¼ teaspoon salt
⅛ teaspoon hot sauce

Position knife blade in food processor bowl; add avocado and lemon juice. Process until smooth, scraping sides of processor bowl occasionally. Add buttermilk and remaining ingredients; process until smooth. Serve with salad greens or Mexican salad. Yield: 3½ cups (9 calories per tablespoon).

PROTEIN 0.3 / FAT 0.7 / CARBOHYDRATE 0.6 / CHOLESTEROL 1 / IRON 0.0 / SODIUM 16 / CALCIUM 3

BANANA FRUIT DRESSING

1 medium banana, peeled
¼ cup low-fat sour cream
3 tablespoons plain nonfat yogurt
3 tablespoons freshly squeezed orange juice
1 tablespoon freshly squeezed lemon juice
1 tablespoon honey

Position knife blade in food processor bowl; add banana. Process until smooth, scraping sides of processor bowl occasionally. Add sour cream and remaining ingredients; process until mixture is smooth. Cover and chill 1 hour. Serve with fresh fruit salad. Yield: 1¼ cups (16 calories per tablespoon).

PROTEIN 0.3 / FAT 0.4 / CARBOHYDRATE 3.1 / CHOLESTEROL 1 / IRON 0.0 / SODIUM 3 / CALCIUM 8

For a warm and hearty sandwich, serve Grilled Pork Tenderloin with Sweet-and-Sour Red Cabbage (page 195).

Sandwiches & Snacks

Take a bite of The Californian Sandwich for a tasty surprise that's sure to please—there's jalapeño jelly inside.

THE CALIFORNIAN SANDWICH

2 tablespoons light cream cheese product
4 (¾-ounce) slices reduced-calorie whole wheat
    bread
2 tablespoons hot jalapeño jelly
6 (1-ounce) slices turkey breast
½ cup alfalfa sprouts

Spread 1 tablespoon cream cheese on 1 slice whole wheat bread; spread 1 tablespoon jelly on cream cheese. Top with 3 slices turkey breast and ¼ cup alfalfa sprouts. Top with 1 slice whole wheat bread.

Repeat procedure with remaining ingredients. Serve sandwiches immediately. Yield: 2 servings (292 calories per serving).

PROTEIN 26.5 / FAT 7.4 / CARBOHYDRATE 32.6 / CHOLESTEROL 56 / IRON 2.8 / SODIUM 870 / CALCIUM 36

BROILED CHICKEN SANDWICH WITH FRESH SALSA

4 (4-ounce) skinned, boned chicken breast halves
1 clove garlic, minced
½ teaspoon ground cumin
½ teaspoon chili powder
⅛ teaspoon ground red pepper
2 teaspoons lime juice
Olive oil-flavored vegetable cooking spray
4 red leaf lettuce leaves
8 (¾-ounce) slices reduced-calorie wheat bread, toasted
Fresh Salsa

Place chicken between 2 sheets of heavy-duty plastic wrap, and flatten to ¼-inch thickness, using a meat mallet or rolling pin. Place chicken in a 13- x 9- x 2-inch baking dish.

Combine garlic and next 4 ingredients; stir well. Rub garlic mixture over entire surface of each chicken breast. Cover and chill 3 hours.

Place chicken, skinned side down, on a rack of a broiler pan coated with cooking spray. Broil 5½ inches from heat 3 to 4 minutes on each side or until tender. Place a lettuce leaf on each of four slices of bread, and top each with a chicken breast. Spoon ¼ cup Fresh Salsa over each broiled chicken breast, and top with remaining bread slices. Yield: 4 servings (258 calories per serving).

Fresh Salsa:

1 cup peeled, seeded, and chopped tomato
2½ tablespoons finely chopped purple onion
2 teaspoons seeded, minced jalapeño pepper
1½ teaspoons chopped fresh cilantro
1 clove garlic, minced
⅛ teaspoon salt
½ teaspoon red wine vinegar

Combine tomato, onion, and pepper in a small bowl; toss gently. Add remaining ingredients, stirring well to combine. Cover salsa and chill at least 1 hour. Yield: 1 cup.

PROTEIN 32.2 / FAT 3.7 / CARBOHYDRATE 25.9 / CHOLESTEROL 70 / IRON 3.2 / SODIUM 353 / CALCIUM 120

BUFFALO CHICKEN SANDWICH

2 cups thinly sliced cabbage
¼ cup minced radish
3 tablespoons plain nonfat yogurt
1 tablespoon reduced-calorie mayonnaise
4 (4-ounce) skinned, boned chicken breast halves
2 tablespoons hot sauce
2 tablespoons water
Vegetable cooking spray
2 ounces blue cheese, crumbled
4 (2-ounce) kaiser rolls, split and toasted

Combine first 4 ingredients in a medium bowl; toss gently. Cover and chill at least 30 minutes.

Place chicken between 2 sheets of heavy-duty plastic wrap, and flatten to ¼-inch thickness, using a meat mallet or rolling pin. Place chicken in a zip-top heavy-duty plastic bag.

Combine hot sauce and water; pour over chicken. Marinate in refrigerator 15 minutes.

Remove chicken breasts from plastic bag, and discard hot sauce mixture.

Coat a large nonstick skillet with cooking spray; place over medium-high heat until hot. Add chicken, and cook 5 minutes on each side or until lightly browned. Remove chicken from skillet; drain and pat dry with paper towels. Wipe drippings from skillet with a paper towel.

Return chicken to skillet; sprinkle with blue cheese. Cover and cook over low heat until cheese melts. Place a chicken breast half on bottom half of a kaiser roll; spoon ½ cup cabbage mixture over chicken. Top with remaining half of roll. Repeat procedure with remaining rolls, chicken, and cabbage mixture. Yield: 4 servings (295 calories per serving).

PROTEIN 31.9 / FAT 9.2 / CARBOHYDRATE 18.9 / CHOLESTEROL 82 / IRON 1.2 / SODIUM 558 / CALCIUM 131

SLIDERS

1 pound ground chuck
16 Small Hamburger Buns
16 leaf lettuce leaves
2 large plum tomatoes (about ½ pound), sliced
2 small boiling onions, sliced

Shape ground chuck into 16 (3-inch) patties. Place a large nonstick skillet over medium-high heat until hot. Add 8 patties; cook 1 minute on each side or until browned. Remove patties from skillet; drain and pat dry with paper towels. Wipe drippings from skillet with a paper towel. Repeat procedure with remaining 8 patties.

Place each patty on a Small Hamburger Bun. Top each with a lettuce leaf, tomato slice, and onion slice. Yield: 16 servings (135 calories per serving).

Small Hamburger Buns:

1 (1-pound) loaf frozen bread dough, thawed
Vegetable cooking spray
1 egg, beaten
1 tablespoon water
1 tablespoon sesame seeds

Divide dough into 16 equal portions; shape each portion into a ball, and flatten slightly. Place on a baking sheet coated with cooking spray. Cover; let rise in a warm place (85°), free from drafts, 1½ hours or until doubled in bulk.

Combine egg and water; stir well. Brush dough with egg mixture, and sprinkle with sesame seeds. Bake at 350° for 10 to 12 minutes or until golden. Remove from oven, and let cool on a wire rack. Yield: 16 buns.

PROTEIN 8.8 / FAT 5.0 / CARBOHYDRATE 13.9 / CHOLESTEROL 30 / IRON 1.5 / SODIUM 147 / CALCIUM 32

THE MELTING POT

6 canned medium-size mild Greek peppers
6 large, thin onion slices, separated into rings
3 tablespoons commercial oil-free Italian dressing
1 tablespoon plus 1 teaspoon prepared mustard
4 (2-ounce) whole wheat French bread rolls, split lengthwise
8 ounces thinly sliced cooked roast beef
2 ounces provolone cheese, cut into thin strips

Remove stems from peppers; discard stems. Cut peppers into ¼-inch slices; set aside.

Combine onion and Italian dressing in a small saucepan; bring to a boil. Reduce heat and simmer just until onion is transparent. Set mixture aside. (Do not drain.)

Spread 1 teaspoon mustard on bottom half of each roll; top each with 2 ounces roast beef. Spoon reserved onion mixture evenly over sandwiches; top with pepper slices and cheese. Top with remaining halves of rolls. Wrap each sandwich individually in aluminum foil. Bake at 350° for 10 minutes or until sandwiches are thoroughly heated. Serve warm. Yield: 4 servings (347 calories per serving).

PROTEIN 28.7 / FAT 9.7 / CARBOHYDRATE 36.1 / CHOLESTEROL 57 / IRON 2.1 / SODIUM 638 / CALCIUM 133

BARBECUE BEEF SANDWICHES

1 (3-pound) lean boneless beef rump roast
Vegetable cooking spray
½ cup no-salt-added tomato sauce
¼ cup reduced-calorie catsup
¼ cup red wine vinegar
2 tablespoons brown sugar
2 tablespoons chili powder
2 tablespoons no-salt-added tomato paste
1 teaspoon liquid smoke
2 bay leaves
¼ teaspoon salt
¼ teaspoon pepper
¼ teaspoon ground red pepper
12 reduced-calorie whole wheat hamburger buns

Trim fat from roast; set roast aside. Coat a large Dutch oven with cooking spray; place over medium heat until hot. Add roast, and cook on all sides until browned. Remove roast from pan; drain and pat dry with paper towels. Wipe drippings from pan with a paper towel. Return roast to pan. Set aside.

Combine tomato sauce and next 10 ingredients in a small bowl; pour over roast. Bring to a boil; cover, reduce heat, and simmer 2½ to 3 hours or until roast is tender. Remove and discard bay leaves.

Remove roast, and shred meat. Return shredded meat to sauce in pan; stir well. Cook over low heat until thoroughly heated. Serve warm on buns. Yield: 12 servings (281 calories per serving).

PROTEIN 28.4 / FAT 9.3 / CARBOHYDRATE 18.4 / CHOLESTEROL 79 / IRON 3.1 / SODIUM 328 / CALCIUM 9

GRILLED PORK TENDERLOIN WITH SWEET-AND-SOUR RED CABBAGE

½ cup canned no-salt-added beef broth, undiluted
¼ cup unsweetened apple juice
¼ cup chopped onion
2 tablespoons cider vinegar
2 tablespoons low-sodium Worcestershire sauce
1 tablespoon chili powder
2 cloves garlic, chopped
2 (½-pound) pork tenderloins
¼ teaspoon freshly ground pepper
⅛ teaspoon salt
Vegetable cooking spray
2 tablespoons no-salt-added tomato paste
2 (6-ounce) French bread baguettes
Sweet-and-Sour Red Cabbage

Combine first 7 ingredients in a large zip-top heavy-duty plastic bag; seal bag, and shake well. Add pork to bag; seal bag, and shake until pork is well coated. Marinate in refrigerator 8 hours, shaking bag occasionally.

Remove pork from marinade, reserving marinade. Sprinkle pork with pepper and salt. Coat grill rack with cooking spray; place on grill over medium-hot coals. Place pork on rack, and insert meat thermometer into thickest part of pork, if desired. Cook 25 minutes or until meat thermometer registers 170°, turning frequently. Let pork stand 10 minutes. Slice diagonally across grain into thin slices.

Place reserved marinade in a saucepan; bring to a boil. Reduce heat; simmer 3 minutes. Whisk in tomato paste; cook an additional 3 minutes.

Cut each baguette in half lengthwise; cut each loaf into quarters crosswise to make 8 sandwich rolls. Divide sliced pork evenly among bottom halves of rolls. Spread each with 1½ tablespoons marinade mixture. Spoon Sweet-and-Sour Red Cabbage evenly onto each roll, and place tops of rolls on sandwiches. Yield: 8 servings (256 calories per serving).

Sweet-and-Sour Red Cabbage:

8 cups shredded red cabbage
1 large purple onion, thinly sliced
½ cup water
½ cup red wine vinegar
3 tablespoons sugar
⅛ teaspoon salt
¼ teaspoon freshly ground pepper
Vegetable cooking spray

Combine first 7 ingredients in a large saucepan coated with vegetable cooking spray. Cover and cook red cabbage mixture over medium heat 55 minutes or until red cabbage is tender, stirring occasionally. Serve red cabbage mixture warm or chilled. Yield: 3 cups.

PROTEIN 17.3 / FAT 3.4 / CARBOHYDRATE 37.5 / CHOLESTEROL 40 / IRON 2.3 / SODIUM 383 / CALCIUM 70

OPEN-FACED CANADIAN BACON SANDWICHES

Vegetable cooking spray
⅓ cup chopped green onions
⅓ cup low-sugar orange marmalade
1 tablespoon Dijon mustard
⅛ teaspoon ground ginger
2 whole wheat English muffins, split and toasted
⅓ cup alfalfa sprouts
4 (1-ounce) slices Canadian bacon
¼ cup (1-ounce) finely shredded part-skim reduced-sodium semi-soft Swiss cheese
2 tablespoons sliced green onions

Coat a small saucepan with cooking spray, and place saucepan over medium-high heat until hot. Add ⅓ cup green onions, and sauté until tender. Stir in orange marmalade, Dijon mustard, and ginger; cook over low heat until mixture is thoroughly heated.

Spread marmalade mixture evenly over each muffin half; top with sprouts and Canadian bacon. Sprinkle evenly with Swiss cheese and 2 tablespoons green onion. Broil 5½ inches from heat 2 to 3 minutes or until Swiss cheese melts. Serve immediately. Yield: 4 servings (150 calories per serving).

PROTEIN 11.4 / FAT 4.9 / CARBOHYDRATE 15.2 / CHOLESTEROL 21 / IRON 0.4 / SODIUM 608 / CALCIUM 86

CRAB CAKES WITH RED PEPPER PUREE

2 (6-ounce) cans crabmeat, drained and flaked
1 cup soft breadcrumbs
1 cup diced sweet red pepper
1 egg, beaten
1 tablespoon reduced-calorie mayonnaise
1 teaspoon Dijon mustard
⅛ teaspoon ground white pepper
⅛ teaspoon dry mustard
3 drops of hot sauce
Vegetable cooking spray
4 red leaf lettuce leaves
8 (¾-ounce) slices reduced-calorie wheatberry
    bread, toasted
Sweet Red Pepper Puree

Combine crabmeat, breadcrumbs, sweet red pepper, and egg in a large bowl; stir well. Add mayonnaise, Dijon mustard, white pepper, dry mustard, and hot sauce stirring gently. Shape into 4 (4½-inch-round) patties; place crab cakes on a rack of a broiler pan coated with cooking spray. Cover and chill 2 hours (cakes will be slightly loose).

Broil crab cakes 5½ inches from heat 4 to 5 minutes on each side or until golden.

Place a lettuce leaf and crab cake on each of 4 bread slices. Top each crab cake with 2 tablespoons Sweet Red Pepper Puree. Top with remaining bread slices. Serve immediately. Yield: 4 servings (325 calories per serving).

Sweet Red Pepper Puree:

1 medium-size sweet red pepper, seeded
Olive oil-flavored vegetable cooking spray
1 clove garlic, minced
2 tablespoons Chablis or other dry white wine
Dash of pepper
Dash of hot sauce

Cut sweet red pepper into 1-inch pieces. Place in a shallow 1-quart casserole coated with cooking spray; add minced garlic and white wine. Cover and bake at 400° for 20 minutes or until red pepper is soft, stirring once; drain.

Position knife blade in food processor bowl; add red pepper mixture. Process until smooth, scraping sides of processor bowl twice. Stir in pepper and hot sauce. Yield: ½ cup.

PROTEIN 22.2 / FAT 7.4 / CARBOHYDRATE 41.7 / CHOLESTEROL 108 / IRON 4.6 / SODIUM 719 / CALCIUM 103

JAPANESE TUNA SANDWICH

¾ pound tuna fillet
¼ cup reduced-sodium soy sauce
2 tablespoons lemon juice
2 tablespoons dry sherry
1 tablespoon grated ginger
2 teaspoons to 1 tablespoon freshly ground pepper
Vegetable cooking spray
½ teaspoon wasabi powder
1 teaspoon water
2 tablespoons reduced-calorie mayonnaise
4 (¾-ounce) slices reduced-calorie whole wheat
    bread, toasted
½ cup alfalfa sprouts

Place tuna in an 11- x 7- x 2-inch baking dish. Combine soy sauce and next 3 ingredients in a small bowl; stir well, and pour soy sauce mixture over tuna fillet. Cover tightly, and marinate in refrigerator 1 to 2 hours.

Remove tuna from marinade; discard marinade. Press freshly ground pepper onto each side of tuna fillet.

Place tuna fillet on rack of a broiler pan coated with cooking spray. Broil 5½ inches from heat 5 minutes on each side or until fish flakes easily when tested with a fork. Transfer tuna to a medium bowl. Flake tuna fillet with a fork, and set aside.

Combine wasabi powder and water in a small bowl; add mayonnaise, stirring well with a wire whisk. Spread 1½ teaspoons mayonnaise mixture on each slice of toasted bread. Divide flaked tuna evenly among prepared bread. Top each sandwich with 2 tablespoons alfalfa sprouts. Serve immediately. Yield: 4 servings (207 calories per serving).

PROTEIN 25.2 / FAT 7.0 / CARBOHYDRATE 10.5 / CHOLESTEROL 40 / IRON 1.4 / SODIUM 196 / CALCIUM 7

OPEN-FACED EGGPLANT SANDWICHES

1 large eggplant (about 1¾ pounds)
½ cup fine, dry breadcrumbs
¼ cup minced fresh parsley
2 tablespoons grated Parmesan cheese
1 egg, beaten
2 cloves garlic, minced
1 teaspoon dried whole oregano
¼ teaspoon salt
¼ teaspoon freshly ground pepper
¼ cup all-purpose flour
Olive oil-flavored vegetable cooking spray
2 teaspoons olive oil
1 cup peeled, seeded, and chopped tomato
½ cup no-salt-added tomato sauce
¼ cup chopped fresh basil
4 (¾-ounce) slices reduced-calorie Italian bread, toasted
Fresh basil sprigs (optional)

Pierce eggplant with a knife in several places. Place eggplant on a baking sheet, and bake at 425° for 30 minutes or until eggplant is tender when pierced with a knife. Remove eggplant from oven and cool. Remove and discard peel, and cut eggplant into chunks. Place eggplant chunks in a colander, and press lightly with paper towels to remove excess moisture. Let eggplant chunks drain 10 to 15 minutes.

Chop eggplant into small pieces, and place in a large bowl. Add breadcrumbs and next 7 ingredients; stir well. Shape eggplant mixture into 4 (½-inch-thick) patties. Gently dredge eggplant patties in flour.

Coat a large nonstick skillet with cooking spray; add oil. Place skillet over medium-high heat until hot. Place eggplant patties in skillet, and cook 3 to 4 minutes on each side or until lightly browned. Remove eggplant patties from skillet. Drain and pat dry with paper towels. Set aside, and keep warm.

Combine tomato, tomato sauce, and basil in a small bowl; stir well.

Place an eggplant patty on each slice of bread. Spoon tomato mixture evenly over eggplant. Garnish each sandwich with a fresh basil sprig, if desired. Serve warm. Yield: 4 servings (223 calories per serving).

PROTEIN 9.3 / FAT 5.3 / CARBOHYDRATE 37.3 / CHOLESTEROL 52 /
IRON 2.6 / SODIUM 408 / CALCIUM 128

FRENCH BREAD PIZZA

½ (16-ounce) loaf French bread, split
Olive oil-flavored vegetable cooking spray
½ pound sliced fresh mushrooms
1 (8-ounce) can no-salt-added tomato sauce
2 teaspoons dried Italian seasoning
⅛ teaspoon salt
1¼ cups (5 ounces) shredded part-skim mozzarella cheese
1½ tablespoons sliced ripe olives
1½ tablespoons freshly grated Parmesan cheese

Lightly spray cut sides of bread with cooking spray. Place bread on rack of a broiler pan, cut sides up. Broil 5½ inches from heat 2 to 3 minutes or until golden.

Spray a large nonstick skillet with cooking spray; place over medium-high heat until hot. Add mushrooms, and sauté until tender. Remove from heat, and set aside.

Combine tomato sauce, Italian seasoning, and salt; stir well. Spread tomato sauce mixture evenly over toasted bread. Sprinkle mozzarella cheese evenly over tomato sauce mixture. Top with sautéed mushrooms and olives. Sprinkle Parmesan cheese over olives. Place on a baking sheet, and bake at 450° for 5 to 6 minutes or until cheese melts. Serve warm. Yield: 4 servings (311 calories per serving).

PROTEIN 16.7 / FAT 8.7 / CARBOHYDRATE 40.7 / CHOLESTEROL 24 /
IRON 3.1 / SODIUM 674 / CALCIUM 316

 ## TONING OLDER MUSCLES

Many people assume that muscles become weaker with age. However, studies show that even at the age of 60, 75, or 90, people can firm and strengthen their muscles. The main reason muscles become weak is lack of activity. A lot of what's blamed on old age—stiffening of the joints included—is often the result of nonuse. Luckily, the damage is reversible. Certain conditions, such as arthritis or other chronic illnesses, necessitate a check with your doctor first. Still, the bottom line is that it's never too late to get in shape. Firm, strong muscles can be developed at any age. Even better, stronger muscles will make the tasks of daily living easier. Everything from making the bed to lifting a bag of groceries will be simpler.

Reduced-calorie mayonnaise and nonfat yogurt add a low-fat creaminess to Curried Deviled Eggs.

CURRIED DEVILED EGGS

6 hard-cooked eggs, peeled
2 tablespoons reduced-calorie
    mayonnaise
1½ tablespoons plain nonfat yogurt
2 teaspoons grated onion
1 teaspoon Dijon mustard
½ teaspoon curry powder
⅛ teaspoon paprika

Slice eggs in half lengthwise, and carefully remove yolks. Mash yolks; add mayonnaise and next 4 ingredients; stir well. Pipe yolk mixture evenly into egg whites, using a No. 1B star tip. Sprinkle eggs with paprika. Yield: 12 servings (44 calories per serving).

PROTEIN 3.2 / FAT 3.2 / CARBOHYDRATE 0.8 / CHOLESTEROL 101 / IRON 0.5 / SODIUM 64 / CALCIUM 16

CRISP MIX

1½ cups small unsalted pretzels
1 cup bite-size shredded whole wheat cereal
  biscuits
1 cup bite-size corn and rice cereal squares
¾ cup bite-size crispy bran squares
2 tablespoons reduced-calorie margarine
1 tablespoon low-sodium Worcestershire
  sauce
2 teaspoons dried Italian seasoning
¼ teaspoon pepper
⅛ teaspoon salt
2 tablespoons grated Parmesan cheese

Combine pretzels, whole wheat cereal biscuits, corn and rice cereal squares, and crispy bran squares in a large bowl. Toss well, and set mixture aside.

Combine margarine, Worcestershire sauce, Italian seasoning, pepper, and salt in a small saucepan. Place over medium heat, and cook until margarine melts, stirring frequently. Pour margarine mixture over pretzel mixture; toss well. Add cheese, and toss well. Place mixture in a 13- x 9- x 2-inch baking dish. Bake at 275° for 45 minutes or until crisp. Yield: 4 cups (78 calories per ½-cup serving).

PROTEIN 1.9 / FAT 2.5 / CARBOHYDRATE 13.3 / CHOLESTEROL 1 /
IRON 1.7 / SODIUM 175 / CALCIUM 33

INDIAN POPCORN

2½ teaspoons reduced-calorie margarine,
  melted and cooled
½ teaspoon ground cumin
½ teaspoon curry powder
¼ teaspoon ground cardamom
⅛ teaspoon salt
⅛ teaspoon ground nutmeg
4 cups popped corn (cooked without salt or fat)

Combine first 6 ingredients in a small bowl; stir well.

Place popcorn in a large bowl; add spice mixture, tossing to coat. Yield: 4 cups (38 calories per 1-cup serving).

PROTEIN 0.9 / FAT 1.9 / CARBOHYDRATE 5.0 / CHOLESTEROL 0 /
IRON 0.4 / SODIUM 97 / CALCIUM 5

ORANGE STICKY POPCORN

3 quarts popped corn (cooked without salt or fat)
¾ cup granola cereal
1½ tablespoons reduced-calorie margarine
¾ cup low-sugar orange marmalade
¼ cup honey
1 teaspoon vanilla extract
1 teaspoon almond extract
Vegetable cooking spray

Combine popcorn and granola in a large bowl; set aside.

Melt margarine in a medium saucepan; add marmalade and honey. Bring to a boil; cook over medium heat 5 minutes, stirring frequently. Remove from heat; stir in flavorings. Pour over popcorn mixture, and toss until well coated. Place mixture on a baking sheet coated with cooking spray. Bake at 225° for 50 minutes. Turn oven off; cool popcorn in oven 1 hour. Spread popcorn on wax paper, and cool completely. Store in an airtight container. Yield: 5½ cups (87 calories per ½-cup serving).

PROTEIN 1.5 / FAT 2.2 / CARBOHYDRATE 15.9 / CHOLESTEROL 0 /
IRON 0.4 / SODIUM 25 / CALCIUM 12

NACHO WONTONS

20 fresh or frozen wonton skins, thawed
Vegetable cooking spray
1 teaspoon chili powder
1 teaspoon paprika
⅛ teaspoon garlic powder
2 teaspoons water
2 teaspoons olive oil
2 tablespoons grated Parmesan cheese

Cut wonton skins in half diagonally to form 40 triangles. Place on two baking sheets coated with cooking spray.

Combine chili powder and next 4 ingredients in a small bowl; stir well. Brush triangles evenly on one side with chili powder mixture. Sprinkle cheese evenly over triangles. Bake at 375° for 6 minutes. Remove from oven, and cool. Yield: 10 servings (29 calories per serving).

PROTEIN 1.0 / FAT 1.6 / CARBOHYDRATE 2.5 / CHOLESTEROL 13 /
IRON 0.2 / SODIUM 51 / CALCIUM 17

SWEET TORTILLA CRISPS

4 (8-inch) flour tortillas
1 tablespoon reduced-calorie margarine, melted
1 tablespoon sugar
½ teaspoon ground cinnamon

Brush tortillas with margarine; cut each tortilla into 8 wedges, and place on an ungreased baking sheet. Combine sugar and cinnamon, stirring well. Sprinkle sugar mixture evenly over tortilla wedges. Bake at 425° for 4 to 6 minutes or until tortilla wedges are lightly browned. Yield: 32 wedges (23 calories per wedge).

PROTEIN 0.4 / FAT 0.6 / CARBOHYDRATE 4.3 / CHOLESTEROL 0 / IRON 0.1 / SODIUM 3 / CALCIUM 5

QUESADILLAS

4 (8-inch) flour tortillas
¾ cup (3 ounces) reduced-fat Monterey Jack cheese
¼ cup commercial salsa

Place 2 tortillas on an ungreased baking sheet. Sprinkle evenly with cheese. Spoon 2 tablespoons salsa onto each tortilla. Top with remaining tortillas. Bake tortillas at 450° for 4 minutes on each side. To serve, cut each tortilla into 8 wedges. Yield: 16 wedges (49 calories per wedge).

PROTEIN 2.3 / FAT 1.7 / CARBOHYDRATE 6.8 / CHOLESTEROL 4 / IRON 0.3 / SODIUM 34 / CALCIUM 51

BANANA-CHOCOLATE CHIP FLURRIES

4 medium-size ripe bananas, peeled and sliced
3 tablespoons semisweet chocolate mini-morsels
6 (5-ounce) paper cups

Place banana slices in a large zip-top heavy-duty plastic bag. Press out excess air, and seal bag. Freeze bananas 2 hours or until firm.
Position knife blade in food processor bowl; add bananas. Process 1 minute or until pureed. Place pureed banana in a medium bowl; add chocolate morsels, and stir well. Spoon mixture

evenly into paper cups. Freeze until firm. Yield: 6 servings (96 calories per serving).

PROTEIN 1.0 / FAT 2.0 / CARBOHYDRATE 21.0 / CHOLESTEROL 0 / IRON 0.4 / SODIUM 1 / CALCIUM 6

FROZEN FRUIT POPS

3 cups fresh strawberries
1 envelope unflavored gelatin
1¼ cups cold water
1½ cups unsweetened pineapple juice
3 tablespoons lemon juice
1 tablespoon sugar
9 (5-ounce) paper cups
9 wooden sticks

Place strawberries in container of an electric blender or food processor; top with cover, and process until smooth. Set aside.
Sprinkle gelatin over cold water in a medium saucepan; let stand 1 minute. Add juices and sugar; stir well. Cook mixture over low heat, stirring until gelatin and sugar dissolve. Stir in pureed strawberries.
Pour strawberry mixture evenly into paper cups. Cover tops of cups with aluminum foil, and insert a wooden stick through foil into center of each cup. Freeze until firm. To serve, remove foil, and peel paper cup away from fruit pop. Yield: 9 servings (47 calories per serving).

PROTEIN 1.1 / FAT 0.2 / CARBOHYDRATE 11.0 / CHOLESTEROL 0 / IRON 0.3 / SODIUM 2 / CALCIUM 14

Stock up on fresh vegetables and melons to make these condiments (from left): Melon, Cucumber, and Tomato Relish (page 207), Pickled Asparagus Spears (page 208), and Two-Tomato Relish (page 207). They can accompany any entrée.

Sauces & Condiments

Creamy Mocha Sauce is guaranteed to be a winner when served over vanilla ice milk.

CREAMY MOCHA SAUCE

2 tablespoons unsweetened cocoa
1 tablespoon cornstarch
1 tablespoon instant coffee granules
1 cup plus 1 tablespoon skim milk
3 tablespoons light-colored corn
  syrup
2 tablespoons Kahlúa or other
  coffee-flavored liqueur

Combine cocoa, cornstarch, and coffee granules in a small saucepan. Gradually stir in milk, corn syrup, and liqueur. Cook over medium heat, stirring constantly, until thickened. Serve warm over ice milk or angel food cake. Yield: 1½ cups (17 calories per tablespoon).

PROTEIN 0.5 / FAT 0.1 / CARBOHYDRATE 3.6 / CHOLESTEROL 0 / IRON 0.2 / SODIUM 8 / CALCIUM 15

MAPLE-NUT SAUCE

¾ cup plus 2 tablespoons skim milk
3 tablespoons dark brown sugar
1 tablespoon cornstarch
3½ tablespoons chopped walnuts, toasted
½ teaspoon vanilla extract
½ teaspoon maple flavoring

Combine skim milk, brown sugar, and cornstarch in a small saucepan, stirring well. Cook over medium heat, stirring constantly, until milk mixture comes to a boil; cook an additional 2 minutes.

Remove milk mixture from heat. Stir in walnuts and flavorings. Serve warm or chilled over ice milk, custard, or angel food cake. Yield: 1 cup (23 calories per tablespoon).

PROTEIN 0.8 / FAT 0.9 / CARBOHYDRATE 3.0 / CHOLESTEROL 0 / IRON 0.1 / SODIUM 7 / CALCIUM 19

BRANDIED BLACKBERRY SAUCE

2 cups fresh blackberries
¼ cup blackberry-flavored brandy
¼ cup sugar
1 teaspoon vanilla extract
2 teaspoons grated orange rind

Combine first 3 ingredients in a medium saucepan; let stand 2 hours. Place over medium heat; bring mixture to a boil, stirring frequently. Reduce heat, and simmer 10 to 15 minutes or until slightly thickened. Remove from heat. Stir in vanilla and orange rind. Cool completely. Serve over ice milk. Yield: 1 cup (23 calories per tablespoon).

PROTEIN 0.1 / FAT 0.1 / CARBOHYDRATE 5.8 / CHOLESTEROL 0 / IRON 0.1 / SODIUM 0 / CALCIUM 7

STRAWBERRY-RHUBARB SAUCE

2 cups sliced fresh strawberries
1 cup diced rhubarb
1 cup water
¼ cup sugar
2 tablespoons cornstarch
¼ teaspoon ground cinnamon
⅛ teaspoon ground cloves
⅛ teaspoon ground cardamom
1 teaspoon grated orange rind

Combine strawberries, rhubarb, and water in a saucepan. Cook over medium heat 6 minutes or until rhubarb is tender. Add sugar and next 4 ingredients. Cook, stirring constantly, until thickened. Stir in orange rind. Serve warm or chilled over angel food cake or pancakes. Yield: 2¾ cups (8 calories per tablespoon).

PROTEIN 0.1 / FAT 0.0 / CARBOHYDRATE 2.1 / CHOLESTEROL 0 / IRON 0.0 / SODIUM 0 / CALCIUM 4

BARBECUE SAUCE

1 (8-ounce) can no-salt-added tomato sauce
⅔ cup sliced green onions
¼ cup red wine vinegar
¼ cup lime juice
2 jalapeño peppers, seeded and minced
1 clove garlic, minced
1 tablespoon dark brown sugar
1½ teaspoons ground allspice
1 teaspoon minced fresh thyme
1 bay leaf
½ teaspoon liquid smoke

Combine first 5 ingredients in a medium saucepan, stirring well to combine. Add garlic, brown sugar, allspice, thyme, bay leaf, and liquid smoke; stir well. Place over medium heat; bring mixture to a boil, stirring frequently. Reduce heat, and simmer 10 minutes. Remove and discard bay leaf. Use sauce for basting grilled beef, pork, or chicken. Yield: 1½ cups (7 calories per tablespoon).

PROTEIN 0.2 / FAT 0.0 / CARBOHYDRATE 1.7 / CHOLESTEROL 0 / IRON 0.1 / SODIUM 3 / CALCIUM 3

VEGETABLE PASTA SAUCE

Olive oil-flavored vegetable cooking spray
1 teaspoon olive oil
½ cup chopped onion
½ cup chopped green pepper
½ cup chopped celery
1 clove garlic, minced
1 (8-ounce) can no-salt-added tomato sauce
1 (6-ounce) can no-salt-added tomato paste
½ cup water
2 tablespoons Burgundy or other dry red wine
1 cup sliced fresh mushrooms
2 tablespoons chopped fresh parsley
½ teaspoon dried whole oregano
½ teaspoon dried whole basil
7½ cups peeled, cubed eggplant (about 2 medium)
2¾ cups coarsely chopped tomato
¼ cup grated Parmesan cheese

Coat a Dutch oven with cooking spray; add oil. Place over medium-high heat until hot. Add onion, pepper, celery, and garlic; sauté 5 minutes or until vegetables are tender. Stir in tomato sauce and next 7 ingredients. Bring to a boil; cover, reduce heat, and simmer 30 minutes. Add eggplant and tomato; cook an additional 15 minutes, stirring occasionally. Stir in cheese. Serve warm over hot cooked pasta. Yield: 8 cups (6 calories per tablespoon).

PROTEIN 0.3 / FAT 0.1 / CARBOHYDRATE 1.0 / CHOLESTEROL 0 / IRON 0.1 / SODIUM 5 / CALCIUM 5

CREAMY HERB SAUCE

1 cup 1% low-fat cottage cheese
¼ cup reduced-calorie mayonnaise
¼ cup skim milk
2 tablespoons red wine vinegar
¼ cup chopped green onions
¼ cup chopped fresh parsley
1 clove garlic, minced
½ teaspoon minced fresh oregano
½ teaspoon minced fresh basil
¼ teaspoon pepper
⅛ teaspoon ground red pepper

Combine cottage cheese, mayonnaise, skim milk, and red wine vinegar in container of an electric blender or food processor; top with cover, and process until smooth. Add green onions, parsley, minced garlic, oregano, basil, pepper, and red pepper; process until blended. Serve herb sauce with seafood. Yield: 1⅔ cups (15 calories per tablespoon).

PROTEIN 1.2 / FAT 0.9 / CARBOHYDRATE 0.6 / CHOLESTEROL 0 / IRON 0.0 / SODIUM 54 / CALCIUM 9

HERBED AIOLI

½ cup canned low-sodium chicken broth, undiluted
2 tablespoons water
1 tablespoon cornstarch
1 egg yolk, beaten
½ cup chopped fresh parsley
¼ cup loosely packed fresh basil leaves
2 cloves garlic, minced
2½ tablespoons fresh lemon juice
2 teaspoons Dijon mustard
¼ teaspoon salt
⅛ teaspoon freshly ground pepper

Combine chicken broth, water, and cornstarch in a small saucepan, stirring well. Cook over medium-high heat, stirring constantly, until broth mixture comes to a boil. Cook an additional minute or until thickened. Remove broth mixture from heat. Gradually stir about one-fourth of hot mixture into egg yolk; add to remaining hot mixture, stirring constantly. Cook mixture over low heat, stirring constantly, until thickened. Transfer mixture to a small bowl; let cool to room temperature.

Position knife blade in food processor bowl. Add parsley and basil; process until finely chopped. Add garlic, lemon juice, and mustard; process until smooth.

Combine cooled broth mixture and parsley mixture in a small bowl; stir well. Stir in salt and pepper. Cover and chill thoroughly. Serve with fish or steamed fresh vegetables. Yield: ¾ cup (14 calories per tablespoon).

PROTEIN 0.4 / FAT 0.6 / CARBOHYDRATE 1.7 / CHOLESTEROL 23 / IRON 0.5 / SODIUM 76 / CALCIUM 22

The flavors of garlic, ginger, green onions, and tomato blend together in tasty Ginger Mayonnaise. Enjoy it served with your favorite cut of pork.

GINGER MAYONNAISE

½ cup reduced-calorie mayonnaise
1 clove garlic, minced
1 teaspoon peeled, grated ginger
2 drops of hot sauce
⅔ cup seeded, diced tomato
2 tablespoons thinly sliced green
  onions

Combine mayonnaise, minced garlic, grated ginger, and hot sauce in a small bowl; stir well to mix thoroughly. Cover mayonnaise mixture, and refrigerate at least 3 hours.

Stir in diced tomato and green onions. Serve mayonnaise with pork or fish. Yield: 1 cup (22 calories per tablespoon).

PROTEIN 0.2 / FAT 2.0 / CARBOHYDRATE 0.9 / CHOLESTEROL 2 /
IRON 0.1 / SODIUM 56 / CALCIUM 1

RÉMOULADE SAUCE

½ cup reduced-calorie mayonnaise
2 tablespoons no-salt-added tomato paste
2 tablespoons minced onion
1 tablespoon minced dill pickle
2 teaspoons minced fresh parsley
1 teaspoon prepared mustard
1 teaspoon anchovy paste
¼ teaspoon dried whole tarragon
⅛ teaspoon ground red pepper

Combine all ingredients in a small bowl; stir well. Cover and refrigerate at least 3 hours. Serve sauce with chilled cooked shrimp or mixed salad greens. Yield: ¾ cup (31 calories per tablespoon).

PROTEIN 0.4 / FAT 2.8 / CARBOHYDRATE 1.3 / CHOLESTEROL 3 /
IRON 0.1 / SODIUM 155 / CALCIUM 2

HONEY-MUSTARD SPREAD

½ cup Dijon mustard
2 tablespoons reduced-calorie mayonnaise
2 tablespoons honey
½ teaspoon grated lemon rind
⅛ teaspoon ground cinnamon
⅛ teaspoon ground cloves
⅛ teaspoon hot sauce

Combine all ingredients in a small bowl; stir well. Cover and refrigerate at least 3 hours. Serve with meat or as a sandwich spread. Yield: ¾ cup (30 calories per tablespoon).

PROTEIN 0.0 / FAT 1.3 / CARBOHYDRATE 3.8 / CHOLESTEROL 1 / IRON 0.0 / SODIUM 316 / CALCIUM 1

CURRY SEASONING

2 tablespoons ground ginger
1 tablespoon plus 2 teaspoons ground coriander
1 tablespoon plus 2 teaspoons ground turmeric
1 tablespoon plus 1 teaspoon ground cumin
2 teaspoons pepper
1 teaspoon ground cardamom
1 teaspoon ground fenugreek

Combine all ingredients in a small bowl; stir well. Store in an airtight container. Use to season chicken, beef, or vegetables before cooking. Yield: ½ cup (6 calories per teaspoon).

PROTEIN 0.2 / FAT 0.2 / CARBOHYDRATE 1.1 / CHOLESTEROL 0 / IRON 0.6 / SODIUM 1 / CALCIUM 7

BLUEBERRY VINEGAR

1 cup fresh blueberries
1¼ cups white wine vinegar
Additional fresh blueberries (optional)

Place 1 cup blueberries in a pint jar. Place vinegar in a small saucepan; bring to a boil. Pour vinegar over blueberries; cover. Let stand at room temperature at least 3 days.

Strain vinegar into decorative jars, discarding blueberries. Add additional fresh blueberries, if desired. Seal jars with a cork or other airtight lid.

Serve with salad greens or fruit salads. Yield: 1 cup (8 calories per tablespoon).

PROTEIN 0.1 / FAT 0.0 / CARBOHYDRATE 1.5 / CHOLESTEROL 0 / IRON 0.0 / SODIUM 3 / CALCIUM 1

FLAVORING THE VINEGAR

When steeped or stored with herbs, fruits, and spices, vinegar takes on intense flavors that add spark to everything from soups to salads to side dishes. These infused vinegars can be purchased in specialty or gourmet food shops. Or you can make them yourself.

Start with fresh herbs or fruits—a bunch of fresh rosemary, a handful of raspberries, or a few hot peppers—and a vinegar such as champagne, sherry, or rice vinegar. Keep in mind that mild vinegars such as white wine or rice wine allow the herb flavor to come through. Crush or bruise the herbs so that flavoring oils can escape, and place them in a bottle with the vinegar. Cap the bottle with a cork or screw cap because a tight seal is important. Then store the vinegar in a cool, dry place. A strong herb such as rosemary will impart a nice flavor after only a few days, but delicately flavored herbs may take a week or longer.

Another way to make vinegar infusions is to use heat. If the bottle of vinegar is placed in the sun, the warmth will draw out the flavoring oils. The vinegar can also be heated before it's poured into the bottles, yielding a stronger, more intense flavor. Experiment with different herb, fruit, and vinegar combinations; the variety of flavors possible is limited only by your imagination.

FRESH SALSA RELISH

2 tablespoons red wine vinegar
2 tablespoons lime juice
2 teaspoons olive oil
1 medium-size sweet red pepper
1¾ cups peeled, seeded, and chopped tomato
¾ cup minced shallots
1 jalapeño pepper, seeded and minced
2 tablespoons minced fresh cilantro
1 clove garlic, minced
¼ teaspoon salt
¼ teaspoon freshly ground pepper

Combine vinegar, lime juice, and olive oil in a small bowl. Beat well with a wire whisk; set mixture aside.

Cut sweet red pepper in half lengthwise; remove and discard seeds and membrane. Place pepper, skin side up, on a baking sheet; flatten with palm of hand. Broil 5½ inches from heat 15 to 20 minutes or until charred. Place in ice water, and chill 5 minutes. Remove pepper from water; peel and discard skin. Dice pepper, and place in a medium bowl.

Add tomato and remaining ingredients to pepper; toss well. Pour reserved vinegar mixture over tomato mixture; toss to combine. Serve with beef, pork, chicken or unsalted tortilla chips. Yield: 3 cups (6 calories per tablespoon).

PROTEIN 0.2 / FAT 0.2 / CARBOHYDRATE 0.9 / CHOLESTEROL 0 / IRON 0.1 / SODIUM 13 / CALCIUM 2

MELON, CUCUMBER, AND TOMATO RELISH

1 cup diced cucumber
1 cup diced cantaloupe
1 cup diced tomato
¼ cup finely chopped onion
¼ cup white wine vinegar
2 tablespoons minced fresh mint
¼ teaspoon salt
¼ teaspoon pepper

Combine all ingredients in a medium bowl; toss well. Cover and refrigerate at least 2 hours. Serve with fish or chicken. Yield: 3 cups (3 calories per tablespoon).

PROTEIN 0.1 / FAT 0.0 / CARBOHYDRATE 0.7 / CHOLESTEROL 0 / IRON 0.1 / SODIUM 13 / CALCIUM 2

TWO-TOMATO RELISH

1½ cups seeded, finely chopped red tomato (about 1 large)
1½ cups seeded, finely chopped yellow tomato (about 1 large)
½ cup plus 2 tablespoons finely chopped onion
½ cup finely chopped celery
½ cup finely chopped green pepper
3 tablespoons prepared mustard
2 tablespoons white wine vinegar
1 tablespoon brown sugar
½ teaspoon mustard seeds
½ teaspoon celery seeds
½ teaspoon salt
¼ teaspoon freshly ground pepper

Combine tomato, onion, celery, and green pepper in a medium bowl; toss gently. Set aside.

Combine mustard and remaining ingredients in a small saucepan; stir well. Place saucepan over medium heat, and cook 2 to 3 minutes or just until mixture simmers. Pour mustard mixture over vegetables, tossing gently to coat. Cover and refrigerate 8 hours. Serve relish over fresh vegetables, steak, or hamburgers. Yield: 4¼ cups (3 calories per tablespoon).

PROTEIN 0.1 / FAT 0.1 / CARBOHYDRATE 0.6 / CHOLESTEROL 0 / IRON 0.1 / SODIUM 27 / CALCIUM 2

COPPER CARROT RELISH

3 cups chopped carrot
1 cup finely chopped onion
½ cup thinly sliced celery
½ cup finely chopped sweet red pepper
½ cup water
¾ cup no-salt-added tomato juice
2 tablespoons white wine vinegar
1 tablespoon prepared mustard
1 teaspoon low-sodium Worcestershire sauce
1 tablespoon sugar
½ teaspoon dried whole dillweed
¼ teaspoon salt
¼ teaspoon ground red pepper

Combine first 5 ingredients in large saucepan. Bring to a boil; cover, reduce heat, and cook 5 minutes or until crisp-tender. Drain well; transfer mixture to a medium bowl, and set aside.

Combine tomato juice and remaining ingredients in a small bowl; stir well. Pour over carrot mixture; toss gently. Cover and refrigerate 24 hours, stirring occasionally. Serve with beef, pork, or poultry. Yield: 4 cups (5 calories per tablespoon).

PROTEIN 0.1 / FAT 0.0 / CARBOHYDRATE 1.2 / CHOLESTEROL 0 / IRON 0.1 / SODIUM 16 / CALCIUM 3

PICKLED ASPARAGUS SPEARS

2 pounds fresh asparagus spears
2 cups water
2 cups white wine vinegar (5% acidity)
2¼ teaspoons mustard seeds
1 teaspoon salt
1 teaspoon crushed red pepper
4 cloves garlic, sliced
4 jalapeño peppers, seeded and
  sliced lengthwise

Snap off tough ends of asparagus. Remove scales from stalks with a knife or vegetable peeler, if desired. Cut asparagus into 4½-inch pieces; set aside.

Combine water and next 4 ingredients in a small saucepan; bring mixture to a boil, and remove from heat.

Pack asparagus into hot sterilized jars. Add 1 garlic slice and 1 jalapeño pepper slice to each jar. Cover asparagus with boiling vinegar mixture, leaving ¼-inch headspace. Remove air bubbles; wipe jar rims. Cover at once with metal lids, and screw on bands. Let cool. Store in refrigerator 3 days before serving. Yield: 4 pints (10 calories per 2-spear serving).

PROTEIN 0.8 / FAT 0.1 / CARBOHYDRATE 1.2 / CHOLESTEROL 0 / IRON 0.2 / SODIUM 44 / CALCIUM 8

SWEET POTATO CHUTNEY

2¾ cups peeled, cubed sweet potato (about 1
  pound)
1 cup unsweetened orange juice
1 small onion, thinly sliced
¼ cup sugar
¼ cup raisins
1 tablespoon grated orange rind
1 teaspoon ground ginger
½ teaspoon ground cinnamon
¼ teaspoon ground allspice
⅛ teaspoon ground cardamom

Combine all ingredients in a large saucepan; stir well. Bring mixture to a boil; cover, reduce heat, and simmer 10 minutes. Uncover and cook 40 to 45 minutes or until thickened, stirring occasionally. Let cool 30 minutes. Cover and chill thoroughly. Serve with beef or pork. Yield: 2⅔ cups (21 calories per tablespoon).

PROTEIN 0.3 / FAT 0.0 / CARBOHYDRATE 5.4 / CHOLESTEROL 0 / IRON 0.0 / SODIUM 3 / CALCIUM 3

PINEAPPLE-DATE CHUTNEY

2 cups cubed fresh pineapple
1 cup chopped dates
¼ cup cider vinegar
1 teaspoon peeled, minced ginger
½ teaspoon ground allspice
¼ teaspoon fennel seeds
¼ teaspoon crushed red pepper
¼ teaspoon ground cumin

Combine all ingredients in a medium saucepan; stir well. Bring mixture to a boil; reduce heat, and simmer 25 to 30 minutes or until thickened, stirring occasionally. Serve with beef, pork, poultry, or fish. Yield: 2 cups (17 calories per tablespoon).

PROTEIN 0.1 / FAT 0.1 / CARBOHYDRATE 4.4 / CHOLESTEROL 0 / IRON 0.1 / SODIUM 0 / CALCIUM 3

Colorful Three-Pepper Stir-Fry (page 214) is a simple yet dramatic dish.

GRECIAN ARTICHOKE HEARTS

2 (9-ounce) packages frozen artichoke hearts, thawed
Vegetable cooking spray
1 teaspoon olive oil
½ cup minced shallots
3 tablespoons crumbled feta cheese
2 tablespoons sliced ripe olives
1 (2-ounce) jar diced pimiento, drained
1 teaspoon dried whole basil
½ teaspoon dried whole thyme
¼ teaspoon cracked pepper

Arrange artichoke hearts in a vegetable steamer over boiling water. Cover and steam 5 minutes or until artichoke hearts are tender. Set aside, and keep warm.

Coat a large nonstick skillet with cooking spray; add oil. Place over medium-high heat until hot. Add shallots, and sauté until tender. Remove from heat. Add artichoke hearts, feta cheese, and remaining ingredients; toss gently. Serve warm. Yield: 7 servings (61 calories per ½-cup serving).

PROTEIN 3.0 / FAT 2.5 / CARBOHYDRATE 8.3 / CHOLESTEROL 5 / IRON 0.9 / SODIUM 121 / CALCIUM 51

BLUE CHEESE ASPARAGUS

1½ pounds fresh asparagus spears
Vegetable cooking spray
2 teaspoons reduced-calorie margarine
2 tablespoons cider vinegar
3 tablespoons crumbled blue cheese
2 tablespoons chopped pecans, toasted

Snap off tough ends of asparagus. Remove scales from stalks with a knife or vegetable peeler, if desired.

Coat a large nonstick skillet with cooking spray; add margarine. Place over medium heat until margarine melts. Add asparagus, and sauté 3 to 4 minutes. Add vinegar; cover and simmer 2 to 3 minutes or until asparagus is crisp-tender. Add blue cheese and chopped pecans; toss gently. Serve warm. Yield: 6 servings (49 calories per serving).

PROTEIN 2.9 / FAT 3.4 / CARBOHYDRATE 3.4 / CHOLESTEROL 2 / IRON 0.6 / SODIUM 47 / CALCIUM 29

MUSTARD GREEN BEANS

1 pound fresh green beans
1 large sweet red pepper, cut into julienne strips
2 teaspoons reduced-calorie margarine
1 tablespoon coarse-grained mustard
2 tablespoons chopped walnuts, toasted

Wash beans; trim ends, and remove strings. Arrange beans and red pepper strips in a vegetable steamer over boiling water. Cover and steam 3 minutes or until crisp-tender.

Melt margarine in a large nonstick skillet over medium heat; add mustard, and stir well. Add steamed vegetables, and toss gently. Transfer mixture to a serving dish, and sprinkle with chopped walnuts. Yield: 8 servings (38 calories per ½-cup serving).

PROTEIN 1.5 / FAT 1.8 / CARBOHYDRATE 4.8 / CHOLESTEROL 0 / IRON 0.7 / SODIUM 68 / CALCIUM 22

QUICK COMPANY GREEN BEANS

1 pound fresh green beans
Vegetable cooking spray
½ cup chopped purple onion
¼ cup sliced green onions
1 (16-ounce) can whole potatoes, drained and halved
2 tablespoons lemon juice
2 teaspoons olive oil
½ teaspoon dried whole thyme
2 tablespoons lemon zest (optional)

Wash beans; trim ends, and remove strings. Cook beans, covered, in a small amount of boiling water 5 minutes or until crisp-tender. Drain and set aside.

Coat a large nonstick skillet with cooking spray; place over medium-high heat until hot. Add onions, and sauté until tender. Add reserved green beans and potato halves; cook until thoroughly heated. Transfer mixture to a serving dish, and keep warm.

Combine lemon juice, olive oil, and thyme; pour over vegetable mixture, tossing well. Sprinkle with lemon zest, if desired. Yield: 6 servings (75 calories per ½-cup serving).

PROTEIN 2.3 / FAT 1.8 / CARBOHYDRATE 14.0 / CHOLESTEROL 0 / IRON 1.7 / SODIUM 164 / CALCIUM 37

SPICED BEETS

1½ pounds medium beets
½ cup low-sugar apricot spread
2 tablespoons lemon juice
½ teaspoon ground ginger
¼ teaspoon ground nutmeg

Leave root and 1 inch of stem on beets; scrub with a vegetable brush. Place beets in a large saucepan; add water to cover. Bring to a boil; cover, reduce heat, and simmer beets 35 to 40 minutes or until tender. Drain; pour cold water over beets, and drain. Trim off stems and roots, and rub off skins; dice beets, and set aside.

Combine apricot spread and remaining ingredients in a medium nonstick skillet; stir well. Cook over low heat until apricot spread melts. Add beets, and cook until thoroughly heated. Yield: 6 servings (67 calories per ½-cup serving).

PROTEIN 1.0 / FAT 0.5 / CARBOHYDRATE 16.1 / CHOLESTEROL 0 / IRON 0.5 / SODIUM 63 / CALCIUM 11

ELEGANT CHEESY BROCCOLI

1½ pounds fresh broccoli
1 tablespoon cornstarch
¼ teaspoon paprika
1 cup skim milk
¾ cup (3 ounces) light Havarti cheese

Trim off large leaves of broccoli, and remove tough ends of lower stalks. Wash broccoli thoroughly, and cut into spears. Arrange spears in a vegetable steamer over boiling water. Cover and steam 10 to 15 minutes or until broccoli is crisp-tender. Drain; transfer broccoli to a serving dish, and keep warm.

Combine cornstarch and paprika in a small saucepan; gradually add milk, stirring constantly. Cook over medium heat, stirring constantly, until mixture thickens. Add cheese; cook until cheese melts, stirring constantly. Pour sauce over broccoli. Serve immediately. Yield: 6 servings (98 calories per serving).

PROTEIN 7.9 / FAT 4.4 / CARBOHYDRATE 8.5 / CHOLESTEROL 15 / IRON 0.9 / SODIUM 142 / CALCIUM 99

CARROT AND ZUCCHINI SAUTÉ

Vegetable cooking spray
1 cup shredded carrot
½ cup chopped green pepper
3 cups shredded zucchini
⅓ cup chopped unsweetened pitted dates
2 tablespoons lemon juice
¾ teaspoon minced fresh thyme or
　¼ teaspoon dried whole thyme
¼ teaspoon pepper

Coat a nonstick skillet with cooking spray; place over medium-high heat until hot. Add carrot and green pepper; sauté until crisp-tender. Add zucchini; sauté 3 minutes or until thoroughly heated. Stir in dates and remaining ingredients. Yield: 6 servings (46 calories per ½-cup serving).

PROTEIN 1.1 / FAT 0.3 / CARBOHYDRATE 11.1 / CHOLESTEROL 0 / IRON 0.6 / SODIUM 8 / CALCIUM 17

 GROW YOUR OWN HERBS

Save a stop at the supermarket by growing your own herbs. All you need to have for a culinary garden is a windowsill or small space that gets some sunshine.

Herbs need very little care or feeding. If planted in well-drained garden soil with some sunlight, herbs will sprout quickly. And be sure to keep watering to a minimum; keeping the soil somewhat dry encourages the development of volatile oils, compounds that give distinct flavor to herbs.

A few easy-to-grow herbs include sage, tarragon, parsley, basil, dillweed, rosemary, and chives. For quicker results, set out full grown plants rather than planting seeds.

A sweet pineapple glaze gives Hawaiian Carrots a tropical flair.

HAWAIIAN CARROTS

1 (20-ounce) can pineapple tidbits in juice, undrained
1 tablespoon honey
½ teaspoon dried whole oregano
¼ teaspoon onion powder
4 large carrots (about ½ pound), scraped and cut diagonally into ½-inch pieces
1 tablespoon cornstarch
2 tablespoons water
2 tablespoons unsalted roasted cashews, chopped

Drain pineapple tidbits, reserving juice; set pineapple tidbits aside.

Combine pineapple juice, honey, oregano, and onion powder in a medium saucepan; bring to a boil. Add carrot; cover, reduce heat, and simmer 10 minutes. Stir in reserved pineapple tidbits, and cook an additional 5 minutes or until carrot is tender.

Combine cornstarch and water; stir until smooth. Stir cornstarch mixture into carrot mixture; cook 1 minute or until thickened. Transfer to a serving dish; sprinkle with cashews. Yield: 6 servings (110 calories per ½-cup serving).

PROTEIN 2.1 / FAT 4.0 / CARBOHYDRATE 18.6 / CHOLESTEROL 0 / IRON 1.1 / SODIUM 16 / CALCIUM 31

FESTIVE CELERY BAKE

3 cups diagonally sliced celery
½ cup sliced water chestnuts, drained
¼ cup slivered almonds, toasted
3 tablespoons finely chopped sweet red pepper
1 cup boiling water
1 teaspoon chicken-flavored bouillon granules
½ teaspoon dried whole tarragon
¼ teaspoon garlic powder

Combine celery, water chestnuts, almonds, and sweet red pepper in a 1½-quart ceramic heatproof dish; stir well. Combine water and remaining ingredients in a small bowl; stir well. Pour bouillon mixture over celery mixture. Cover and bake at 350° for 40 to 50 minutes or until crisp-tender. Serve with a slotted spoon. Yield: 6 servings (56 calories per ½-cup serving).

PROTEIN 1.8 / FAT 3.2 / CARBOHYDRATE 6.1 / CHOLESTEROL 0 / IRON 0.6 / SODIUM 187 / CALCIUM 38

OVEN-FRIED EGGPLANT OLÉ

1 cup finely chopped tomato
1 teaspoon seeded, minced jalapeño pepper
⅛ teaspoon garlic powder
Dash of freshly ground pepper
2 teaspoons minced fresh cilantro
1 small eggplant (about ¾ pound)
½ cup plain nonfat yogurt
¼ cup grated Parmesan cheese
1½ tablespoons minced fresh cilantro
½ teaspoon dried whole oregano
½ teaspoon ground cumin
¼ teaspoon hot sauce
1 cup soft breadcrumbs
Vegetable cooking spray

Combine tomato, jalapeño pepper, garlic powder, and freshly ground pepper in a small nonstick skillet; bring to a boil. Reduce heat, and simmer 15 minutes or until slightly thickened. Stir in 2 teaspoons cilantro. Set aside, and keep warm.

Peel eggplant, and cut crosswise into 12 (½-inch-thick slices). Combine yogurt and next 5 ingredients in a small bowl. Thinly spread yogurt mixture on both sides of eggplant slices. Dredge lightly in breadcrumbs. Place eggplant slices on a baking sheet coated with cooking spray. Bake at 425° for 15 minutes. Turn eggplant slices, and bake an additional 10 minutes or until golden and tender. Spoon 1 tablespoon reserved tomato mixture over each eggplant slice. Yield: 6 servings (71 calories per serving).

PROTEIN 4.1 / FAT 1.6 / CARBOHYDRATE 10.8 / CHOLESTEROL 3 / IRON 1.0 / SODIUM 125 / CALCIUM 115

MEXICAN LIMA BEANS

2 (10-ounce) packages frozen baby lima beans
Vegetable cooking spray
¼ cup chopped onion
1 (4-ounce) can chopped green chiles, drained
1 (2-ounce) jar diced pimiento, undrained
1½ cups peeled, seeded, and chopped tomato
½ teaspoon ground cumin
⅓ cup plain nonfat yogurt

Cook lima beans according to package directions, omitting salt and fat; drain and set aside.

Coat a large nonstick skillet with cooking spray; place over medium-high heat until hot. Add onion, chiles, and pimiento; sauté until tender. Stir in reserved lima beans, tomato, and cumin. Cook over low heat just until thoroughly heated. Top each serving with 2 teaspoons yogurt. Serve immediately. Yield: 8 servings (105 calories per ½-cup serving).

PROTEIN 6.5 / FAT 0.4 / CARBOHYDRATE 19.9 / CHOLESTEROL 0 / IRON 2.3 / SODIUM 114 / CALCIUM 53

SPICY MUSHROOMS

¼ cup water
2 teaspoons olive oil
2 teaspoons hot sauce
½ teaspoon onion powder
¼ teaspoon dried whole thyme
20 medium-size fresh mushrooms

Combine first 5 ingredients in a large nonstick skillet; bring to a boil. Add mushrooms; cover and cook 6 to 8 minutes or until tender, stirring occasionally. Serve with a slotted spoon. Yield: 4 servings (39 calories per serving).

PROTEIN 1.5 / FAT 2.5 / CARBOHYDRATE 3.5 / CHOLESTEROL 0 / IRON 1.0 / SODIUM 20 / CALCIUM 6

MINTED MANDARIN PEAS

1 (10-ounce) package frozen English peas
1 (11-ounce) can mandarin oranges in water,
    drained
1 cup peeled, seeded, and diced cucumber
2 tablespoons chopped fresh mint
1 tablespoon chopped fresh chives

Cook peas in a medium saucepan according to package directions, omitting salt and fat. Drain well.

Add oranges, diced cucumber, fresh mint, and fresh chives to peas; stir well. Cook just until thoroughly heated. Transfer to a serving dish. Serve warm. Yield: 7 servings (47 calories per ½-cup serving).

PROTEIN 2.6 / FAT 0.2 / CARBOHYDRATE 9.0 / CHOLESTEROL 0 / IRON 0.9 / SODIUM 6 / CALCIUM 16

THREE PEPPER STIR-FRY

Vegetable cooking spray
3 tablespoons Chablis or other dry white
    wine
1 medium-size green pepper, cut into
    julienne strips
1 medium-size sweet red pepper, cut into
    julienne strips
1 medium-size sweet yellow pepper, cut into
    julienne strips
¼ cup plus 2 tablespoons sliced green onions
1½ teaspoons minced fresh basil or ½ teaspoon
    dried whole basil
¼ teaspoon dill seeds
¼ teaspoon celery seeds
Fresh basil sprigs (optional)

Coat a wok or large nonstick skillet with cooking spray; place over medium-high heat until hot. Add Chablis, peppers, sliced green onions, dried basil, dill seeds, and celery seeds; stir-fry 2½ to 3 minutes or until vegetables are crisp-tender. Transfer mixture to a serving dish, and garnish with fresh basil, if desired. Yield: 4 servings (21 calories per serving).

PROTEIN 0.8 / FAT 0.4 / CARBOHYDRATE 4.5 / CHOLESTEROL 0 / IRON 1.2 / SODIUM 3 / CALCIUM 15

SHERRIED MASHED POTATOES

6 cups peeled, cubed potato
½ cup skim milk
¼ cup grated Parmesan cheese, divided
¼ cup low-fat sour cream
2 tablespoons minced fresh chives
2 tablespoons dry sherry
Vegetable cooking spray
¼ teaspoon paprika

Cook potato in boiling water to cover 30 minutes or until tender. Drain potato, and mash. Add milk, 2 tablespoons Parmesan cheese, sour cream, chives, and sherry; stir well. Spoon mixture into a 1½-quart ceramic heatproof dish coated with cooking spray. Combine remaining 2 tablespoons Parmesan cheese and paprika. Sprinkle evenly over potato mixture. Bake, uncovered, at 350° for 25 minutes. Yield: 8 servings (117 calories per ½-cup serving).

PROTEIN 4.1 / FAT 1.9 / CARBOHYDRATE 21.6 / CHOLESTEROL 5 / IRON 0.9 / SODIUM 65 / CALCIUM 70

DEVILED OVEN FRIES

2 (8-ounce) baking potatoes
1 teaspoon olive oil
Vegetable cooking spray
¾ teaspoon chili powder
½ teaspoon garlic powder
½ teaspoon dry mustard
¼ teaspoon salt

Wash potatoes; cut each potato lengthwise into 8 wedges. Place wedges in a medium bowl; add cold water to cover. Let stand 30 minutes; drain. Pat dry with paper towels.

Combine potato wedges and oil in a medium bowl; toss well. Place wedges, skin side down, on a baking sheet coated with cooking spray. Combine chili powder and remaining ingredients; sprinkle evenly over potato wedges. Bake at 400° for 50 minutes or until potato wedges are lightly browned and tender. Yield: 4 servings (99 calories per serving).

PROTEIN 2.7 / FAT 1.5 / CARBOHYDRATE 19.4 / CHOLESTEROL 0 / IRON 1.5 / SODIUM 159 / CALCIUM 18

SAUTÉED SPINACH

1 pound fresh spinach
Vegetable cooking spray
2 cups thinly sliced fresh mushrooms
3 tablespoons diced pimiento, drained
1 teaspoon olive oil
1 tablespoon lemon juice
1 tablespoon prepared mustard

Remove stems from spinach; wash leaves, and pat dry thoroughly with paper towels. Set spinach aside.

Coat a Dutch oven with cooking spray; place over medium-high heat until hot. Add mushrooms and pimiento; sauté 2 to 3 minutes or until tender. Remove from Dutch oven, and keep warm.

Coat Dutch oven with cooking spray; add oil. Place over medium heat until hot. Add half of spinach; cook until spinach begins to wilt, stirring occasionally. Add remaining spinach, and cook 3 minutes or until spinach wilts, stirring occasionally. Remove from heat. Stir in reserved mushroom mixture, lemon juice, and mustard; toss gently. Serve immediately. Yield: 4 servings (41 calories per ½-cup serving).

PROTEIN 2.7 / FAT 2.0 / CARBOHYDRATE 4.9 / CHOLESTEROL 0 / IRON 2.2 / SODIUM 98 / CALCIUM 62

SESAME SQUASH MEDLEY

Vegetable cooking spray
3 cups sliced yellow squash
1¾ cups sliced fresh mushrooms
½ cup sliced green onions
2 tablespoons rice vinegar
1 tablespoon reduced-sodium soy sauce
2 teaspoons sesame seeds, toasted
1 teaspoon dark sesame oil
¼ teaspoon crushed red pepper

Coat a large nonstick skillet with cooking spray; place over medium-high heat until hot. Add yellow squash, sliced mushrooms, and sliced green onions; sauté 10 minutes or until vegetables are tender.

Combine vinegar and remaining ingredients in a small bowl; stir well. Pour over vegetable mixture, tossing gently. Transfer vegetable mixture to a large serving bowl, and serve immediately. Yield: 6 servings (34 calories per ½-cup serving).

PROTEIN 1.5 / FAT 1.6 / CARBOHYDRATE 4.4 / CHOLESTEROL 0 / IRON 0.8 / SODIUM 103 / CALCIUM 26

TURNIPS AU GRATIN

3½ cups sliced turnips (about 1 pound)
Vegetable cooking spray
1 cup chopped sweet red pepper
1 tablespoon reduced-calorie margarine
1 tablespoon all-purpose flour
1 cup skim milk
¼ teaspoon ground nutmeg
⅛ teaspoon ground red pepper
½ cup (2 ounces) shredded Gruyère cheese
2 tablespoons fine, dry breadcrumbs
¼ teaspoon paprika

Place turnips in a large saucepan; add water to cover, and bring to a boil. Cover, reduce heat, and simmer 8 minutes or until crisp-tender. Drain well, and set aside.

Coat a small nonstick skillet with cooking spray; place over medium-high heat until hot. Add sweet red pepper, and sauté until crisp-tender. Set aside.

Melt margarine in a small heavy saucepan over medium heat; add flour. Cook 1 minute, stirring constantly with a wire whisk. Gradually add milk, stirring constantly. Cook, stirring constantly, an additional 10 minutes or until thickened and bubbly. Add nutmeg, ground red pepper, and cheese; stir until cheese melts. Remove cheese sauce from heat.

Place half of turnips in a 1-quart casserole coated with cooking spray. Spoon half of sautéed pepper over turnips, and top with half of cheese sauce; repeat layers with remaining turnips, pepper, and cheese sauce. Combine breadcrumbs and paprika; sprinkle evenly over top. Bake at 350° for 25 minutes or until thoroughly heated and bubbly. Yield: 8 servings (79 calories per ½-cup serving).

PROTEIN 4.1 / FAT 3.7 / CARBOHYDRATE 8.0 / CHOLESTEROL 8 / IRON 0.5 / SODIUM 104 / CALCIUM 130

Zucchini Italienne is a quick and easy way to serve summer vegetables at their finest.

ZUCCHINI ITALIENNE

Vegetable cooking spray
2½ cups sliced zucchini (about 2 medium)
1 cup diced tomato
1½ teaspoons minced fresh basil or ½ teaspoon dried whole basil
¾ teaspoon minced fresh oregano or ¼ teaspoon dried whole oregano
¼ cup (1 ounce) shredded part-skim mozzarella cheese
Fresh basil sprig (optional)

Coat a large nonstick skillet with cooking spray; place over medium-high heat until hot. Add zucchini, and sauté 3 to 4 minutes or until crisp-tender. Add tomato, minced basil, and oregano; cook until thoroughly heated. Transfer to a serving dish, and sprinkle with cheese. Garnish with fresh basil, if desired. Yield: 4 servings (39 calories per ½-cup serving).

PROTEIN 3.0 / FAT 1.5 / CARBOHYDRATE 4.4 / CHOLESTEROL 4 / IRON 0.6 / SODIUM 39 / CALCIUM 65

WINTER SQUASH AND APPLE SAUTÉ

Vegetable cooking spray
4¾ cups grated butternut squash (about 1 large)
½ cup unsweetened apple juice
1 tablespoon lemon juice
¼ teaspoon ground cinnamon
2½ cups coarsely chopped cooking apple
1 tablespoon honey

Coat a large nonstick skillet with cooking spray; place over medium-high heat until hot.

Add grated squash, and sauté 3 minutes. Add apple juice, lemon juice, and cinnamon; cover, reduce heat, and simmer 2 minutes. Add chopped apple and honey; cover and cook squash mixture over medium heat 5 minutes or until squash is tender. Yield: 8 servings (62 calories per ½-cup serving).

PROTEIN 0.7 / FAT 0.3 / CARBOHYDRATE 16.0 / CHOLESTEROL 0 / IRON 0.5 / SODIUM 3 / CALCIUM 36

TARRAGON APPLE WEDGES

4 Granny Smith apples, peeled and cored
Vegetable cooking spray
2 teaspoons minced fresh tarragon
1 teaspoon brown sugar
2 tablespoons tarragon vinegar
½ cup unsweetened apple juice

Cut each apple into 12 wedges.
Coat a large nonstick skillet with cooking spray; place over medium-high heat until hot. Add apple wedges; sauté 5 minutes. Reduce

heat; stir in tarragon and brown sugar. Cook, stirring frequently, 10 minutes or until apples are lightly browned and tender.

Add vinegar, and cook over medium heat until vinegar evaporates. Add apple juice, and bring to a boil; reduce heat, and simmer 2 minutes or until apple juice evaporates. Serve immediately. Yield: 4 servings (116 calories per serving).

PROTEIN 0.3 / FAT 0.7 / CARBOHYDRATE 29.7 / CHOLESTEROL 0 / IRON 0.4 / SODIUM 2 / CALCIUM 11

BAKED BANANAS

3 medium bananas, peeled, split lengthwise,
  and halved
¼ cup reduced-calorie apricot spread, melted
3 tablespoons unsweetened orange juice
¼ teaspoon ground cardamom

Place bananas in an 11- x 7- x 2-inch baking dish. Combine apricot spread, orange juice, and

cardamom in a small bowl; stir well. Pour apricot mixture over bananas. Bake at 400° for 10 to 12 minutes or to desired degree of doneness. Serve immediately. Yield: 6 servings (77 calories per serving).

PROTEIN 0.7 / FAT 0.3 / CARBOHYDRATE 19.7 / CHOLESTEROL 0 / IRON 0.2 / SODIUM 11 / CALCIUM 5

BROILED GRAPEFRUIT

3 medium grapefruit
2 tablespoons honey
2 tablespoons dark rum
½ teaspoon ground cinnamon

Cut grapefruit in half crosswise; remove seeds, and loosen sections. Place grapefruit, cut side up, on a rack in a roasting pan. Combine honey,

rum, and cinnamon in a small bowl; drizzle 2 teaspoons honey mixture over each grapefruit half. Broil 5½ inches from heat 6 to 8 minutes or until thoroughly heated. Yield: 6 servings (58 calories per serving).

PROTEIN 0.7 / FAT 0.1 / CARBOHYDRATE 15.1 / CHOLESTEROL 0 / IRON 0.2 / SODIUM 0 / CALCIUM 16

A tasty combination of cinnamon schnapps and citrus zest flavors Sautéed Citrus.

218   Fruits

SAUTÉED CITRUS

2 medium-size pink grapefruit
2 large oranges
Vegetable cooking spray
1 tablespoon reduced-calorie margarine
¼ cup cinnamon schnapps
¼ teaspoon orange zest
¼ teaspoon grapefruit zest
Fresh mint sprigs (optional)

Peel and section pink grapefruit and oranges. Set fruit aside.

Coat a large nonstick skillet with vegetable cooking spray; add margarine. Place over medium heat until margarine melts. Add cinnamon schnapps, and cook 1 minute.

Stir in fruit sections, and cook 2 to 3 minutes or until thoroughly heated.

Transfer mixture to a serving dish. Sprinkle with zests. Garnish with fresh mint, if desired. Yield: 8 servings (64 calories per ½-cup serving).

PROTEIN 0.8 / FAT 1.1 / CARBOHYDRATE 14.0 / CHOLESTEROL 0 / IRON 0.1 / SODIUM 14 / CALCIUM 26

CURRIED PEACHES

7 cups peeled, sliced fresh peaches
¼ cup plus 2 tablespoons peach nectar
2 tablespoons brown sugar
½ teaspoon curry powder

Arrange peach slices in an 11- x 7- x 2-inch baking dish. Combine peach nectar, brown

sugar, and curry powder in a small bowl, stirring well. Pour mixture over peach slices. Bake at 350° for 30 minutes or until thoroughly heated. Yield: 8 servings (66 calories per ½-cup serving).

PROTEIN 0.9 / FAT 0.1 / CARBOHYDRATE 17.1 / CHOLESTEROL 0 / IRON 0.3 / SODIUM 2 / CALCIUM 9

GINGER-GLAZED PEACHES

1 (16-ounce) can peach halves in juice, undrained
Vegetable cooking spray
1 tablespoon plus 1 teaspoon reduced-calorie margarine, melted
1 tablespoon honey
½ teaspoon ground ginger
⅛ teaspoon ground red pepper

Drain peaches, reserving 2 tablespoons juice. Arrange peaches in an 8-inch square baking

dish coated with cooking spray. Combine reserved peach juice, margarine, and remaining ingredients in a small bowl; stir well. Pour mixture over peaches.

Broil peach halves 5½ inches from heat 6 minutes or until thoroughly heated. Serve warm. Yield: 4 servings (70 calories per serving).

PROTEIN 0.5 / FAT 2.7 / CARBOHYDRATE 12.4 / CHOLESTEROL 0 / IRON 0.4 / SODIUM 41 / CALCIUM 3

BAKED PEARS AND DRIED FRUIT

2½ cups peeled, chopped fresh pears
¼ cup mixed dried fruit
½ cup pear nectar
½ teaspoon vanilla extract
⅛ teaspoon ground cloves
⅛ teaspoon ground mace

Combine all ingredients in a 1-quart baking dish; stir well. Cover and bake at 350° for 1 hour or until fruit is tender. Yield: 4 servings (111 calories per ½-cup serving).

PROTEIN 1.0 / FAT 0.5 / CARBOHYDRATE 26.5 / CHOLESTEROL 0 / IRON 0.5 / SODIUM 10 / CALCIUM 12

EASY PINEAPPLE CASSEROLE

1 (20-ounce) can pineapple tidbits in juice, undrained
Vegetable cooking spray
2 tablespoons all-purpose flour
1½ tablespoons sugar
½ cup (2 ounces) shredded reduced-fat Cheddar cheese

Drain pineapple, reserving juice. Place pineapple in a shallow 1-quart baking dish coated with cooking spray. Combine reserved juice, flour, and sugar in a small bowl; stir well. Pour juice mixture over pineapple. Bake at 325° for 30 minutes. Top with cheese, and broil 5½ inches from heat 2 to 3 minutes or until cheese melts. Serve immediately. Yield: 4 servings (120 calories per ½-cup serving).

PROTEIN 5.2 / FAT 3.0 / CARBOHYDRATE 19.4 / CHOLESTEROL 9 / IRON 0.8 / SODIUM 106 / CALCIUM 134

CURRIED FRUIT COMPOTE

1 (16-ounce) can peach halves in light syrup, drained
1 (16-ounce) can pear halves in juice, drained
1 (8-ounce) can pineapple slices in juice, drained
1 (8-ounce) can apricot halves in light syrup, drained
⅓ cup Chablis or other dry white wine
3½ tablespoons brown sugar
2 teaspoons curry powder

Combine first 4 ingredients in a 1½-quart baking dish; toss gently. Combine wine, brown sugar, and curry powder in a small bowl, stirring well. Pour over fruit mixture. Cover and bake at 350° for 35 minutes or until thoroughly heated. Serve with a slotted spoon. Yield: 6 servings (122 calories per ½-cup serving).

PROTEIN 1.1 / FAT 0.4 / CARBOHYDRATE 31.4 / CHOLESTEROL 0 / IRON 1.1 / SODIUM 9 / CALCIUM 27

FRUITED RHUBARB

3 cups sliced fresh rhubarb (about 1 pound)
1 cup unsweetened grapefruit juice
2 medium-size pink grapefruit, peeled and sectioned
3 tablespoons sugar
1 tablespoon reduced-calorie margarine
¼ teaspoon ground allspice

Combine rhubarb and grapefruit juice in a medium saucepan; bring to a boil. Cover and reduce heat; simmer rhubarb mixture 10 minutes or until very tender. Drain and return rhubarb to saucepan.

Add grapefruit sections and remaining ingredients, tossing well to combine. Transfer rhubarb mixture to a serving dish, and serve warm. Yield: 6 servings (79 calories per ½-cup serving).

PROTEIN 1.0 / FAT 1.4 / CARBOHYDRATE 16.8 / CHOLESTEROL 0 / IRON 1.0 / SODIUM 22 / CALCIUM 66

Center your meal around Vegetarian Chili (page 230); it's thick with vegetables. Be sure to put cheese and nonfat yogurt on top for an extra twist.

CHILLED BLUEBERRY SOUP

4 cups fresh blueberries
3 cups water, divided
2 tablespoons Triple Sec or other orange-flavored liqueur
3 tablespoons lemon juice
3 tablespoons crème de cassis
2 tablespoons honey
2 (1-inch) sticks cinnamon
2 tablespoons cornstarch
3 tablespoons plus 2 teaspoons low-fat sour cream
Grated orange rind (optional)

Combine blueberries, 2½ cups water, and next 5 ingredients in a large saucepan. Bring to a boil over medium heat; cover, reduce heat, and simmer 15 minutes. Combine cornstarch and remaining ½ cup water, stirring until smooth. Add cornstarch mixture to blueberry mixture; bring to a boil. Boil 1 minute, stirring constantly. Remove from heat; let cool 15 minutes. Remove and discard cinnamon sticks.

Pour blueberry mixture into container of an electric blender or food processor; top with cover, and process until smooth. Cover and chill thoroughly. Ladle into individual soup bowls. Top each serving with 1 teaspoon sour cream, and garnish with orange rind, if desired. Yield: 5 cups (149 calories per 1-cup serving).

PROTEIN 1.0 / FAT 1.1 / CARBOHYDRATE 36.7 / CHOLESTEROL 2 / IRON 0.3 / SODIUM 11 / CALCIUM 13

CREAMY MANGO SOUP

3 cups coarsely chopped ripe mango (about 2 pounds)
½ cup unsweetened orange juice
2 tablespoons sugar
2 tablespoons lime juice
1 teaspoon vanilla extract
1½ cups skim milk
Fresh raspberries (optional)

Combine mango, orange juice, sugar, lime juice, and vanilla in container of an electric blender or food processor; top with cover, and process until smooth. Transfer mixture to a large bowl. Add milk, and stir well. Cover and chill thoroughly.

Stir soup before serving. Ladle soup into individual bowls, and garnish each serving with fresh raspberries, if desired. Yield: 5 cups (149 calories per 1-cup serving).

PROTEIN 3.4 / FAT 0.5 / CARBOHYDRATE 35.2 / CHOLESTEROL 1 / IRON 0.2 / SODIUM 41 / CALCIUM 107

MINTED PINEAPPLE-CHAMPAGNE SOUP

1 fresh pineapple (about 5¼ pounds)
½ cup unsweetened pineapple juice
¼ cup water
1 tablespoon sugar
1½ teaspoons lemon juice
¼ teaspoon ground cinnamon
⅛ teaspoon ground ginger
¼ cup loosely packed fresh mint sprigs
1¼ cups champagne, chilled
Fresh mint sprigs (optional)

Peel and trim eyes from pineapple; remove core. Cut pineapple into 2-inch chunks. Combine pineapple chunks, pineapple juice, and next 5 ingredients in a medium saucepan. Bring to a boil; cover, reduce heat, and simmer 20 to 25 minutes or until pineapple is tender. Let cool.

Position knife blade in food processor bowl; add pineapple mixture and ¼ cup mint sprigs; process until smooth. Pour mixture into a large bowl. Cover and refrigerate at least 8 hours.

To serve, combine pineapple mixture and champagne; stir gently. Ladle soup into individual bowls, and garnish with fresh mint sprigs, if desired. Serve immediately. Yield: 5 cups (148 calories per 1-cup serving).

PROTEIN 0.9 / FAT 0.7 / CARBOHYDRATE 26.7 / CHOLESTEROL 0 / IRON 1.2 / SODIUM 5 / CALCIUM 22

CHILLED CREAM OF TOMATILLO SOUP

1 pound fresh tomatillos
1 (10½-ounce) can low-sodium chicken broth, undiluted
1½ cups skim milk
1 tablespoon all-purpose flour
¼ teaspoon salt
¼ teaspoon ground cumin
1 tablespoon plus 1 teaspoon minced fresh cilantro
¼ teaspoon chili powder

Remove and discard husks from tomatillos. Combine tomatillos and chicken broth in a medium saucepan. Bring to a boil; cover, reduce heat, and simmer 10 minutes or until tomatillos are tender.

Pour mixture into container of an electric blender or food processor; top with cover, and process until smooth.

Return mixture to saucepan. Combine milk and flour, stirring until smooth. Gradually stir milk mixture into tomatillo mixture. Stir in salt and cumin. Cook over medium heat, stirring constantly, until thickened and bubbly. Remove from heat. Cover and chill thoroughly.

Stir soup with a wire whisk before serving. Ladle soup into individual bowls. Top each with 1 teaspoon cilantro and a dash of chili powder. Yield: 4 cups (68 calories per 1-cup serving).

PROTEIN 4.5 / FAT 0.5 / CARBOHYDRATE 11.6 / CHOLESTEROL 2 / IRON 0.8 / SODIUM 207 / CALCIUM 125

SPICY TOMATO-CORN SOUP

2½ cups spicy hot vegetable juice cocktail
1½ cups chopped tomato
1 cup fresh corn cut from cob (about 2 ears)
1 cup diced zucchini
3 tablespoons lime juice
2 tablespoons minced fresh basil
2 green onions, thinly sliced

Combine all ingredients in a large bowl. Cover and refrigerate at least 2 hours. To serve, ladle soup into individual bowls. Yield: 5 cups (69 calories per 1-cup serving).

PROTEIN 2.5 / FAT 0.5 / CARBOHYDRATE 15.2 / CHOLESTEROL 0 / IRON 1.1 / SODIUM 423 / CALCIUM 16

TASTY TOMATILLOS

Tomatillos can be eaten raw, but cooking brings out a more intense, less acidic flavor. Cooking also helps to soften the tough outer skin. These small, firm fruits come enclosed in thin papery husks which can be easily peeled away before chopping or cooking. Look for fresh tomatillos in the produce section of the supermarket or in specialty food shops or Latin markets. Once purchased, tomatillos can be stored in the refrigerator for up to one month.

FIRE AND ICE TOMATO SOUP

Vegetable cooking spray
5 cups peeled, seeded, and chopped tomato
¼ cup chopped sweet red pepper
1 cup chopped onion
½ cup thinly sliced carrot
2 cups water
½ cup thinly sliced celery
¼ cup chopped fresh parsley
1 jalapeño pepper, seeded and chopped
1 tablespoon lemon juice
1 tablespoon prepared horseradish
1 teaspoon low-sodium Worcestershire sauce
½ teaspoon salt
½ teaspoon hot sauce
Thinly sliced cucumber (optional)

Coat a Dutch oven with cooking spray; place over medium-high heat until hot. Add tomato, sweet red pepper, onion, and carrot; sauté until tender. Stir in water and next 7 ingredients. Bring mixture to a boil; cover, reduce heat, and simmer 30 minutes, stirring occasionally. Stir in hot sauce.

Position knife blade in food processor bowl; add hot tomato mixture in batches. Process until smooth. Transfer mixture to a large bowl. Cover and chill thoroughly. To serve, ladle soup into individual bowls, and garnish with cucumber slices, if desired. Yield: 2 quarts (47 calories per 1-cup serving).

PROTEIN 2.0 / FAT 0.5 / CARBOHYDRATE 10.1 / CHOLESTEROL 0 / IRON 1.1 / SODIUM 167 / CALCIUM 32

TOMATO AND RED PEPPER SOUP

Olive oil-flavored vegetable cooking spray
1 teaspoon olive oil
1 large onion, thinly sliced
2 cloves garlic, minced
4 cups water
3 medium-size sweet red peppers, seeded and cut into thin strips
2 cups diced carrot
¼ cup Burgundy or other dry red wine
3 tablespoons chopped fresh parsley
2 teaspoons chicken-flavored bouillon granules
1 teaspoon dried Italian seasoning
¼ teaspoon ground red pepper
½ cup wagon wheel pasta, uncooked
5½ cups peeled, seeded, and chopped tomato
1 (9-ounce) package frozen cut green beans, thawed

Coat a large Dutch oven with cooking spray; add oil. Place over medium-high heat until hot. Add onion and garlic; sauté until tender. Stir in water and next 7 ingredients. Bring to a boil; cover, reduce heat, and simmer 20 minutes. Add pasta; bring to a boil. Cover, reduce heat, and simmer 5 minutes. Stir in tomato and green beans. Cook over medium heat, stirring frequently, 15 to 20 minutes or until vegetables are tender. Ladle soup into individual bowls. Yield: 3 quarts (70 calories per 1-cup serving).

PROTEIN 2.7 / FAT 1.1 / CARBOHYDRATE 13.9 / CHOLESTEROL 0 / IRON 1.6 / SODIUM 153 / CALCIUM 39

SCANDINAVIAN MUSHROOM SOUP

Vegetable cooking spray
2 teaspoons vegetable oil
1 pound sliced fresh mushrooms
1½ cups chopped onion
2 cups water
½ cup Chablis or other dry white wine
2 teaspoons beef-flavored bouillon granules
2 teaspoons low-sodium Worcestershire sauce
1 bay leaf
¼ teaspoon ground nutmeg
¼ teaspoon pepper
3 tablespoons all-purpose flour
1 cup skim milk, divided
½ cup low-fat sour cream

Coat a Dutch oven with cooking spray; add oil. Place over medium-high heat until hot. Add mushrooms and onion; sauté until tender. Stir in water and next 6 ingredients. Bring to a boil; cover, reduce heat, and simmer 15 minutes, stirring occasionally.

Combine flour and ¼ cup milk; stir until smooth. Add flour mixture to mushroom mixture. Cook over medium heat, stirring constantly, until mixture is slightly thickened. Stir in remaining ¾ cup milk and sour cream. Cook until thoroughly heated. Remove and discard bay leaf. Ladle soup into individual bowls. Yield: 1½ quarts (109 calories per 1-cup serving).

PROTEIN 4.5 / FAT 4.9 / CARBOHYDRATE 12.9 / CHOLESTEROL 8 / IRON 1.4 / SODIUM 356 / CALCIUM 88

SAVORY TURNIP AND RUTABAGA SOUP

Vegetable cooking spray
1 teaspoon vegetable oil
2 medium onions, thinly sliced
8 cups water
2 cups peeled, chopped turnips
2 cups peeled, chopped rutabaga
1 cup shredded carrot
2 tablespoons chopped fresh parsley
2 teaspoons beef-flavored bouillon granules
1 bay leaf
¼ teaspoon salt
¼ teaspoon pepper
¼ cup all-purpose flour
¼ cup water
¼ cup plus 1 tablespoon grated Parmesan cheese

Coat a Dutch oven with cooking spray; add oil. Place over medium-high heat until hot. Add onion, and sauté until tender. Stir in 8 cups water and next 8 ingredients. Bring to a boil; cover, reduce heat, and simmer 35 minutes.

Combine flour and ¼ cup water; stir until smooth. Add flour mixture to vegetable mixture; cook, stirring constantly, 10 minutes. Remove and discard bay leaf. Ladle soup into individual bowls, and sprinkle each serving with 1½ teaspoons grated Parmesan cheese. Yield: 2½ quarts (66 calories per 1-cup serving).

PROTEIN 2.6 / FAT 1.8 / CARBOHYDRATE 10.6 / CHOLESTEROL 2 / IRON 0.6 / SODIUM 326 / CALCIUM 79

CURRIED VEGETABLE-RICE SOUP

Vegetable cooking spray
1 teaspoon vegetable oil
1 cup cubed yellow squash
1 medium onion, thinly sliced and
  separated into rings
¾ cup thinly sliced carrot
1 clove garlic, minced
6 cups water
1 tablespoon chicken-flavored bouillon
  granules
1½ teaspoons curry powder
1 teaspoon ground coriander
¼ teaspoon ground cumin
1 cup fresh broccoli flowerets
1 cup fresh cauliflower flowerets
½ cup long-grain rice, uncooked

Coat a Dutch oven with cooking spray; add oil. Place over medium-high heat until hot. Add squash, onion, carrot, and garlic; sauté until vegetables are crisp-tender. Stir in water, bouillon granules, curry powder, coriander, and cumin. Bring mixture to a boil; cover, reduce heat, and simmer 30 minutes. Add broccoli, cauliflower, and rice.

Cover and cook an additional 25 to 30 minutes or until rice is tender. Ladle soup into individual bowls. Yield: 2 quarts (74 calories per 1-cup serving).

PROTEIN 2.2 / FAT 1.3 / CARBOHYDRATE 14.2 / CHOLESTEROL 0 / IRON 1.0 / SODIUM 317 / CALCIUM 27

COCK-A-LEEKIE SOUP

Vegetable cooking spray
1 teaspoon vegetable oil
8 cups thinly sliced leeks (about 5 leeks)
6 cups water
1½ cups thinly sliced celery
¾ cup diced carrot
3 tablespoons chopped fresh parsley
2 teaspoons beef-flavored bouillon granules
1 bay leaf
½ teaspoon pepper
1½ cups diced cooked chicken breast (skinned
  before cooking and cooked without salt or fat)

Coat a Dutch oven with cooking spray; add oil. Place over medium-high heat until hot. Add leeks, and sauté until tender. Stir in water and next 6 ingredients; stir well. Bring mixture to a boil; cover, reduce heat, and simmer 40 minutes or until vegetables are tender. Add chicken, stirring well. Cover and cook until thoroughly heated. Remove and discard bay leaf. Serve warm. Yield: 2 quarts (123 calories per 1-cup serving).

PROTEIN 12.5 / FAT 2.5 / CARBOHYDRATE 13.1 / CHOLESTEROL 30 / IRON 2.3 / SODIUM 298 / CALCIUM 64

CAULIFLOWER-CHEESE CHOWDER

Vegetable cooking spray
1 teaspoon vegetable oil
1 cup chopped onion
1 cup sliced fresh mushrooms
¾ cup finely chopped green pepper
¾ cup finely chopped sweet red pepper
2 cloves garlic, minced
2½ cups fresh cauliflower flowerets
2 cups water
3 tablespoons dry sherry
1 teaspoon chicken-flavored bouillon granules
½ teaspoon ground white pepper
1 cup evaporated skimmed milk
3½ tablespoons all-purpose flour
2 cups skim milk
¾ cup (3 ounces) shredded reduced-fat Cheddar
  cheese

Coat a Dutch oven with cooking spray; add oil. Place over medium-high heat until hot. Add onion and next 4 ingredients; sauté until tender. Stir in cauliflower, water, sherry, bouillon granules, and white pepper. Bring to a boil; cover, reduce heat, and simmer 20 minutes. Combine evaporated milk and flour; stir until smooth. Add flour mixture and skim milk to vegetable mixture; stir well. Cook over medium heat, stirring constantly, 10 minutes or until thickened. Add cheese, and stir until cheese melts. Serve chowder immediately. Yield: 7 cups (139 calories per 1-cup serving).

PROTEIN 10.6 / FAT 3.7 / CARBOHYDRATE 16.7 / CHOLESTEROL 11 / IRON 1.2 / SODIUM 292 / CALCIUM 308

HARVEST VEGETABLE BISQUE

1 (2-pound) butternut squash
Vegetable cooking spray
1 teaspoon vegetable oil
2 cups thinly sliced leek
1 cup coarsely chopped sweet red pepper
4 cups water
3 cups diced carrot
3 cups diced potato
1½ cups diced parsnip
1 tablespoon chicken-flavored bouillon granules
1 tablespoon chopped fresh parsley
1 teaspoon chopped fresh thyme
¼ teaspoon pepper
½ cup low-fat sour cream
½ cup skim milk
Fresh chives (optional)

Cut squash in half lengthwise; place squash, cut side down, in a 13- x 9- x 2-inch baking dish. Add hot water to dish to a depth of ½ inch. Cover and bake at 350° for 45 minutes or until squash is tender. Drain. Let cool to touch. Remove and discard seeds. Scoop out and reserve pulp; discard shells.

Coat a large Dutch oven with cooking spray; add oil. Place over medium-high heat until hot. Add leeks and sweet red pepper; sauté until tender. Stir in water and next 7 ingredients. Bring to a boil; cover, reduce heat, and simmer 20 to 25 minutes or until vegetables are tender.

Position knife blade in food processor bowl. Add reserved squash pulp and 2 cups vegetable mixture; process until smooth. Add vegetable puree to remaining vegetable mixture. Stir in sour cream and milk. Cook over medium-low heat until thoroughly heated. Ladle bisque into individual bowls, and garnish with chives, if desired. Yield: 3 quarts (127 calories per 1-cup serving).

PROTEIN 3.2 / FAT 2.2 / CARBOHYDRATE 25.9 / CHOLESTEROL 4 / IRON 1.5 / SODIUM 236 / CALCIUM 87

BAKED MEATBALL STEW

1 pound ground chuck
½ cup soft breadcrumbs
2 teaspoons low-sodium Worcestershire sauce
½ teaspoon garlic powder
2 cups chopped onion
2 cups chopped potato
1 cup sliced carrot
½ teaspoon dried whole basil
¼ teaspoon dried whole thyme
½ teaspoon pepper
3 cups canned low-sodium beef broth, undiluted
3 tablespoons chopped fresh parsley

Combine first 4 ingredients in a medium bowl; stir well. Shape mixture into 21 meatballs, using about 1 tablespoon mixture for each meatball. Place meatballs in a large nonstick skillet, and cook over medium heat 8 to 10 minutes or until browned, turning frequently. Drain and pat dry with paper towels.

Arrange half of meatballs in a 3-quart casserole. Layer half of onion, potato, and carrot over meatballs. Combine basil, thyme, and pepper; sprinkle half of basil mixture over vegetables. Repeat layers with remaining meatballs, onion, potato, carrot, and basil mixture. Pour beef broth over layered vegetable mixture. Cover and bake at 350° for 1 hour and 15 minutes or until vegetables are tender. Ladle stew into individual bowls, and sprinkle with parsley. Yield: 7 cups (207 calories per 1-cup serving).

PROTEIN 15.2 / FAT 8.2 / CARBOHYDRATE 17.6 / CHOLESTEROL 40 / IRON 2.2 / SODIUM 64 / CALCIUM 32

Pureed butternut squash and diced vegetables make Harvest Vegetable Bisque thick and rich.

BEEF STEW BALSAMICO

1½ pounds lean boneless round steak
    (½-inch thick)
Vegetable cooking spray
1 large onion, sliced
1 clove garlic, minced
3¼ cups water
½ cup balsamic vinegar
1 tablespoon chopped fresh oregano
1 teaspoon chopped fresh parsley
1 teaspoon chopped fresh basil
2 teaspoons beef-flavored bouillon granules
½ teaspoon cracked pepper
2 medium-size sweet red peppers, cut into
    1-inch pieces
2 medium-size sweet yellow peppers, cut into
    1-inch pieces
1 cup sliced fresh mushrooms
¼ pound snow pea pods, trimmed and cut into
    1-inch pieces

Trim fat from boneless round steak, and cut steak into 1-inch pieces.

Coat a Dutch oven with cooking spray; place over medium-high heat until hot. Add steak pieces; cook until browned on all sides, stirring frequently. Drain steak pieces, and pat dry with paper towels. Wipe drippings from Dutch oven with a paper towel.

Coat pan with cooking spray, and place over medium-high heat until hot. Add onion and garlic; sauté until onion is tender. Stir in steak, water, vinegar, oregano, parsley, and basil, stirring well to combine. Add bouillon granules and pepper, stirring well. Bring to a boil; cover, reduce heat, and simmer 1 hour and 15 minutes.

Add pepper pieces and mushrooms; cover and cook 15 minutes. Add snow peas; cover and cook an additional 15 minutes or until crisp-tender. To serve, ladle beef stew into individual serving bowls. Yield: 9 cups (145 calories per 1-cup serving).

PROTEIN 17.8 / FAT 5.3 / CARBOHYDRATE 6.2 / CHOLESTEROL 47 / IRON 2.9 / SODIUM 250 / CALCIUM 25

FRENCH CHICKEN STEW

4 (4-ounce) skinned, boned chicken breast halves
2 teaspoons olive oil
1 cup thinly sliced green onions
½ cup sliced onion
4 cloves garlic, minced
2 cups peeled, chopped tomato
1½ cups canned no-salt-added chicken broth,
    undiluted
1 cup Chablis or other dry white wine
1 bay leaf
1 teaspoon dried whole thyme
½ teaspoon fennel seeds, crushed
¼ teaspoon salt
⅛ teaspoon saffron powder
Dash of ground red pepper
2⅓ cups sliced new potatoes
Freshly ground pepper (optional)

Place chicken in a large saucepan; cover with cold water. Bring to a boil over high heat; cover, reduce heat, and simmer 15 minutes or until done. Drain chicken, reserving broth for another use. Set chicken aside.

Heat olive oil in a Dutch oven over medium-high heat until hot. Add onions and garlic; sauté until onion is tender.

Shred chicken into bite-size pieces. Add chicken, tomato, chicken broth, wine, and bay leaf to onion mixture, stirring well to combine. Add thyme, fennel seeds, salt, saffron, and red pepper, stirring well. Bring to a boil; cover, reduce heat, and simmer 20 minutes.

Stir in sliced potatoes. Cover and cook an additional 25 to 30 minutes or until potatoes are tender. Remove and discard bay leaf. Ladle stew into individual bowls, and garnish with freshly ground pepper, if desired. Yield: 2 quarts (137 calories per 1-cup serving).

PROTEIN 15.1 / FAT 3.2 / CARBOHYDRATE 11.6 / CHOLESTEROL 35 / IRON 1.8 / SODIUM 137 / CALCIUM 36

Spoon up a bowl of California Seafood Stew for a flavorful treat.

CALIFORNIA SEAFOOD STEW

Vegetable cooking spray
½ cup chopped onion
½ cup chopped sweet red pepper
1 clove garlic, minced
1 (14½-ounce) can no-salt-added whole tomatoes, undrained and chopped
1 (8-ounce) can no-salt-added tomato sauce
¼ cup Burgundy or other dry red wine
¼ cup chopped fresh oregano
2 tablespoons chopped fresh parsley
1 teaspoon low-sodium Worcestershire sauce
¼ teaspoon crushed red pepper
½ pound bay scallops
½ pound medium-size fresh shrimp, peeled and deveined
1 (10-ounce) can whole baby clams, drained

Coat a Dutch oven with cooking spray; place over medium-high heat until hot. Add chopped onion, sweet red pepper, and minced garlic; sauté until vegetables are tender.

Add tomato, tomato sauce, and Burgundy, stirring well to combine. Add oregano and next 3 ingredients; stir well. Bring vegetable mixture to a boil over medium heat; cover, reduce heat, and simmer 20 minutes. Add scallops, shrimp, and clams to vegetable mixture; bring to a boil. Reduce heat, and simmer 7 to 8 minutes or until scallops and shrimp are done. To serve, ladle stew into individual bowls. Yield: 1½ quarts (146 calories per 1-cup serving).

PROTEIN 20.9 / FAT 1.6 / CARBOHYDRATE 11.5 / CHOLESTEROL 77 / IRON 9.4 / SODIUM 160 / CALCIUM 92

PORTUGUESE FISH STEW

Olive oil flavored-vegetable cooking spray
1 teaspoon olive oil
1½ cups chopped onion
⅓ cup sliced carrot
2 cloves garlic, minced
2¼ cups peeled, seeded, and chopped tomato
2 cups peeled, cubed potato
2 cups thinly sliced leek
1 cup chopped green pepper
¾ cup water
¼ cup Chablis or other dry white wine
2 teaspoons grated lemon rind
½ teaspoon dried whole thyme
¼ teaspoon salt
¼ teaspoon pepper
1 pound flounder fillets, cut into 1-inch pieces
1 pound medium-size fresh shrimp, peeled and
  deveined
Chopped fresh parsley (optional)

Coat a Dutch oven with cooking spray; add
oil. Place over medium-high heat until hot. Add
onion, carrot, and garlic; sauté until vegetables
are crisp-tender. Add tomato and next 9 ingredients, stirring well. Bring mixture to a boil over
medium heat; cover, reduce heat, and simmer
20 minutes.

Add flounder fillets and shrimp to vegetable
mixture, stirring well. Cover and simmer an additional 10 to 15 minutes or until fish flakes easily
when tested with a fork and shrimp are done.
Ladle stew into individual bowls. Garnish stew
with parsley, if desired. Yield: 2 quarts (163 calories per 1-cup serving).

PROTEIN 21.3 / FAT 2.4 / CARBOHYDRATE 14.1 / CHOLESTEROL 92 /
IRON 2.4 / SODIUM 191 / CALCIUM 60

VEGETARIAN CHILI

Vegetable cooking spray
1 teaspoon vegetable oil
2 cups chopped onion
2 cups sliced fresh mushrooms
1½ cups diced carrot
2 cloves garlic, minced
2 cups sliced yellow squash
1 cup diced sweet red pepper
2 (14½-ounce) cans no-salt-added whole tomatoes,
  undrained and chopped
2 cups water
1 jalapeño pepper, seeded and chopped
1 tablespoon chili powder
1 teaspoon ground cumin
⅛ teaspoon ground red pepper
2 cups fresh broccoli flowerets
1 (16-ounce) can red kidney beans, rinsed and
  drained
½ cup plus 2 tablespoons plain nonfat yogurt
½ cup plus 2 tablespoons (2½ ounces) shredded
  40% less-fat Cheddar cheese

Coat a Dutch oven with cooking spray; add
oil. Place over medium-high heat until hot. Add
onion, mushrooms, carrot, and garlic; sauté until
vegetables are crisp-tender. Stir in squash and
next 7 ingredients; stir well. Bring mixture to a
boil; cover, reduce heat, and simmer 15 minutes. Stir in broccoli and kidney beans; cover
and simmer an additional 20 minutes. Ladle
chili into individual bowls. Top each serving with
1 tablespoon yogurt, and sprinkle each with 1
tablespoon cheese. Yield: 2½ quarts (123 calories per 1-cup serving).

PROTEIN 7.2 / FAT 2.2 / CARBOHYDRATE 21.3 / CHOLESTEROL 4 /
IRON 2.4 / SODIUM 81 / CALCIUM 145

*When it's time for dessert, no one
will be able to resist these light
offerings. Take your pick of two
different ways to serve angel food
cake: (from back) Ribbon Cakes and
Chocolate-Raspberry Torte (recipes,
page 246).*

"FRIED" BANANAS

3 large bananas, peeled and split lengthwise
1 tablespoon lemon juice
½ cup unsweetened pineapple-orange-banana juice
3 tablespoons brown sugar
3 tablespoons brandy
2 tablespoons reduced-calorie margarine
1½ cups vanilla ice milk
Fresh mint sprigs (optional)

Brush bananas with lemon juice; set aside.
Combine pineapple-orange-banana juice and next 3 ingredients in a large nonstick skillet; cook over medium heat, stirring until margarine melts. Place bananas in skillet, cut side down. Cover and cook 5 to 6 minutes or until bananas are tender. Transfer bananas to individual dessert dishes with a slotted spatula. Cook remaining juice mixture, uncovered, 5 minutes or until liquid evaporates and sugar begins to caramelize. Spoon caramel mixture over bananas. Top each serving with ¼ cup ice milk. Garnish with mint sprigs, if desired. Serve immediately. Yield: 6 servings (131 calories per serving).

PROTEIN 1.8 / FAT 4.1 / CARBOHYDRATE 24.0 / CHOLESTEROL 5 / IRON 0.4 / SODIUM 65 / CALCIUM 51

BERRY AMBROSIA WITH MIMOSA SAUCE

2 oranges, peeled, seeded, and sectioned
1½ cups fresh blueberries
1½ cups fresh raspberries
¾ cup fresh orange juice
1 tablespoon cornstarch
⅓ cup dry champagne
1 tablespoon light-colored corn syrup

Combine orange sections, blueberries, and raspberries; toss gently. Cover and chill.

Combine orange juice and cornstarch in a saucepan. Stir in champagne. Bring to a boil; stir constantly. Reduce heat; simmer 1 minute, stirring constantly. Remove from heat; stir in corn syrup. Cool to room temperature.
To serve, spoon ½ cup fruit mixture into each of 8 individual dessert dishes. Spoon 2 tablespoons sauce over each serving. Yield: 8 servings (68 calories per ½-cup serving).

PROTEIN 0.9 / FAT 0.3 / CARBOHYDRATE 16.8 / CHOLESTEROL 0 / IRON 0.4 / SODIUM 5 / CALCIUM 23

FRUIT PLATTER WITH KIWIFRUIT SAUCE

1 cup unsweetened pineapple juice
2 tablespoons cornstarch
2 teaspoons grated lime rind
3 tablespoons fresh lime juice
2 tablespoons light rum
1 tablespoon light-colored corn syrup
1 kiwifruit, peeled and quartered
1 small cantaloupe (about 2 pounds)
8 (¾-inch-thick) slices fresh pineapple, peeled and cored
2 cups fresh strawberries

Combine pineapple juice and cornstarch in a small saucepan, stirring well. Add lime rind and next 3 ingredients; stir well. Cook over medium heat until thickened and bubbly. Remove from heat, and set aside.
Position knife blade in food processor bowl; add kiwifruit. Process until smooth. Stir kiwifruit puree into reserved pineapple juice mixture; set mixture aside.
Peel cantaloupe; cut in half lengthwise. Scoop out seeds. Slice cantaloupe into 16 slices.
Cut pineapple slices in half. Arrange cantaloupe, pineapple, and strawberries on a serving platter. Spoon reserved kiwifruit sauce over fruit. Yield: 8 servings (124 calories per serving).

PROTEIN 1.5 / FAT 0.9 / CARBOHYDRATE 30.4 / CHOLESTEROL 0 / IRON 0.9 / SODIUM 10 / CALCIUM 31

PEACHES WITH ALMOND CUSTARD SAUCE

½ cup peach nectar
½ cup water
1 (1½-inch) vanilla bean
½ teaspoon almond extract
4 peaches, peeled, pitted, and halved crosswise
1 cup skim milk
¼ cup sugar
2½ teaspoons cornstarch
2 eggs, beaten
¼ teaspoon almond extract

Combine first 4 ingredients in a large saucepan. Place over medium heat, and bring to a boil, stirring constantly. Add peaches; cover, reduce heat, and simmer 5 minutes or until peaches are tender. Remove from heat; let cool. Remove and discard vanilla bean.

Combine skim milk, sugar, and cornstarch in a medium saucepan; stir well. Cook over medium heat, stirring constantly, until mixture comes to a boil. Cook an additional minute, stirring constantly, until mixture thickens. Reduce heat. Gradually stir about one-fourth of hot mixture into eggs; add to remaining hot mixture; stir constantly. Cook 1 minute. Remove from heat; stir in almond extract. Cover and chill.

Transfer peach halves into dessert dishes with a slotted spoon. Spoon custard sauce over fruit. Yield: 8 servings (89 calories per serving).

PROTEIN 3.0 / FAT 1.4 / CARBOHYDRATE 17.1 / CHOLESTEROL 50 / IRON 0.3 / SODIUM 33 / CALCIUM 47

SPICED PEACHES IN CHAMPAGNE

4 medium-size fresh peaches, peeled (about 1¼ pounds)
1 tablespoon lemon juice
2 cups water
8 whole cloves
6 whole allspice
2 (3-inch) sticks cinnamon
2 ounces Neufchâtel cheese, softened
1 tablespoon sugar
1 teaspoon skim milk
⅛ teaspoon ground cardamom
½ cup dry champagne

Brush peaches with lemon juice; set aside.

Combine water, and next 3 ingredients in a large saucepan. Bring to a boil, and cook 5 minutes, stirring occasionally. Reduce heat to low; add peaches. Cover and simmer 10 minutes or until peaches are tender. Remove peaches with a slotted spoon; let cool.

Strain spice mixture, discarding spices. Return liquid to saucepan; cook over medium-high heat or until mixture is reduced to ½ cup. Remove from heat; cover and chill thoroughly.

Combine Neufchâtel cheese, sugar, milk, and cardamom in a small bowl. Stir well until mixture is smooth.

Cut peaches in half; remove pit. Spoon Neufchâtel cheese mixture evenly into peach halves; set aside.

Combine chilled spice mixture and champagne; stir well. Pour champagne mixture evenly into 4 individual dessert dishes. Place two peach halves in each dish. Serve immediately. Yield: 4 servings (102 calories per serving).

PROTEIN 2.0 / FAT 3.4 / CARBOHYDRATE 11.8 / CHOLESTEROL 11 / IRON 0.3 / SODIUM 58 / CALCIUM 17

 TELEVISION AND COUCH POTATOES

Scientists say your television viewing habits provide a good clue to your weight. The more television you watch, the more likely you are to be overweight, according to studies of both children and adults. Researchers theorize that people who watch television for hours at a time set themselves up with weight problems for two reasons.

First, they aren't exercising, unless you count the finger workout from the remote control. To make matters worse, this negative training can actually change muscle fibers physically, making them weaker and less durable.

Second, snacking often increases during viewing time. As commercials urge viewers to eat, many follow that advice. Seeing a gooey chocolate brownie or a crunchy snack on the screen is too tempting for many viewers.

Fortunately, there is a possible remedy for this weight problem. Turn off the television and do something active instead. Save viewing for special shows rather than slouching on the couch watching anything. And if you must snack, choose a piece of fresh fruit or some plain popcorn.

POACHED PEARS WITH RASPBERRY-CHOCOLATE SAUCE

6 medium-size ripe pears (about 2 pounds)
1½ tablespoons lemon juice
6 cups water
3 tablespoons grated orange rind
1 teaspoon almond extract
¼ cup frozen unsweetened raspberries
3 ounces light process cream cheese product, softened
1 tablespoon crème de framboises or other raspberry-flavored liqueur
Raspberry-Chocolate Sauce

Peel pears, and core just from the bottom, cutting to but not through the stem end. Brush pears with lemon juice.

Bring water to boil in a Dutch oven. Add rind and almond extract; boil 5 minutes. Place pears, stem end up, in pan; cover, reduce heat, and simmer 12 to 15 minutes or just until pears are tender. Remove pan from heat; let pears cool in cooking liquid. Remove pears from liquid with a slotted spoon.

Thaw raspberries, and reserve juice. Mash raspberries in juice with a fork. Add cream cheese and liqueur; stir until smooth. Pipe filling into cavity of pears, using a pastry bag.

Spoon 1 tablespoon Raspberry-Chocolate Sauce into each of 6 individual dessert dishes; place pears in sauce. Drizzle 1 tablespoon Raspberry-Chocolate Sauce over each pear. Yield: 6 servings (174 calories per serving).

Raspberry-Chocolate Sauce:

⅓ cup sifted powdered sugar
2 tablespoons unsweetened cocoa
1½ teaspoons cornstarch
½ cup plus 3 tablespoons water
1 tablespoon crème de framboises or other raspberry-flavored liqueur
1 teaspoon vanilla extract

Combine first 3 ingredients in a small saucepan. Gradually add water, stirring well. Place over medium heat, and cook until slightly thickened, stirring constantly. Remove from heat; stir in liqueur and vanilla. Yield: ¾ cup.

PROTEIN 2.6 / FAT 3.2 / CARBOHYDRATE 33.0 / CHOLESTEROL 8 / IRON 0.7 / SODIUM 81 / CALCIUM 40

FLOATING ISLANDS IN FRUIT SAUCE

1 (16-ounce) package frozen unsweetened raspberries, thawed
4 cups peeled and sliced nectarines (about 1½ pounds)
3 tablespoons fresh lime juice
1 tablespoon corn syrup
1 tablespoon kirsch or other cherry-flavored brandy
2 egg whites
¼ teaspoon cream of tartar
¼ teaspoon almond extract
½ cup sugar
Fresh raspberries (optional)
Fresh mint sprigs (optional)

Position knife blade in food processor bowl; add half of raspberries, nectarines, and lime juice. Process until smooth. Press berry mixture through a sieve; discard seeds and pulp. Pour mixture into a medium bowl. Repeat procedure with remaining raspberries, nectarines, and lime juice. Stir in corn syrup and kirsch. Cover mixture, and chill.

Beat egg whites (at room temperature), cream of tartar, and almond extract in a medium bowl at high speed of an electric mixer until foamy. Gradually add sugar, 1 tablespoon at a time, beating until stiff peaks form and sugar dissolves (2 to 4 minutes).

Pour boiling water into a 13- x 9- x 2-inch baking pan to a depth of 1 inch. Drop egg white mixture in 8 equal portions into boiling water. Bake at 350° for 15 to 18 minutes or until lightly browned. Remove islands with a slotted spoon, and drain on paper towels. Chill islands until ready to serve.

Spoon raspberry mixture evenly into 8 individual dessert dishes, and top each with an island. If desired, garnish with fresh raspberries and mint sprigs. Serve immediately. Yield: 8 servings (142 calories per serving).

PROTEIN 1.8 / FAT 0.8 / CARBOHYDRATE 34.2 / CHOLESTEROL 0 / IRON 0.3 / SODIUM 21 / CALCIUM 6

Serve Floating Islands in Fruit Sauce in stemmed dishes; garnish with fresh mint sprigs and raspberries for a formal touch.

MERINGUE-TOPPED NECTARINES

2 medium-size firm fresh nectarines, halved and
    pitted (about ¾ pound)
Vegetable cooking spray
1 tablespoon kirsch or other cherry-flavored brandy
1 egg white
⅛ teaspoon cream of tartar
2 tablespoons sugar
¼ teaspoon almond extract
¼ teaspoon coconut extract
2 tablespoons finely chopped almonds, lightly
    toasted

Place nectarine halves, cut side up, in an 8-inch square baking dish coated with cooking spray. Gently brush cut sides of nectarines evenly with kirsch.

Beat egg white (at room temperature) and cream of tartar in a medium bowl at high speed of an electric mixer until foamy. Gradually add sugar, 1 tablespoon at a time, beating until stiff peaks form (2 to 4 minutes). Fold in flavorings.

Spread each nectarine half with 2 tablespoons meringue. Sprinkle 1½ teaspoons almonds over each nectarine half. Bake at 375° for 15 minutes or until meringue is lightly browned, and nectarines are tender. Yield: 4 servings (88 calories per serving).

PROTEIN 2.1 / FAT 2.3 / CARBOHYDRATE 16.1 / CHOLESTEROL 0 /
IRON 0.2 / SODIUM 20 / CALCIUM 14

RUBY STRAWBERRIES

1 (10-ounce) package frozen raspberries in light
    syrup, thawed
1 tablespoon plus 1 teaspoon cornstarch
1 tablespoon lemon juice
1 tablespoon Cointreau or other orange-flavored
    liqueur
1 quart fresh strawberries, hulled
2 tablespoons sugar
¼ cup sliced almonds, toasted
Fresh mint sprigs (optional)

Press raspberries through a sieve, and discard seeds. Combine strained raspberries and cornstarch in a small saucepan; stir well. Bring raspberry mixture to a boil over medium heat, and cook until thickened, stirring constantly. Remove raspberry mixture from heat, and stir in lemon juice and liqueur.

Combine strawberries and sugar in a large bowl, tossing gently to coat. Pour raspberry sauce over strawberries; cover and chill strawberry mixture 3 to 4 hours. Toss strawberry mixture gently, and spoon evenly into individual dessert dishes. Sprinkle each serving with 1½ teaspoons toasted almonds. Garnish strawberries with fresh mint sprigs, if desired. Yield: 8 servings (104 calories per ½-cup serving).

PROTEIN 1.4 / FAT 2.2 / CARBOHYDRATE 20.3 / CHOLESTEROL 0 /
IRON 0.7 / SODIUM 2 / CALCIUM 25

PEACH CARDINALE SHERBET

1 (16-ounce) package frozen unsweetened
    raspberries, thawed and undrained
½ cup peach nectar
4 cups peeled, sliced fresh peaches
½ cup low-fat sour cream
2 tablespoons instant nonfat dry milk powder
1 (6-ounce) can frozen unsweetened pineapple
    juice concentrate, thawed and undiluted
1 cup water
¼ teaspoon almond extract
Fresh mint sprigs (optional)

Place raspberries and peach nectar in container of an electric blender or food processor; top with cover, and process until smooth. Press raspberry puree through a sieve, and discard seeds. Transfer raspberry mixture to a large bowl; set aside.

Place sliced peaches, sour cream, and milk powder in container of electric blender or food processor; top with cover, and process peach mixture until smooth. Add peach mixture to reserved raspberry puree, stirring well to combine. Add pineapple juice concentrate, water, and almond extract; stir well.

Pour mixture into freezer can of a 2-quart hand-turned or electric freezer. Freeze according to manufacturer's instructions. Let ripen 1 hour, if desired. Scoop sherbet into individual dessert bowls. Garnish with fresh mint sprigs, if desired. Serve immediately. Yield: 6 cups (87 calories per ½-cup serving).

PROTEIN 1.6 / FAT 1.5 / CARBOHYDRATE 18.1 / CHOLESTEROL 4 /
IRON 0.4 / SODIUM 12 / CALCIUM 42

For a bright and attractive dessert, garnish Rainbow Fruit Bombe with edible flowers.

MINT DAIQUIRI SHERBET

1 (6-ounce) can frozen limeade concentrate,
    thawed and undiluted
¼ cup fresh mint sprigs
1¾ cups skim milk
3 tablespoons instant nonfat dry milk powder
½ teaspoon rum extract

Combine limeade concentrate and mint sprigs in container of an electric blender or food processor; top with cover, and process 30 seconds or until smooth. Add milk, milk powder, and rum extract; process just until blended.

Pour mixture into freezer can of a 2-quart hand-turned or electric ice cream freezer. Freeze according to manufacturer's instructions. Let ripen 1 hour, if desired. Scoop sherbet into individual dessert bowls, and serve immediately. Yield: 2½ cups (113 calories per ½-cup serving).

PROTEIN 4.7 / FAT 0.2 / CARBOHYDRATE 23.5 / CHOLESTEROL 3 / IRON 0.4 / SODIUM 70 / CALCIUM 167

RAINBOW FRUIT BOMBE

2 cups peach sorbet, softened
1 cup raspberry sherbet, softened
3 cups frozen unsweetened whole raspberries
2 egg whites
2 tablespoons sugar
2 tablespoons kirsch or other cherry-flavored brandy
Raspberry Sauce
Edible flowers (optional)

Line a 12-cup mold or large bowl with plastic wrap. Spoon sorbet and sherbet alternately into prepared bowl; swirl with a knife to make a marbled design. Freeze 1 hour or until firm.

Position knife blade in food processor bowl; add frozen raspberries. Process until fruit is finely chopped and of a powdery consistency. Transfer fruit to a large bowl. Add egg whites, sugar, and kirsch; beat at high speed of an electric mixer for 10 minutes or until mixture is thick and fluffy. Pour fruit mixture over sorbet mixture. Smooth top; cover and freeze 8 hours or until firm.

Using the tip of a knife, loosen edges of bombe from mold. Invert mold onto a chilled serving platter. Wrap a warm towel around mold for 30 seconds. Remove towel, and firmly hold plate and mold together. Shake gently, and slowly lift off the mold. Remove plastic wrap. Smooth rough edges with a knife.

Slice into wedges, and serve with Raspberry Sauce. Garnish with edible flowers, if desired. Yield: 12 servings (67 calories per serving).

Raspberry Sauce:

1 (16-ounce) package frozen unsweetened
    raspberries, thawed
¼ cup water
2 teaspoons cornstarch
2 tablespoons kirsch or other cherry-flavored brandy

Position knife blade in food processor bowl; add raspberries, and process until smooth. Strain raspberries and discard seeds. Combine water and cornstarch; stir well. Combine raspberry puree, cornstarch mixture, and kirsch in a medium saucepan. Cook over medium heat, stirring constantly until thickened and bubbly. Remove from heat; cool completely. Yield: 2 cups.

PROTEIN 1.5 / FAT 0.8 / CARBOHYDRATE 14.4 / CHOLESTEROL 0.3 / IRON 0.4 / SODIUM 18.8 / CALCIUM 27

BLACKBERRY ICE MILK

2 cups fresh blackberries
3 cups skim milk
½ cup sugar
1 egg, beaten
¼ cup instant nonfat dry milk powder
1 (12-ounce) can evaporated skimmed milk
½ teaspoon vanilla extract

Place blackberries in container of an electric blender or food processor; top with cover, and process until smooth. Press blackberry puree through a sieve; discard seeds. Chill blackberry puree at least 30 minutes.

Combine milk, sugar, egg, and milk powder in a medium saucepan. Cook over medium-low heat, stirring constantly with a wire whisk until mixture is slightly thickened. Remove from heat, and chill thoroughly.

Combine blackberry puree, milk mixture, evaporated milk, and vanilla extract in a large bowl; stir well.

Pour mixture into freezer can of a 1-gallon hand-turned or electric freezer. Freeze according to manufacturer's instructions. Let ripen 1 hour, if desired. Scoop ice milk into individual dessert bowls, and serve immediately. Yield: 7½ cups (81 calories per ½-cup serving).

PROTEIN 4.6 / FAT 0.5 / CARBOHYDRATE 14.8 / CHOLESTEROL 16 / IRON 0.2 / SODIUM 67 / CALCIUM 158

PEANUT BUTTER-CHOCOLATE ICE MILK

1 cup skim milk
¾ cup water
½ cup instant nonfat dry milk powder
¼ cup no-sugar-added creamy peanut butter
¼ cup honey
3 cups 2% low-fat chocolate milk

Combine first 5 ingredients in container of an electric blender or food processor; top with cover, and process until smooth.

Pour mixture into freezer can of a 1-gallon hand-turned or electric freezer; add chocolate milk, stirring well. Freeze according to manufacturer's instructions. Let ripen 1 hour, if desired.

Scoop ice milk into individual dessert bowls, and serve immediately. Yield: 7 cups (106 calories per ½-cup serving).

PROTEIN 5.2 / FAT 3.5 / CARBOHYDRATE 14.3 / CHOLESTEROL 5 / IRON 0.2 / SODIUM 65 / CALCIUM 138

HAZELNUT TORTONI

¼ cup cold water
1 egg white
¼ cup plus 1 tablespoon powdered sugar
½ cup instant nonfat dry milk powder
1 tablespoon Frangelico or other hazelnut-flavored liqueur
2 tablespoons chopped hazelnuts, toasted
2 tablespoons shredded unsweetened coconut, toasted

Place water in a small, narrow glass or stainless steel bowl; freeze 25 minutes or until a ⅛-inch-thick layer of ice forms on surface.

Beat egg white (at room temperature) in a large bowl at high speed of an electric mixer until soft peaks form. Gradually add powdered sugar, 1 tablespoon at a time, beating until stiff peaks form (do not overbeat). Set aside.

Add milk powder to partially frozen water; beat at high speed of electric mixer 5 minutes or until stiff peaks form. Stir in liqueur. Gently fold milk mixture into egg white mixture.

Combine hazelnuts and coconut. Sprinkle 1 teaspoon nut mixture into each of 6 paper-lined muffin pans; spoon whipped mixture evenly into cups. Sprinkle evenly with remaining nut mixture. Freeze at least 8 hours. Yield: 6 servings (87 calories per serving).

PROTEIN 3.6 / FAT 2.8 / CARBOHYDRATE 11.4 / CHOLESTEROL 1 / IRON 0.2 / SODIUM 47 / CALCIUM 95

AMARETTO FREEZE

¼ cup plus 1 tablespoon amaretto
1 tablespoon brown sugar
5 cups vanilla ice milk
1 tablespoon grated semisweet chocolate

Combine amaretto and brown sugar in a small bowl; stir until sugar dissolves. Combine amaretto mixture and ice milk in container of an electric blender; top with cover, and process until smooth.

Spoon mixture into 8 individual freezer-proof bowls; sprinkle evenly with grated chocolate. Cover and freeze until firm. Yield: 8 servings (156 calories per ½-cup serving).

PROTEIN 3.3 / FAT 4.1 / CARBOHYDRATE 22.7 / CHOLESTEROL 11 / IRON 0.2 / SODIUM 66 / CALCIUM 111

GINGER-RAISIN ICE MILK SANDWICHES

½ cup boiling water
½ teaspoon brandy extract
¾ cup raisins
3 cups vanilla ice milk, softened
16 (2-inch-round) thin gingersnaps

Combine boiling water and brandy extract in a small bowl; stir in raisins. Let stand 15 minutes. Drain well.

Fold raisins into ice milk. Spread ⅓ cup ice milk mixture onto each of 8 gingersnaps; top with remaining gingersnaps. Place on a baking sheet, and freeze until firm. Wrap sandwiches in plastic wrap, and store in freezer. Yield: 8 servings (115 calories per serving).

PROTEIN 2.5 / FAT 3.5 / CARBOHYDRATE 18.6 / CHOLESTEROL 10 / IRON 0.5 / SODIUM 51 / CALCIUM 82

TROPICAL PUDDING

1 envelope unflavored gelatin
1¾ cups papaya nectar
2 tablespoons sugar
2 teaspoons grated lime rind
1 (8-ounce) carton plain nonfat yogurt
1 (8-ounce) can crushed pineapple in juice, drained
¼ teaspoon coconut extract
1 medium mango (about ¾ pound)
1 tablespoon fresh lime juice

Sprinkle gelatin over papaya nectar in a medium saucepan, and let stand 1 minute. Add sugar, and cook papaya mixture over medium heat, stirring constantly, until gelatin and sugar

dissolve. Remove mixture from heat, and stir in lime rind. Chill papaya mixture until consistency of unbeaten egg white. Add plain yogurt, crushed pineapple, and coconut extract, stirring well. Spoon ½ cup fruit mixture into each of 6 individual dessert bowls, and set aside.

Peel and slice mango; brush mango slices with lime juice. Arrange mango slices evenly over each serving. Yield: 6 servings (122 calories per ½-cup serving).

PROTEIN 3.6 / FAT 0.4 / CARBOHYDRATE 27.9 / CHOLESTEROL 1 / IRON 0.4 / SODIUM 35 / CALCIUM 89

MOCHA CUSTARD

2½ cups water
¼ cup coffee beans
1 (2-inch) vanilla bean
⅔ cup instant nonfat dry milk powder
¼ cup plus 1 tablespoon sugar
¼ cup unsweetened cocoa
2½ tablespoons cornstarch
⅛ teaspoon salt
⅔ cup frozen egg substitute, thawed
2½ tablespoons Kahlúa

Bring water to a boil in a medium saucepan; remove from heat, and add coffee beans. Split vanilla bean in half, and remove seeds; add vanilla bean and seeds to water. Let mixture stand 1 hour. Strain, reserving liquid. Discard vanilla and coffee beans.

Combine milk powder, sugar, unsweetened cocoa, cornstarch, and salt in a medium saucepan, stirring well. Gradually add reserved vanilla liquid, stirring mixture until smooth. Bring mixture to a boil over medium heat, stirring constantly; boil 1 minute.

Gradually stir about one-fourth of hot mixture into egg substitute; add to remaining hot mixture, stirring constantly. Add Kahlúa, and cook mixture over low heat, stirring constantly, 1 to 2 minutes or until mixture is smooth and slightly thickened (do not boil).

Spoon mixture into 6 individual dessert dishes. Cover and chill thoroughly. Yield: 6 servings (144 calories per ½-cup serving).

PROTEIN 8.6 / FAT 0.6 / CARBOHYDRATE 26.0 / CHOLESTEROL 3 / IRON 1.2 / SODIUM 165 / CALCIUM 183

SPICED CUSTARD

3 cups water
¼ cup sugar
20 whole cloves
3 (3-inch) sticks cinnamon
1 cup instant nonfat dry milk powder
2 tablespoons cornstarch
⅛ teaspoon salt
2 eggs, lightly beaten
1 teaspoon vanilla extract
Freshly grated nutmeg

Combine first 4 ingredients in a medium saucepan. Bring to a boil over medium heat; reduce heat, and simmer until mixture is reduced to 2 cups. Strain and discard cloves and cinnamon sticks. Let spiced water mixture cool 15 minutes.

Combine milk powder, cornstarch, and salt in medium saucepan. Gradually add spiced water mixture, stirring until smooth. Cook mixture over medium heat, stirring constantly, until mixture comes to a boil. Cook 1 minute, stirring mixture constantly.

Gradually stir about one-fourth of hot mixture into eggs; add to remaining hot mixture, stirring constantly. Cook over low heat 1 to 2 minutes, stirring constantly. Remove mixture from heat, and stir in vanilla.

Spoon custard into 6 individual dessert dishes. Sprinkle with nutmeg. Serve warm. Yield: 6 servings (141 calories per ⅓-cup serving).

PROTEIN 9.3 / FAT 1.8 / CARBOHYDRATE 21.6 / CHOLESTEROL 71 / IRON 0.4 / SODIUM 177 / CALCIUM 260

BAKED LIME SOUFFLÉ

½ cup sugar
¼ cup all-purpose flour
¼ teaspoon salt
2 eggs, separated
⅔ cup skim milk
1½ teaspoons grated lime rind
¼ cup lime juice
2 egg whites

Combine sugar, flour, and salt in a small bowl; stir well, and set aside.

Combine egg yolks, milk, lime rind, and lime juice; beat at low speed of an electric mixer until smooth. Add flour mixture; beat well.

Beat 4 egg whites (at room temperature) at high speed of electric mixer until stiff peaks form. Gently fold egg whites into lime mixture.

Spoon mixture into a 1-quart soufflé dish. Place dish in an 8-inch square baking pan; pour hot water into pan to a depth of 1 inch. Bake at 350° for 45 to 50 minutes or until top of soufflé looks like a cake and springs back when touched (bottom of soufflé will be a sauce).

Remove dish from water. Spoon cake-like top into serving dishes, and spoon sauce from bottom of dish over each serving. Yield: 6 servings (123 calories per serving).

PROTEIN 4.7 / FAT 1.7 / CARBOHYDRATE 22.9 / CHOLESTEROL 67 / IRON 0.5 / SODIUM 150 / CALCIUM 46

CHOCOLATE-MINT ICE MILK PIE

3 ounces semisweet chocolate
2 tablespoons reduced-calorie margarine
¼ cup green crème de menthe, divided
1½ teaspoons vanilla extract, divided
1¼ cups crispy rice cereal
½ cup evaporated skim milk
2 tablespoons unsweetened cocoa
2 tablespoons light-colored corn syrup
1 teaspoon cornstarch
2 pints vanilla ice milk, softened
Chocolate curls (optional)
Fresh mint sprigs (optional)

Line a 9-inch pieplate with aluminum foil; fold excess under edge of pieplate. Combine 3 ounces chocolate and margarine in top of a double boiler; bring water to a boil. Reduce heat to low; cook until chocolate and margarine melt. Add 1 tablespoon crème de menthe; cook 1 minute, stirring constantly. Remove from heat; add 1 teaspoon vanilla and cereal, stirring well.

Spoon chocolate mixture into prepared pieplate. Spread evenly over bottom and up sides of pieplate. Freeze 30 minutes or until firm. Remove chocolate shell from pieplate; peel foil from shell, and return shell to pieplate. Return pieplate to freezer.

Chocolate and crème de menthe make a luscious combination for Chocolate-Mint Ice Milk Pie.

Combine milk, cocoa, corn syrup, and cornstarch in a small saucepan; stir well. Cook over medium heat, stirring constantly, until mixture thickens and comes to a boil. Add 1 tablespoon crème de menthe, and cook an additional minute. Remove from heat, and add remaining ½ teaspoon vanilla; let cool completely.

Combine softened ice milk and remaining 2 tablespoons crème de menthe in a large bowl. Remove pieplate from freezer, and spread half the ice milk mixture evenly over pieshell. Return to freezer for 30 minutes. Remove from freezer, and top ice mixture with chocolate mint filling; freeze 10 minutes. Remove from freezer, and top with remaining ice milk mixture. Cover and freeze at least 8 hours.

If desired, garnish each serving with chocolate curls and fresh mint sprigs. Let stand 5 minutes before serving. Yield: 10 servings (188 calories per serving).

PROTEIN 4.0 / FAT 6.6 / CARBOHYDRATE 27.7 / CHOLESTEROL 8 / IRON 0.9 / SODIUM 108 / CALCIUM 115

STRAWBERRY AND CHOCOLATE PHYLLO NESTS

8 sheets commercial frozen phyllo pastry, thawed
Vegetable cooking spray
3 cups sliced strawberries
3 tablespoons unsweetened orange juice
2 tablespoons light rum
1 tablespoon grated orange rind
Chocolate Sauce

Place 1 sheet of phyllo on a damp towel (keep remaining phyllo covered). Lightly coat phyllo with cooking spray. Layer 3 more sheets of phyllo on first sheet, lightly coating each sheet with cooking spray. Cut stack of phyllo into 12 (approximately 4-inch) squares with kitchen shears. Repeat procedure with remaining phyllo.

Coat 12 muffins cups with cooking spray. Layer 2 portions of phyllo squares in each muffin cup, pressing gently in center to form a pastry shell. Prick bottom of each pastry shell with a fork. Bake at 350° for 8 to 10 minutes or until golden. Gently remove from pan, and let cool on wire racks.

Place strawberries in a large bowl. Combine orange juice, rum, and orange rind. Sprinkle over strawberries, and toss gently. Let stand 15 minutes. Spoon ¼ cup strawberry mixture into each pastry nest. Drizzle 1 tablespoon Chocolate Sauce evenly over each serving. Yield: 12 servings (106 calories per serving).

Chocolate Sauce:

3 tablespoons unsweetened cocoa
3 tablespoons brown sugar
1½ teaspoons cornstarch
½ cup plus 1 tablespoon water
3 tablespoons honey
⅛ teaspoon salt
1 tablespoon reduced-calorie margarine
1½ teaspoons vanilla extract

Combine first 3 ingredients in a small saucepan; add water, and stir well. Add honey and salt. Cook over medium heat, stirring constantly, until mixture comes to a boil; boil 1 minute. Add margarine, stirring until melted. Remove from heat, and stir in vanilla. Serve at room temperature. Yield: ¾ cup.

PROTEIN 2.1 / FAT 1.6 / CARBOHYDRATE 19.8 / CHOLESTEROL 0 / IRON 0.8 / SODIUM 36 / CALCIUM 11

SWEET CHERRY CREAM TART

1 cup sifted cake flour
¼ cup cold margarine
2 to 3 tablespoons cold water
1 cup low-fat sour cream
2 eggs, beaten
¼ cup all-purpose flour
¼ cup sugar
1 tablespoon kirsch or other cherry-flavored brandy
1 pound fresh sweet cherries, pitted

Place flour in a medium bowl; cut in margarine with a pastry blender until mixture resembles coarse meal. Sprinkle cold water, 1 tablespoon at a time, evenly over surface; stir with a fork until dry ingredients are moistened. Shape into a ball.

Place dough between 2 sheets of heavy-duty plastic wrap, and gently press dough to a 4-inch circle. Chill 15 minutes. Roll dough to a 10-inch circle. Place in freezer 5 minutes or until plastic wrap can be removed easily. Remove top sheet of plastic wrap; invert and fit pastry into a 9-inch tart pan. Remove remaining sheet of plastic wrap. Prick bottom of pastry with a fork. Bake at 425° for 20 minutes. Remove from oven, and cool completely.

Combine sour cream and next 4 ingredients in a medium bowl. Beat at medium speed of an electric mixer until smooth. Arrange cherries in tart shell. Pour sour cream mixture over cherries. Bake at 400° for 25 minutes or until filling is set. Let cool completely on a wire rack. Yield: 10 servings (188 calories per serving).

PROTEIN 3.7 / FAT 9.0 / CARBOHYDRATE 24.1 / CHOLESTEROL 49 / IRON 1.2 / SODIUM 76 / CALCIUM 41

LEMON AND BERRY TART

1 cup all-purpose flour
½ teaspoon ground cardamom
¼ cup margarine
2 to 3 tablespoons cold water
1 tablespoon sugar
¾ cup water
⅓ cup sugar
1 tablespoon grated lemon rind
3 tablespoons lemon juice
Dash of salt
1 tablespoon cornstarch
3 tablespoons water
1 teaspoon reduced-calorie margarine
2 eggs, beaten
1 cup strawberries, halved
1 small kiwifruit, sliced
¼ cup fresh blackberries

Combine flour and cardamom in a large bowl; cut in margarine with a pastry blender until mixture resembles coarse meal. Sprinkle cold water, 1 tablespoon at a time, evenly over surface; stir with a fork until dry ingredients are moistened. Shape into a ball.

Place dough between 2 sheets of heavy-duty plastic wrap; gently press dough to a 4-inch circle. Chill 15 minutes. Roll dough to a 10-inch circle. Place in freezer 5 minutes or until plastic wrap can be removed easily. Remove top sheet of plastic wrap; invert and fit pastry into a 9-inch tart pan. Remove remaining sheet of plastic wrap. Prick bottom of pastry with a fork. Sprinkle with 1 tablespoon sugar. Bake at 400° for 15 minutes or until lightly browned. Remove from oven, and cool completely.

Combine ¾ cup water, ⅓ cup sugar, lemon rind, lemon juice, and salt in a medium saucepan; bring to a boil over medium heat. Combine cornstarch and 3 tablespoons water, stirring until smooth. Add cornstarch mixture to lemon mixture, stirring until smooth. Stir in reduced-calorie margarine. Cook over medium-low heat, stirring constantly, until mixture comes to a boil. Remove from heat. Gradually stir about one-fourth of hot mixture into eggs; add to remaining hot mixture. Cook over low heat, stirring constantly, 1 minute or until mixture thickens. Remove from heat, and cool completely.

Spoon filling into tart shell. Arrange fruit over lemon filling. Yield: 8 servings (181 calories per serving).

PROTEIN 3.4 / FAT 7.5 / CARBOHYDRATE 25.6 / CHOLESTEROL 50 / IRON 1.1 / SODIUM 107 / CALCIUM 19

ALMOND-NECTARINE COBBLER

3½ cups sliced ripe nectarines
1 cup fresh raspberries
¼ cup sugar
2 tablespoons amaretto
1½ teaspoons cornstarch
Vegetable cooking spray
¾ cup all-purpose flour
2 tablespoons ground unsalted almonds
1 tablespoon sugar
¾ teaspoon baking powder
⅛ teaspoon salt
3 tablespoons cold margarine
½ teaspoon almond extract
1 to 2 tablespoons cold water

Combine nectarines, raspberries, sugar, amaretto, and cornstarch in a medium bowl; toss gently. Spoon into an 8-inch square baking dish coated with cooking spray. Set aside.

Combine flour and next 4 ingredients in a medium bowl; stir well. Cut in margarine with a pastry blender until mixture resembles coarse meal. Sprinkle almond extract and water, 1 tablespoon at a time, evenly over surface; stir with a fork until dry ingredients are moistened.

Roll dough between 2 sheets of heavy-duty plastic wrap to ¼-inch thickness. Remove plastic wrap. Cut pastry into decorative shapes. Place pastry cutouts on top of fruit mixture. Bake at 425° for 35 minutes or until pastry is golden and filling is bubbly. Yield: 8 servings (167 calories per serving).

PROTEIN 2.2 / FAT 5.8 / CARBOHYDRATE 27.8 / CHOLESTEROL 0 / IRON 0.8 / SODIUM 116 / CALCIUM 32

SPICED GERMAN PANCAKE WITH POACHED FRUIT

1½ cups water
12 whole cloves
2 (3-inch) sticks cinnamon
2 tablespoons sugar
2 tablespoons unsweetened orange juice
2 cups fresh peach slices
2 cups fresh pear slices
1½ teaspoons cornstarch
2 teaspoons water
1½ teaspoons all-purpose flour
¼ teaspoon apple pie spice
⅛ teaspoon salt
½ cup skim milk
½ cup frozen egg substitute, thawed
Vegetable cooking spray
2 teaspoons margarine

Combine first 5 ingredients in a large nonstick skillet; bring to a boil over medium heat. Reduce heat, and simmer, uncovered, until mixture is reduced to 1 cup. Remove and discard spices. Add peaches and pears to skillet. Cover and simmer 5 minutes or until fruit is tender, stirring occasionally.

Combine cornstarch and 2 teaspoons water, stirring well; add to fruit mixture. Cook, stirring constantly, 1 minute or until mixture is slightly thickened. Set aside, and keep warm.

Combine flour, apple pie spice, salt, milk, and egg substitute in a medium bowl; stir with a wire whisk until smooth. Set aside.

Coat a 9-inch pieplate with cooking spray; add margarine. Preheat pieplate in oven at 425° for 4 minutes or until margarine melts and pieplate is hot. Pour flour mixture into hot pieplate. Bake at 425° for 15 to 20 minutes or until puffy and browned. Remove from oven; top with poached fruit mixture. Cut into 6 wedges, and serve immediately. Yield: 6 servings (147 calories per serving).

PROTEIN 4.4 / FAT 1.8 / CARBOHYDRATE 29.8 / CHOLESTEROL 0 / IRON 1.1 / SODIUM 107 / CALCIUM 45

LEMON PHYLLO DANISH

8 sheets commercial frozen phyllo pastry, thawed
Vegetable cooking spray
½ cup water
2 tablespoons margarine
½ cup all-purpose flour
⅛ teaspoon salt
2 eggs
1 teaspoon lemon extract
½ cup sifted powdered sugar
1 teaspoon grated lemon rind
2 teaspoons lemon juice

Place 1 sheet of phyllo on a damp towel (keep remaining phyllo covered). Lightly coat phyllo with cooking spray. Layer second sheet of phyllo on first sheet, lightly coating with cooking spray. Cut stack of phyllo into 4 rectangles (approximately 9- x 6½-inches) with a sharp knife. Working with one rectangle at a time, roll edges toward center to form a 3-inch circle with a rim of turned-up phyllo. Transfer to an ungreased baking sheet; spray rim with cooking spray. Repeat procedure with remaining phyllo.

Combine water and margarine in a medium saucepan; bring to a boil. Add flour and salt all at once, stirring vigorously over low heat about 1 minute or until mixture leaves sides of pan and forms a smooth ball. Remove from heat, and cool 4 to 5 minutes.

Position knife blade in food processor bowl; add flour mixture, eggs, and lemon extract; process until smooth and glossy. Spoon dough evenly onto 16 phyllo rounds. Bake at 350° for 20 to 25 minutes or until puffed and golden.

Combine powdered sugar, lemon rind, and lemon juice in a small bowl; stir well. Drizzle glaze over pastries. Yield: 16 servings (86 calories per serving).

PROTEIN 2.2 / FAT 2.5 / CARBOHYDRATE 13.3 / CHOLESTEROL 25 / IRON 0.5 / SODIUM 43 / CALCIUM 4

ANGEL FOOD CAKE WITH RASPBERRY SAUCE

1¼ cups sugar, divided
¾ cup all-purpose flour
⅛ teaspoon ground cardamom
11 egg whites
1½ teaspoons cream of tartar
¼ teaspoon salt
¼ teaspoon brandy extract
Raspberry Sauce

Sift together ¾ cup sugar, flour, and cardamom in a small bowl; set aside.

Beat egg whites (at room temperature) in an extra-large bowl at high speed of an electric mixer until foamy. Add cream of tartar and salt; beat until soft peaks form. Gradually add remaining ½ cup sugar, 2 tablespoons at a time, beating until stiff peaks form. Sift flour mixture over egg white mixture, ¼ cup at a time, folding in carefully after each addition. Gently fold in brandy extract.

Spoon batter into an ungreased 10-inch tube pan; spread evenly with a spatula. Break large air pockets by cutting through batter with a knife. Bake at 375° for 30 to 35 minutes or until cake springs back when lightly touched. Remove cake from oven. Invert pan; cool 1 hour. Loosen cake from sides of pan, using a narrow metal spatula; remove from pan.

To serve, cut cake into 12 slices, and place slices on individual dessert plates. Spoon Raspberry Sauce evenly over cake slices. Yield: 12 servings (153 calories per serving).

Raspberry Sauce:

¼ cup water
3 tablespoons sugar
1 (16-ounce) package unsweetened frozen raspberries, thawed and undrained

Combine water and sugar in a small saucepan. Cook over medium heat, stirring until sugar dissolves (about 2 to 3 minutes).

Pour sugar mixture into container of an electric blender. Add unsweetened raspberries; top with cover, and process until smooth. Strain raspberry puree, and discard seeds. Cover and chill thoroughly. Yield: 1¾ cups.

PROTEIN 4.2 / FAT 0.3 / CARBOHYDRATE 34.1 / CHOLESTEROL 0 / IRON 0.6 / SODIUM 121 / CALCIUM 13

AUTUMN ANGEL FOOD CAKE

1¼ cups sugar, divided
¾ cup all-purpose flour
1 tablespoon pumpkin pie spice
11 egg whites
1½ teaspoons cream of tartar
¼ teaspoon salt
½ teaspoon brandy extract

Sift together ¾ cup sugar, flour, and pumpkin pie spice in a small bowl; set aside.

Beat egg whites (at room temperature) in an extra-large mixing bowl at high speed of an electric mixer until foamy. Add cream of tartar and salt; beat until soft peaks form. Gradually add remaining ½ cup sugar, 2 tablespoons at a time, beating until stiff peaks form. Sift flour mixture over egg white mixture, ¼ cup at a time, folding in carefully after each addition. Gently fold in brandy extract.

Spoon batter into an ungreased 10-inch tube pan; spread evenly with a spatula. Break large air pockets by cutting through batter with a knife. Bake at 350° for 45 to 50 minutes or until cake springs back when lightly touched. Remove cake from oven. Invert pan; cool 1 hour. Loosen cake from sides of pan, using a narrow metal spatula; remove from pan. Yield: 12 servings (124 calories per serving).

PROTEIN 3.8 / FAT 0.1 / CARBOHYDRATE 27.0 / CHOLESTEROL 0 / IRON 0.4 / SODIUM 121 / CALCIUM 8

MUSIC TO DINE BY

Researchers at Johns Hopkins Institution in Baltimore have found that the music people listen to during mealtime can affect how much a person eats. Strains of Bach or Brahms seem to have a way of putting diners at ease, according to the researchers. They've found that soft music slows down the pace of eating and may cause people to eat less. Rock and roll tunes, on the other hand, pick up the pace. Diners tend to eat faster—nearly twice as fast—and, subsequently, eat more.

The weight control message here: Save the pulsating rhythms of rock and roll, the upbeat Sousa marches, and the German polkas for the dance floor. Choose the slow tunes for a more controlled, pleasurable mealtime.

RIBBON CAKES

1 (10¾-ounce) loaf commercial angel food cake
¼ cup low-sugar orange marmalade spread
1 tablespoon plus 1 teaspoon amaretto
¼ cup low-sugar raspberry spread
1 tablespoon plus 1 teaspoon amaretto
2 ounces semisweet chocolate

Scrape brown edges off cake with a small metal spatula. Slice cake horizontally into 6 equal layers (about ⅜-inch thick), using a long serrated knife. (Keep layers covered with plastic wrap to prevent drying.)

Combine orange marmalade with 1 tablespoon plus 1 teaspoon amaretto in a small bowl. Stir well, and set aside.

Combine raspberry spread with 1 tablespoon plus 1 teaspoon amaretto in a small bowl. Stir well, and set aside.

Spread half of orange marmalade mixture on 1 cake layer; top with another cake layer, and spread with half of raspberry spread mixture. Top with cake layer. Place layers in a 9-inch square pan. Repeat procedure with remaining 3 cake layers and remaining spread mixtures, spreading raspberry mixture first then orange mixture, and place in pan. Cover tightly with plastic wrap, and chill at least 8 hours.

Remove cakes from pan, and place on a cutting board. Cut each cake into 8 squares.

Place chocolate in a small zip-top freezer bag; place bag in hot water until chocolate melts. Cut ⅛-inch edge off corner of bag; pipe chocolate over each cake square in a zig-zag design. Yield: 16 servings (75 calories per serving).

PROTEIN 1.3 / FAT 1.2 / CARBOHYDRATE 14.4 / CHOLESTEROL 0 / IRON 0.2 / SODIUM 29 / CALCIUM 21

CHOCOLATE-RASPBERRY TORTE

1 (10¾-ounce) loaf commercial angel food cake
3 tablespoons low-sugar raspberry spread
2 tablespoons raspberry schnapps, divided
2 tablespoons unsweetened cocoa
2 teaspoons cornstarch
¼ cup plus 2 tablespoons water
3 tablespoons light corn syrup
Dash of salt
1 tablespoon reduced-calorie margarine
Whipped Frosting
Edible flowers (optional)

Slice cake horizontally into 6 equal layers (about ⅜-inch thick). (Keep layers covered with plastic wrap to prevent drying.)

Place raspberry spread in a small saucepan; bring to a boil over medium heat. Remove from heat; add 1 tablespoon schnapps, stirring well.

Combine cocoa and cornstarch in a small saucepan; stir in water. Add corn syrup and salt. Cook over medium heat, stirring constantly, until mixture comes to a boil; boil 1 minute. Remove from heat, and add remaining 1 tablespoon raspberry schnapps and margarine; stir until margarine melts.

Spread 2 teaspoons raspberry mixture and 2 tablespoons chocolate filling between each cake layer. Stack layers; cover tightly with plastic wrap, and chill at least 8 hours. To serve, remove cake from refrigerator. Spread top and sides of cake with Whipped Frosting. Garnish with edible flowers, if desired. Yield: 10 servings (193 calories per serving).

Whipped Frosting:

⅓ cup water
1 teaspoon unflavored gelatin
¼ cup cold water
⅓ cup instant nonfat dry milk powder
3 tablespoons sifted powdered sugar
¼ teaspoon almond extract

Place water in a small, narrow glass or stainless steel bowl; freeze 25 minutes or until a ⅛-inch-thick layer of ice forms on surface.

Sprinkle gelatin over ¼ cup cold water in a small saucepan. Let stand 1 minute. Place over medium heat, stirring to dissolve. Let cool.

Add milk powder, sugar, almond extract, and gelatin mixture to partially frozen water. Beat at high speed of an electric mixer 5 minutes or until stiff peaks form. Yield: 1⅓ cups.

PROTEIN 3.7 / FAT 1.0 / CARBOHYDRATE 29.2 / CHOLESTEROL 1 / IRON 0.5 / SODIUM 97 / CALCIUM 84

FRESH APPLE SNACK CAKE

½ cup sugar
¼ cup frozen egg substitute, thawed
3 tablespoons reduced-calorie margarine, melted
1 cup all-purpose flour
1 teaspoon apple pie spice
¾ teaspoon baking soda
⅛ teaspoon salt
2 cups peeled, cored, and chopped cooking apple
¼ cup chopped dates
Vegetable cooking spray

Combine sugar, egg substitute, and margarine in a mixing bowl, beating well at medium speed of an electric mixer.

Combine flour and next 3 ingredients in a small bowl; stir well. Add flour mixture to sugar mixture, stirring well. Fold in apple and dates. (Batter will be stiff.)

Spread batter into an 8-inch square baking dish coated with cooking spray. Bake at 325° for 45 to 55 minutes or until golden. Serve warm. Yield: 9 servings (139 calories per serving).

PROTEIN 2.1 / FAT 2.7 / CARBOHYDRATE 27.8 / CHOLESTEROL 0 / IRON 0.8 / SODIUM 148 / CALCIUM 23

MOCHA SWIRL CHEESECAKE

Vegetable cooking spray
2 tablespoons graham cracker crumbs
1 (16-ounce) carton low-fat sour cream
1 (8-ounce) package Neufchâtel cheese, softened
2 teaspoons vanilla extract
⅔ cup sugar
1 tablespoon cornstarch
1 (8-ounce) carton frozen egg substitute, thawed
¼ cup unsweetened cocoa
1½ teaspoons instant espresso coffee granules
2 tablespoons Kahlúa or other coffee-flavored liqueur

Coat bottom of a 9-inch springform pan with cooking spray. Dust with cracker crumbs.

Combine sour cream, Neufchâtel cheese, and vanilla in a large bowl; beat at medium speed of an electric mixer until smooth. Add sugar and cornstarch; beat until well blended. Add egg substitute, ¼ cup at a time, beating at low speed just until blended.

Transfer 1½ cups batter to a medium bowl. Add cocoa, espresso granules, and Kahlúa; beat at low speed of electric mixer until well blended.

Spoon batters alternately into prepared pan. Cut through mixture with a knife to create a marbled effect. Bake at 300° for 35 to 40 minutes. Turn oven off, and partially open oven door; leave cheesecake in oven 1 hour. Remove from oven; cover and chill 8 hours. Yield: 12 servings (178 calories per serving).

PROTEIN 5.7 / FAT 9.5 / CARBOHYDRATE 17.5 / CHOLESTEROL 29 / IRON 0.9 / SODIUM 128 / CALCIUM 64

DAIQUIRI CHEESECAKE

½ cup vanilla wafer crumbs
1 tablespoon reduced-calorie margarine, softened
½ teaspoon grated lime rind
Vegetable cooking spray
1 (15-ounce) carton part-skim ricotta cheese
1 (8-ounce) carton plain nonfat yogurt, drained
¾ cup sugar
¼ cup frozen limeade concentrate, thawed and undiluted
2½ tablespoons all-purpose flour
2 tablespoons grated lime rind
1 (8-ounce) carton light process cream cheese product, softened
½ cup frozen egg substitute, thawed
2 egg whites
1 teaspoon rum extract

Combine wafer crumbs, margarine, and ½ teaspoon lime rind in a small bowl. Spread in a 9-inch springform pan coated with cooking spray. Bake at 350° for 6 minutes; cool.

Position knife blade in food processor bowl; add ricotta cheese and next 5 ingredients. Process until smooth.

Beat cream cheese at medium speed of an electric mixer until smooth. Add egg substitute, egg whites, and rum extract; beat well. Gradually add ricotta mixture; beat until smooth. Slowly pour mixture over crumb crust. Bake at 325° for 50 minutes. Remove from oven, and let cool to room temperature on a wire rack. Cover and chill 8 hours. Yield: 14 servings (175 calories per serving).

PROTEIN 7.8 / FAT 6.7 / CARBOHYDRATE 21.1 / CHOLESTEROL 19 / IRON 0.5 / SODIUM 187 / CALCIUM 144

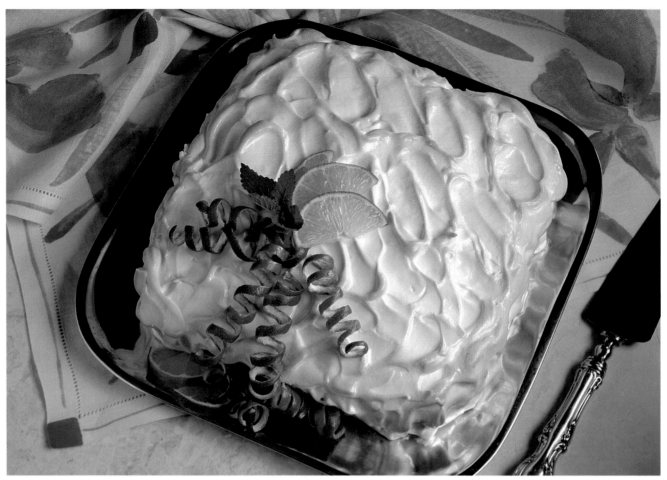

Your guests will be pleasantly surprised to discover cake with a lime filling under this golden meringue. Lime Meringue Cake, decorated with lemon balm and lime, makes a pretty dessert.

LIME MERINGUE CAKE

¼ cup frozen egg substitute, thawed
½ cup sugar
2 tablespoons margarine, melted
1½ cups sifted cake flour
2 teaspoons baking powder
½ teaspoon grated lime rind
¼ teaspoon salt
½ cup skim milk
¼ teaspoon lemon extract
Vegetable cooking spray
4 egg whites
½ teaspoon cream of tartar
½ cup sugar
Lime Custard
Lime slices and rind curls (optional)

Beat egg substitute in a bowl at high speed of an electric mixer until foamy. Gradually add ½

cup sugar and melted margarine; beat well, and set aside.

Combine flour, baking powder, ½ teaspoon lime rind, and salt; add to sugar mixture alternately with milk, beginning and ending with flour mixture. Mix well after each addition. Stir in lemon extract.

Pour batter into a 9-inch square cakepan coated with cooking spray. Bake at 350° for 25 to 30 minutes or until a wooden pick inserted in center comes out clean. Cool in pan 10 minutes. Remove cake from pan; cool completely on a wire rack.

Beat egg whites (at room temperature) and cream of tartar in a large bowl at high speed of electric mixer until soft peaks form. Gradually add ½ cup sugar, 1 tablespoon at a time, beating until stiff peaks form and sugar dissolves.

Place cake on an ovenproof serving platter. Spoon Lime Custard onto cake. Spread meringue over filling. Bake at 350° for 12 minutes or until meringue peaks are lightly browned. If desired, garnish with lime slices and rind curls. Yield: 12 servings (189 calories per serving).

Lime Custard:

1 cup water
½ cup frozen egg substitute, thawed
½ cup sugar
3 tablespoons cornstarch
2 tablespoons grated lime rind
¼ cup lime juice
1 tablespoon reduced-calorie margarine

Combine water and ½ cup egg substitute; set aside. Combine ½ cup sugar and cornstarch in a heavy saucepan. Add egg substitute mixture, lime rind, and lime juice, stirring constantly to dissolve cornstarch. Cook over medium heat, stirring constantly, until mixture comes to a boil; boil 1 minute or until slightly thickened. Remove from heat, and stir in reduced-calorie margarine. Cover and chill. Yield: 1¼ cups.

PROTEIN 4.0 / FAT 2.7 / CARBOHYDRATE 37.7 / CHOLESTEROL 0 / IRON 1.2 / SODIUM 184 / CALCIUM 55

GINGER COOKIES

⅓ cup reduced-calorie margarine, softened
½ cup firmly packed brown sugar
1 egg white
1 teaspoon vanilla extract
2 cups all-purpose flour
½ teaspoon baking soda
¼ teaspoon ground cinnamon
¼ teaspoon ground cloves
¼ teaspoon ground nutmeg
1 ounce crystallized ginger, pulverized

Cream margarine; gradually add brown sugar, beating at medium speed of an electric mixer until light and fluffy. Add egg white and vanilla, beating well.

Combine flour and next 4 ingredients, stirring well. Gradually add flour mixture to creamed mixture, mixing well. Stir in crystallized ginger. Press dough from a cookie press onto ungreased cookie sheets, making 2-inch ribbon-like strips.

Bake at 400° for 7 to 8 minutes or until edges are lightly browned. Remove from cookie sheets; let cool on wire racks. Yield: 3 dozen (47 calories each).

PROTEIN 0.8 / FAT 1.2 / CARBOHYDRATE 8.6 / CHOLESTEROL 0 / IRON 0.6 / SODIUM 31 / CALCIUM 8

CHOCOLATE-STRIPED ORANGE LOGS

⅓ cup margarine, softened
¼ cup sugar
¼ cup sifted powdered sugar
1 egg white
1 teaspoon grated orange rind
1 teaspoon orange extract
2¼ cups all-purpose flour
½ teaspoon baking soda
½ teaspoon cream of tartar
⅛ teaspoon salt
Vegetable cooking spray
Chocolate Glaze

Cream margarine; gradually add sugars, beating at medium speed of an electric mixer until light and fluffy. Add egg white, orange rind, and orange extract, beating well.

Combine flour, soda, cream of tartar, and salt; add to creamed mixture, beating at low speed of electric mixer until well blended. Divide dough in half. Shape each half into a ball, and wrap in plastic wrap; chill 1 hour.

Shape each ball into 24 (2-inch) logs. Place on cookie sheets coated with cooking spray. Flatten each cookie lengthwise with a fork to ¼-inch thickness. Bake at 375° for 8 minutes. Cool on wire racks. Drizzle ¼ teaspoon Chocolate Glaze over each cookie. Yield: 4 dozen cookies (46 calories each).

Chocolate Glaze:

¾ cup sifted powdered sugar
1 tablespoon unsweetened cocoa
½ teaspoon orange extract
Dash of salt
1 tablespoon plus 1 teaspoon hot water

Combine all ingredients in a small bowl. Stir until smooth. Yield: ¼ cup.

PROTEIN 0.7 / FAT 1.4 / CARBOHYDRATE 7.7 / CHOLESTEROL 0 / IRON 0.3 / SODIUM 36 / CALCIUM 3

Calorie/Nutrient Chart

FOOD	APPROXIMATE MEASURE	FOOD ENERGY (CALORIES)	PROTEIN (GRAMS)	FAT (GRAMS)	CARBOHYDRATES (GRAMS)	CHOLESTEROL (MILLIGRAMS)	IRON (MILLIGRAMS)	SODIUM (MILLIGRAMS)	CALCIUM (MILLIGRAMS)
Apple									
Fresh, with skin	1 medium	81	0.2	0.5	21.0	0	0.2	0	10
Juice, unsweetened	½ cup	58	0.1	0.1	14.5	0	0.5	4	9
Applesauce, unsweetened	½ cup	52	0.2	0.1	13.8	0	0.1	2	4
Apricot									
Fresh	1 each	18	0.4	0.1	4.1	0	0.2	0	5
Dried, uncooked	1 each	17	0.3	0.0	4.3	0	0.3	1	3
Canned, peeled, in water	½ cup	25	0.8	0.0	6.2	0	0.6	12	9
Canned, with skin in juice	½ cup	58	0.8	0.0	15.0	0	0.4	5	15
Canned, in light syrup	½ cup	75	0.7	0.1	19.0	—	0.3	1	12
Nectar	½ cup	70	0.5	0.1	18.0	0	0.5	4	9
Artichoke									
Fresh, cooked	1 each	53	2.6	0.2	12.4	0	1.6	79	47
Hearts, cooked	½ cup	37	1.8	0.1	8.7	0	1.1	55	33
Asparagus, fresh, cooked	½ cup	23	2.3	0.3	4.0	0	0.6	4	22
Arugula	3 ounces	21	2.2	0.5	3.1	0	—	23	136
Avocado	1 medium	322	3.9	30.6	14.8	0	2.0	20	22
Bacon									
Canadian-style	1 ounce	45	5.8	2.0	0.5	14	0.2	399	2
Cured, broiled	1 slice	43	2.3	3.7	0.0	6	0.1	120	1
Bamboo shoots, cooked	½ cup	7	0.9	0.1	1.1	0	0.1	2	7
Banana									
Mashed	½ cup	101	1.1	0.5	25.8	0	0.3	1	7
Whole	1 medium	109	1.2	0.5	27.6	0	0.4	1	7
Barley, dry	½ cup	352	9.9	1.2	77.7	0	2.5	9	29
Basil, fresh, raw	¼ cup	1	0.1	0.0	0.1	0	0.1	0	3
Bean sprouts, raw	½ cup	16	1.6	0.1	3.1	0	0.5	3	7
Beans, cooked and drained									
Black	½ cup	114	7.6	0.5	20.4	0	1.8	1	23
Cannellini, canned	½ cup	96	5.5	0.5	16.1	—	1.8	—	21
Garbanzo	½ cup	134	7.3	2.1	22.5	0	2.4	6	40
Great Northern	½ cup	132	9.3	0.5	23.7	0	2.4	2	76
Green, fresh	½ cup	22	1.2	0.2	4.9	0	0.8	2	29
Green, canned, regular pack	½ cup	18	1.0	0.1	4.2	0	1.0	442	29
Kidney or red	½ cup	112	7.7	0.4	20.2	0	2.6	2	25
Lima, frozen, baby	½ cup	94	6.0	0.3	17.5	0	1.8	26	25
Pinto	½ cup	117	7.0	0.4	21.9	0	2.2	2	41
White	½ cup	127	8.0	0.6	23.2	0	2.5	2	65
Wax, canned	½ cup	14	0.8	0.1	3.1	0	0.5	171	18
Beef, trimmed of fat									
Flank steak, broiled	3 ounces	207	21.6	12.7	0.0	60	2.2	71	5
Ground, extra-lean, broiled	3 ounces	218	21.5	13.9	0.0	71	2.0	60	6
Liver, braised	3 ounces	137	20.7	4.2	2.9	331	5.7	60	6
Roast, roasted	3 ounces	204	23.1	11.7	0.0	69	2.2	63	9
Round, bottom, braised	3 ounces	189	26.9	8.2	0.0	82	2.9	43	4
Round, top, lean, broiled	3 ounces	162	27.0	5.3	0.0	71	2.4	52	5
Round, eye of, cooked	3 ounces	156	24.7	5.5	0.0	59	1.7	53	4
Sirloin, broiled	3 ounces	177	25.8	7.4	0.0	76	2.9	56	9

Dash (—) indicates insufficient data available

FOOD	APPROXIMATE MEASURE	FOOD ENERGY (CALORIES)	PROTEIN (GRAMS)	FAT (GRAMS)	CARBOHYDRATES (GRAMS)	CHOLESTEROL (MILLIGRAMS)	IRON (MILLIGRAMS)	SODIUM (MILLIGRAMS)	CALCIUM (MILLIGRAMS)
Beets									
Fresh, diced, cooked	½ cup	26	0.9	0.4	5.7	0	0.5	42	9
Canned, regular pack	½ cup	30	0.8	0.1	7.2	—	0.5	209	15
Beverages									
Beer	12 fluid ounces	146	1.1	0.0	13.1	0	0.1	18	18
Beer, light	12 fluid ounces	95	0.7	0.0	4.4	0	0.1	10	17
Brandy, bourbon, gin, rum, vodka, or|whiskey, 80 proof	1 fluid ounce	65	0.0	0.0	0.0	0	0.0	0.0	0
Champagne	6 fluid ounces	129	0.5	0.0	2.0	0	0.9	7	5
Club soda	8 ounces	0	0.0	0.0	0.0	0	—	48	11
Coffee, black	1 cup	5	0.2	0.0	0.9	0	1.0	5	5
Coffee liqueur	1 fluid ounce	99	0.0	0.1	13.9	0	0.0	2	0
Cognac brandy	1 fluid ounce	69	—	—	—	—	—	—	—
Crème de menthe liqueur	1 tablespoon	105	0.0	0.1	11.8	0	0.0	1	0
Sherry, sweet	1 fluid ounce	39	0.1	0.0	2.0	0	0.1	4	2
Vermouth, dry	1 fluid ounce	35	0.0	0.0	1.6	0	0.1	5	2
Vermouth, sweet	1 fluid ounce	45	0.0	0.0	4.7	0	0.1	8	2
Wine, port	6 fluid ounces	279	0.2	0.0	21.3	0	0.7	7	7
Wine, red	6 fluid ounces	121	0.4	0.0	0.5	0	1.4	18	12
Wine, white, dry	6 fluid ounces	112	0.2	0.0	1.0	0	0.9	7	15
Blackberries, fresh	½ cup	37	0.5	0.3	9.2	0	0.4	0	23
Blueberries, fresh	½ cup	41	0.5	0.3	10.2	0	0.1	4	4
Bouillon, dry									
Beef-flavored cubes	1 cube	3	0.1	0.0	0.2	—	—	400	—
Beef-flavored granules	1 teaspoon	10	0.0	1.0	0.0	—	—	945	—
Chicken-flavored cubes	1 cube	7	0.2	0.1	0.5	—	—	800	—
Chicken-flavored granules	1 teaspoon	10	0.5	1.0	0.5	—	0.0	819	—
Bran									
Oat, dry, uncooked	½ cup	153	8.0	3.0	23.5	0	2.6	1	31
Wheat, crude	½ cup	65	4.7	1.3	19.4	0	3.2	1	22
Bread									
Bagel, plain	1 each	161	5.9	1.5	30.5	—	1.4	196	23
Biscuit, homemade	1 each	127	2.3	6.4	14.9	2	0.6	224	65
Bun, hamburger or hot dog	1 each	136	3.2	3.4	22.4	13	0.8	112	19
Cornbread	2-ounce square	154	3.5	6.0	21.1	56	0.7	273	96
English muffin	1 each	182	5.9	3.6	30.9	32	1.5	234	41
French/vienna	1 slice	73	2.3	0.5	13.9	1	0.6	145	11
Light, wheatberry or 7-grain	1 slice	40	2.0	1.0	7.0	5	0.7	11	20
Pita, whole wheat	1 medium	122	2.4	0.9	23.5	0	1.4	—	39
Pumpernickel	1 slice	76	2.8	0.4	16.4	0	0.7	176	26
Raisin	1 slice	66	1.6	0.7	13.4	1	0.3	91	18
Rye	1 slice	61	2.3	0.3	13.0	0	0.4	139	19
White	1 slice	67	2.2	0.8	12.6	1	0.6	127	18
Whole wheat	1 slice	61	2.6	0.8	11.9	1	0.6	132	25
Breadcrumbs									
Fine, dry	½ cup	196	6.3	2.2	36.7	2	1.7	368	61
Seasoned	½ cup	214	8.4	1.5	41.5	—	1.9	1590	59
Bread stick, plain	1 each	17	0.4	0.5	2.7	—	0.2	20	1
Broccoli, fresh, chopped, cooked	½ cup	12	1.3	0.1	2.3	0	0.6	12	21
Broth									
Beef, canned, diluted	1 cup	32	4.8	0.6	2.6	24	0.4	782	0
Chicken, low-sodium	1 cup	22	0.4	0.0	2.0	0	0.0	4	0
Chicken, no-salt-added	1 cup	16	1.0	1.0	0.0	—	—	67	—
Brussels sprouts, fresh, cooked	½ cup	30	2.0	0.4	6.8	0	0.9	16	28
Bulgur, uncooked	½ cup	239	8.6	0.9	53.1	0	1.7	12	25
Butter									
Regular	1 tablespoon	102	0.1	11.5	0.0	31	0.0	117	3
Whipped	1 tablespoon	68	0.1	7.7	0.0	21	0.0	78	2

FOOD	APPROXIMATE MEASURE	FOOD ENERGY (CALORIES)	PROTEIN (GRAMS)	FAT (GRAMS)	CARBOHYDRATES (GRAMS)	CHOLESTEROL (MILLIGRAMS)	IRON (MILLIGRAMS)	SODIUM (MILLIGRAMS)	CALCIUM (MILLIGRAMS)
Cabbage									
Bok choy	1 cup	9	1.0	0.1	1.5	0	0.6	45	73
Common varieties, raw, shredded	½ cup	8	0.4	0.1	1.9	0	0.2	6	16
Cake, without frosting									
Angel food	2-ounce slice	147	3.2	0.1	33.7	—	0.2	83	54
Pound	1-ounce slice	305	3.6	17.5	33.7	134	0.5	245	27
Sponge, cut into 12 slices	1 slice	183	3.6	5.0	30.8	221	0.8	99	44
Yellow, cut into 12 slices	1 slice	190	2.8	7.5	28.0	40	0.2	157	79
Candy									
Fudge, chocolate	1 ounce	113	0.8	3.4	21.3	0	0.3	54	22
Gumdrops	1 ounce	98	0.0	0.2	24.8	0	0.1	10	2
Hard	1 each	27	0.0	0.0	6.8	0	0.1	2	1
Jelly beans	1 ounce	104	0.0	0.1	26.4	0	0.3	3	3
Milk chocolate	1 ounce	156	2.1	9.1	16.1	—	0.5	26	54
Cantaloupe, raw, diced	½ cup	28	0.7	0.2	6.7	0	0.2	7	9
Capers	1 tablespoon	4	0.4	0.0	0.6	0	—	670	—
Carambola (starfruit)	1 medium	42	0.7	0.4	9.9	0	0.3	3	5
Carrot									
Raw	1 medium	31	0.7	0.1	7.3	0	0.4	25	19
Cooked, sliced	½ cup	33	0.8	0.1	7.6	0	0.4	48	22
Juice, canned	½ cup	66	1.6	0.2	15.3	0	0.8	48	40
Catsup									
Regular	1 tablespoon	18	0.3	0.1	4.3	0	0.1	178	4
No-salt-added	1 tablespoon	15	0.0	0.0	4.0	—	—	6	—
Reduced-calorie	1 tablespoon	7	0.0	0.0	1.2	—	0.0	3	0
Cauliflower									
Raw, flowerets	½ cup	12	1.0	0.1	2.5	0	0.3	7	14
Cooked, flowerets	½ cup	15	1.2	0.1	2.8	0	0.2	4	17
Caviar	1 tablespoon	40	3.9	2.8	0.6	94	—	240	—
Celeriac, raw, shredded	½ cup	30	1.2	0.2	7.2	0	0.5	78	34
Celery, raw, diced	½ cup	10	0.4	0.1	2.2	0	0.3	53	23
Cereal									
Bran flakes	½ cup	64	2.5	0.4	15.3	0	5.6	182	10
Bran, whole	½ cup	104	6.0	1.5	32.7	0	6.7	387	30
Corn flakes	½ cup	44	0.9	0.0	9.8	0	0.7	140	0
Crispy rice	½ cup	55	0.9	0.1	12.4	0	0.3	103	3
Granola	½ cup	242	5.8	8.9	34.7	0	1.8	66	29
Puffed wheat	½ cup	22	0.9	0.1	4.8	0	0.3	0	2
Raisin bran	½ cup	77	2.7	0.5	18.6	0	3.0	179	9
Shredded wheat miniatures	½ cup	76	2.3	0.5	17.0	0	0.9	2	8
Toasted oat	½ cup	44	1.7	0.7	7.8	0	1.8	123	19
Whole-grain wheat flakes	½ cup	72	2.0	0.0	15.7	—	0.2	1	—
Cheese									
American, processed, light	1 ounce	50	6.9	2.0	1.0	—	—	407	198
American, processed, skim	1 ounce	69	6.0	5.0	1.0	10	—	—	149
American, processed	1 ounce	106	6.3	8.9	0.5	27	0.1	405	175
Blue	1 ounce	100	6.0	8.1	0.7	21	0.1	395	150
Brie	1 ounce	95	5.9	7.8	0.1	28	0.1	178	52
Camembert	1 ounce	85	5.6	6.9	0.1	20	0.1	239	110
Cheddar	1 ounce	114	7.0	9.4	0.3	30	0.2	176	204
Cheddar, light, processed	1 ounce	50	6.9	2.0	1.0	—	—	442	198
Cheddar, 40% less-fat	1 ounce	71	5.0	4.1	6.0	15	0.1	150	192
Cottage, dry curd, no-salt-added	½ cup	62	12.5	0.3	1.3	5	0.2	9	23
Cottage, low-fat (1% milk-fat)	½ cup	81	14.0	1.1	3.1	5	0.2	459	69
Cottage, low-fat (2% milk-fat)	½ cup	102	15.5	2.2	4.1	9	0.2	459	77
Cottage (4% milk-fat)	½ cup	108	13.1	4.7	2.8	16	0.1	425	63
Cream, light	1 ounce	62	2.9	4.8	1.8	16	0.0	160	38
Farmer	1 ounce	40	4.0	3.0	1.0	—	—	—	30

Dash (—) indicates insufficient data available

FOOD	APPROXIMATE MEASURE	FOOD ENERGY (CALORIES)	PROTEIN (GRAMS)	FAT (GRAMS)	CARBOHYDRATES (GRAMS)	CHOLESTEROL (MILLIGRAMS)	IRON (MILLIGRAMS)	SODIUM (MILLIGRAMS)	CALCIUM (MILLIGRAMS)
Cheese (continued)									
Feta	1 ounce	75	4.0	6.0	1.2	25	0.2	316	139
Fontina	1 ounce	110	7.3	8.8	0.4	33	0.1	—	156
Gouda	1 ounce	101	7.1	7.8	0.6	32	0.1	232	198
Gruyère	1 ounce	117	8.4	9.2	0.1	31	—	95	287
Monterey Jack	1 ounce	106	6.9	8.6	0.2	22	0.2	152	211
Monterey Jack, reduced-fat	1 ounce	83	8.4	5.4	0.5	19	0.1	181	227
Mozzarella, part-skim	1 ounce	72	6.9	4.5	0.8	16	0.1	132	183
Mozzarella, whole milk	1 ounce	80	5.5	6.1	0.6	22	0.0	106	147
Muenster	1 ounce	104	6.6	8.5	0.3	27	0.1	178	203
Neufchâtel	1 ounce	74	2.8	6.6	0.8	22	0.1	113	21
Parmesan, grated	1 ounce	111	10.1	7.3	0.9	19	0.2	454	336
Provolone	1 ounce	100	7.2	7.5	0.6	20	0.1	248	214
Ricotta, part-skim	1 ounce	39	3.2	2.2	1.5	9	0.1	35	77
Romano, grated	1 ounce	110	9.0	7.6	1.0	29	—	340	302
Swiss	1 ounce	107	8.1	7.8	1.0	26	0.0	74	272
Swiss, reduced-fat	1 ounce	85	9.6	5.0	0.5	18	0.1	44	334
Cherries									
Fresh, sweet	½ cup	52	0.9	0.7	12.0	0	0.3	0	11
Sour, unsweetened	½ cup	39	0.8	0.2	9.4	0	0.2	2	12
Sour, in light syrup	½ cup	94	0.9	0.1	24.3	0	1.7	9	13
Chicken, skinned, boned, and roasted									
White meat	3 ounces	147	26.1	3.8	0.0	72	0.9	65	13
Dark meat	3 ounces	163	22.1	7.6	0.0	75	1.2	63	12
Liver	3 ounces	134	20.7	4.6	0.7	537	7.2	43	12
Chili sauce	1 tablespoon	18	0.4	0.1	4.2	0	0.1	228	3
Chives, raw, chopped	1 tablespoon	1	0.1	0.0	0.1	0	0.0	0	2
Chocolate									
Chips, semisweet	¼ cup	215	1.7	15.2	24.2	0	1.1	1	13
Sweet	1 ounce	150	1.2	9.9	16.4	0	0.4	9	27
Syrup, fudge	1 tablespoon	64	0.9	2.5	9.6	—	0.2	22	19
Unsweetened, baking	1 ounce	141	3.1	14.7	8.5	0	2.0	1	23
Chutney, apple	1 tablespoon	41	0.2	0.0	10.5	—	0.2	34	5
Cilantro, fresh, minced	1 tablespoon	1	0.1	0.0	0.3	0	0.2	1	5
Clams									
Raw	½ cup	92	15.8	1.2	3.2	42	17.3	69	57
Canned, drained	½ cup	118	20.4	1.6	4.1	54	22.4	90	74
Cocoa powder, unsweetened	1 tablespoon	24	1.6	0.7	2.6	—	0.9	0	8
Coconut									
Fresh, grated	1 cup	460	4.3	43.5	19.8	0	3.2	26	18
Dried, unsweetened, shredded	1 cup	526	5.5	51.4	18.8	0	2.6	30	21
Dried, sweetened, shredded	1 cup	463	2.7	32.8	44.0	0	1.8	242	14
Cookies									
Brownie	2-ounce bar	243	2.7	10.1	39.0	10	1.3	153	25
Chocolate	1 each	72	1.0	3.4	9.4	13	0.4	61	18
Chocolate chip, homemade	1 each	69	0.9	4.6	6.8	7	0.3	30	7
Fortune	1 each	23	0.3	0.2	5.0	—	0.1	—	1
Gingersnaps	1 each	36	0.5	1.3	5.4	3	0.4	11	14
Oatmeal, plain	1 each	57	0.9	2.7	7.2	9	0.3	46	13
Sandwich, with creme	1 each	40	0.3	1.7	6.0	—	0.2	41	2
Sugar	1 each	50	0.3	2.7	6.6	—	0.1	38	2
Vanilla wafers	1 each	13	0.2	0.4	2.3	—	0.1	10	2
Corn									
Fresh, kernels, cooked	½ cup	89	2.6	1.0	20.6	0	0.5	14	2
Cream-style, regular pack	½ cup	92	2.2	0.5	23.2	0	0.5	365	4
Cornmeal									
Enriched, dry	1 cup	442	9.9	4.4	93.8	0	4.2	43	7
Self-rising	1 cup	407	10.1	4.1	85.7	0	7.0	1521	440
Cornstarch	1 tablespoon	31	0.0	0.0	7.3	0	0.0	1	0

FOOD	APPROXIMATE MEASURE	FOOD ENERGY (CALORIES)	PROTEIN (GRAMS)	FAT (GRAMS)	CARBOHYDRATES (GRAMS)	CHOLESTEROL (MILLIGRAMS)	IRON (MILLIGRAMS)	SODIUM (MILLIGRAMS)	CALCIUM (MILLIGRAMS)
Couscous, cooked	½ cup	98	3.5	0.0	20.6	—	0.5	—	10
Crab									
Blue, cooked	3 ounces	87	17.2	1.5	0.0	85	0.8	237	88
King, cooked	3 ounces	82	16.5	1.3	0.0	45	0.6	912	50
Imitation	3 ounces	76	10.2	0.0	8.5	—	0.5	—	255
Crackers									
Butter	1 each	17	0.0	1.0	2.0	—	0.1	32	4
Graham, plain	1 square	27	0.6	0.7	5.2	0	0.1	47	3
Melba rounds, plain	1 each	11	0.4	0.2	2.0	—	0.1	26	—
Saltine	1 each	13	0.3	0.3	2.0	—	0.1	43	5
Whole wheat	1 each	27	0.5	1.0	3.5	—	0.1	50	0
Cranberry									
Fresh, whole	½ cup	23	0.2	0.1	6.0	0	0.1	0	3
Juice cocktail, reduced-calorie	½ cup	24	0.0	0.0	5.9	—	2.8	4	7
Juice cocktail, regular	½ cup	75	0.0	0.1	19.2	0	0.2	5	4
Sauce, sweetened	¼ cup	105	0.1	0.1	26.9	0	0.1	20	3
Cream									
Half-and-half	1 tablespoon	20	0.5	1.7	0.7	6	0.0	6	16
Sour	1 tablespoon	31	0.5	3.0	0.6	6	0.0	8	17
Sour, reduced-calorie	1 tablespoon	20	0.4	1.8	0.6	6	0.0	6	16
Whipping, unwhipped	1 tablespoon	51	0.3	5.5	0.4	20	0.0	6	10
Creamer, non-dairy, powder	1 teaspoon	11	0.1	0.7	1.1	0	0.0	4	16
Croutons, seasoned	1 ounce	139	3.0	5.0	18.9	—	0.3	—	20
Cucumbers, raw, whole	1 medium	32	1.3	0.3	7.1	0	0.7	5	34
Currants	1 tablespoon	25	0.3	0.2	6.7	—	0.3	1	8
Dandelion greens, raw	3 ounces	38	2.3	0.6	7.8	0	2.6	65	159
Dates, pitted, unsweetened	5 each	114	0.8	0.2	30.5	0	0.5	1	13
Doughnut									
Cake type	1 each	156	1.8	7.4	20.6	24	0.5	200	16
Plain, yeast	1 each	166	2.5	10.7	15.1	10	0.6	94	15
Egg									
White	1 each	16	3.2	0.0	0.4	0	0.0	49	4
Whole	1 each	75	6.4	5.1	0.6	213	1.0	69	28
Yolk	1 each	59	2.8	5.1	0.0	213	0.9	8	26
Substitute	¼ cup	30	6.0	0.0	1.0	0	1.1	90	20
Eggplant, cooked without salt	½ cup	13	0.4	0.1	3.2	0	0.2	1	3
Extract, vanilla	1 teaspoon	12	—	—	—	—	—	—	—
Fennel, leaves, raw	½ cup	13	1.2	0.2	2.3	0	1.2	4	45
Figs									
Fresh	1 medium	37	0.4	0.2	9.9	0	0.2	1	18
Dried	1 each	48	0.6	0.2	12.2	0	0.4	2	27
Fish, cooked									
Catfish, farm-raised	3 ounces	195	15.4	11.3	6.8	69	1.2	238	37
Cod	3 ounces	89	19.4	0.7	0.0	47	0.4	66	12
Flounder	3 ounces	100	20.5	1.3	0.0	58	0.3	89	15
Grouper	3 ounces	100	21.1	1.1	0.0	40	1.0	45	18
Haddock	3 ounces	95	20.6	0.8	0.0	63	1.1	74	36
Halibut	3 ounces	119	22.7	2.5	0.0	35	0.9	59	51
Mackerel	3 ounces	134	20.1	5.4	0.0	62	0.6	56	11
Perch	3 ounces	100	21.1	1.0	0.0	98	1.0	67	87
Pollock	3 ounces	96	20.0	1.0	0.0	82	0.2	99	5
Pompano	3 ounces	179	20.1	10.3	0.0	54	0.6	65	37
Salmon	3 ounces	184	23.2	9.3	0.0	74	0.5	56	6

Dash (—) indicates insufficient data available

FOOD	APPROXIMATE MEASURE	FOOD ENERGY (CALORIES)	PROTEIN (GRAMS)	FAT (GRAMS)	CARBOHYDRATES (GRAMS)	CHOLESTEROL (MILLIGRAMS)	IRON (MILLIGRAMS)	SODIUM (MILLIGRAMS)	CALCIUM (MILLIGRAMS)
Fish (continued)									
Scrod	3 ounces	89	19.4	0.7	0.0	47	0.4	66	12
Snapper	3 ounces	109	22.4	1.5	0.0	40	0.2	48	34
Sole	3 ounces	100	20.5	1.3	0.0	58	0.3	89	15
Swordfish	3 ounces	132	21.6	4.4	0.0	43	0.9	98	5
Trout	3 ounces	128	22.4	3.7	0.0	62	2.1	29	73
Tuna, canned in water	3 ounces	116	22.7	2.1	0.0	36	0.5	333	—
Tuna, canned in oil	6½ ounces	343	48.9	14.9	0.0	57	1.2	730	7
Flour									
All-purpose, unsifted	1 cup	455	12.9	1.2	95.4	0	5.8	3	19
Bread, sifted	1 cup	495	16.4	2.3	99.4	0	6.0	3	21
Cake, sifted	1 cup	395	8.9	0.9	85.1	0	8.0	2	15
Rye, light, sifted	1 cup	374	8.6	1.4	81.8	0	1.8	2	21
Whole wheat, unsifted	1 cup	401	12.0	1.0	86.3	0	4.5	5	0
Frankfurter									
All-meat	1 each	130	5.8	11.2	1.1	29	0.8	484	3
Chicken	1 each	113	5.7	8.6	3.0	44	0.9	603	42
Turkey	1 each	99	6.3	7.8	0.7	47	0.8	627	47
Fruit bits, dried	1 ounce	93	1.3	0.0	20.0	0	0.5	24	—
Fruit cocktail, canned, packed in juice	½ cup	57	0.6	0.0	14.6	0	0.2	5	10
Garlic, raw	1 clove	4	0.2	0.0	1.0	0	0.1	1	5
Gelatin									
Flavored, prepared with water	½ cup	61	1.4	0.0	14.4	0	0.0	52	2
Unflavored	1 teaspoon	10	2.6	0.0	0.0	—	—	3	—
Ginger									
Fresh, grated	1 teaspoon	1	0.0	0.0	0.3	0	0.0	0	0
Crystallized	1 ounce	96	0.1	0.1	24.7	0	6.0	17	65
Grape juice, concord	½ cup	77	0.7	0.1	18.9	0	0.3	4	11
Grapefruit									
Fresh	1 medium	77	1.5	0.2	19.3	0	0.2	0	29
Juice, unsweetened	½ cup	47	0.6	0.1	11.1	0	2.5	1	9
Grapes, green, seedless	1 cup	114	1.1	0.9	28.4	0	0.4	3	18
Grits, cooked	½ cup	73	1.7	0.2	15.7	0	0.8	0	0
Ham, cured, roasted, extra-lean	3 ounces	123	17.8	4.7	1.3	45	1.3	1023	7
Hominy									
Golden	½ cup	80	1.5	0.5	17.1	0	0.6	—	—
White	½ cup	58	1.2	0.7	11.4	0	0.5	168	8
Honey	1 tablespoon	64	0.1	0.0	17.5	0	0.1	1	1
Honeydew, raw, diced	1 cup	59	0.8	0.2	15.6	0	0.1	17	10
Horseradish, prepared	1 tablespoon	6	0.2	0.0	1.4	0	0.1	14	9
Hot sauce, bottled	¼ teaspoon	0	0.0	0.0	0.0	0	0.0	9	0
Ice cream									
Vanilla, regular	½ cup	134	2.3	7.2	15.9	30	0.0	58	88
Vanilla, gourmet	½ cup	175	2.0	11.8	16.0	44	0.1	54	75
Ice milk, vanilla	½ cup	92	2.6	2.8	14.5	9	0.1	52	88
Ice, cherry	½ cup	82	0.2	0.0	10.3	—	—	0	—
Jams and Jellies									
Regular	1 tablespoon	54	0.1	0.0	14.0	0	0.2	2	4
Reduced-calorie	1 tablespoon	29	0.1	0.0	7.4	0	0.0	16	1
Jicama	1 cup	49	1.6	0.2	10.5	0	0.7	7	18
Kiwifruit	1 each	44	1.0	0.5	8.9	0	0.4	0	20
Kumquat	1 each	12	0.2	0.0	3.1	0	0.1	1	8

FOOD	APPROXIMATE MEASURE	FOOD ENERGY (CALORIES)	PROTEIN (GRAMS)	FAT (GRAMS)	CARBOHYDRATES (GRAMS)	CHOLESTEROL (MILLIGRAMS)	IRON (MILLIGRAMS)	SODIUM (MILLIGRAMS)	CALCIUM (MILLIGRAMS)
Lamb									
Ground, cooked	3 ounces	241	21.0	16.7	0.0	82	1.5	69	19
Leg, roasted	3 ounces	162	24.1	6.6	0.0	76	1.8	58	7
Loin or chop, broiled	3 ounces	184	25.5	8.3	0.0	81	1.7	71	16
Lard	1 tablespoon	116	0.0	12.8	0.0	12	0.0	0	0
Leeks, bulb, raw	½ cup	32	0.8	0.2	7.3	0	1.0	10	31
Lemon									
Fresh	1 each	22	1.3	0.3	11.4	0	0.6	3	66
Juice	1 tablespoon	4	0.1	0.0	1.3	0	0.0	0	1
Lemonade, sweetened	1 cup	99	0.2	0.0	26.0	0	0.4	7	7
Lentils, cooked	½ cup	115	8.9	0.4	19.9	0	3.3	2	19
Lettuce									
Boston or Bibb, shredded	1 cup	7	0.7	0.1	1.3	0	0.2	3	—
Belgian endive	1 cup	14	0.9	0.1	2.9	0	0.5	6	—
Curly endive or escarole	1 cup	8	0.6	0.1	1.7	0	0.4	11	26
Iceberg, chopped	1 cup	7	0.5	0.1	1.1	0	0.3	5	10
Radicchio, raw	1 ounce	7	0.4	0.1	1.3	0	—	6	6
Romaine, chopped	1 cup	9	0.9	0.1	1.3	0	0.6	4	20
Lime									
Fresh	1 each	20	0.4	0.1	6.8	0	0.4	1	21
Juice	1 tablespoon	4	0.1	0.0	1.4	0	0.0	0	1
Lobster, cooked, meat only	3 ounces	83	17.4	0.5	1.1	61	0.3	323	52
Luncheon meats									
Bologna, all meat	1 slice	90	3.3	8.0	0.8	16	0.4	289	3
Deviled ham	1 ounce	78	4.3	6.7	0.0	—	0.3	—	1
Salami	1 ounce	71	3.9	5.7	0.6	18.3	0.7	302	3.7
Turkey ham	1 ounce	35	5.6	1.4	0.0	16	0.8	196	3
Turkey pastrami	1 ounce	40	5.2	1.8	0.5	—	0.5	296	3
Lychees, raw	1 each	6	0.1	0.0	1.6	0	0.0	0	0
Mango, raw	½ cup	54	0.4	0.2	14.0	0	0.1	2	8
Margarine									
Regular	1 tablespoon	101	0.1	11.4	0.1	0	0.0	133	4
Reduced-calorie, stick	1 tablespoon	60	0.0	7.3	0.0	0	0.0	110	0
Marshmallows, miniature	½ cup	73	0.5	0.0	18.5	0	0.4	9	4
Mayonnaise									
Regular	1 tablespoon	99	0.2	10.9	0.4	8	0.1	78	2
Reduced-calorie	1 tablespoon	40	0.0	4.0	1.0	5	—	85	—
Milk									
Buttermilk, nonfat	1 cup	90	9.0	1.0	12.0	—	—	255	285
Buttermilk, low-fat	1 cup	120	9.0	4.0	12.1	—	—	126	301
Chocolate, low-fat 2%	1 cup	180	8.0	5.0	25.8	18	0.6	150	285
Condensed, sweetened	1 cup	982	24.2	26.3	166.5	104	0.5	389	869
Evaporated, skim, canned	1 cup	200	19.3	0.5	29.1	10	0.7	294	742
Low-fat, 2% fat	1 cup	122	8.1	4.7	11.7	20	0.1	122	298
Low-fat, 1% fat	1 cup	102	8.0	2.5	11.6	10	0.1	122	300
Nonfat dry	⅓ cup	143	14.3	0.3	20.6	8	0.1	212	498
Powder, malted	1 tablespoon	35	1.0	0.6	6.2	—	0.1	43	26
Skim	1 cup	86	8.3	0.4	11.9	5	0.1	127	301
Whole	1 cup	149	8.0	8.1	11.3	34	0.1	120	290
Millet, cooked	½ cup	143	4.2	1.2	28.4	0	0.8	2	4
Mint	¼ cup	1	0.1	0.0	0.1	0	0.1	0	4
Molasses, cane, light	1 tablespoon	52	0.0	0.0	13.3	0	0.9	3	34
Mushrooms									
Fresh	½ cup	9	0.7	0.1	1.6	0	0.4	1	2
Canned	½ cup	19	1.5	0.2	3.9	0	0.6	—	—
Shiitake, dried	1 each	14	0.3	0.0	2.6	0	0.1	0	0

Dash (—) indicates insufficient data available

FOOD	APPROXIMATE MEASURE	FOOD ENERGY (CALORIES)	PROTEIN (GRAMS)	FAT (GRAMS)	CARBOHYDRATES (GRAMS)	CHOLESTEROL (MILLIGRAMS)	IRON (MILLIGRAMS)	SODIUM (MILLIGRAMS)	CALCIUM (MILLIGRAMS)
Mussels, blue, cooked	3 ounces	146	20.2	3.8	6.3	48	5.7	314	28
Mustard									
Dijon	1 tablespoon	18	0.0	1.0	1.0	0	—	446	—
Prepared, yellow	1 tablespoon	12	0.7	0.7	1.0	0	0.3	196	13
Nectarine, fresh	1 each	67	1.3	0.6	16.1	0	0.2	0	7
Nuts									
Almonds, chopped	1 tablespoon	48	1.6	4.2	1.7	0	0.3	1	22
Cashews, dry roasted	1 tablespoon	49	1.3	4.0	2.8	0	0.5	1	4
Hazelnuts, chopped	1 tablespoon	45	0.9	4.5	1.1	0	0.2	0	14
Macadamia, roasted, unsalted	1 tablespoon	60	0.6	6.4	1.1	0	0.1	1	4
Peanuts, roasted, unsalted	1 tablespoon	53	2.4	4.5	1.7	0	0.2	1	8
Pecans, chopped	1 tablespoon	50	0.6	5.0	1.4	0	0.2	0	3
Pine	1 tablespoon	52	2.4	5.1	1.4	0	0.9	0	3
Pistachio nuts	1 tablespoon	46	1.6	3.9	2.0	0	0.5	0	11
Walnuts, black	1 tablespoon	47	1.9	4.4	0.9	0	0.2	0	5
Oats									
Cooked	1 cup	145	6.1	2.3	25.3	0	1.6	374	19
Rolled, dry	½ cup	156	6.5	2.6	27.1	0	1.7	2	21
Oil									
Canola (rapeseed)	1 tablespoon	117	0.0	13.6	0.0	0	0.0	0	0
Olive or peanut	1 tablespoon	119	0.0	13.5	0.0	0	0.0	0	0
Vegetable or sesame	1 tablespoon	121	0.0	13.6	0.0	0	0.0	0	0
Okra, cooked	½ cup	26	1.5	0.1	5.8	0	0.3	4	50
Olives									
Green, stuffed	1 each	4	0.0	0.4	0.1	—	—	290	—
Ripe	1 medium	5	0.0	0.4	0.3	0	0.1	35	4
Onions									
Green	1 tablespoon	2	0.1	0.0	0.3	0	0.1	0	4
Raw, chopped	½ cup	29	1.0	0.2	6.2	0	0.3	2	21
Cooked, yellow or white	½ cup	15	0.4	0.1	3.3	0	0.1	4	14
Orange									
Fresh	1 medium	62	1.2	0.2	15.4	0	0.1	0	52
Juice	½ cup	56	0.8	0.1	13.4	0	0.1	1	11
Mandarin, canned, packed in water	½ cup	37	0.0	0.0	8.4	—	0.4	11	—
Mandarin, canned, packed in juice	½ cup	46	0.7	0.0	12.0	0	0.4	6	14
Mandarin, canned, packed in light syrup	½ cup	79	0.0	0.0	19.7	0	0.3	7	—
Oysters, raw	3 ounces	59	6.0	2.1	3.3	47	5.7	95	38
Papaya									
Fresh, cubed	½ cup	27	0.4	0.1	6.9	0	0.1	2	17
Nectar, canned	½ cup	71	0.3	0.3	18.1	0	0.4	6	13
Parsley, raw	1 tablespoon	1	0.1	0.0	0.3	0	0.2	1	5
Parsnips, cooked, diced	½ cup	63	1.0	0.2	15.1	0	0.4	8	29
Passion fruit	1 medium	17	0.4	0.1	4.2	0	0.3	5	2
Pasta, cooked									
Macaroni or lasagna noodles	½ cup	99	3.3	0.5	19.8	0	1.0	1	5
Medium egg noodles	½ cup	106	3.8	1.2	19.9	26	1.3	6	10
Rice noodles	½ cup	138	3.1	1.3	28.6	0	2.2	—	40
Spinach noodles	½ cup	100	3.8	1.0	18.9	0	1.8	22	46
Spaghetti or fettuccine	½ cup	99	3.3	0.5	19.8	0	1.0	1	5
Whole wheat	½ cup	100	3.7	1.4	19.8	0	1.0	1	12
Peaches									
Fresh	1 medium	37	0.6	0.1	9.7	0	0.1	0	4
Canned, packed in water	½ cup	29	0.5	0.1	7.5	0	0.4	4	2
Canned, packed in juice	½ cup	55	0.8	0.0	14.3	0	0.3	5	7
Canned, packed in light syrup	½ cup	69	0.6	0.0	18.6	0	0.5	6	4

FOOD	APPROXIMATE MEASURE	FOOD ENERGY (CALORIES)	PROTEIN (GRAMS)	FAT (GRAMS)	CARBOHYDRATES (GRAMS)	CHOLESTEROL (MILLIGRAMS)	IRON (MILLIGRAMS)	SODIUM (MILLIGRAMS)	CALCIUM (MILLIGRAMS)
Peanut butter									
Regular	1 tablespoon	95	4.6	8.3	2.6	0	0.3	79	5
No-salt-added	1 tablespoon	95	4.6	8.3	2.6	0	0.3	3	5
Pear									
Fresh	1 medium	97	0.6	0.7	24.9	0	0.4	0	18
Canned, packed in juice	½ cup	62	0.4	0.1	16.0	0	0.3	5	11
Canned, packed in light syrup	½ cup	71	0.2	0.0	19.6	0	0.3	6	6
Juice	½ cup	57	0.0	0.0	13.6	—	—	6	—
Nectar, canned	½ cup	64	0.4	0.2	16.1	—	0.1	1	4
Peas									
Black-eyed, cooked	½ cup	90	6.7	0.7	15.0	0	1.2	3	23
English, cooked	½ cup	62	4.1	0.2	11.4	0	1.2	70	19
Snow pea pods	½ cup	34	2.6	0.2	5.6	0	1.6	3	34
Split, cooked	½ cup	116	8.2	0.4	20.7	0	1.3	2	14
Peppers									
Chile, hot, green, chopped	1 tablespoon	4	0.2	0.0	0.9	0	0.1	1	2
Jalapeño, green	1 each	4	0.2	0.0	0.8	0	0.1	1	2
Sweet, raw, green, red, or yellow	1 medium	19	0.6	0.4	3.9	0	0.9	2	4
Phyllo strudel dough, raw	1 each	63	2.1	0.2	13.3	—	0.5	—	—
Pickle									
Dill, sliced	¼ cup	4	0.2	0.1	0.9	0	0.4	553	10
Relish, chopped, sour	1 tablespoon	3	0.1	0.1	0.4	0	0.2	207	4
Sweet, sliced	¼ cup	57	0.2	0.2	14.1	0	0.5	276	5
Pie, baked, 9-inch diameter, cut into 8 slices									
Apple, fresh	1 slice	409	3.3	15.3	67.7	12	0.8	229	37
Chocolate meringue	1 slice	354	6.8	13.4	53.8	109	1.2	307	130
Egg custard	1 slice	248	7.3	11.6	28.6	149	0.9	229	129
Peach	1 slice	327	3.2	11.0	55.1	0	1.0	339	35
Pecan	1 slice	478	5.8	20.3	71.1	141	2.4	324	51
Pumpkin	1 slice	181	4.0	6.8	27.0	61	1.1	210	78
Pimiento, diced	1 tablespoon	5	0.2	0.1	1.1	0	0.3	5	1
Pineapple									
Fresh, diced	½ cup	38	0.3	0.3	9.6	0	0.3	1	5
Canned, packed in juice	½ cup	75	0.5	0.1	19.6	0	0.4	1	18
Canned, packed in light syrup	½ cup	66	0.5	0.2	16.9	0	0.5	1	18
Juice, unsweetened	½ cup	70	0.4	0.1	17.2	0	0.3	1	21
Plum, fresh	1 medium	35	0.5	0.4	8.3	0	0.1	0	3
Popcorn, hot-air popped	1 cup	23	0.8	0.3	4.6	0	0.2	0	1
Poppy seeds	1 tablespoon	47	1.6	3.9	2.1	0	0.8	2	127
Pork, cooked									
Chop, center-loin	3 ounces	204	24.2	11.1	0.0	77	0.9	59	5
Roast	3 ounces	204	22.7	11.7	0.0	77	1.0	59	8
Sausage link or patty	1 ounce	105	5.6	8.8	0.3	24	0.3	367	9
Spareribs	3 ounces	338	24.7	25.7	0.0	103	1.5	79	40
Tenderloin	3 ounces	141	24.5	4.1	0.0	79	1.3	57	8
Potatoes									
Baked, with skin	1 each	218	4.4	0.2	50.4	0	2.7	16	20
Boiled, diced	½ cup	67	1.3	0.1	15.6	0	0.2	4	6
Potato chips									
Regular	10 each	105	1.3	7.1	10.4	0	0.2	94	5
No-salt-added	10 each	105	1.3	7.1	10.4	0	0.2	2	5
Pretzel sticks, thin	10 each	25	0.5	0.5	4.4	—	0.3	83	4
Prunes									
Dried, pitted	1 each	20	0.2	0.0	5.3	0	0.2	0	4
Juice	½ cup	91	0.8	0.0	22.3	0	1.5	5	15

Dash (—) indicates insufficient data available

FOOD	APPROXIMATE MEASURE	FOOD ENERGY (CALORIES)	PROTEIN (GRAMS)	FAT (GRAMS)	CARBOHYDRATES (GRAMS)	CHOLESTEROL (MILLIGRAMS)	IRON (MILLIGRAMS)	SODIUM (MILLIGRAMS)	CALCIUM (MILLIGRAMS)
Pumpkin									
Canned	½ cup	42	1.3	0.3	9.9	0	1.7	6	32
Seeds, dry	1 ounce	153	7.0	13.0	5.0	0	4.2	5	12
Radish, fresh, sliced	½ cup	10	0.3	0.3	2.1	0	0.2	14	12
Raisins	1 tablespoon	27	0.3	0.0	7.2	0	0.2	1	4
Raisins, golden	1 tablespoon	31	0.4	0.1	8.2	0	0.2	1	5
Raspberries									
Black, fresh	½ cup	33	0.6	0.4	7.7	0	0.4	0	15
Red, fresh	½ cup	30	0.6	0.3	7.1	0	0.3	0	14
Rhubarb									
Raw, diced	½ cup	13	0.5	0.1	2.8	0	0.1	2	52
Cooked, with sugar	½ cup	157	0.5	0.1	42.1	0	0.3	1	196
Rice cake, plain	1 each	36	0.7	0.2	7.7	0	0.2	1	1
Rice, cooked without salt or fat									
Brown	½ cup	108	2.5	0.9	22.4	0	0.4	5	10
White, long-grain	½ cup	100	2.0	0.2	21.6	0	1.0	3	17
Wild	½ cup	84	2.3	0.6	17.1	—	1.2	12	8
Roll									
Croissant	1 each	272	4.6	17.3	24.6	47	1.1	384	32
Hard	1 each	156	4.9	1.6	29.8	2	1.1	313	24
Kaiser, small	1 each	92	3.0	1.8	16.0	—	1.3	192	7
Plain, brown-and-serve	1 each	82	2.2	2.0	13.7	2	0.5	141	13
Whole wheat	1 each	72	2.3	1.8	12.0	9	0.5	149	16
Rutabaga, cooked, cubed	½ cup	29	0.9	0.2	6.6	0	0.4	15	36
Salad dressing									
Blue cheese	1 tablespoon	84	0.4	9.2	0.3	0	0.0	216	3
Blue cheese, low-calorie	1 tablespoon	14	0.7	1.1	1.0	3	0.0	307	18
French	1 tablespoon	96	0.3	9.4	2.9	8	0.1	205	6
French, low-calorie	1 tablespoon	22	0.0	0.9	3.5	1	0.1	128	2
Italian	1 tablespoon	84	0.1	9.1	0.6	0	0.0	172	1
Italian, no-oil, low-calorie	1 tablespoon	8	0.1	0.0	1.8	0	0.0	161	1
Thousand Island	1 tablespoon	59	0.1	5.6	2.4	—	0.1	109	2
Thousand Island, low-calorie	1 tablespoon	24	0.1	1.6	2.5	2	0.1	153	2
Salsa, commercial	1 tablespoon	4	0.2	0.0	0.8	0	0.1	1	2
Salt, iodized	1 teaspoon	0	0.0	0.0	0.0	0	0.0	2343	15
Sauerkraut, canned	½ cup	13	0.7	0.1	3.2	—	0.4	560	27
Scallops, raw, large	3 ounces	75	14.3	0.6	2.0	28	0.2	137	20
Sesame seeds, dry, whole	1 teaspoon	17	0.5	1.5	0.7	0	0.4	0	29
Sherbet									
Lime or raspberry	½ cup	104	0.9	0.9	23.8	0	0.0	67	39
Orange	½ cup	135	1.1	1.9	29.3	7	0.1	44	52
Shortening	1 tablespoon	94	0.0	10.6	0.0	—	—	—	—
Shrimp									
Fresh, peeled and deveined	½ pound	240	46.1	3.9	2.1	345	5.5	336	118
Canned, drained	3 ounces	102	19.6	1.7	0.9	147	2.3	144	50
Soy sauce									
Regular	1 tablespoon	8	0.8	0.0	1.2	0	0.3	829	2
Reduced-sodium	1 tablespoon	8	0.8	0.0	1.2	0	0.3	484	2
Low-sodium	1 tablespoon	6	0.0	0.0	0.0	—	—	390	—
Soup, condensed, made with water									
Beef broth	1 cup	31	4.8	0.7	2.6	24	0.5	782	0
Chicken noodle	1 cup	75	4.0	2.4	9.3	7	0.7	1106	17
Chili, beef	1 cup	168	18.4	7.9	6.1	59	3.9	606	36
Cream of chicken	1 cup	117	2.9	7.3	9.0	10	0.6	986	34
Cream of mushroom	1 cup	129	2.3	9.0	9.0	2	0.5	1032	46

FOOD	APPROXIMATE MEASURE	FOOD ENERGY (CALORIES)	PROTEIN (GRAMS)	FAT (GRAMS)	CARBOHYDRATES (GRAMS)	CHOLESTEROL (MILLIGRAMS)	IRON (MILLIGRAMS)	SODIUM (MILLIGRAMS)	CALCIUM (MILLIGRAMS)
Soup (continued)									
Cream of potato	1 cup	73	1.7	2.3	11.0	5	0.5	1000	20
Onion	1 cup	58	3.7	1.7	8.2	0	0.7	1053	27
Tomato	1 cup	85	2.0	1.9	16.6	0	1.7	871	12
Vegetable, beef	1 cup	78	5.4	2.0	9.8	5	1.2	956	17
Spinach									
Fresh	1 cup	12	1.6	0.2	2.0	0	1.5	44	55
Cooked	½ cup	21	2.7	0.2	3.4	0	3.2	63	122
Canned, regular pack	½ cup	27	3.0	0.7	3.9	—	2.8	381	132
Squash, cooked									
Acorn	½ cup	57	1.1	0.1	14.9	0	1.0	4	45
Butternut	½ cup	41	0.8	0.1	10.7	0	0.6	4	42
Spaghetti	½ cup	22	0.5	0.2	5.0	0	0.3	14	16
Summer	½ cup	21	1.0	0.3	4.5	0	0.4	1	28
Squid, raw	4 ounces	104	17.7	1.6	3.5	264	0.8	50	36
Strawberries, fresh	1 cup	45	0.9	0.6	10.5	0	0.6	1	21
Sugar									
Granulated	1 tablespoon	48	0.0	0.0	12.4	0	0.0	0	0
Brown, packed	1 tablespoon	51	0.0	0.0	13.3	0	0.5	4	12
Powdered	1 tablespoon	29	0.0	0.0	7.5	0	0.0	0	0
Sunflower kernels	¼ cup	205	8.2	17.8	6.8	0	2.4	1	42
Sweet potatoes									
Whole, baked	½ cup	103	1.7	0.1	24.3	0	0.4	10	28
Mashed	½ cup	172	2.7	0.5	39.8	0	0.9	21	34
Syrup									
Chocolate-flavored	1 tablespoon	49	0.6	0.2	11.0	—	0.3	13	3
Corn, dark or light	1 tablespoon	60	0.0	0.0	15.4	0	0.8	14	9
Maple, reduced-calorie	1 tablespoon	6	0.0	0.0	2.0	0	—	4	—
Pancake	1 tablespoon	50	0.0	0.0	12.8	0	0.2	2	20
Taco shell	1 each	52	0.7	2.8	5.9	—	0.4	62	—
Tangerine									
Fresh	1 medium	38	0.5	0.1	9.6	0	0.1	1	12
Juice, unsweetened	½ cup	53	0.6	0.2	12.5	0	0.2	1	22
Tapioca, dry	1 tablespoon	32	0.1	0.0	7.8	0	0.0	0	1
Tofu									
Firm	4 ounces	164	17.9	9.9	4.9	—	11.9	16	232
Soft	4 ounces	65	6.0	4.0	2.0	—	1.4	2	193
Tomato									
Fresh	1 medium	23	1.1	0.2	5.3	0	0.6	10	9
Cooked	½ cup	30	1.3	0.3	6.8	0	0.7	13	10
Juice, regular	1 cup	41	1.8	0.1	10.3	0	1.4	881	22
Juice, no-salt-added	1 cup	49	2.4	0.0	12.1	—	—	27	—
Paste, regular	1 tablespoon	14	0.6	0.1	3.1	0	0.5	129	6
Paste, no-salt-added	1 tablespoon	11	0.5	0.0	2.6	0	0.2	6	4
Sauce, regular	½ cup	37	1.6	0.2	8.8	0	0.9	741	17
Sauce, no-salt-added	½ cup	42	1.2	0.0	9.7	—	—	27	—
Stewed, canned, no-salt-added	½ cup	32	1.3	0.0	7.5	—	0.7	20	33
Whole, canned, peeled	½ cup	22	0.9	0.0	5.2	—	0.5	424	38
Whole, canned, no-salt-added	½ cup	22	0.9	0.0	5.2	—	0.5	15	38
Tortilla									
Chips, plain	10 each	135	2.1	7.3	16.0	0	0.7	24	3
Corn, 6" diameter	1 each	67	2.1	1.1	12.8	0	1.4	53	42
Flour, 6" diameter	1 each	111	2.4	2.3	22.2	0	0.8	0	27
Turkey, skinned, boned, and roasted									
White meat	3 ounces	115	25.6	0.6	0.0	71	1.3	44	10

Dash (—) indicates insufficient data available

FOOD	APPROXIMATE MEASURE	FOOD ENERGY (CALORIES)	PROTEIN (GRAMS)	FAT (GRAMS)	CARBOHYDRATES (GRAMS)	CHOLESTEROL (MILLIGRAMS)	IRON (MILLIGRAMS)	SODIUM (MILLIGRAMS)	CALCIUM (MILLIGRAMS)
Turkey *(continued)*									
Dark meat	3 ounces	159	24.3	6.1	0.0	72	2.0	67	27
Smoked	3 ounces	126	20.4	4.9	0.0	48	2.3	506	9
Turnip greens, cooked	½ cup	14	0.8	0.2	3.1	0	0.6	21	99
Turnips, cooked, cubed	½ cup	14	0.6	0.1	3.8	0	0.2	39	17
Veal, loin, cooked	3 ounces	149	22.4	5.9	0.0	90	0.7	82	18
Vegetable juice cocktail									
Regular	1 cup	46	1.5	0.2	11.0	0	1.0	883	27
Low-sodium	1 cup	48	2.4	0.2	9.7	—	1.7	48	34
Venison, raw	4 ounces	136	26.0	2.7	0.0	96	3.9	58	6
Vinegar, distilled	1 tablespoon	2	0.0	0.0	0.8	0	0.0	0	0
Water chestnuts, canned, sliced	½ cup	35	0.6	0.0	8.7	0	0.6	6	3
Watercress, fresh	½ cup	2	0.4	0.0	0.2	0	0.0	7	20
Watermelon, raw, diced	1 cup	51	1.0	0.7	11.5	0	0.3	3	13
Wheat bran, crude	1 tablespoon	8	0.6	0.2	2.4	0	0.4	0	3
Wheat germ	1 tablespoon	26	1.7	0.7	3.7	0	0.5	1	3
Whipped cream	1 tablespoon	26	0.2	2.8	0.2	10	0.0	3	5
Whipped topping, non-dairy, frozen	1 tablespoon	15	0.1	1.2	1.1	0	0.0	1	0
Wonton wrappers	1 each	6	0.2	0.1	0.9	5	0.1	12	1
Worcestershire sauce									
Regular	1 tablespoon	12	0.3	0.0	2.7	0	0.0	147	15
Low-sodium	1 tablespoon	12	0.0	0.0	3.0	0	—	57	—
Yeast, active, dry	1 package	20	2.6	0.1	2.7	0	1.1	4	3
Yogurt									
Coffee and vanilla, low-fat	1 cup	193	11.2	2.8	31.3	11	0.2	150	388
Plain, nonfat	1 cup	127	13.0	0.4	17.4	5	0.2	173	452
Plain, low-fat	1 cup	143	11.9	3.5	16.0	14	0.2	159	415
Fruit varieties, low-fat	1 cup	225	9.0	2.6	42.3	9	0.1	120	313
Frozen	½ cup	124	3.1	2.1	23.7	—	—	51	—
Zucchini									
Raw	½ cup	9	0.7	0.1	1.9	0	0.3	2	10
Cooked	½ cup	9	0.7	0.1	1.9	0	0.3	2	10

Source of Data:

Computrition, Inc., Chatsworth, California. Primarily comprised of *The Composition of Foods: Raw, Processed, Prepared.* Handbooks - 8 series. United States Department of Agriculture, Human Nutrition Information Service, 1976-1989.

Recipe Index

Subject Index